Fabiano Caruana: 60 Memorable Games

Andrew Soltis

BATSFORD

First published in the United Kingdom in 2022 by
B.T. Batsford
43 Great Ormond Street
London WC1N 3HZ

An imprint of B.T. Batsford Holdings Ltd

ISBN: 9781849947213

A CIP catalogue record for this book is available from the
British Library.

27 26 25 24 23 22
10 9 8 7 6 5 4 3 2 1

Reproduction by Rival Ltd, UK
Printed and bound by CPI Mackays, Chatham, UK

This book can be ordered direct from the publisher at
www.batsford.com, or try your local bookshop

Contents

Page

Introduction
The Caruana Difference

It reads like a Hollywood script:

A Brooklyn boy dreams of becoming the world chess champion. He makes the unheard-of decision to become a professional player at age 12. His family moves to Europe so he can learn from the best teachers. He studies and plays constantly. In two years he is a grandmaster. By age 16, sponsors from Azerbaijan to Germany are bidding to have him play for their teams.

As in any good movie plot, this is the first stage of a narrative arc. There is a roller coaster of changes to come:

His great victories are followed by severe reverses. His progress is halted. Younger players seem to surpass him. He talks of giving up chess. Then he registers the greatest winning streak in chess history. Major media outlets flock to interview him. Gossip web sites claim he has amassed a fortune of more than $10 million. His return to play for the United States is an international news story. He finally wins the right to challenge the world champion. He battles undefeated through the most-watched championship match in history. Then in a dramatic playoff he wins and becomes history's 17th world champion.

Yes, it's a typical Hollywood fantasy. But except for the final sentence, Fabiano Caruana's story is true.

And if he had a celebrity personality – that of a Magnus Carlsen, a Bobby Fischer or a Garry Kasparov – his story would be known well beyond chess circles. But Caruana is Caruana. "He is shy and modest, like a conservatory student," one of his teachers said. He is content to let his moves do most of the talking.

To appreciate how he accomplished what he did in his first 30 years, it helps to understand why he is different in so many ways from Carlsen, Kasparov and rivals such as Ian Nepomniachtchi and Hikaru Nakamura.

Concrete Plus

"Caruana is a very concrete player," Carlsen said. In grandmaster jargon, this means someone who relies primarily on calculation to choose his moves. All of the world's elite players are excellent calculators. "A pretty damned good one," Maxime Vachier-Lagrave said of himself.

By the time Caruana reached the world's number two rating he had beaten the number one, Carlsen, by crunching variations."When the position gets out of control, he can be out-calculated. I've out-calculated him in the past," he told the *New Yorker* in 2016.

His analytical skill began early. At age six, his teacher gave him positions to analyze, typically tactical quizzes. "The one proviso he had to honor, no matter what, was always to analyze in his head, never moving the pieces until he had completed analysis," recalled the teacher, Bruce Pandolfini.

Carlsen is much more intuitive than "concrete." His instinct for moving the *right* piece to the *right* square at the *right* time is unrivaled.

But Caruana will choose the same move as Carlsen 90 percent of the time, sometimes more. Yet Magnus acknowledges that there are some of Fabiano's moves he would never consider.

Wojtaszek – Caruana
Wijk aan Zee 2021

Black to play

Caruana played his previous moves quickly. Here he paused. After six minutes he played **13...♗xc3**.

Black sometimes gives up his cherished g7-bishop for the knight in this opening, the King's Indian Defense. But in return he inflicts doubled pawns (bxc3) and often wins a pawn.

This is quite different. Caruana's grandmaster colleagues were horrified.

"If this decision is good for Black, I need to learn chess again," GM Ivan Sokolov tweeted.

The great King's Indian authority Yefim Geller "is probably turning in his grave," he said.

Caruana's intuition was different. He wasn't certain 13...♗xc3 was right. "But I had seen it some *similar* examples where White can't really free himself," he said afterward.

This became clearer after play continued **14 ♕xc3 ♕f6 15 ♕c1 ♘c5 16 ♕b1 ♕e6**.

White to play

Black must win a pawn (17...♘xe4 or 17...♕xc4). Caruana later switched to a crushing kingside attack.

The tenor of grandmaster tweets also switched. "Brilliant! Thanks for the lesson in the King's Indian," wrote GM Rauf Mamedov.

No Clone

Carlsen has expressed astonishment in the way many of his colleagues honed their skills. "I think his entire training has been with a computer," he said of Wesley So.

Caruana also grew up during the engine era. He's been called a computer clone, another "son of Fritz." Or of Stockfish, or even AlphaZero. But since his earliest international successes he has made moves that few machines would recommend.

Caruana – van der Wiel
Wijk aan Zee, C Group 2008

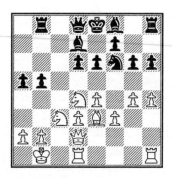

White to play

Stockfish recommends 16 ♘ce2, to get White's knight out of the path of onrushing Black pawns.

Second best, according to various engines, is 16 ♖c1. Also good is 16 ♖he1. Each of these moves earns a plus evaluation from software.

Caruana put another piece in the way of Black's pawns, **16 ♘b3**. Computers reversed their evaluations. Black is much better now, they said. "One might think that White has committed some sort of oversight," Caruana wrote in *Chessbase*.

After **16...a4 17 ♘c1 b4 18 ♘3e2** the machines appreciate how White can keep the files in front of the king closed. He will answer ...a3 with b2-b3!, and ...b3 with a2-a3!.

However Caruana's centralization of force didn't impress them until **18...♗g7 19 d4 h5 20 g5 ♘g8 21 d5!**.

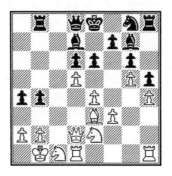

But now White's superiority is obvious, at least to humans. Play went **21...e5 22 ♘d3 b3 23 a3 ♘e7 24 f4! exf4 25 ♗d4** and after mutual inexact play, White won.

What makes Caruana's study habits different from Carlsen's is not technology but dedication. Magnus is easily bored. There are days he doesn't look at all at chess. When his father Henrik Carlsen was asked how the young Magnus studied, he replied, "He does what he likes...It's curiosity as opposed to discipline."

Fabiano has the same driving curiosity of all great players. But he also has self-discipline. "What is most striking about Caruana is a fantastic concentration," said Yuri Razuvaev, one of his grandmaster trainers. He has the ability to examine a chess position to the exclusion of all else, for as long as he needed to understand it.

"Only the great ones have this," Razuvaev said, mentioning Bobby Fischer, Viktor Korchnoi and Anatoly Karpov. "Caruana's concentration does not wane in six hours of studying."

Believing the Board

To Carlsen, Hikaru Nakamura and other elite players, chess is more sport than science. The tournament scoretable takes precedence over the position on the board. Carlsen will try to win any position, even a dead drawn endgame, if it means moving up in the standings.

Caruana is superb in last rounds as this book's Games 8, 32, 40 and others attest. But he is guided, most of all, by what he sees on the board. If the pieces and pawns tell him he is justified in taking risks, he may. Otherwise, he probably won't.

Dominguez – Caruana
FIDE Grand Prix, Paris 2013

Black to play

The stakes were huge for Caruana in this final-round game. A win would get him into the 2014 Candidates tournament, the last stop before a world championship match.

But his opponent had little to play for. After **15...♕c6** he repeated the position, **16 ♘a7 ♕c7 17 ♘b5**.

Caruana wanted to play on. But the position wouldn't let him. He again rejected 17...♕d8 18 ♕a7! and 17...♕b8 18 ♕xd7+.

The game ended with **17...♕c6 18 ♘a7 ♕c7 19 ♘b5 ♕c6**, draw. His world championship hopes had to wait three years.

Caruana was sharply criticized by several colleagues. He should have played to win, they said – without saying how.

Jan Timman came to his defense. "Every top player has his or her values in a position," he wrote in *New In Chess*. "If you think the position is objectively balanced, forcing things goes against the grain."

Caruana was in a similar situation a year before, in the last round of the Grand Slam Final. He was tied with Carlsen for the tournament lead.

Vallejo Pons – Caruana
São Paulo 2012

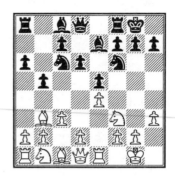

Black to play

Caruana played **9...♖e8**, an invitation to the Zaitsev Variation, 10 d4.

His opponent replied **10 ♘g5**. This virtually forced him to play **10...♖f8**. Then came **11 ♘f3 ♖e8**.

This repetition of moves is a common device by grandmasters. It shortens the distance to the time control and helps avoid time trouble 30 moves later. White usually continues 12 d4! and heads for a complex middlegame.

But Vallejo Pons continued **12 ♘g5 ♖f8** and then **13 d4 ♗b7 14 ♘f3 ♖e8 15 ♘g5 ♖f8**.

Caruana was described as stunned as White's knight shifted back and forth from g5 to f3. But he felt trapped.

The game ended with **16 ♘f3 ♖e8 17 ♘g5 ♖f8 18 ♘f3 ♖e8 19 ♘g5 draw**.

Of course, there were sound ways for him to vary at move 9 – and again at 11, 14, 16 and 18.

But at the time, Caruana considered anything but the Zaitzev Variation somewhat dicey. He didn't know those positions well and didn't trust them.

Because of the draw, he ended up in a playoff with Carlsen and lost.

Carlsen relishes impossible tasks, when he *has* to win with Black. Fabiano doesn't. He found himself in that situation in the last round of the 2016 Candidates tournament. He couldn't afford to meet Sergey Karjakin's 1 e4 with 1...e5. A draw would allow Karjakin to clinch first place.

So Caruana played the Richter-Rauzer Variation of the Sicilian Defense. It was "an opening that I hate," he said. He lost and once again had to wait for the next championship cycle.

Disciplined Nerves

Even after he became a grandmaster, Caruana was a mystery to older colleagues. They included Viktor Korchnoi, who lost his first three games to him.

"In recent time it became hard for me to play with youngsters,"

Korchnoi wrote. "I stopped understanding from where they got their moves. Do they think them up out of their heads or remember what was shown in books, or by their trainers or the computers?"

He found an answer on his fourth try with Caruana.

Caruana – Korchnoi
Gibraltar 2011

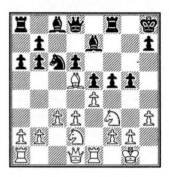

Black to move

Caruana's last move, 14 h3, weakened the kingside before it comes under attack. This violates basic principles, Korchnoi said. "Obviously," he said, 14 ♘c4 was the main alternative.

To justify the knight move, White would have to investigate 14...g4 15 ♘fd2 f4 16 a4, he added. He carried his analysis well past move 20 in variations that continued 16...♕c7 17 ♕b3 ♗d8 and 16...♘a7 17 ♕b3 b5. "Robert Fischer would approve" of this, he said.

Korchnoi concluded his young opponent was *not* primarily a calculator. "Caruana chose a position that was better known to him and, perhaps, demands less nervous tension," he wrote.

Unlike Korchnoi at 70, Caruana at 18 had learned to manage his nerves, his emotions and his clock. "Of course, I was nervous," he recalled, about his last-round game at Thessaloniki 2013.

His opponent, Gata Kamsky, needed a draw to clinch first prize and extend his career comeback. If Caruana won he might finish first. He sensed Kamsky "would experience more pressure than me."

So, Caruana complicated. Kamsky "made correct moves but spent too much time," he said. The position "became impossible to defend" and Caruana won.

Tournament pressure "can be debilitating," he said in a later interview. But "If you learn to deal with it, it can be motivating." He cited the example of Karjakin, who plays better when the stakes are higher, such as in Candidates tournaments.

In the fourth round of the 2018 Candidates tournament he survived several near-death experiences:

Kramnik – Caruana
Candidates tournament,
Berlin 2018

Black to move

Caruana could have kept roughly even chances with 52...♗e7 or 52...♘d5.

But he has a splendid sense of when his opponent is uncomfortable with the position or his side of the clock. Vladimir Kramnik had less than three minutes to reach the next control at move 60.

Caruana had 15 minutes left and spent more than half of it on **52...♘c2! 53 ♖c1 ♘d4**.

Computers called this insane. They said 54 ♗g4 would win after 54...h2 55 ♖e1+ ♔d5 56 ♖xf6.

They were wrong. When prompted to consider a possible perpetual check, 56...♖a4+ 57 ♔b2 ♖b4+ 58 ♔c1 ♖c4+, engines see 59 ♔d1 ♖a4 60 ♖h6 ♔c4!.

What might have been

Engines realize Black is threatening ...♔d3 and ...♖a1 mate!.

Instead of this, Kramnik refused to give up the prospect of a win. He forged ahead with **54 ♗d3 ♖a4+ 55 ♔b1 ♘b3 56 ♖e1+ ♔d5 57 ♔c2 ♘d4+ 58 ♔b1? ♘f3!**.

He had vowed "to play every game to the end." But, he acknowledged afterwards, "When you play 6-7 hours every day you get very tired."

Now he had to try for a draw (59 ♖xf6! ♘xe1 60 ♗f1).

But with less than a minute he blundered, **59 ♖d1?? ♖a1+ 60 ♔c2 ♖xd1** (61 ♔xd1 h2!), and resigned in a few moves.

Kramnik never recovered in the tournament. It turned out to be his final bid to regain the world championship. Caruana, on the other hand, was destined to hold and fall out of the tournament lead until the end.

"There was no moment when it wasn't incredibly tense," he said. "I was playing catch-up or trying to hold on to my very thin edge at the top." When the tournament ended, he had finished first and qualified to challenge Carlsen.

Discomfort Zone

When the position doesn't strongly suggest a particular candidate move, Caruana and his rivals will choose the one that makes it easier to find good subsequent moves. Caruana will also place a priority on a candidate that makes it harder for his opponent to find good moves, as in the Kramnik game.

This also guides his opening preparation. He wants to push his opponent out of his comfort zone.

In the following hyper-sharp line of the Najdorf Variation, White has had promising results with 15 ♕h3 and double-edged results with 15 e5 and 15 g5.

Caruana – Nakamura
Stavanger 2017

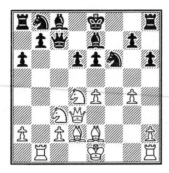

Caruana played **15 ♖g1** instead. He acknowledged it was no better than the other moves. But it makes it harder for "Black to navigate the maze of options over the board."

Play went **15...♗d7 16 g5 hxg5 17 ♖xg5** and Nakamura sank into 45 minutes' thought. He apparently considered 17...♖h7, 17...♗f8 and a few other candidates.

When Nakamura chose **17...♘c6!?** "I knew the move was decent for Black," Caruana wrote. "But it is so risky and difficult to calculate that I never expected anyone to play it."

What he meant was it allowed **18 ♖xg7** and then **18...0-0-0 19 ♘cb5!**. This gave him a forcing path to a slightly favorable endgame, 19...axb5 20 ♘xb5 ♘e5! 21 ♘xc7 ♘xd3+ 22 cxd3. Nakamura quickly erred and lost.

Little Moves

Two generations before, Korchnoi had also been critical of Garry Kasparov. When Kasparov was on the verge of the world championship, Korchnoi said he lacked "a very important quality, patience."

Kasparov tries too hard with every move, he said. "In all his games he plays ♕a4, ♕h5, ♕a6 – always long moves. He plays his pieces as far as they will go." This may work against mere masters but not among the world's best, Korchnoi claimed.

No knowledgeable player would accuse Caruana of this. He has extraordinary patience. It is best illustrated by his quiet, innocuous-looking moves. Often they seem to do next to nothing. But often his position keeps improving, inexplicably, inexorably.

Caruana – Eljanov
Baku 2016

White to move

White is better but far from victory. Forcing moves won't change this quickly.

What White needs is an optimum formation of his three pieces.

If he can get his rook to e5, his queen to e3 and his king to g2, the evaluation of the position jumps from +1 to well over +2, that is from "may win" range to "probable win."

He began with **38 ♕e3!** so that 38...♚g8 39 ♖e4 ♖e8 40 ♖e5 approaches the desired formation.

Play went **38...♖f8 39 ♖e4! ♖f7** and now **41 ♖e5!** so he could push the a-pawn without concern.

None of his moves seemed dramatic. They were "little." But after **40...♕d6 41 a5 ♕d1+ 42 ♚g2 ♕a1 43 ♕e2!** and a5-a6 they had transformed a merely good endgame into a winning position.

Caruana's annotations typically do not credit how his little moves

change a position. In analyzing Game 16 he described how a balanced endgame somehow deteriorated into a loss for Kramnik without a detectable error by him.

In the Eljanov game only the final moves drew expressions of admiration from his fans. Black resigned soon after **43...e6 44 a6 ♕d4 45 ♖xe6 c5 46 ♖e7!**.

Deep Prep

Carlsen is the first world champion in decades who did not consider the opening a very important part of the game. He would be happy to get past the first dozen moves and reach a middlegame position in which he can out-think his opponent.

Caruana also wants to out-think his opponent. But it would be nice if his opponent was the first to start thinking. When he won Game 59 he blitzed off his first 25 moves, many of them highly complex and some strikingly original. His opponent had taken nearly an hour and was beginning to make mistakes.

A typical Caruana game is no easier to define than a typical game of Carlsen, Nepo, Vachier-Lagrave or Wesley So, to name a few. One that comes to mind began this way.

Caruana – Georg Meier
Baden-Baden 2013
French Defense,
Rubinstein Variation (C10)

**1 e4 e6 2 d4 d5 3 ♘c3 dxe4
4 ♘xe4 ♘d7 5 ♘f3 ♘gf6
6 ♘xf6+ ♘xf6 7 ♗e3 ♘d5 8 ♗d2
c5 9 ♗b5+ ♗d7 10. ♗xd7+ ♕xd7
11 c4 ♘b6 12 ♖c1 f6 13 0-0 cxd4**

White to move

Opening databases at the time stopped here with the conclusion that chances are roughly balanced. This is a typical evaluation of a position when 21st century masters start thinking.

"With the computers we are all almost equal in the beginning," Veselin Topalov said. "And then you have a margin of like 20 moves when you have to make the difference."

Play went **14 ♖e1 ♖c8 15 ♕b3**. After the game, Caruana pointed out in detail how 15...e5? would lose to 16 ♘xe5 fxe5 17 ♖xe5+.

Better is 15...♔f7 when 16 ♕d3 and 17 b4, with the idea of c4-c5, offers chances for an initiative.

Black, a French Defense expert, preferred **15...♗e7** and Caruana answered **16 c5! ♖xc5 17 ♖xc5 ♗xc5 18 ♖xe6+ ♔d8 19 ♖e1**.

Caruana had analyzed as far as this position, six moves past the last "book" move.

He didn't believe White was significantly better. What he liked about the position is that it is hard for Black to defend.

This became evident as the game went **19...♕d5 20 ♕d3 ♘d7 21 b4 ♗b6 22 a4 a6 23 a5 ♗a7?**

Computers suggest improvements (20...♘c4 and later 22...♖e8). So did Caruana (20...♔c8 and later 23...♗c7 and 24...♘f8).

In any case, by the time Black regained his sacrificed pawn, he was lost, **24 ♗f4! ♘b8 25 ♗xb8 ♗xb8 26 ♘xd4**.

But it took several more moves, **26...♕d6 27 ♘e6+ ♔e7 28 ♘c5+ ♔f7 29 ♕c4+ ♔g6 30 g3 h5 31 ♕e4+ ♔h6 32 ♕xb7**, before the outcome of the game was clear.

Caruana downplays the significance of his opening preparation. "It's been greatly exaggerated that this is a strength of mine." He joked that Anish Giri "always manages to out-prepare me in the opening."

"Sometimes he ends up four pawns up after the opening, and usually the game ends in a draw," he said with a laugh.

Wounding, Not Killing

Caruana is not Kasparov. His most evident flaw is an occasional failure to deliver the knockout blow.

Twice in the 2018 world championship match – the event he had devoted his life to winning – he failed to play critical, if not decisive moves. He wounded Carlsen. He didn't kill him.

Caruana joked about this failing when he commented on his game with Meier (above). "I could have finished it off faster," he wrote after 26 moves. "But the advantage is so overwhelming it's hard to ruin it, even for me!"

He doesn't ruin dead-won positions. But a promising position can be a problem. Even when he takes an enormous amount of time to calculate a killer, he may step back.

Firouzja – Caruana
Wijk aan Zee 2021

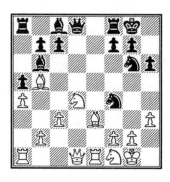

Black to move

He was way ahead on the clock and could afford his first "big think" of the game. Natural candidates include 18...♕f6, 18...♕g5 and 18...c6. But a master's intuition tells him there is one other move that could be much better.

18

"I spent at least 50 minutes, maybe more, just calculating 18...♘xg2," Caruana said after the game. "It was the only move I was thinking about."

The easy part, after 19 ♔xg2 ♘h4+, was dispensing with 20 ♔h2? or 20 ♔g1?. Then 20...♕d5 21 f3 ♗xd4 and ...♘xf3+ would win.

And it was not difficult to visualize the remaining move, 20 ♔h1, and then 20...♕d5+ 21 f3.

Not pulling the trigger

But here he hit a wall of uncertainty. There was no clear continuation to 21...♗xh3 22 ♘h2.

Neither was there one for 21...c5 22 ♘c2 ♕f5 23 ♘h2.

"I didn't quite see how to follow up," he said. He eventually chose **18...c6.**

Then came **19 ♗c4 ♗c7**, when 19...♘xg2! 20 ♔xg2 ♕h4 would have been strong.

Caruana eventually drew – with some difficulty – after **20 ♘g3 ♘d5?** (20...♘xg2!).

"Every part of me wanted to take on g2," he said later. But he wanted to be certain and his calculation couldn't find certainty.

Emotional Stamina

Caruana takes disappointments well. He has what Bent Larsen called "emotional stamina." He readily concedes when he is outplayed and when he doesn't know exactly how it happened.

"It was kind of funny," he said after he lost a rook-and-bishop endgame wonderfully played by Carlsen at Bilbao 2012. "Because after the game I couldn't even point out a clear mistake." He wondered if his only error was making a neutral seventh move of the game – and laughed when he said it.

Privately, he is not so unflappable, according to former trainer Alexander Chernin. During his drive to the grandmaster title, Fabiano had had mood swings, he said.

They ranged "from elation and seeing himself as world champion after a significant win to wanting to quit chess completely after a disastrous tournament," Chernin told journalist Diana Mihajlova.

But like a true professional, Caruana accepts the inevitability of mistakes and what we call "luck." He knows luck tends to balance out. "I saved some truly awful positions," he said after the Moscow 2016 Candidates tournament.

Then he added, "And I saved some truly awful positions for my opponents as well."

First Moves

It may surprise Fabianistas, his devoted fans, that he was first encouraged to learn chess as a remedial assignment. He learned the moves at age 5 when he joined an after-school program near his Brooklyn home. "I was a decent student but had some disciplinary problems, and they thought that would help me out," he told *Interview* magazine.

Fabiano was so tiny when he started to play that his feet could not reach the floor when he sat in a tournament chair. Instead, he sat hunched up on his knees. In his first tournament, two months shy of his sixth birthday, he lost his first game, won his second, finished 1-3 and was given a US chess federation rating of 473.

In late 1997, he met Bruce Pandolfini, the best-known chess teacher in America. Pandolfini had been portrayed, by Ben Kingsley, in the movie *Searching for Bobby Fischer* and was later the technical advisor for the TV series *The Queen's Gambit*.

When Pandolfini eventually spoke to Fabiano's parents, he agreed to give him regular lessons. That day Pandolfini wrote a note to himself: "This kid has great promise...It's obvious he loves chess and is extremely gifted. You can see it in his eyes."

He gradually came to understand Fabiano's character. "His greatest strength is that he has the courage of his convictions," Pandolfini told the *New Yorker*. "He is stubborn and sticks to his ideas, come hell or high water," Pandolfini said. "That serves him well in tournament play – you need to believe in yourself. But it makes him harder to teach."

When Fabiano turned 7, he was rated over 1100. He demonstrated tactical skill but also a feeling of where pieces belong. A year later, when his rating had soared to 1575, he began a game in a weekend tournament against a slightly higher-rated opponent, Thomas Murphy. It went **1 e4 d6 2 d4 ♘f6 3 ♘c3 g6 4 ♘f3 ♗g7 5 ♗c4 0-0 6 0-0 c6** and now **7 e5! ♘e8 8 ♖e1 d5 9 ♗b3 ♔h8**.

Here most 1500 players would choose a developing move such as 10 ♗f4.

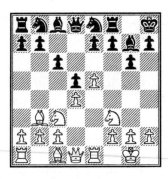

White to move

You can find the best move by realizing two of White's two developed minor pieces are misplaced. Or by foreseeing that Black's best source of counterplay lies in ...f6.

Caruana chose **10 ♘e2!** so he could play ♘f4, c2-c3 and ♗c2.

After **10...f6 11 ♘f4** he had a substantial advantage, e.g. 11...♘c7 12 exf6 exf6 13 c3 and ♗c2!.

He won after **11...fxe5? 12 ♘xe5 ♘c7? 13 ♘exg6+! hxg6 14 ♘xg6+ ♔g8 15 ♘xe7+** (15...♔f7 16 ♕h5+ and mates).

Soon Caruana was studying with a different teacher, Miron Sher. His rating broke 2000 when he was 9. His progress was expensive, costing his family $70,000 a year.

This figure shocks people outside the chess community. But another young American, Daniel Naroditsky, became a grandmaster after his father spent more than $50,000 a year and amassed a library of more than 1,000 chess books. And in 2021, when Abhimanyu Mishra became the youngest grandmaster in history, his father said he had already spent more than $270,000 on his son's chess career.

Caruana was on the verge of becoming a master when his parents moved the family to Europe. He told *Deadspin*:

"That was my parents' decision entirely. I wanted to stay in the U.S. *[laughs]* I had friends in the U.S. and my family was there and my home was there, but my parents wanted to visit Europe and explore a few countries for a few years, and it ended up being pretty much a decade that we were in Europe."

Soviet School

Anatoly Karpov saw Caruana for the first time at a French tournament in 2008. After playing a series of rapid games with him, Karpov said he recognized not only what Fabiano knew about chess but how he was taught. Caruana is a product of the Soviet school, Karpov concluded.

Caruana's first foreign teacher, Boris Zlotnik, like Sher, was a Soviet émigré. In fact, Zlotnik had attended the same chess classes as Karpov, given by

Mikhail Botvinnik. Living in Spain, Zlotnik had never heard of Caruana when they met near Madrid in December 2004. Zlotnik asked his parents where Fabiano would be going to school. "We want Fabiano to become a professional chessplayer and therefore he will not go," Zlotnik said he was told.

Zlotnik proposed giving Fabiano two lessons a week and having him play one tournament a month. The lessons covered different aspects of chess. For example in November 2005, he gave him a homework task:

In the starting position White plays 1 f3, 2 ♔f2, 3 ♔g3 and 4 ♔h4. How does Black deliver mate on the fourth move?

Caruana quickly emailed him back: "Boris, the answer is 1 f3 e5 2 ♔f2 ♛f6 3 ♔g3 ♛xf3+ 4 ♔h4 ♗e7 mate," he said. "This puzzle took me about 10 minutes."

Yuri Razuvaev later cited a Soviet chess joke: No matter how bad things are going, it can always be made worse by a change of trainers. But this didn't apply to Caruana. By 2007, he had moved on and kept improving. Among his new Soviet-trained teachers were Alexander Chernin and Vladimir Chuchelov.

Perhaps the most important quality he took from the Soviet players was their attitude towards study. "I inherited their work ethic, which is pretty good," he said years later. "If there is one way to play chess, it is probably the Russians'." Pandolfini adds that he taught Fabiano never to give up if there was any play left. He did this by repeating a mantra, "Fight like Botvinnik."

Caruana later summed up his European apprenticeship: "I started working pretty much all day, working with coaches in Spain and Hungary and Switzerland. We travelled Europe for about 10 years, and I pretty much played chess non-stop. I would play 100 games a year or something, for 10 years. And I went from a decent, talented kid level, to pretty much a strong grandmaster level by the time I came back."

But that's getting ahead of the Caruana script. Let's begin with the early games of that boy from Brooklyn.

1
Risk Lessons

Fabiano was a veteran of international chess before his ninth birthday. That is, at the same age when Magnus Carlsen was playing his very first tournament games.

When he was eight years and ten months old, Caruana finished second in a Pan American Under-10 Championship in a field that was composed mainly of older boys, including three other future grandmasters. His play in games like the following, from another youth tournament, was far more mature than Carlsen at the same age. Caruana was learning the rules of positional risk.

Levan Bregadze – Caruana
World Under-10 Championship,
Heraklion 2002
Dzhindzi-Indian Defense (A40)

1	d4	g6
2	c4	♝g7
3	♞c3	c5

Caruana was already familiar with some move-order finesses. This is a way to prod a 1 d4 player out of his comfort zone.

If White defends his d-pawn with 4 ♞f3, then 4...cxd4 5 ♞xd4 ♞c6 may be unfamiliar to him. It's an English Opening position and a harmless one, after 6 e3 ♞f6 and ...0-0/...d5.

| 4 | d5! | ♝xc3+? |

This is a high-risk weapon of GM Roman Dzhindzhichashvili, rather than transposing into a Benoni opening (4...♞f6).

| 5 | bxc3 | f5 |

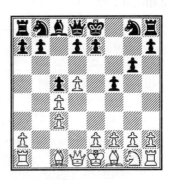

And this raises the stakes. If Black had allowed e2-e4 – such as with 5...♞f6 6 ♛c2 d6 7 e4 – White's advantage in space would count more than the doubling of his c-pawns.

| 6 | h4! |

Black's gamble pays off if White responds routinely, such as with 6 ♞f3.

Then Black can handle the position in the style of a 1930s

23

Aron Nimzovich game. He could play 6...♕a5, place knights on b6 and f6 and try to squeeze White with ...♘e4, ...♕a4 or ...♘a4.

But Black doesn't have time for this after 6 h4! because it threatens 7 h5 and 8 hxg6.

6 ... ♘f6

7 ♘h3

White should double the bet with 7 h5! and 7...♘xh5 8 e4.

Then Black can lose a miniature (8...fxe4? 9 ♖xh5! gxh5 10 ♕xh5+ and mates).

His alternatives are heading to the inferior middlegames of 7...♖g8 8 hxg6 hxg6 9 ♘f3 or 7...gxh5 8 ♘h3 and ♘f4.

7 ... ♘e4

Caruana could have killed off the remaining tactical gremlins with 7...♕a5!, followed by 8...♘bd7.

8 ♕c2 ♕a5

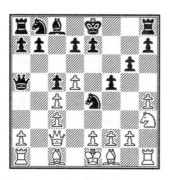

9 ♗d2

White's second lost opportunity was 9 ♘g5!.

He would win by pinning after 9...♕xc3+? 10 ♕xc3 ♘xc3 11 ♗b2 and 9...♘xc3? 10 ♗d2.

And he would renew the h4-h5 idea after 9...♘xg5 10 ♗xg5 or 9...d6 10 h5.

9 ... d6

10 ♘g5 ♘xd2

11 ♕xd2 h6!

12 ♘f3 ♘d7

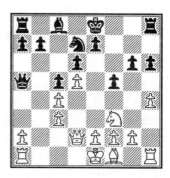

Twelve moves old and this game could teach Caruana a lot:

He didn't realize how great a strategic gamble (...♗xc3+) he was taking.

But when it was not punished, the reward was nearly as great as when you get away with an unsound attacking sacrifice.

Black has an emerging positional advantage.

13	e3	♞f6
14	♖c1	♗d7

He prepares to castle queenside. This is more solid than 13...♞b6 and ...♕a4.

He might have tried 14...0-0 because 15 h5 g5 is a safer kingside than it looks. But it was not worth calculating 15 e4 fxe4 16 ♕xh6 when there was a simple alternative.

15	♗d3	0-0-0

Both sides have weak pawns and poorly placed pieces.

But the position will not seem double-edged if Black understands the power of ...e5!.

If White lets that pawn structure stand, he would be strategically lost.

For example, 16 0-0 e5 (threat: ...e4) 17 ♗e2 e4!.

Then 18 ♞h2 g5! or 18 ♞e1 g5!.

16	♕b2	e5!
17	dxe6	♗xe6
18	0-0	

Black's minor pieces are superior to White's. But this will not be evident until he repositions his bishop on c6. Then it defends his weakest point (b7) and also aims at the kingside.

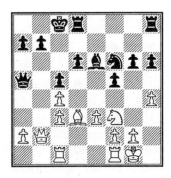

In addition, White's h4-pawn is exploitable. It can't be won by force. Rather, Black can use it to open the kingside (...h5 and a well-prepared ...g5!).

18	...	♗d7!
19	♞d2	♗c6
20	♖fe1	♖he8

White needs play. But e3-e4 would be met by ...f4!.

Then Black can prepare the knockout plan of ...g5 that succeeds in the game.

21	f3	♕c7

Another way Black can improve his pieces is ...♞d7-e5. But here 21...♞d7 22 h5! gives White chances his position does not warrant.

22	♘f1	h5!
23	♕c2	♘d7
24	♕f2	♘e5
25	♗e2	

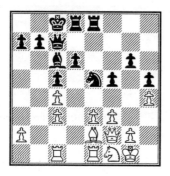

A young player who reads his Nimzovich would be strongly tempted by ...♕f7 and ...♘xc4.

Uncle Aron was a superb tactician and he would have approved of 25...♕f7 26 ♘d2 f4!.

For example, 27 exf4 ♕xf4 28 ♖cd1 ♖f8 with a threat of 29...♘g4!.

White would nearly be in a middlegame zugzwang after 29 g3 ♕f5 30 f4 ♔b8 in view of 31 ♘f1? ♕e4!, for example.

Caruana was capable of working out at least some of these lines. He was "a little calculating machine," as his former teacher Bruce Pandolfini said.

25	...	♕a5

But after 25...♕f7, White can play 26 ♕g3! rather than 26 ♘d2.

Then on 26...♘xc4 27 ♗xc4 ♕xc4 28 ♕xg6 Black would keep his advantage.

For example, after 28...♕xh4 29 ♕xf5+ ♔b8 30 e4 d5.

But Caruana's position is so good he can try other ways to win before he starts knocking pieces and pawns off the board. First, he teases the idea of capturing the a2-pawn.

26	♖ed1	♕a3
27	♕e1	♔b8
28	♔h1	

Even with Black's a7-pawn protected, he couldn't play 28...♕xa2 because the queen comes under perpetual rook attack (29 ♖a1 ♕c2 30 ♖dc1).

With his king on h1, White seems impervious to tactics.

28	...	f4!

At first, 29 exf4 seems safe because 29...♘xf3? 30 gxf3 ♗xf3+ turns the tables after 31 ♗xf3! ♖xe1 32 ♖xe1.

However, 29...♘xc4! followed by doubling rooks on the e-file should be decisive (30 ♕f2 ♕xa2).

29 e4?

White's best try was 29 ♕f2, with a difficult defense ahead after, say, 29...fxe3 30 ♘xe3 ♖e6.

29	...	♕a5
30	♘h2	♕c7!

In retrospect we can see White was lost after 29 e4?.

There is no good answer to the opening of the g-file after ...g5, supported by ...♕e7.

31	♕f2	♕e7
32	♖g1	g5
33	hxg5	♕xg5

Black's simplest plan is to double rooks (...♖g8-g6,...♖dg8) and break through with his h-pawn.

For example, 34 ♖cd1 ♖g8 35 ♖d2 ♖g6 36 ♗f1 ♖dg8 37 ♕e1 h4 and ...h3.

34	g3	fxg3
35	♕xg3	♕e3

36	♕e1	♘g4!

This is the neatest finisher (37 fxg4 ♗xe4+ wins).

Or 37 ♖g2 ♘xh2 38 ♖xh2 ♖xe4!.

37	♘f1	♕f4

An immediate killer is 37...♘f2+ 38 ♔h2 ♕f4+ 39 ♔g2 ♘xe4!.

38	♖g2	♘e5

And here 38...♖xe4! was prettier.

39	♕d2	♕f7
40	♖f2	♗xe4
41	♘g3	♗c6

42 White resigns.

There was nothing to be done about ...♖g8, for example.

Shortly before this game, Caruana began entering the strongest regular tournaments in America, the New York Masters, held every Tuesday at the Marshall Chess Club. This meant playing four 30-minute games in an evening, against opponents who typically outrated him by 300 points.

Fabiano did not stand out. In December 2002, for example, he finished last in the field of 20. Hikaru Nakamura, who had just turned 15, took first prize.

He often lost all of the games he played in a tournament. This happened even after his rating rose above 2200, and he was an official master, in January 2004.

But Caruana persisted. "I went practically every Tuesday," he recalled. When he moved from New York later in 2004 he had played in some 30 New York Masters tournaments and earned just $80 in prize money. In contrast, GM Leonid Yudasin pocketed more than $16,000 in them. But Caruana was learning.

2
When Not To Calculate

One of the things he learned was how patience is a weapon. Many youngsters, especially those with a gift for tactics, regard forcing moves as their only way of making a good position better. It often takes years for them to appreciate that slow progress makes a forcing move more powerful when its time comes.

Sergio Garza Marco – Caruana
Lorca 2005
Queen Pawn's Game (A48)

1	d4	♘f6
2	♘f3	g6
3	c3	♗g7
4	♗g5	

White's move order, a favorite of Vladimir Kramnik, allows him to shift play into a Pirc Defense after 4...0-0 5 ♘bd2 d6 6 e4!.

4	...	d5

Databases indicate this position occurred most often in the games of Garry Kasparov. He generated counterplay with ...e5 or ...♘e4.

Caruana goes instead for the equally good ...c5.

5	♘bd2	0-0
6	e3	♘bd7
7	♗e2	c5
8	0-0	b6

Those databases also show that *this* position, reached via different move orders, occurred most often in the games of Caruana.

In one of his First Saturday tournaments in 2004, he used all three of Black's basic ideas (...c5, ...♘e4 and ...e5).

His game with Laszlo Eperjesi went 9 a4 a6 10 ♕b1 ♗b7 11 ♖c1 ♖e8 12 b4! c4! 13 h3 b5 14 ♗f4 ♘e4! 15 ♘xe4 dxe4.

Now instead of 16 ♘e5 ♘b6 and ...♘d5, White spiraled downward after 16 ♘d2? e5!.

9	b4	

29

This and a2-a4-a5 are White's most promising sources of play.

Ten years after this game, when Caruana was a world-class player, Kramnik tested him with 9 a4.

Then 9...♗b7 10 a5! would have expanded nicely on the queenside (10...bxa5 11 ♘b3 or 11 ♕a4 regains the pawn with advantage).

Caruana replied 9...a6, so that 10 a5 b5 with play like the current game.

Instead, Kramnik obtained a nice edge with 10 b4 ♗b7 11 a5! and 11...cxb4 12 cxb4 b5 13 ♖c1. (But Caruana won.)

9 ... ♗b7

In this and similar ♗g5 variations of the King's Indian Defense, Black can seek the two-bishop advantage. Here this means 9...h6 10 ♗h4 g5 11 ♗g3 ♘h5.

But by 2005 Caruana had shied away from the kind of committal kingside pushes he adopted in Game 1.

10 ♕b3

More in tune with the queenside plan is 10 bxc5! bxc5 11 ♖b1.

For example, 11...♕c8 12 ♕b3 ♗a6 13 ♗xa6 ♕xa6 14 ♕b7 is a small White plus.

10 ... ♗c6

To meet the threat of 11 bxc5 bxc5 12 ♕xb7, Caruana had to evaluate two pawn structures.

Exchanging c-pawns, 10...cxb4 11 cxb4 as in the Kramnik game, means White will have the better long-term chances of exploiting the c-file.

Sealing the file, 10...c4, as in the Eperjesi game, is better. But after 11 ♕c2 it would not be clear where Black's middlegame play lies.

For instance, 11...♘e4? turns out badly now (12 ♘xe4 dxe4 13 ♘d2).

So, Caruana delays a decision about the queenside. He looks at ...e5.

11 a4

White might have tried 11 ♗a6, which threatens to trap the bishop with 12 b5.

But it is White's bishop that is trapped after 11...c4 and 12...♘b8.

11 ... ♖e8

Now 12 ♗a6 works better, e.g. 12...♘b8 13 ♘e5! ♘xa6 14 ♘xc6 ♕d7 15 b5.

12 a5

Here 12 ♘e5 would likely have led to 12...♘xe5 13 dxe5 ♘d7 14 f4.

Then 14...f6 15 exf6? exf6 favors Black.

But 15 ♗h4! can be the reverse (15...fxe5? 16 e4!).

Black should maintain the balance with 15...e6.

12 ... c4

There was a tactical point to 12 a5. White can refute 12...e5 with 13 b5! (13...♗b7 14 a6 ♗c8 15 ♗xf6! ♘xf6 16 ♘xe5).

Black can insert ...c4 to avert that. But that gives White a potential outpost at d4.

For example, 13...c4 14 ♕b4 ♗b7 15 a6 ♗c8 and now 16 dxe5 ♘xe5 17 ♘xe5 ♖xe5 18 ♘f3 confers a lasting plus-over-equals advantage.

13 ♕c2 b5

The next few moves show what happens in a closed position when one player has a plan and the other doesn't.

14 ♖fe1 ♕c8

15 ♕b2? ♘e4!

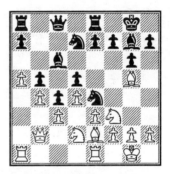

Black's previous move becomes understandable after 16 ♘xe4? dxe4 17 ♘d2 and then 17...e5!.

He could continue with ...♕b7, ...f5, ...h6 with an avalanche of advancing kingside pawns.

16 ♗f4 ♕b7

17 ♗d1 a6

18 ♖e2

White could have held Black's edge to a minimum by swapping knights with ♘e5 on one of the

31

last two moves. Caruana, in turn, could have stopped that with …f6.

18   …   f6!

Now that …e5 is coming, his superiority should steadily grow.

For example, 19…e5 20 ♗g3 ♘xg3 21 hxg3 e4 followed by …f5 lays the groundwork for a winning breakthrough with …f4.

Occupying d4 wouldn't be enough to save White after 20 dxe5 (instead of 20 ♗g3).

For instance, 20…fxe5 21 ♗g3 ♘xg3 22 hxg3 e4 23 ♘d4 ♘e5 and a later …♘d3.

19   h3!   e5

20   dxe5   fxe5

21   ♗h2

It was natural for a "little calculating machine" to take a long look at 21…d4 or 21…♘xd2 followed by 22…d4.

Opening the center would win in some scenarios (21…♘xd2 22 ♘xd2? d4! 23 exd4 ♗xg2).

But it is not convincing in others (22 ♖xd2 d4 23 exd4 exd4 24 cxd4).

21   …   ♘d6

A maturing master knows when he can – and when he should – take his time. Here Black has many more ways to improve his position than White does before …d4.

As James Mason said more than a century ago, "Don't play a good move too soon."

22   ♗c2

In addition, there are more ways for White to err and make …d4 stronger. For example, 22 ♘f1? d4! and …♗xf3.

22   …   ♖ad8

23   ♖d1

Again, Black could try to calculate his way to a quick finish, with 23…e4 24 ♗xd6 exf3 25 ♘xf3 d4!.

23   …   ♘f7

But calculating is unnecessary. There is no White antidote to 24…d4 or 24…e4 25 ♘d4 ♘de5 and …♘d3.

24   e4?

A bad move in a bad position.

24   …   d4

25	cxd4	exd4
26	♘xd4	♘de5!

White may have foreseen this position when he played 24 e4. He could have seen how Black could win his queen with 27...♖xd4 28 ♕xd4 ♘f3+.

But he would get nearly enough compensation for it after 29 ♘xf3 ♗xd4 30 ♘xd4.

The reason White is lost in the diagram is that the real threat is 27...♘d3!.

For example, 27 ♕a1 ♘d3 28 ♘2f3 ♖xe4 or 28...♗xe4, and his position collapses.

27	♘xc6	♘f3+

Now 28 ♘xf3 ♖xd1+! makes it easy.

28	gxf3	♗xb2

29	♘xd8	♖xd8

Black will have three connected passed pawns after ...♗c3xb4xa5.

30	f4	♗c3
31	e5	

But it was still possible to lose if he allowed 32 e6! ♘d6?? 33 ♘e4! or 32...♘h6 33 e7.

31	...	♗xb4

The bishop guards e7 and d6 so 32 e6 ♘d6 33 ♘e4 ♕e7 or 32...♘h6 33 ♘e4 ♖xd1+ is harmless.

32	♘e4	♖xd1+
33	♗xd1	♗e7
34	♘f6+	♗xf6
35	exf6	♕c6
36	**White resigns.**	

By the end of 2005, Caruana had added 200 points to his rating and was above 2400. But he wasn't certain he would devote his life to chess. Before switching federations to Italy, he told *Chess Life* his goals were to become a grandmaster … and, perhaps, a real estate investor.

3

Second Chances to Sparkle

"Back then I preferred to attack all the time," Fabiano recalled about his adolescent style. "I really loved sacrificing pieces to get at the enemy king. I played like that for quite a long time."

He was allowed to win that way because his opponents were often poor defenders. Sloppy defense can make any tactician a Tal. In this game, he rushed his attack and was granted a second – and then a third – chance to sparkle.

Caruana – Adalberto Villavicencio
Andorra la Vella 2006
*Sicilian Defense,
Najdorf Variation (B96)*

1	e4	c5
2	♘f3	d6
3	d4	cxd4
4	♘xd4	♘f6
5	♘c3	a6

In Europe, Caruana faced opponents who knew more about trendy, sharp openings than Americans.

There were about three times as many FIDE-rated players in Spain than in the United States when he moved in 2004.

But even in his first strong Spanish tournaments he often faced opponents who ran out of memorized book moves long before he did.

For example, Raphael Cortes Jurado – Caruana, Madrid Championship 2005 went: 1 e4 c5 2 ♘f3 ♘c6 3 d4 cxd4 4 ♘xd4 ♘f6 5 ♘c3 e5 6 ♘db5 d6 7 ♗g5 a6 8 ♘a3 b5 9 ♗xf6 gxf6 10 ♘d5 ♗g7 11 c3 ♘e7 12 ♘xe7 ♕xe7 13 ♘c2 ♗b7 14 ♗d3 f5 15 ♘e3 fxe4 16 ♘f5 ♕f6 17 ♗xe4 d5 18 ♗c2? (*The first new move, in place of 18 ♗xd5 ♖d8 19 ♕g4*) ♗f8 19 a4 b4 20 a5 0-0-0 21 ♘g3 ♔b8 22 0-0 h5 23 ♖e1 h4 24 ♘f1 ♖g8 25 ♕e2 e4 (*25...b3!*) 26 c4 b3 27 ♗xb3 d4 28 c5 ♗xc5 29 ♕h5 e3 30 f3 ♗xf3 31 ♕xc5 ♖xg2+ 32 ♔h1 ♖f2+ White resigned.

Yet the following game is the first Najdorf Sicilian of his that you will find in many databases. He soon finds himself improvising in a rare sideline.

6	♗g5	e6
7	f4	♕c7

By far the main lines of the 6 ♗g5 Najdorf are 7...♗e7, 7...♘bd7 and the Poisoned Pawn 7...♕b6.

8	♗xf6	gxf6

9	♕e2	

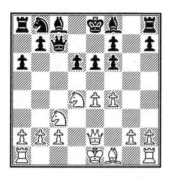

Even in the heavily vetted Najdorf, some early ad libbing is possible. There is nothing wrong with doubling Black's pawns, rather than the book 8 ♕f3.

Or with preparing for 0-0-0 this way, rather than with the Rauzer Variation-like 9 ♕d2.

9	...	♘c6

10	0-0-0	♗d7

Now 11 ♕h5 is tempting because it stops 11...0-0-0 12 ♕xf7.

But 11...♘xd4 12 ♖xd4 ♕c5! would force the queen to retreat or trade into a balanced endgame.

11	g3

This protects the f4-pawn and enables White to apply pressure to e6 with ♗h3/f4-f5.

For example, 11...♖c8 12 ♗h3 ♗e7? 13 f5 and even 13...e5 14 ♘e6! favors him.

11	...	♘xd4

Black's best counterplay lies on the c-file and with ...b5.

But the immediate 11...b5 makes 12 ♘d5! possible. The reason is 12...exd5 13 ♘xc6! and exd5+.

Or 12...♕d8 13 ♘xc6 ♗xc6 14 f5 with a sizable edge.

12	♖xd4	♖c8

13	♗h3	h5

Black's last move does two things. It creates the possibility of ...h4xg3 counterplay. And it prevents the inhibiting ♕h5, e.g. 13...♗c6? 14 ♕h5!, when White threatens ♗xe6.

14	♖hd1

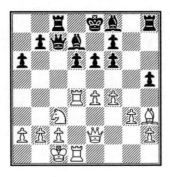

Now 14...b5 15 ♔b1 looks like the opening act of a typical Sicilian Defense melodrama.

But White would be ready to blow up the center with 16 e5!.

This is a thematic sacrifice in this pawn structure, based in part on prospects for ♘e4!.

Black would stand well after 16...fxe5 17 fxe5 d5 – if it were not for more sacrifices.

Good enough is 18 ♘e4 dxe4 19 ♖xd7.

But better is 18 ♘xd5! exd5 19 e6!.

For instance, 19...fxe6 20 ♖xd5 and ♖xd7. Or 19...♗xe6? 20 ♗xe6 fxe6? 21 ♕xg6+ ♗e7 22 ♕g6+ and mates.

14   ...   h4

15   g4

A more mature Caruana would likely have chosen 15 ♗g4 and ♗h5.

But keeping the h-file closed – and eyeing the possibility of a g4-g5 sacrifice – was tempting.

15   ...   ♕a5

16   ♕e3

Now the threatened 16...♖xc3 and ...♕xa2 would lose to 17 ♕xc3 ♕xa2 18 ♕c7!.

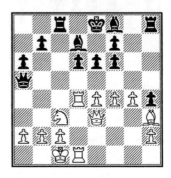

16   ...   ♕c5!

Clever play.

If Black had played the direct 15...♕c5 White would have had that thematic sack, 16 e5 fxe5 17 fxe5 d5 18 ♘xd5! exd5 19 ♖xd5 and wins.

But by inducing ♕e3, Black stopped the sacrifice (17 e5? dxe5 18 ♖xd7? ♕xe3+).

He also threatens to get into a good endgame with 17...e5.

17   ♕d3   b5

18   a3

The Sicilian is fun to play because there are game-changing tactics for both sides.

Here White would lose after 18...♗h6 19 ♖xd6?? ♗xf4+.

But he would win after 19 g5! fxg5 30 ♖xd6!.

18 ... ♗c6?

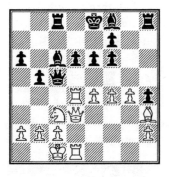

Consistent and good was 18...a5! with the idea of 19...b4.

Black may have rejected it because the b5-square is vulnerable (19 ♗f1 b4? 20 axb4 axb4 21 ♘b5! with advantage).

But 19...♖b8 would have put the onus back on White.

Instead, Black was tempted by the idea of trapping the d4-rook with 18...♗c6 and 19...e5.

19 g5?!

This is an attacking move with a positional goal, to undermine Black's weakest point, his e6-pawn, with 20 g6!.

But more accurate was a waiting move, 19 ♔b1!.

Then 19...e5 20 ♖d5! is a good sacrifice, 20...♗xd5 21 ♘xd5

and ♘xf6+ or g4-g5.

Routine replies like 19...♗e7 would make g4-g5 stronger.

For example, 19...♗e7 20 g5! fxg5 21 ♘d5! exd5? 22 ♗xc8.

Or 21...gxf4 22 b4! ♛a7 23 ♘xe7 and 24 ♖xd6 with a bind.

19 ... fxg5

20 e5!

Now 20...dxe5?? 21 ♖d8+ or 20...d5 21 ♘e4! wins.

Also 20...gxf4 21 exd6 ♖b8 22 ♗xe6!.

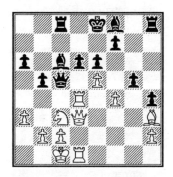

20 ... ♖g8?

Remarkably safe was 20...♗g7!.

Then 21 ♖xd6 0-0! and Black lives to play a middlegame (22 ♖xe6! gxf4!).

It looks like White must have a forced win with 21 ♗xe6 fxe6 22 ♛g6+ ♔f8.

But 23 ♖xd6 ♛e3+ 24 ♔b1 ♛xf4! is a dead end.

With a clock ticking, you can drive yourself crazy trying to find the mate that doesn't exist. For example, 25 ♖d8+ ♖xd8 26 ♖xd8+ ♔e7.

Or 25 ♖xc6 ♖xc6 26 ♖d8+ ♔e7 27 ♖d6! looks like a killer.

But Black is not worse after 27...♕xe5!.

21   exd6

The threat of 22 d7+ wins – and so would 21 b4 ♕a7 22 f5!.

21   ...   ♔d7

Or 21...♗d7 22 ♘e4! and 21...♖d8 22 d7+ ♔e7 23 b4 ♕a7 24 f5!.

A defensive slip has given Caruana a second chance to sparkle.

22   f5!

The vulnerable e6-square is ultimately decisive, as 22...♗g7 23 fxe6+ fxe6 24 ♕g6 shows.

Or 22...♕e5 23 fxe6+ fxe6 24 ♖f1 and ♖f7+ or ♘e4.

22   ...   g4

This sets a trap (23 fxe6+ fxe6+ 24 ♖xg4? ♖xg4 25 ♗xg4 ♕g5+) and provides a way for the queen to defend the kingside.

23   fxe6+   fxe6

24   ♗xg4   ♕g5+

25   ♔b1

Now 25...♕g6 would temporarily stanch the tactics and prompt Caruana to try to win with low-wattage moves.

For instance, 26 ♘e4 ♔d8! 27 ♘c5! ♕xd3 28 ♖1xd3, followed by a capture on e6.

25   ...   ♗g7

But now he has a choice of pretty wins. One is 26 ♘e4! ♕e5 27 ♗xe6+! so that 27...♕xe6 28 ♘c5+ or 27...♔xe6 28 ♕b3+.

26   ♗xe6+!   ♔xe6

Now 27 ♘e4! ♕e5 28 ♕b3+ would transpose into the last line.

27   d7!

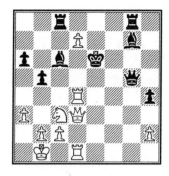

Black would only be a pawn down after 27...♗xd4 28 dxc8(♕)+ ♖xc8 29 ♕xd4.

But with his king on e6 he would be doomed by 30 ♖g1 or 30 ♘e4.

For example, 29...♔f7 30 ♖f1+ ♔g8 31 ♕f2 and ♖g1.

27	...	♖c7
28	d8(♕)	♖xd8
29	♖xd8	♗e5

Also 29...♕e5 30 ♕g6+.

| 30 | ♖d6+ | ♔f7 |

And **Black resigned** before 31 ♕h7+.

In the year this was played, the Caruana family moved to Hungary and found new teachers. He had become one of the world's more than 2,500 international masters in December 2005 and was about to join a more selective club.

His bright future was recognized in May 2006 when he was invited to Russia to play in the fourth edition of a tournament titled "Young Stars of the World." In the field of several grandmasters-to-be he tied for third place and drew with the second-place finisher, Ian Nepomniachtchi.

4
Norm Harvesting

When Caruana became a player to watch, he was competing with other youngsters with a future. His most frequent opponent had become Tamas Fodor Jr., a Hungarian one year older than him. Fodor won their first game easily, in the World Under-10 Championship of 2001, where he shared first place. They went on to meet six times in the First Saturday tournaments of Budapest. It was just a matter of amassing the norms needed for the GM title. They were both grandmaster strength by then.

Caruana – Tamas Fodor Jr.
Budapest 2007
Bishop's Opening (C24)

1	e4	e5
2	♗c4	♘f6

Opening books virtually ignored the Bishop's Opening for most of the 20th century. An authoritative 1965 opening encyclopedia by the respected analyst Alexey Sokolsky didn't contain a word about it in its 463 pages.

3	d3	c6

The reason is 4...d5 was regarded as the refutation.

The most popular English-language opening text, *Modern Chess Openings,* dispensed with the Bishop's Opening in its 1982 edition with a simple comment "3...c6! 4 ♕e2 ♗e7 5 f4 d5!."

4	♘f3	d5
5	♗b3	

This retreat, based on 5...dxe4 6 ♘g5! and its threat to f7, is what textbooks ignored for so long.

Instead, they claimed the best White could do was fight for equality with 5 exd5 cxd5 6 ♗b3.

5	...	♗d6

For decades after the Morphy era of 1 e4 e5 games, it was widely assumed that whoever pushed his d-pawn to his fourth rank first had an inherent advantage.

Therefore, Black must be better here as he controls more space.

But White began experimenting with d2-d3, rather than d2-d4, in Ruy Lopez variations at the turn of the 21st century.

This prompted masters to rethink the conventional wisdom.

They realized that ...d5 can be more of a weakness than an asset.

For example, 5...♘bd7 6 exd5! cxd5 7 0-0 and now 7...♗d6 8 ♘c3! ♘b6 9 ♖e1 favors White.

6   ♘c3   ♗e6

White is only slightly better after 6...dxe4 7 ♘g5 0-0 8 ♘gxe4. But that is generally more than he gets in the main lines of 1 e4 e5 openings.

7   ♗g5!   ♗c7

This was a new Black move, rather than 7...d4 8 ♘e2 or 8 ♗xe6 dxc3 9 ♗f5.

8   d4!

This recalls a Caro-Kann Defense line that runs 1 e4 c6 2 d3 d5 3 ♘d2 e5 4 ♘gf3 ♘d7?.

Black cannot defend his e5-pawn with ...♘c6. This makes 5 d4! strong. The favorable liquidation of the center was made famous in a Tal – Smyslov brilliancy.

8   ...   exd4

The story is similar here since 8...♘bd7? drops a pawn (9 exd5 cxd5 10 ♗xd5).

Another point of 8 d4! is shown by the simplifying 8...dxe4? 9 ♘xe4 ♗xb3? 10 axb3.

It takes a while to realize Black is nearly lost. For example, 10...♕e7 11 0-0 ♘bd7 12 dxe5 ♘xe5 13 ♘xe5 ♗xe5 14 ♖e1 and White threatens 15 f4.

9   ♘xd4

White should not sell his superiority cheaply with 9 ♕xd4 dxe4! (10 ♗xe6 exf3).

If he wants to retake with his queen on d4 he should insert 9 exd5! cxd5 and then 10 ♕xd4!, so that 10...♘c6 11 ♕h4 and 0-0-0.

Also good for him is 9 exd5 dxc3 in view of 10 dxe6 fxe6 11 ♕e2.

9   ...   0-0

10   ♕e2   h6!

11   ♗h4

White's e4-pawn becomes a problem now. The best way to target it is 11...♖e8 with the idea of 12...♗a5 or just retreating the e6-bishop, to d7 or c8.

A cute tactic is 12 ♘xe6 ♖xe6 13 0-0-0 ♗f4+! and then 14 ♔b1 ♘xe4! (15 ♗xd8? ♘xc3+ and ...♖xe2).

White would be better after 15 ♕xe4! but not as much as in the game.

11   ...   ♗a5?

The pin threatens 12...g5 13 ♗g3 ♗xc3 and ...♘xe4.

Black would have an excellent middlegame after 12 e5 g5 13 ♗g3 ♘e4.

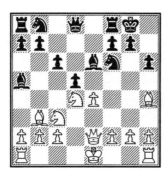

12   0-0!

To play this, Caruana had to calculate at least four moves ahead, to make sure a piece sacrifice was sound.

He had started this tournament poorly, with two losses in the first three rounds. To make a grandmaster norm he would need

to win almost every one of his remaining six games.

12   ...   g5

What made his calculation easier is Black's moves are more or less forced now. White's two bishops would have given him the upper hand after 12...♗xc3 13 bxc3 g5 14 exd5! ♗xd5 15 ♗g3, for example.

13   exd5   gxh4

14   ♘xe6!

Caruana would not have enough compensation for a piece after 14 dxe6? ♕xd4.

14   ...   fxe6

15   dxe6!   ♕e7

16   ♖ad1

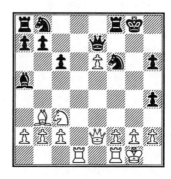

But he does here. The immediate threat is 17 ♖d7!, winning the queen.

His long-term compensation will come from doubling rooks on the d-file.

16 ...   ♔g7?

Black needed to move his king off of the discovered check diagonal.

He decided to protect the h6-pawn. But 16...♔h8 17 ♖d4 ♘g8 was fairly harmless.

Better is 17 ♘e4 ♘bd7 18 ♕e3!.

That forces 18...♘g4 and the favorable endgame of 19 ♖xd7! ♕xd7! 20 exd7 ♘xe3 21 fxe3.

17   ♘e4

Black's king makes 18 ♘d6 and ♘f5+ a danger.

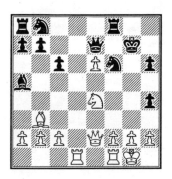

17 ...   ♗c7

In principle, Black benefits from a trade of knights. But 17...♘xe4 18 ♕xe4 sets up another fork, ♕e5+ and ♕xa5.

After 18...♗c7 19 ♖fe1 he would be getting paralyzed:

He can never play ...♘a6 because of ♖d7.

He cannot trade rooks, 19...♖d8? 20 ♕g4+ ♔h7 21 ♖xd8 ♗xd8 22 ♖e3 and ♖f3-f7+.

He could temporize, such as 19...♖f4 20 ♕e3 ♖f6, but White is bound to find a winning plan.

18   ♘xf6

Black's recapture will misplace one of his pieces.

It is the queen after 18...♕xf6 19 ♖fe1 and, for example, 19...♖e8 20 ♖d3 ♖e7 21 ♖f3 ♕g6 22 c3 and ♗c2.

Or after 19...♕e7 20 ♕g4+ ♔h7 21 c3 and ♗c2+.

18 ...   ♖xf6

Now the rook is misplaced and cannot help Black oppose White rooks if they double on the d-file.

19   ♖d3

White had a second good plan, f2-f4-f5 and Qh5xh4.

19 ... a5

20 a4

Black may have intended 20...♖a6 so this rook can become active on b6 and go to b4.

But 21 ♖fd1! then threatens 22 ♖d7.

After 21...♔h8 White would have a choice of winning with 22 ♕h5 followed by 23 ♖d7.

Or the immediate 22 ♖d7 ♘xd7 23 ♖xd7 ♕c5 24 ♖xc7 followed by e6-e7.

20 ... b6

Instead, Black's rook will go to a7 and protect his bishop.

21 ♖fd1 ♖a7

Black had set a trap: 22 ♖d7? ♘xd7 23 ♖xd7 walks into 24...♗xh2+! and ...♖xd7.

22 ♔h1

The alternative way of preparing ♖d7 is 22 g3. That has the benefit of avoiding 22...♗f4.

White would win after, for example, 22 g3 hxg3 23 hxg3 ♔h8 24 ♖d7! ♘xd7 25 ♖xd7 and then 25...♕e8 26 ♕d3! ♕g6 27 e7.

Computers have a fondness for 22 ♕g4+ and ♕xh4. But we know what they're like.

22 ... ♗f4

23 g3 hxg3

24 hxg3 ♗g5

25 f4

This wins the bishop but also opens the Black kingside, e.g. 25...♖f8 26 fxg5 ♕xg5 27 ♖f1 followed by invasion on the f-file.

25 ... ♗xf4

26 gxf4 ♖xf4

Also lost is 26...♖g6 27 ♕h5 and ♖d8.

27 ♖g3+ ♔h7

28	♕d3+	♚h8
29	♕g6	

Computers point out an elaborate forced mate beginning with 29 ♖g8+! ♚xg8 30 ♕g6+ ♚f8 31 ♕xh6+ ♚e8 32 ♕h5+.

Caruana finds a simpler sacrifice that frees his e-pawn to queen.

29	...	♕f8

30	♕g8+!	♕xg8
31	♖xg8+	♚xg8
32	e7+	♚h7
33	e8(♕)	♖g7

Cheapo alert (34...♖f4 mate).

Caruana could have gone into "calculating machine" mode to see if 34 ♖d2 ♖h4+ 35 ♖h2 ♖hg4 works.

He would have seen 34 ♕d8 ♘d7 35 ♖xd7?? ♖f1+ 36 ♚h2 ♖f2+.

It's not worth the trouble when you can get a piece-up ending by force.

34	♕xb8	♖h4+
35	♕h2	♖xh2+
36	♚xh2	b5
37	♖d6	♖c7
38	♚g3	resigns.

Caruana did win his final six games in the tournament and earned his second grandmaster norm. Garnering the necessary third norm seemed just a matter of time.

His trainer Yuri Razuvaev expressed a consensus view: If you don't become a grandmaster by 16, you will not have a great future in chess.

Caruana pressured himself to do it before he was 15, in July 2007.

"It was like a goal," he told Macauley Peterson in *Chess Life*. He wanted to replace Hikaru Nakamura as the youngest-ever American GM. "Yeah, actually, I did want to break his record," he said.

He made his final norm one week before his 15th birthday.

His new colleagues were unimpressed. "These days, if you are not a GM by 13 you are nobody," Peter Svidler had said in February.

45

5
Strategic Cake

As he moved into the grandmaster ranks, Fabiano still won an occasional Morphy game. For example, **Caruana – Neubauer,** Szeged 2007 went: **1 e4 e6 2 d4 d5 3 ♘c3 ♘f6 4 ♗g5 ♗e7 5 e5 ♘fd7 6 h4 ♘c6 7 ♘f3 ♘b6 8 ♗d3 ♗d7 9 a3 a6 10 ♖h3 h6 11 ♗e3! ♘a7 12 ♖g3 ♗f8 13 ♘e2 ♗b5 14 ♘f4 ♘d7 15 ♘h5! g6 16 ♖xg6! fxg6 17 ♗xg6+ ♔e7 18 ♘g5! ♗g7 19 ♘xe6! ♕g8** (19...♔xe6 20 ♘xg7+ ♔e7 21 ♘f5+ ♔e6 22 ♕g4 wins) **20 ♘exg7 ♖f8 21 f4 ♔d8 22 f5 ♔c8 23 ♕g4 c5 24 0-0-0 cxd4 25 ♗f4 ♘c6 26 f6! resigns.**

But, he recalled, "When I moved up, it turned out that you can far from always win with a direct attack. I had to become universal, to learn to maneuver and defend and so on."

When he sacrificed his queen it was more likely to be the icing on an impressive strategic cake. Here's an example, played just before he achieved his final GM norm.

Caruana – Florian Jenni
Mitropa Cup, Szeged 2007
Ruy Lopez, Berlin Defense (C65)

1	e4	e5
2	♘f3	♘c6
3	♗b5	♘f6
4	d3	d6
5	0-0	♗d7

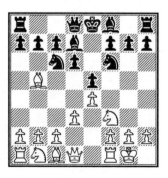

This resembles the old Steinitz Defense (3...d6). That has a dubious reputation because White can seize the initiative with 4 d4!.

Here 6 d4 is playable although White has spent an extra tempo (4 d3).

He retains the same space advantage of the Steinitz after 6...exd4 7 ♘xd4 or 6...♗e7 7 d5. But 6 d4 remains a rarity.

6	c3	g6
7	♖e1	♗g7
8	♘bd2	0-0

White benefits by delaying d3-d4 because he has more useful preparatory moves (such as ♘f1-g3) than Black.

46

9   ♗a4

How is this useful? One answer is tactical:

If White had pushed 9 d4?, Black has 9...♘xd4!.

Then 10 ♗xd7 ♘xf3+ costs White a pawn.

Or 10 cxd4 and the less-than-equal 10...♗xb5 11 dxe5 dxe5 12 ♘xe5 ♖e8.

9   ...   ♘h5

Another explanation of 9 ♗a4 is strategic.

When cramped for space in a Lopez, Black benefits by a swap of minor pieces, such as the light-squared bishops.

But now a move of the c6-knight, to a5, b8 or e7, would be favorably answered by 10 ♗c2, leaving his knight misplaced.

Instead, Black drops hints of ...f5 or ...♘f4.

10   ♘f1   h6

He needs ...h6 because 10...f5? 11 exf5 costs material after 11...gxf5 12 ♗b3+ and 13 ♘g5.

11   h3   ♔h7

12   ♗c2

Another retreat of this bishop is explained by another tactic, 12...f5? 13 exf5!.

Black drops material after 13...♗xf5 14 g4.

What does this have to do with 12 ♗c2?

The answer is 13...gxf5 14 ♘xe5! so that 14...♘xe5 15 ♕xh5 and 15...♘xd3 is not possible.

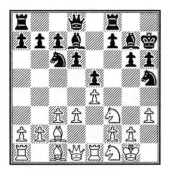

An improving player may wonder: What's the big deal about the Ruy Lopez? Why is White supposed to be better in a position like this?

Black's pieces are somewhat restricted. But not much more than White's – or more than

47

Black's in other major openings such as the King's Indian Defense.

12 ... ♛f6

The answer is White has more ways of improving his chances in a middlegame than Black here.

Black lacks the inherent counterplay of a King's Indian. Instead, he needed this clumsy queen move to prevent White's expansion with 13 d4!.

13 ♘e3

13 ... ♘f4?

Black wanted to meet ♘d5 with ...♘xd5.

But 13...♖ae8 14 ♘d5 ♛d8 is the kind of flexible defense that once made versions of the Steinitz Variation popular with elite players, such as Paul Keres and José Capablanca.

Then 15 d4 exd4 16 cxd4 f5! allows counterplay.

For example, 17 exf5 ♖xe1+ 18 ♛xe1 ♗xf5 and the d5-knight is hanging after 19 ♗xf5 ♖xf5.

Instead of 15 d4 White would stand well after 15 ♗e3 and, for instance, 15...♘e7 16 ♘xe7 and 17 d4!.

14 ♘g4! ♛e7

He would make quick progress after 14...♗xg4? 15 hxg4 followed by 16 g3, 17 ♔g2 and ♖h1 with a ready-made attack on the h-file.

15 d4! ♖ae8

16 ♗e3

Black's queen is uncomfortable on the same e-file as White's rook, as 16...f5 17 exf5 gxf5? 18 ♗xf4 shows.

Black would be somewhat worse after 17...♗xf5 18 ♗xf4 ♗xc2 19 ♛xc2 ♖xf4 20 dxe5.

16 ... a6

He adopts a wait-and-see policy. Hs move is as good as 16...♛d8 and other passes.

17 ♛d2

48

The best thing about Black's game seemed to be the f4-knight.

But it has become a liability because 18 ♗xf4 is threatened.

Clearly 17...♘h5 18 ♗xh6 was bad.

17 ... g5

A temporary measure is 17...h5 18 ♘gh2 ♗h6 because 19 ♔h1 and g2-g3 is strong.

18 dxe5 dxe5

That diagonal is closed but wouldn't be after 18...♘xe5 20 ♗xf4 ♘xf3+? 21 gxf3 gxf4 22 e5+!.

White no longer has a superior pawn center. The exchange of pawns on e5 would turn out to be a grave error after 19 ♖ad1? ♖d8, when, if anything, Black is slightly better.

19 ♗c5! ♕xc5

20 ♕xd7

The chief benefit of Caruana's little combination is that it makes his next moves easy to find.

Black now misses 20...♕b5! with the idea of 21...♘d4! 22 ♕xb5 ♘xf3+.

20 ... ♘e7?

21 ♖ad1 ♔g8

Both players understood that ...♖d8 at any point would allow a very favorable trade of the White queen for two rooks.

If they needed proof, they could calculate 21...♖d8 22 ♕xd8 ♖xd8 23 ♖xd8.

They could look further at, say, 23...♘eg6 24 ♖ed1 ♘e6 25 ♖8d7 ♔g8 26 ♗b3 ♘gf8 27 ♖7d5 ♕e7 28 ♘e3.

That's far from decisive but gives the outline of a slowly deteriorating Black position.

22 ♗b3 ♘fg6

23 ♘e3 ♗f6

24 ♘f5!

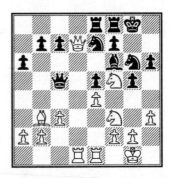

Now 24...♘xf5? 25 ♗xf7+ ♖xf7 26 ♕xe8+ is lost and so is 24...♔h7 25 ♗xf7!.

49

| 24 | ... | ♖d8 |

Did Black suddenly have doubts about the ♛-for-♖s swap?

No, he was probably becoming desperate after looking at 24...♗g7 and seeing how strong 25 h4, 25 ♘h2 (and ♘g4) or just 25 ♖d2 and ♖ed1 was.

| 25 | ♛xd8! | |

This is simpler than 25 ♘xh6+ ♔g7! (not 25...♔h7 26 ♘g4! ♖xd7 27 ♘xf6+ and ♘xd7) 26 ♘f5+ ♘xf5 27 ♛xf5 ♛e7.

| 25 | ... | ♖xd8 |

| 26 | ♖xd8+ | ♔h7 |

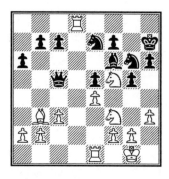

| 27 | ♘xe7 | |

Caruana begins to relax, perhaps thinking the position can be won with routine moves.

Not yet. But it would be getting there if he had preserved his knight (27 ♘e3 or 27 ♘g3) or calculated 27 ♗xf7!.

| 27 | ... | ♛xe7 |

| 28 | ♖ed1 | |

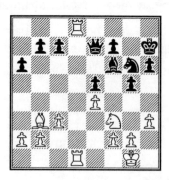

| 28 | ... | ♘f8 |

The pawn-down endgame, 28...♛xd8 29 ♖xd8 ♗xd8 30 ♗xf7, is lost after 30...♗f6 31 ♗xg6+ ♔xg6 32 ♔f1.

| 29 | ♘h2 | ♔g6 |

| 30 | ♖8d3 | |

This rook is better on the eighth rank, such as after 30 ♖b8 c6 31 ♘g4.

| 30 | ... | h5 |

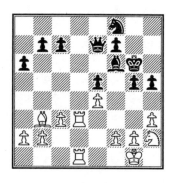

| 31 | ♘f1! | c6? |

Black mistakenly believed he had to control d5, rather than d6.

Passing, such as 31...♕c5 32 ♘e3 ♕b5, held out remote hopes.

32 ♘g3 ♕c5

33 ♘f5

It's not necessary but White can even sacrifice the Exchange.

For example, 33...a5 34 ♖d7! ♗xd7 35 ♖xd7 ♔h7 36 ♗xf7.

Then 36...h4 37 ♖d6! (37...♗e7 38 ♖h6 mate or 37...♗g7 38 ♖g6 ♗f8 39 ♖xg5 and ♖h5+).

33 ... ♘e6

34 ♖d6! ♘f4

35 ♖d7 ♘e6

After 35...♘d5 the simplest is 36 g4!, rather than 36 exd5 ♔xf5.

36 ♖1d6 g4

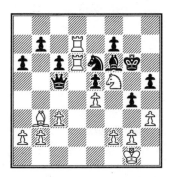

This allows a neat finish.

37 ♗xe6 fxe6

38 ♖xe6 g3

39 ♖g7 mate

Caruana had yet to gain much attention in major events. He finished in a tie for 48th place at Gibraltar 2007, for example. His new trainer, Alexander Chernin, later described his thinking as quick but "impulsive and very chaotic." But his potential was beginning to be noticed.

6
New Era Novelties

In the Internet age, the value of introducing a new opening move was transformed. A novelty still forced an opponent to think for himself. But the TN (theoretical novelty) that turned an equal position into a very favorable one was increasingly rare.

Information was shared too widely to allow even mild improvements to remain secret for long. When Garry Kasparov was asked about his storehouse of thousands of theoretical innovations he shrugged it off. "Everyone has a computer," he said.

Instead, what a new move could do is force an opponent to come up with a reply that was hard to find. By 2008 Caruana was able to do this in various openings.

**Oscar de la Riva Aguado –
Caruana**
Olympiad, Dresden 2008
*Sicilian Defense,
English Attack (B80)*

1	e4	c5
2	♘f3	d6
3	d4	♘f6
4	♘c3	cxd4
5	♘xd4	a6
6	♗e3	e6
7	♕d2	

Caruana's opponent had helped popularize this queen move, in place of 7 f3.

Unlike the similar and more popular 6...♘g4 7 ♗g5 h6 8 ♗h4 g5, Black just loses time after 6...e6 7 ♕d2 ♘g4 8 ♗g5.

7	...	b5

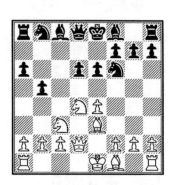

8	f3	♘bd7

Black would be able to coordinate his pieces faster after 9 a3 ♗b7 10 g4 h6 11 0-0-0 ♖c8, for example. Then he is poised for 12...d5!.

9	g4	

52

What helped strengthen the English Attack in the 1990s was the realization that White need not spend a tempo on 9 a3 to stop ...b4.

If White doesn't go for g2-g4-g5, he has to rely on massing pieces in the center.

A game of Caruana's from the 2008 Italian Championship (by transposition) illustrated the problems with this.

After 9 0-0-0 ♗b7 10 ♗d3 ♘e5 11 ♖he1 he was able to generate a queenside initiative and won after 11...♖c8 12 ♔b1 ♗e7 13 g4 ♘fd7 14 g5 ♘b6 and 15...♘bc4.

9 ... h6

10 0-0-0 ♗b7

In one of the few times he had played this position, Caruana was White and chose 11 h4. Then came 11...b4 12 ♘a4.

Moving the knight to the side has tactical pluses and minuses.

One critical continuation goes 12...♕a5 13 b3.

Then the thematic 13...d5 can be met by 14 e5.

This is justified by 14...♘xe5 15 ♘xe6! and the threatened queen trap, 16 ♗b6.

But the offsides knight also invites 13...♘c5! (14 ♘xc5? dxc5) and immense complications after 14 a3! ♘xa4 15 axb4 ♕c7 16 bxa4 d5.

11 ♗d3 ♘e5

12 ♖he1

White is daring his opponent to open the center with ...b4/...d5.

If Black continues instead with development, such as ...♖c8 and ...♗e7, White also has useful incremental moves, such as ♔b1 and h2-h4/g4-g5.

12 ... b4!

13 ♘ce2

A year later, de la Riva Aguado tried 13 ♘a4 and then 13...d5 14 exd5 ♘xd5 15 f4!.

His idea was that 15...♘xg4? 16 ♘xe6! fxe6 17 ♗g6+ unleashes a deadly attack.

Better is 15...♘xd3+ 16 ♕xd3 with unclear chances.

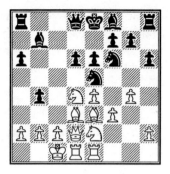 

13 ... d5!

If you look solely at the two central files, this move looks suicidal.

But without ...d5 to worry about, White would be freed to choose one of two powerful plans.

One is preparing a crushing sacrifice (♘f4 and ♘fxe6).

The other is taking slow aim at the kingside (h2-h4 and g4-g5-g6).

For example, 13...♕a5 14 ♔b1 ♗e7 15 ♘f4 ♖c8 16 h4 with a nice game.

14 exd5

Black's main idea was not 14...dxe4 but 14...♘xf3! 15 ♘xf3 dxe4.

14 ... ♘xd5

15 ♘f4

The point of retreating the knight to e2 was to prepare a knight sacrifice on e6.

Chances would be mixed after 15...♗d6 16 ♘dxe6 fxe6 17 ♘xe6 ♕f6 18 ♗d4, for example.

"For that reason the great Sicilianist Lev Polugaevsky played 15...♕d7 here," Yuri Razuvaev said. "But Fabiano had prepared a surprise for his opponent."

15 ... ♕a5

We are still in "book." The natural 16 ♔b1? allows 16...♘xf3! and 17 ♘xf3 ♘c3+! 18 bxc3 bxc3, as in a 2002 game.

16 ♘b3 ♕xa2

17 ♗e4!

Both players knew other games that had gone 17...0-0-0? 18 ♕d4! with a winning advantage to White.

For example, 18...♗e7 19 ♗xd5 ♗xd5 20 ♘xd5 ♖xd5 21 ♕a7!.

17 ... ♘c3!

Black would also be losing after 17...♖d8 18 ♘xd5 ♗xd5 19 ♕d4!.

18 bxc3 ♗xe4

19 fxe4

Even this position was known, from a game that had gone 19...♖c8 20 c4 ♗e7 21 c5 with no clear verdict to make.

19 ... a5!

An astonishing innovation. Can Black really attack with just a pawn – while his king sits unguarded on e8?

The quick answer is 20 ♕e2 and 21 ♕b5+ is simply met by 20...♖b8.

Then it is Black's turn to threaten (...bxc3 or ...a4xb3).

There are 20 ♕e2 ♖b8 scenarios in which White escapes, such as 21 c4 a4 22 ♗d4 axb3?? 23 ♗xe5.

But 22...♘c6 or 22...♗c7 is solidly in Black's favor.

There is more punch to 21 ♘d5. Then 21...exd5? 22 ♖xd5 wins.

But 21...♗e7 prepares 22...exd5 safely.

20 ♘d5!

Caruana's new move did not win. It just imposed a multi-part quiz on White.

This move, threatening 21 ♘c7+, gets the first answer right.

White would win after 20...exd5?? 21 ♕xd5.

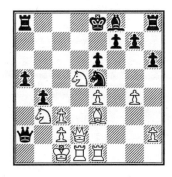

20 ... ♗d6

Black had three safe moves.

One was 20...f6 21 ♘c7+ ♔f7 because 22 ♘xa8? allows 22...bxc3 23 ♕xc3 ♗a3+ 24 ♔d2 ♗b4. But 22 c4 is unclear (22...♖c8 23 ♗f4).

Another was 20...♗e7 so that 21 ♘xe7 a4! 22 ♘c6 (threat of ♕d8+) 0-0!.

Caruana's move may not be best. But it makes the quiz longer and harder for White to pass.

21 ♘f6+!

He would be lost after 21 cxb4 a4 or 21 ♘xb4 axb4 22 ♕xd6 bxc3.

21 ... gxf6

22 ♕xd6 bxc3

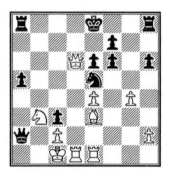

To stop 23...♕b2 mate, White must move his d1-rook.

Engines quickly point out 23 ♖d5 and 23...exd5? 24 ♗c5! wins.

They add that the critical line is 23...♕b2+ 24 ♔d1 ♕b1+.

White should shun 25 ♔e2? ♕xc2+ 26 ♔f1 ♕xe4 or 26...♕xb3.

Instead, 25 ♗c1 exd5 26 ♕xf6 0-0! 27 ♕xe5! dxe4 can be

analyzed with a computer for another dozen moves until the engine finds that a draw is likely.

23 ♖d4??

At first glance, this looks just as good as 23 ♖d5 but...

23 ... a4

24 ♘c5

White resigned when he saw 24...♕a1 mate.

Razuvaev cited this game in a profile of Caruana in the leading Russian magazine, *64*.

He analyzed the critical variation, 23 ♖d5 ♕b2+ 24 ♔d1 ♕b1+, and said the best winning try was 25 ♘c1!.

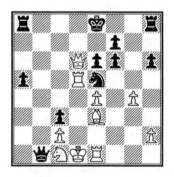

What might have been

Then White's bishop is not pinned and he can mate after 25...exd5? 26 ♕xf6 0-0? 27 ♗xh6.

Razuvaev analyzed 25...♕b7 26 ♗d4 ♘c4 out to an unclear conclusion.

Today's computers point out 26 ♖xe5!.

White would have more than enough material for his queen after 26...♖d8 27 ♕xd8+ ♚xd8 28 ♖xa5.

And his two minor pieces would beat Black's rook after 26...fxe5 27 ♕xe5 followed by ♚e2 and ♖d1.

Razuvaev said the truth about 23 ♖d5!! would come out in future games.

But the variation with 15 ♘f4 has been virtually retired in OTB chess since this game.

Razuvaev also noted that this game was played in the third round of the Olympiad after two disappointing Caruana losses. What he didn't mention is that Caruana scored 7½-1½ in his last nine games, including victories over Viktor Korchnoi and Michael Adams in the next two rounds.

"I've always been good at forgetting about losses relatively quickly. I don't dwell over them too much," he recalled years later to Chess.com. He soon realized he was able to recover from a bad start and still win a tournament. "I was very good at bouncing back," he said.

7
Younger Gen, Second Echelon

By 2009 Caruana was regularly being considered a member of "the younger generation." This took in a lot of territory, including Sergey Karjakin (two years older) and Hikaru Nakamura (five years older). He was not nearly at their level yet.

But he and David Navara were roughly the same rating when they first shook hands at the board. The Czech GM was undergoing a career surge that took him to number 18 in world ratings in July 2010.

He had scored 2½-½ and was leading the second section of Wijk aan Zee 2009 when the following game began.

Caruana – David Navara
Wijk aan Zee, B Section 2009
Ruy Lopez,
Zaitsev Variation (C92)

1	e4	e5
2	♘f3	♘c6
3	♗b5	a6
4	♗a4	♘f6
5	0-0	♗e7
6	♖e1	b5
7	♗b3	d6
8	c3	0-0
9	h3	♗b7

A year before, Caruana played the White side of this variation three times and only scored one draw. He had an excuse: His opponent in all three games was Anatoly Karpov.

They played a series of rapid games at Cap d'Agde. It was in that meeting that the former world champion became impressed with Caruana and his Soviet-school based training.

10	d4	♖e8
11	♘g5	♖f8
12	♘f3	♖e8
13	♘bd2	♗f8

In one of the Karpov games, Caruana closed the position here with d4-d5. Karpov equalized with a quick ...♘b8/...c6.

14	♗c2	g6
15	d5	

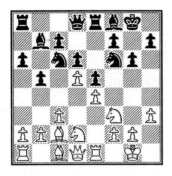

15   ...   ♞b8

Alexander Chernin had imparted Soviet-school wisdom when he told Caruana a Black knight is always badly placed on e7 after d4-d5 in a King's Indian Defense.

This isn't a King's Indian. But the pawn structure is very similar and the same rule applies.

The reason is that after 15 d5 White will play 16 c4 and aim for a queenside breakthrough with c4-c5.

A Black knight on d7, after 15...♞b8!, will help deter that.

After 15...♞e7, Black's best bet is seeking kingside counterplay. The e7-knight should help him there. But it does little after 16 c4 c6 17 b3 ♝g7 18 ♝b2 ♜f8 19 ♞f1 ♞h5 20 ♞e3, for instance.

16   c4   c6

Without ...c6 at some point, Black slowly gets the worst of both wings.

For example, 16...♞bd7 17 b3 ♜b8 18 ♞f1 ♞c5 19 ♞g3 bxc4 20 bxc4 and ♝e3, with the kind of emerging advantage that scored for Caruana in Game 60.

17   b3   ♝h6

This is a book position so old that Black's last move is credited to Svetozar Gligorić. It seeks a trade of the dark-squared bishop.

18   a4!

Thanks to ...♞b8, Black would be fairly secure if he chose the generic b3-b4/♝b2 plan

For example, 18 a3 ♞bd7 19 b4 ♛c7 20 ♝b2 ♞b6 and ...♞a4.

18   ...   b4

Black had to meet the threat of winning a pawn with 19 dxc6.

He would be happy with 18...bxc4 19 bxc4 a5 and ...♞a6 because he might blockade the open file with ...♞b4.

But he can't get that position. White would retake 19 ♘xc4!.

His pieces come alive after 19...♗xc1 20 dxc6! ♘xc6 21 ♖xc1.

Black could try 18...bxa4 instead. That gets him the position he wants after 19 bxa4 a5.

But there are problems after 19 b4! a5 20 b5.

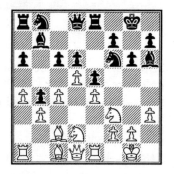

Now, however, Black is poised for a queenside blockade, 19 ♘f1 ♗xc1 20 ♖xc1 c5!.

19   dxc6!

White can pursue two promising plans after this:

He can pressure the d6-pawn with his heavy pieces (♕d2/♖ad1).

At the same time, he can wait for the right moment to plant a knight on d5.

For instance, 19...♘xc6 20 ♘f1 ♗xc1 21 ♖xc1 ♕e7 22 ♕d2 a5 23 ♘e3.

Then 23...♖ad8 anticipates the attack on the d-pawn.

But it makes 24 ♘d5! ♘xd5 25 cxd5 stronger in view of ♗d3-b5 and ♕e3-b6.

Black can counter both of White's plans with the superior 23...♘d8!.

The threat of ...♘xe4 gains time for the knight to land on c5, after 24 ♘d5 ♗xd5 and ...♘b7.

19   ...   ♗xc6

The trade of pawns made a change that grandmasters notice quickly and many amateurs don't: The sacrifice c4-c5 is in the air.

It would clear a square for a knight and partially liberate White's pawn-bound bishop.

20   ♘f1

The sacrifice has to be made before Black blockades with ...♘bd7-c5.

But 20 c5 dxc5 21 ♘c4 leaves White's e-pawn underprotected.

Chances would be roughly equal after 21...♕xd1 22 ♖xd1 ♗xc1 23 ♖axc1 ♗xe4!.

20   ...   ♗xc1

21   ♖xc1

The d6-pawn is the poster child for a backward pawn on an open file.

For example, 21...♕e7 22 ♕d2 a5? would safeguard the b4-pawn.

But it allows 23 ♖cd1 ♖d8 24 c5! (24...d5 25 ♕g5).

21 ... a5

However, if Black evades tactics like that, his position is sound.

His knights match up well with the very bad bishop on c2 and the target pawns at b3 and e4.

Now 22 ♕d2 ♘a6 23 ♖cd1 ♘c5 24 ♘g3! looks dangerous to him (24...♖e6? 25 ♘g5).

But 24...♘b7 is surprisingly solid.

Even the pawn sacrifice 24...♖c8 is sound (25 ♕xd6 ♕xd6 26 ♖xd6 ♔g7), as Caruana pointed out in *64*.

22 c5!

Now or never. Black was one move (...♘a6) away from a permanent veto of this push.

It is not a sacrifice because of 22...dxc5 23 ♕xd8 ♖xd8 24 ♘xe5.

White's knights are hopping after 24...♗b7 25 ♘g3 ♘bd7 26 ♘c4 and 26...♘f8 27 e5/♘d6, for example.

22 ... d5!

"David is a very concrete player," Caruana wrote (echoing what observers had begun to say about *him*).

Navara calculated a second pawn sacrifice, 22...♖a7 23 cxd6 (not 23 ♕xd6?? ♖d7) ♖d7.

But he rejected this because of White's pressure from 24 ♕d2 ♖xd6 25 ♕g5!, as he pointed out in the post-mortem.

23 exd5 ♕xd5

24 ♕xd5 ♗xd5!

Now 25 ♖xe5 ♖c8 is fine for Black (26 ♗d1? ♘bd7! with advantage).

25 ♘xe5 ♘bd7

If White loses his extra pawn, such as after 26 ♘d3 ♖xe1 27 ♖xe1 ♖c8 and ...♘xc5, Black should stand well because of the bad c2-bishop.

26	♘xd7	♘xd7
27	♖xe8+	♖xe8
28	♘e3	♗e6!

Caruana would have a much easier time after 28...♗c6? 29 ♘c4 ♘xc5 30 ♘xa5 because of the protected, passed a5-pawn.

Or after 29...♖a8 30 ♘d6 ♘xc5? 31 ♗xg6 and ♖xc5.

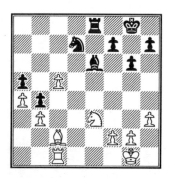

Navara sought this position when he chose 22...d5!.

It will be difficult, and, he hoped, impossible, for White to exploit his extra pawn.

For example, 29 c6? ♘c5 is no winning attempt.

29 ♗d3!

Caruana called this his "best practical chance." This is grandmaster-speak for "the best attempt to win a probably drawn position."

White is offering a pawn to break the blockade.

| 29 | ... | ♖c8 |

He was also tempting Navara to try 29...♗xb3 30 c6 ♘b6 31 c7 ♗xa4? – and fall for 32 ♘d5! ♘xd5 33 c8(♕).

But even then Black would likely draw with 31...♗e6 and 32 ♖c6 ♘c8.

| 30 | c6 | ♖c7 |

Caruana admitted that he was surprised by this move, which averts all scenarios in which c6-c7 is strong.

He had calculated 30...♘b6 31 c7 ♘a8 and now 32 ♗c4!.

If rooks are traded, 32...♖xc7 33 ♖d1! ♖d7 34 ♗xe6 ♖xd1+ 35 ♘xd1 fxe6 35 ♘e3, his king reaches d4.

| 31 | ♗b5 |

More accurate is 31 ♗e4 so that 31...♘b6 allows 32 ♖c5 ♗xb3 33 ♖xa5.

| 31 | ... | ♘b6 |
| 32 | ♖b1 | ♔f8? |

This can be deferred in favor of 32...♘d5!, with the idea of a trade of knights or ...♘c3!.

After 33 ♘xd5 ♗xd5, White's rook is tied to the defense of the b3-pawn. Then Black has time to

neutralize White's chances with
...♚f8-e7-d6.

Another scenario is 33 ♘c4
♘c3.

White's passed pawns would
win after 34 ♖e1 ♗xc4 35 bxc4
♘xb5? 36 cxb5.

But Black can blow this up with
35...b3!.

33   ♘c2!

Caruana was already getting
into time trouble when he found a
winning plan: The knight heads to
d4. This frees his bishop to go to
b7.

33   ...   ♚e7

A swap of pieces, 33...♗f5
34 ♖c1 ♗xc2 35 ♖xc2, would
remove the threat to the b3-pawn.

Then White's king can penetrate
on the kingside or queenside after
35...♚e7 36 ♚f1.

Black's king is limited by
36...♚d6 37 ♖d2+ ♚c5? 38 ♖d7!
and wins.

34	♘d4	♗d5
35	♖d1	♚d6
36	♗a6!	♚c5

37   ♗b7

Short of time, Caruana
distrusted 37 ♘b5! ♖xc6 38 ♖c1+.
He saw how 38...♗c4 39 bxc4??
♘xa4 would throw away the fruits
of four hours work.

White could win a pawn instead
with 39 ♘a7 ♖c7 40 ♗xc4 ♖xa7
41 ♗xf7+. But the rest isn't
clear because there is no passed
pawn.

However, if White passes
instead (39 g4), Black is near
zugzwang.

Then 39...♖e6 or 39...♖f6
would allow White to win the
pinned bishop with 40 ♘a7!.

37	...	♖c7
38	f3	♖e3
39	♚f2	♖c3

63

40 h4!

One of the ironies of putting your pieces on more active squares is that you don't want to move anything – and this brings you closer to zugzwang.

Caruana understood Black was getting close:

He would lose his knight or rook if he moved them. A king move allows ♘b5+. And 40…♗e6 invites 41 c7!.

That leaves pawn moves. For example, 40….h6 41 g4 f6 42 h5 forces Black to create a path for White's king (42…gxh5 43 gxh5 and ♔g3).

Or it runs Black out of moves (42…g5 43 ♔e2).

40 …   ♗xb3

41 ♘xb3+ ♖xb3

42 c7   ♖c3

One last trap. The win would be gone after 43 c8(♕)+?? ♘xc8 44 ♗xc8 b3.

43 ♖d5+! ♔c4

44 ♖xa5

Work remains after 44 ♖b5 ♔b3 45 ♖xb6 ♖xc7.

After **44…♔b3** Navara **resigned**.

Even without a passed a-pawn, White would win after 45 ♖b5 ♖xc7 46 ♖xb6 (46…♔xa4 47 ♗d5). Black could stretch out the game with 45…♘c8 46 ♗xc8 ♖xc7 but he would lose after, for instance, 47 ♖b8 ♔xa4 48 ♗b7 b3? 49 ♗d5.

Navara won the next four decisive games he played with Caruana. There was some doubt who had the brighter future.

But after their ratings fluctuated in 2009 and 2010, Caruana moved ahead of him for good by late 2011.

8
Last Round Nerves

Caruana would earn a substantial reputation over the next decade for winning when it mattered, often in the last round. He had done it before 2009 but the final round of the Wijk aan Zee B section that year made an international impression.

The situation seemed ideal for his opponent, Nigel Short. The English GM needed a draw to secure first prize and an automatic invitation to the prestigious top section in the next year's Wijk aan Zee. It was a perfect opportunity to show that experience counted more than youthful energy. In the end, what mattered most was the stronger nerves.

Caruana – Nigel Short
Wijk aan Zee, B Group 2009
Catalan Opening,
Open Variation (E06)

1	d4	♘f6
2	c4	e6
3	g3	d5
4	♘f3	♗e7
5	♗g2	

Caruana said he played 1 d4 because he was tired of trying to earn a tiny advantage in a Ruy Lopez after 1 e4.

Databases are notoriously incomplete and have few examples of him playing the Catalan before this game.

5	...	0-0
6	0-0	dxc4

The closed variation, 6...c6, had gradually lost its primacy as the Catalan's main line.

7	♕c2	a6
8	♕xc4	b5
9	♕c2	♗b7
10	♗d2	

Catalan specialists had exhausted all of the more natural moves – including 10 ♘c3, 10 ♘bd2, 10 ♖d1, 10 a4, 10 ♗f4 and 10 ♗g5 – with little evidence of a White advantage. Caruana's choice is no better or worse.

10	...	♗d6
11	♘g5	

This move was new, at least to Short, who took some time to make the natural reply.

11	...	♝xg2
12	♔xg2	♛c8

Vishy Anand later demonstrated a direct path to equality – against Caruana – with 12...♘bd7 and 13...e5.

But Short's idea of ...♛b7 is more enterprising. For example, 13 ♘c3 ♛b7+ 14 ♔g1 ♘bd7 15 ♖ac1 ♖ac8 16 ♘ge4 ♝e7 and ...c5!.

13	e4	♛b7
14	♖e1	♘bd7
15	♘f3	

His idea would succeed after 15 ♘c3? c5 16 ♝e3 b4 17 ♘a4 cxd4 18 ♝xd4 e5, when his pieces are better placed than White's.

15	...	e5
16	♝g5	

Or 16 dxe5 ♘xe5 17 ♘xe5 ♝xe5 18 ♝c3 ♖fe8 and ...c5.

16	...	exd4

Now 17 ♝xf6? ♘xf6 18 e5? ♖fe8 is quite bad.

17	♘xd4	♖fe8
18	♘d2	

Evaluating a position and finding a good move are two related but different skills.

During the game Caruana felt he was better here.

But he concluded afterwards that chances were equal.

And computers see a Black advantage from here until move 28.

18	...	c5
19	♘f5	♝f8
20	b3	♖e6
21	f3	♖ae8
22	♖ad1	♘e5

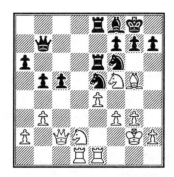

There is another way to evaluate. Whose position is more *playable?* Which player will have an easier time finding good moves?

Caruana gave an answer in *New In Chess*. "Now I realized I had no concept to improve my position."

He was burning a lot of minutes trying to find moves that proved he had an advantage (which didn't exist).

He also had to dodge logical moves that turn out to be blunders. For example, 23 ♘f1? ♘xf3! 24 ♚xf3 ♘xe4 and Black wins.

23	♗f4	♘fd7
24	♕c3	h5
25	♘e3	♘b6

Short prepared ...c4.

Caruana wanted to reply 26 ♘d5, with compensation for a pawn after 26...♘xd5 27 exd5 ♕xd5 28 ♘f1.

But he was concerned about the insertion of 26...b4!.

Then 27 ♕a1 ♘xd5 28 exd5 ♕xd5 29 ♘f1?? ♕xf3+ or 29 ♘e4 ♘d3!.

26	♘df1	♘g6
27	♗g5	

This was a rare case when Caruana did not trust what the board was telling him.

He was worried about 27...♘e5, when he would have nothing more impressive than 28 ♗f4.

But if he repeated the position and drew, his chances of reaching the top section of next year's Wijk aan Zee would evaporate.

"My position on the board (and on the clock) demanded I agree to a draw, but my position in the tournament demanded I play for a win," he wrote.

27	...	c4
28	bxc4	♕c7

29	♖c1	

Caruana was looking to play ♘f5. He would not be worse after 29 ♘f5 ♕xc4 30 ♕b3.

Simpler is 29 ♘d5 ♘xd5 30 ♖xd5, so that the other knight has a square at e3.

After 30...♖c6 31 ♖e2 ♖xc4 32 ♕b2 he would be quite solid.

29	...	bxc4
30	♘f5	♖c8
31	♘d2	f6
32	♗e3	♘e5
33	♖b1	♗c5
34	♗f4	♖d8

Caruana was overly critical of his play in this phase ("The knight doesn't belong on d2!").

Computers point out possibilities such as 35 ♗xe5 ♕xe5 36 ♕c1. But this isn't something a human would do in time pressure.

| 35 | ♖ed1 | g6 |

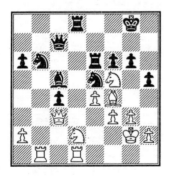

| 36 | ♘h4 |

White has been looking for the optimal time to capture on c4 or e5.

This looked like his opportunity to do both, 36 ♘xc4 ♘bxc4 37 ♗xe5!.

Then 37...♘xe5 38 ♕xc5! ♕xc5 39 ♖xd8+ wins.

But there is a refutation, 36...♖xd1 and then 37 ♗xe5 ♕d7!.

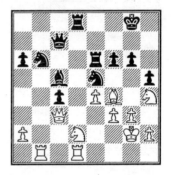

| 36 | ... | ♖ed6? |

Caruana expected 36...g5 37 ♗xe5 ♕xe5 38 ♕xe5 and ♘f5 "when White may survive but Black is playing without risk."

True, but this is not the path an experienced GM like Short was likely to choose when his opponent had seconds left, as Caruana did.

Instead, 36...♔h7! and ...♖ed6 would have been psychologically powerful.

| 37 | ♘xg6! |

This is not desperation because 37...♘xg6? 38 ♗xd6 and ♘xc4 would favor White.

Black's advantage has vanished.

37 ...   &d4

38 ♕a5?

But this revives it. Caruana should have been content with the unclear 38 ♕c2 ♘xg6 39 &xd6 ♖xd6 40 ♘b3!.

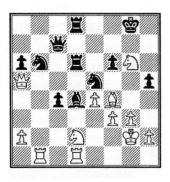

38 ...   ♘xg6

This is the first indication that the tension – of his *opponent's* time pressure – was getting to Short.

He would have won routinely after 38...c3! threatened ...cxd2 as well as ...c2!.

For example, 39 ♖dc1 ♘xg6 40 &xd6 ♖xd6 41 ♖c2 ♘e5 prepares 42...♕d7 43 ♘f1 ♘bc4!.

39 &xd6   ♖xd6

40 ♕xh5   ♔g7

41 ♘f1   c3!

The first time control is over and material is roughly even.

But the c-pawn and the prospect of a Black knight invading at e3 or b2 make it unlikely White would reach the second control.

42 ♖bc1

Caruana entertained the idea of sacrificing the Exchange and playing with two or three extra pawns against Short's extra knight.

This wouldn't work now (42 ♖xd4 ♖xd4 43 ♘e3 ♖d2+) and didn't look good later. And, besides, it was too early to panic.

42 ...   ♘c4

43 f4!   ♕b7

44 ♕e2   f5!

Based on 45 ♕xc4? ♕xe4+ 46 ♔h3 ♘xf4+! and mates.

45 ♖e1   ♕c6

46 ♕f3

White had to anticipate ...♖e6xe4 – and 46 ♔h3? ♘e7 was not the way.

46	...	♘d2!
47	♘xd2	

When he chose his last move, Short had seen 47...cxd2! and the endgame that arises after 48 ♖xc6 dxe1(♘)+.

For example, 49 ♔f1 ♘xf3 50 ♖xd6 fxe4 51 ♖xa6.

But Short simply miscounted the number of minor pieces. He thought he would have two, not three, to battle the rook, he admitted after the game.

47	...	♘h4+??

When Caruana saw this, he felt it must be a mating combination.

48	gxh4	♖g6+

It would have been, after 49 ♔f1? ♕b5+ or 49 ♔h1? cxd2 50 ♖xc6 dxe1(♕)+.

49	♔h3	

Now 49...cxd2 50 ♖xc6 dxe1(♕) 51 ♖xg6+ ♔xg6 52 exf5+ would be a draw at best. White

can win the a6-pawn and Black cannot mate with his queen and bishop.

49	...	♕d7?

50	♕h5!	

The only move but it reverses his fortunes. Short had overlooked 50...fxe4+ 51 f5!.

50	...	cxd2
51	exf5	♖h6

52	♕g5+?	

Second-control time pressure strikes.

White would have the better of 52 ♖g1+! ♗xg1 53 ♖xg1+ ♔h7.

70

Then 54 ♕g5 ♕d3+ is a draw (55 ♖g3 ♕f1+).

But 54 ♕g4! ♕d3+ 55 ♔g2! and ♖d1 is a different story.

52	...	♔f7!
53	♕xh6	♕xf5+
54	♔g3	dxc1(♕)
55	♖xc1	♕d3+
56	♔g4	♕e2+

Now Short must have seen that 57 ♔g5 ♕e7+?? loses to 58 ♔f5 ♕d7+ 59 ♔e4 and he is out of bullets.

But he would also have seen how 57...♕b5+ draws (and 58 f5?? ♗e3+ allows mate).

57	♔f5

| 57 | ... | ♕b5+?? |

"I couldn't believe my eyes," Caruana said.

Black could have forced perpetual check with 57...♕d3+ 58 ♔g5 and then 58...♕b5+! 59 ♔g4 ♕e2+.

58	♔e4!	♕e2+
59	♔d5!	♕xa2+
60	♖c4	

Game over. Short played **60...♗f6 61 ♕h7+ ♔f8 62 ♕e4 ♗xh4 63 ♔e6 ♔g7 64 f5 ♗d8 65 f6+ ♔f8 66 ♕d5 ♕e2+ 67 ♖e4** until he **resigned**.

At least four moves would have changed the result of this game and delayed Caruana's leap into the big leagues of chess.

9
Crafty Old Adolescent

The advantage that older players may have against youngsters lies in endgame skill and craftiness. Caruana's endgame skill against his elders would be on display in games 16, 20 and 21. The following game shows he could match them in time-pressure cunning.

Boris Gelfand – Caruana
Biel 2009
Nimzo-Indian Defense,
Classical Variation (E32)

1	c4	♘f6
2	d4	e6
3	♘c3	♗b4
4	♕c2	0-0

Caruana was on new ground. He had usually played 4...♘c6. But he was learning some of the subtleties of main opening lines that elite GMs play.

5	a3	♗xc3+
6	♕xc3	d5

This is one: The position resembles the trendy 4...d5 5 a3 ♗xc3+ 6 ♕xc3.

Then Black can vary with 6...dxc4 7 ♕xc4 b6.

At the time this game was played, 8 ♗f4 was considered good for White.

But in the game's move order he can't use that idea.

After 7 ♘f3 dxc4 8 ♕xc4 b6 Black could meet 9 ♗f4 with 9...♗a6!.

White would have to play carefully to equalize after 10 ♕xc7 ♕d5.

This is a minor transpositional trick. It matters to grandmasters and to almost nobody else.

But now that Caruana was a GM, it was something worth knowing.

7   cxd5!

This move set Caruana to considering another finesse.

There is nothing fundamentally wrong with 7...exd5 or 7...♛xd5.

But he was inclined to choose 7...♞e4 so that he would avoid the ♝g5 pin after 8 ♛c2 exd5.

While he was thinking, he looked up at the demonstration boards and discovered another game, Morozevich – Alekseev, had also gone 7 cxd5.

He quickly turned away and decided to play his own game.

7 ... exd5

Alekseev chose 7...♞e4 and equalized after 8 ♛c2 exd5.

8 ♝g5 ♛d6

A rule of thumb of the Classical Variation Nimzo is that Black stands well if he can play ...c5 safely. Here he can't.

Instead, he threatens 9...♞e4. There is no reason to fear 9 ♝xf6 ♛xf6 10 ♛xc7? ♛xd4.

9 f3 ♝f5

There were other Classical Variation finesses to learn.

One is that 9...♜e8! is more accurate because the e3-pawn can become a target after 10 e3 h6 11 ♝h4.

White can't play 11 ♝f4? ♛xf4. But in the game, Gelfand will have the option of retreating ♝f4!.

10 e3 ♞bd7

11 ♞e2

Now the space-gaining g2-g4 becomes a dangerous White option.

If Black permits 12 g4 ♝g6? 13 h4 his kingside can be overwhelmed (13...h6 14 ♝f4 ♛e7 15 h5 ♝h7 16 g5!).

11 ... ♜ac8

Caruana holds out hope for ...c5.

The immediate 11...c5? 12 ♝xf6 is awful (12...♞xf6 13 dxc5; 12...gxf6 13 ♞f4).

12 b4 ♜fe8?

Caruana did not indicate afterwards how he got such a questionable middlegame. But we can guess that he was relying on his calculating powers to get him out of an unfamiliar opening.

For example, he was poised to meet 13 g4 with 13...♗xg4 (14 fxg4 ♘e4).

A key point is that on 14 ♗f4! he can reply 14...♗xf3! 15 ♗xd6 cxd6.

He would have so much compensation for the queen after 16...♗xh1 that White should bail out with 16 ♕xc8 ♖xc8 17 ♖g1, and an equal endgame.

Caruana doesn't have time for 15...b6 16 ♘g3 c5? because 17 g5 traps the f6-knight.

16   h5   h6

White played 16 h5 to avoid 16...♘g6. But it will allow the knight to g5 now.

Before that happens, Gelfand can open lines with 17 g5 hxg5 18 ♗xg5.

Caruana couldn't calculate his way to safety because the desperado line 18...♘e4 19 ♗xe7 ♘xc3 20 ♗xf8 ♘xe2 21 ♗xg7 favors White.

17   ♘g3

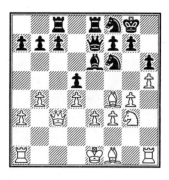

Instead of calculation, let's pause to take in the big picture:

Black cannot achieve ...c5 in the near future (17...b6? 18 ♗a6).

This means White can improve his position slowly, with useful moves, such as ♔f2 and ♗d3.

Then he can decide on a major plan, such as the kingside attack of ♖ag1/g4-g5 or seeking a favorable endgame with ♕c5.

13   ♗f4   ♕e7

14   g4!

This move order gains Gelfand a sizable edge. Again Black would be in serious trouble on the kingside after, say, 14...♗g6 15 h4 h5 16 g5 ♘h7 17 ♗h3.

14   ...   ♗e6

15   h4   ♘f8

The main danger to him in such a favorable situation is that he would lose control – that is, allow counterplay.

17 ... ♘8h7

Both players considered 18 ♗d3 ♘g5 19 ♔f2 and realized Black could go desperate with a piece sacrifice on f3 or g4.

Gelfand was particularly concerned about 19...♗xg4 20 fxg4 ♘xg4+ and ...♘xe3.

But 21 ♔g1! ♘xe3 22 ♘f5! would have defended easily.

And if he didn't trust that, White could have gotten a favorable endgame with 22 ♗b5 c6 22 ♕xe3.

18 ♕c5

Caruana said afterward he was surprised to be given a choice by this move. It was a choice of defending a poor endgame or sacrificing a pawn for scant compensation.

18 ... ♕d8!

Computers jeer but this is a good playability decision.

In an endgame such as 18...♘d7 19 ♕xe7 ♖xe7 20 ♔f2 it is difficult to find good Black moves because his minor pieces are severely restricted by the pawn structure.

On the other hand, White could gradually expand on the queenside with no-think moves such as ♗d3, a3-a4, b4-b5 and ♖fb1.

19 ♕xa7 b6

Black cuts off the queen's best exit and prepares ...♗d7.

20 ♕a4

The rest of game looks like a struggle between a veteran grandmaster who wants to win without a lot of calculation and a young GM who knows he must out-calculate him to survive.

Gelfand would be safe and on his way to victory with 20 ♖c1 ♗d7 21 ♔f2 c6 22 ♖c3.

But he hadn't forgotten about the knight sacrifices that spooked him after 17...♘8h7.

In the last variation, Black should play 21...♘g5 (instead of 21...c6?) so that 22 ♖xc7? can be met by 22...♗xg4!, with enough complications to escape.

If White were Viktor Korchnoi, he would force himself to look further and find that 22 ♕b7! was very promising.

20 ... ♘g5

From now on ♗xg5/...hxg5 looks dubious because it leaves the e3-pawn and other dark squares vulnerable.

21 ♗e2 c5

22 bxc5

Computers recommend 22 ♕d1! so White can recapture on d4 with the queen after ...cxd4.

But Gelfand knew he held a considerable advantage. He wanted to make all potential endgames winnable.

It would be harder to make his extra pawn count after 22 ♕d1 because of 22...c4 and ...♗d7, followed by ...b5 or ...♘e6.

22 ... bxc5

23 dxc5 ♖xc5

White still has control – but not after the explosive ...d4!.

For example, 24 ♔f2 ♗d7 25 ♕d1? d4!.

Then 26 exd4? allows the surprisingly strong 26...♖c3!.

Black would win in view of 27...♗c6! or 27...♘xg4+! 28 fxg4 ♕f6.

Better but still bad for White is 26 ♕xd4 ♘e6 27 ♕b4 ♘d5 and 27 ♕d6 ♖c6 28 ♕d2 ♘xf4.

Instead of 25 ♕d1? White would hold the better winning chances after 25 ♕b4.

That allows 25...♖c2 but Gelfand would have had a better version of what happens in the game after 26 ♗xg5 hxg5 27 ♕d4.

24 &xg5

Caruana confessed he didn't consider this capture, which he gave "?!" in his notes.

24 ... hxg5

25 ♕d4

Nevertheless, he acknowledged 25 h6! would have still kept White on top.

Instead, Gelfand defended e3 and seemed to make h5-h6xg7 stronger.

25 ... ♖c2

Caruana was thinking about a sacrifice on g4. But as he pointed out after the game, he could have prepared it with 25...♕c7!.

Then 26 ♔f2 &xg4! 27 fxg4 ♘e4+ or 27...♖c3 first would equalize.

26 h6

Caruana was beginning to see swindles. For example, 26 ♔f2 ♕a5 27 ♖hd1? looks safe.

But then 27...&xg4! 28 fxg4 ♕c7 makes 29...♘e4+ a winning threat.

Black would escape with a perpetual check after 29 ♖d2 ♘e4+ 30 ♘xe4 ♕h2+.

26 ... ♕a5+

Both players were in time trouble and Caruana knew enough not to make it easy for White by going into an endgame.

That is, with 26...♕b8 27 ♔f2 ♕b2 28 ♕xb2 or 26...♕c7 27 ♔f2 ♕c4 28 ♕xc4.

27 ♔f2

White had ♔f2 on his mind for so long that he didn't notice how different 27 ♔f1! would be.

27 ... ♖d2

With his king on f2, White can meet 28 ♕b4 ♕xb4 29 axb4 ♖b2 with 30 ♖hb1.

But Black has better in 29...d4!.

Then 30 exd4 ♗c4 and a capture on e2 would offer good drawing chances.

But the greater difference between ♔f1 and ♔f2 was revealed by:

28   ♕e5

28   ...   ♘xg4+!

If White had played 27 ♔f1, this would not be a check but rather a blunder that allows 29 ♕xg7 mate.

29   fxg4   f6

Now 30 h7+ ♔h8 looks like a useful interpolation – until you see how much stronger 30 ♕d6 d4! is, now that hxg7 is off the table.

30   ♕d6!

White is still better, in fact, close to winning.

30   ...   d4!

But after this he has the much more difficult decisions to make.

Option number one is 31 exd4 ♗xg4.

This appears to win for Black (32 ♖ae1? ♗xe2 33 ♖xe2 ♖dxe2+ 34 ♘xe2 ♕f5+!).

But White has his own beneficial tactics after 32 ♕c6! or 32 hxg7!.

For example, 32 hxg7! ♔xg7 33 ♔g1 ♖exe2 (33...♗xe2?? 34 ♕d7+ mates) 34 ♔xe2 ♖xe2 35 ♖f1 ♗f5 36 ♖h3!.

31   ♕c6

Another option was to move his king.

Gelfand was wise to reject 31 ♔g1 ♕c3!, when anything can happen.

But 31 ♔f1 had a clever point. Then 31...dxe3 32 ♕c6! is strong because 32...♗d7?? loses to a check of the unpinned bishop.

White can get a promising piece-up endgame after 32...♗f7 33 ♖c1! ♕e5 34 ♕c7.

Is it promising enough to win?

Perhaps, after 34...♕f4+ 35 ♕xf4 gxf4 36 ♘f5.

31	...	♗d7!
32	♕c4+	♗e6
33	♕c6	

Caruana played **33...♗d7** and offered a **draw**.

He had two minutes to Gelfand's one, according to his account in *64*.

Gelfand accepted because 34 ♕xd7?? dxe3+ costs the queen.

Yet there are published accounts that claim the game ended with 33...♗f7 34 hxg7 ♕e5 draw agreed.

Caruana tried to correct the record by pointing out how that "final" position would allow 35 ♖h8+ ♔xg7 36 ♖xe8!.

But the bogus version lives on in some databases.

There was no doubt, after games like this, of Caruana's skills. But there were still glaring gaps in his knowledge. Veteran GMs were able to expose them on occasion.

Alexander Beliavsky – Caruana
"Rising Stars versus Experience,"
Amsterdam 2009
Queen's Indian Defense (E12)

1 d4 ♘f6 2 c4 e6 3 ♘f3 b6 4 a3 ♗a6 5 ♕c2 ♗b7 6 ♘c3 c5 7 e4 cxd4 8 ♘xd4 ♗c5 9 ♘b3 ♗e7?

"It is hard to believe that this was prepared," John Watson wrote on *The Week In Chess*. "Apparently Caruana and his trainer were unaware" of the latest book on this opening, he added. "It was written by – Beliavsky."

Caruana obtained a passive position after **10 ♗f4 d6 11 ♖d1 0-0 12 e5** and was lost after **12...♘h5 13 ♗e3 ♗g5? 14 ♕c1 ♗xe3 15 ♕xe3 ♘c6 16 ♖xd6.** He resigned nine moves later.

10
Hired Gun

A sponsor, who has never been identified, helped enlist Caruana to play on the Italian Olympiad team in the biennial team tournament beginning in 2008. He played four times on first board and his results improved, from a 2696 performance to 2708, then 2722 and 2776 in his final year, 2014. His team went from finishing 41st in his first Olympiad to 15th.

What is often overlooked in accounts of Caruana's career is how he was regularly recruited for other team events. He played in the club team championships of Germany, Spain, France, Switzerland and Italy over the next decade. He even appeared over-the-board for his Bundesliga team in 2020 despite Covid-19. Winning teams were composed of the well-paid cream of the international crop. When he joined the perennial powerhouse Baden-Baden team for the 2008-2009 Bundesliga season Caruana was only the 13th highest rated player on it, well behind Vishy Anand, Magnus Carlsen, Alexei Shirov, Peter Svidler and Michael Adams.

The following game, played on second board in Russia's premier team event, helped establish his reputation as a team member. He scored a spectacular 2896 performance rating in the tournament.

Caruana – Artem Smirnov
Russian Team Championship,
Dagomys 2009
*Ruy Lopez,
Berlin Defense (C65)*

1	e4	e5
2	♘f3	♘c6
3	♗b5	♘f6
4	d3	d6
5	0-0	♗d7

Once White decides against challenging the notorious Berlin Wall endgame (4 0-0 ♘xe4 5 d4 ♘d6 6 ♗xc6 dxc6 7 dxe5 ♘f5 8 ♕xd8+), his next big choice is a middlegame pawn structure.

The usual formula is to insert c2-c3 and shift the b1-knight to g3 so that it protects the e4-pawn. We saw that in Game 5.

| 6 | ♖e1 | g6 |

7   d4

Caruana chooses a more forceful method that saves the c2-c3 tempo. Now 7...exd4? is dubious because of 8 ♗xc6 and 9 e5.

7   ...   ♗g7

And so is 7...♘xd4? 8 ♘xd4 exd4 in view of 9 ♕xd4 ♗xb5 10 e5!.

8   d5

A standard positional strategy. White creates a light-square pawn chain and exchanges his light-squared bishop.

8   ...   ♘e7

9   ♗xd7+   ♘xd7

10   ♗e3   0-0

11   c4   h6

Black's last move is necessary if he wants to avoid the punishing ♘g5-e6 after he fights for space with ...f5.

12   ♘fd2

White will support his e4-pawn with f2-f3. Then on ...f4 he can retreat his bishop to f2 and pursue his strategic goal of c4-c5.

12   ...   f5

13   f3

Common questions in this pawn structure are:

How would White retake on e4 after ...fxe4? And which knight benefits more if he prefers ♘xe4?

After 13 f3 ♘f6 14 ♘c3 fxe4 15 fxe4 Black can play 15...♕d7 and 16...♘g4 (because 16 h3 g5! and ...g4 opens his king position.)

Most masters would prefer 15 ♘dxe4 ♘f5 16 ♗f2. Then Black can plant his knight on d4. But White has greater space and a more achievable (c4-c5) plan.

If Black doesn't exchange on e4 he can choose from among three plans. None quite equalizes.

One is the pawn storm, 13...f4 14 ♗f2 g5.

Experience has shown White's queenside attack shows results

first, after 15 ♘c3 ♘g6 16 b4 ♘f6 17 c5 and ♘c4.

This suggests the second plan, blockading the queenside with 13...c5. White would then shift his aim with 14 ♘c3, 15 a3 and b2-b4.

13 ... ♚h7

Smirnov goes for a third plan, swapping his bad bishop with ...♗f6-g5. He needs to defend his h-pawn first.

14 ♘c3 ♗f6

15 ♗f2!

Black intended to induce a kingside weakness, 15...♗h4 16 g3, and then 16...♗g5, when chances would be roughly equal.

15 ... ♗g5

He could have insisted on ...♗h4 with 15...♘g8.

For example, 16 b4 a5 17 a3 ♗h4 18 ♗xh4 ♕xh4, with a slight plus for White.

Instead, Black relies on a logical but flawed version of the pawn-storm strategy

16 b4 ♗xd2?

17 ♕xd2 f4

With his bad bishop gone, Black feels more confident putting pawns on dark-squares.

He will attack the base of the White pawn chain with ...g5-g4.

This is the plot of gazillions of King's Indian Defenses:

White usually penetrates at the base of the queenside pawn chain first (c5xd6).

But checkmate counts more than winning a queenside pawn. The outcome of the game depends on who inflicts so much damage that he causes his opponent to slow his wing attack.

18 c5! ♘f6

19 ♖ec1 ♕d7

That's what would happen after 19...g5 20 cxd6 cxd6 21 ♘b5!.

Black cannot stop both ♘c7-e6! and ♘xa7.

He would be forced to halt after 21...g4? 22 ♘c7.

His attack would run out of gas after 21...♘e8 22 ♘xa7 g4 23 fxg4 and then 23...f3 24 gxf3 ♖xf3 25 ♕e2.

20 ♕e2 a6

Endgames generally favor White. But so does an opening of the center.

Black had to be concerned about 20...g5 21 ♕b5 c6 22 ♕d3, e.g. 22...g4 23 dxc6 ♘xc6 24 ♘d5.

21 b5!

Now 22 c6 bxc6 23 dxc6! is a big-time threat.

White would easily penetrate the queenside, 23...♕c8 24 b6! cxb6 25 ♘a4 and ♘xb6.

21 ... g5

Not much better is 21...axb5 22 ♕xb5 c6 23 ♕b3.

Black's kingside initiative lags White's queenside play after 23...g5 24 ♖ab1 ♖ab8 25 ♘a4.

For example, 25...g4 26 ♘b6 ♕d8 27 cxd6 ♕xd6 28 ♗c5.

22 ♖ab1

White's position is so good that Caruana may have wanted to be sure about 22 c6 bxc6 23 dxc6 ♕e8 24 bxa6 g4 25 fxg4 ♕c8 before he burned any queenside bridges.

22 ... g4

It almost never pays for Black to capture ...dxc5 in similar positions. Here 22...dxc5 23 ♗xc5 ♖f7 would be close to lost after 24 bxa6 bxa6 25 ♖b7.

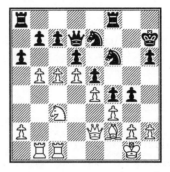

The 21st century brought a controversial new theory about choosing a move:

There is no single "best" move for all playing formats, the theory claims.

The move that is most likely to succeed in a round-robin tournament may not be best if played in a Swiss system tournament, or in a match or a team tournament, according to former FIDE world champion Alexander Khalifman.

Other grandmasters elaborated on the theory and said there is a best move in a "classical" time-limit game, a different one in speed or blitz chess, yet another in bullet (one-minute) games and still two others in Armageddon games, one for White and one for Black.

23 bxa6

Objectively, 23 b6! may be the best move in a round robin. But Caruana must have known that two of his teammates were winning in this match. He didn't need to win his game. But losing would be very bad.

There is some losing risk in 23...c6 24 dxc6 ♘xc6 25 ♖d1 g3!.

For example, 26 hxg3 fxg3 27 ♗xg3? ♘d4.

Or 27 ♗e3 ♕f7 28 ♖xd6? ♕h5.

23 ... bxa6

24 ♖b7

This riskless plan threatens to rip open the c-file, after 25 cxd6 ♕xd6 26 ♘a4.

24 ... g3?

Black also knew about his two losing teammates and this may explain this semi-desperate bid for attack.

His could see his mating dreams would evaporate after 24...gxf3 25 ♕xf3. But he could have minimized Caruana's queenside advantage with 25...dxc5 26 ♗xc5 ♖fb8!.

25 hxg3 fxg3

26 ♗xg3

The ...g3 sacrifice has been played, successfully, in similar positions since Taimanov – Najdorf, Zurich Candidates 1953.

But in that celebrated game Black quickly brought his knights to h5 and h4, and his threats proved insurmountable on the g-file.

Here there is no good follow-up to 26...♘h5 27 ♗h2.

26 ... ♖ab8

27 c6 ♕d8

28 f4

There was nothing wrong with ♕xa6 on either of the last two moves. Caruana's opening of the kingside gives him another way to win, along the f-file and the potentially vulnerable b1-h7 diagonal.

28 ... exf4

Black's e7-knight would finally get into the game after 28...♘g6 29 f5 ♘f4.

But 30 ♗xf4 exf4 31 e5! is quite lost.

29 ♗xf4 ♘g6

30	♗g3	♕e7

Another loss would be 30...♘e5 31 ♗xe5 dxe5 32 ♘a4 and ♘c5 followed by ♘e6 or ♘xa6.

31	♖f1!	♖bc8

32	♖f5

White can abandon the queenside in favor of 33 ♖b1 and 34 ♖bf1/35 ♕f3.

32	...	♘g8

33	♕f3

From now on there are fancy ways to win, based on pushing the center pawns.

For example, 33 ♖xf8 ♕xf8 34 e5 or 33...♖xf8 34 e5! dxe5 35 ♘e4 and 36 d6!.

33	...	♖xf5

34	♕xf5	♖d8

35	♘e2!	♕g7

36	♘f4	♘e7

37	♕h3

Also winning is 37 ♕g4 or 37 ♕e6. Caruana wanted to make h6 his next target...

37	...	♘xf4

38	♗xf4

...as 38...♘g6 39 ♗xh6! would show (39...♕xh6 40 ♖xc7+).

38	...	♖f8

39	♗xh6!	♕xh6

40	♖xc7	♖e8

41	e5!

So that if 41...dxe5 then 42 d6.

41	...	♕xh3

42	gxh3	♔g6

43	♖xe7!	♖xe7

44	exd6	resigns.

Two connected passed pawns on the sixth rank defeat an unaided rook. Even without his d5-pawn Black could not stop queening.

11
Learning To Become Lucky

More often than his colleagues, Caruana acknowledged that the outcome of tension-spiked games was not the result of superior knowledge, training or computer-vetted openings. The determinant was often just plain luck.

Biel 2010 is an example. It was a round-robin tournament of roughly equal youngsters. Caruana qualified for a three-way blitz playoff with Wesley So and Maxime Vachier-Lagrave. "I couldn't calm down and was very nervous," he said afterwards. But he won and credited "luck" – and explained that was typically the case in a speed tie-breaker.

What he didn't say is that you can create the conditions for your good fortune. Tactical awareness and superior clock management can make you lucky, as in this back-and-forth game.

Vladimir Potkin – Caruana
Russian Team Championship,
Dagomys 2010
Slav Defense (D12)

1	d4	♘f6
2	♘f3	d5
3	c4	c6
4	e3!	

During this decade, the quiet advance of the e-pawn earned a reputation as White's most pragmatic way to start a Slav Defense.

The main benefit is what it evades. The more traditional 4 ♘c3 allows the Czech Variation, 4...dxc4, and opens a path to the Meran Variation, after 4...e6.

These are the lines most likely to be prepared by Black with computer-checked improvements.

4	...	♗g4

The chief drawback to delaying ♘c3 is the absence of pressure on d5.

This means Black can solve his traditional problem in 1 d4 d5 openings: How to develop his QB.

5   h3   ♗xf3

The alternative is 5...♗h5 and then 6 g4 ♗g6 7 ♘e5 e6.

White can work with a slight Black disadvantage after 8 ♘d2 ♘bd7 9 ♘xg6 hxg6.

The GM elite is roughly divided on which path is best, 5..♗xf3 or 5...♗h5. And, to no surprise, Magnus Carlsen has played both.

6   ♕xf3   e6

7   ♘c3   ♘bd7

8   ♗d2

White hints at 0-0-0 and g2-g4-g5. But he retains the option of ♗d3, 0-0 and ♖ae1 followed by e3-e4 or something on the queenside.

8   ...   ♗d6

9   cxd5

This simplifies his choice. After 9...cxd5, queenside castling is riskier because the c-file is open.

But it also makes ♗d3, 0-0, ♖fc1 and ♘a4 much more desirable.

9   ...   exd5

Now the e4-square becomes important. Black can contest control of it with ...♕e7/...♗b4.

10   g4

Caruana knew the dangers to Black if White just pushes his g- and h-pawns.

He was White a year before when he got an effortless edge against Erwin L'Ami after 10 ♗d3 ♘f8 11 g4! ♘e6 12 h4.

10   ...   0-0

11   g5

Like 9 cxd5, this forces Black to make a major decision.

The easy choice is 11...♘e4 – easy, because he could count on White responding 12 ♘xe4 and then 12...dxe4 13 ♕xe4 ♕xg5.

87

Then a typical continuation is 14 ♗d3 ♘f6 15 ♕f3.

Black would probably end up in a slightly inferior endgame, after 15...♕d5 16 ♕xd5 or 15...♖fe8 16 h4 ♕h5, for example.

You can make a good case for 11...♘e4 being Black's best move. But the most likely result would be a draw, with a White win close behind. A Black win would be a distant third.

11	...	♘e8

12	h4

It was much harder to calculate the consequences of 11...♘e8 because White can attack with a variety of routine moves.

For instance 12...♘c7 13 ♗d3 ♘e6 14 0-0-0 and 15 ♖dg1/16 h5 is promising.

So is 15 ♕f5 g6 16 ♕h3 and 17 f4 and h4-h5.

12	...	♗b4!

Caruana generates the potential for ...♗xc3/...♘d6-e4 and ...♘b6-c4.

13	0-0-0	♘d6

He also has the orthodox option of blocking kingside attacking lines with ...f5.

If White replies gxf6 en passant, he opens half of the g-file.

In principle that should be promising. But here 13...f5 14 gxf6? ♘dxf6 is a positional error.

Black would get more than enough counterplay after 15 ♕g2 ♘d6 16 ♗d3 ♕e7 and ...♘c4 or ...♗xc3/...♘fe4.

14	♗d3

Caruana wanted to play 14...f5 now but rejected it because of an elaborate line he calculated:

He saw 15 g6 and how 15...hxg6 16 ♖dg1 ♕f6 17 ♕g2 would be good for White.

So he considered the line-closing 15...h6! – and spotted 16 ♘xd5.

He gave up on 14...f5 after he calculated 16...♗xd2+ 17 ♖xd2 17...cxd5? 18 ♕xd5+ and ♕xd6.

He apparently did not notice 17...♘e4!. That would allow him to accept the sacrifice under favorable circumstances (18 ♗xe4 fxe4 19 ♕xe4 cxd5 20 ♕xd5+ ♔h8).

But this was wasted effort. White could avoid complications by meeting 14...f5 with 15 ♘e2!.

A trade of bishops, 15...♗xd2+ 16 ♖xd2, would give him a positional pull after ♘f4.

14 ... a5

Instead, Caruana prepared to push his b-pawn.

The immediate 14...b5 15 ♔b1 ♘b6? 16 ♘xb5! costs a pawn (16...♗xd2 17 ♘xd6).

15 ♔b1 ♛e7

16 ♖dg1 b5

Now 16...f5 would have worked well because 17 ♘e2?? hangs the d2-bishop. White's kingside attacking chances would be smothered after 17 gxf6 ♘xf6 and planting a knight on e4.

After 16...b5 Black could have met 17 ♛h5 with 17...f5 18 g6? h6 or 18 gxf6 ♘xf6 19 ♛g5 ♗xc3 and 20...♘de4!.

17 ♛d1

Vladimir Potkin won the European Championship this year and has served as trainer/second for Ian Nepomniachtchi, Sergey Karjakin, Levon Aronian and the Russian national team. Not a bad résumé.

Here he recognized that his frontal attack on the kingside isn't working. He banks instead on ♛c2.

Then the threat of ♗xh7+ may provoke ...g6 and create a target for h4-h5.

17...♗xc3!

This secures e4 for a knight. It is more promising than 17...f5 18 gxf6 ♘xf6 19 ♖g2, which tends toward equal chances.

18 ♗xc3

Black could open a queenside file after 18 bxc3 ♘e4 19 ♛c2 b4!.

18 ... b4

19 ♗e1 c5!

Black's queenside play would have stalled without this move. White should not now allow 20...c4!.

20 dxc5 ♘xc5

89

If White could get his e1-bishop to d4 he would have a substantial edge.

But it is Black who would exploit the opened c3-f6 diagonal after 21 h5 ♘c4 and 22...♕e5!.

21 ♖g4

While calculating their wing attacks, the players had to consider potential endgames.

For example, 21 ♗c2 ♕e5 22 ♕d4! ♕xd4 23 exd4.

Despite White's bishops Black would be slightly better after 23...♘e6 24 ♗b3 ♘b5! and then 25 ♗xd5 ♖ad8 26 ♗b3 ♘bxd4.

It would be White who is looking for counterplay, such as 24...♘c4? 25 ♗xc4! dxc4 26 d5 and 27 ♖g4.

21 ... ♘xd3

Black can anticipate an attack on the d5-pawn with 21...♖fd8!.

That is not just defensive. He can work with the idea of 22...♕b7 followed by ...d4!, threatening ...♕xh1.

22 ♕xd3 ♖ac8

But Caruana adopted a policy more appropriate for White's time trouble.

Instead of defending the d5-pawn, he relies on tactics that might induce a blunder.

In other words, he is trying to make himself lucky.

He would succeed after 23 ♕xd5? ♖fd8!, for example.

Then 24 ♖d4 ♘b5 25 ♕xb5 ♖xd4 and ...♕e4+.

23 ♖d4! ♘e4

The d-pawn is also toxic after 24 ♖xd5? ♘c5 25 ♕c2 ♘b3! and wins (26 ♕xb3 ♕e4+).

Or 25 ♕d4 ♖fd8 with a threat of 26...♖xd5 27 ♕xd5 ♖d8.

24 f3! ♘c5

25 ♛d2

After the game, Caruana pointed out how 25 ♛d1 protects the key squares f3 and b3 and prepares to reorganize White's pieces with ♝g3!.

Then on 25...♛xe3 26 ♖xd5 ♞e4 he would have tricks such as 27 ♖d3 ♖c1+! and wins (28 ♛xc1 ♛xd3+ and ...♛xf3).

But the dangerous-looking 26...♞e4 threatens nothing.

White could keep the balance if he chooses careful moves such as 27 ♖f1 or 27 ♖h2.

The first thing a tactician notices is how 25...b3 26 axb3 ♞xb3 is a winning fork.

It takes him a while to realize White might be able to play 26 ♖xd5 bxa2+ 27 ♔xa2.

25 ... ♛e6

Now 25...♖fd8 26 ♖xd5? ♖xd5 27 ♛xd5 loses to 27...♖d8. But 26 ♝g3 is safe and roughly equal.

But a tactician also notices the f3-pawn is unprotected.

Black can threaten to win it with either 25...♛e6/...♛f5+ or 25...f6 ...fxg5.

He might calculate a forcing line, 25...f6 26 ♖xd5 fxg5 27 hxg5 ♖xf3.

He would be disappointed to find a fairly simple defense, 28 ♛c2!.

This threatens ♛xh7+, pins the c5-knight and wins time for a bishop move and ♖hc1.

26 ♔a1?

Caruana's 25...♛e6 gave him a better chance to become lucky because the safest-looking moves could lose.

For example, 26 f4? ♞e4 27 ♛-moves ♖c5 and 28...♖fc8.

Or 26 ♛e2 ♛g6+ 27 ♔a1? ♞b3+! and 27 ♛c2 ♞b3! (28 ♛xg6 ♖c1 mate).

The only good move is the one that looks riskiest, 26 ♖xd5! so that 26 ...♛g6+ 27 ♔a1 ♞e4 28 ♛d1! leads to even chances

26 ... b3

White's king move put it in greater danger because of potential last-rank mates. Better

91

was 26...♕f5! since 27 ♖f4 ♕c5 would threaten 28...♘d3!.

No better is 27 ♖f1 ♘e6 28 ♖xd5? ♕xd5 29 ♕xd5 ♖c1 mate. Or 28 ♖d3 ♖c5 and ...♖fc8.

27 ♕d1!

Not 27 a3 because of 27...♘a4! and ...♖c2 (28 ♖xa4 ♕c6! and ...♕c1+ or ...♕xa4).

27 ... bxa2

With ideas that include 28...a4 and 29...♘b3+.

28 ♗xa5

White is not quite lost after 28 ♔xa2 ♖fd8 but it isn't a position you want to play with only seconds left.

28 ... ♕xe3!

Threatening 29...♘b3+ or 29...♕xd4 30 ♕xd4 ♘b3+.

29 ♗c3 ♖a8

30 ♖e1?

This was the best defense to 29...♖b8! but now:

30 ... ♕c1+!

White resigned before 31 ♕xc1 ♘b3 mate.

Yes, the finish was a matter of luck. White should play 30 ♖b4! ♖fd8 and prevent 31...d4! with 31 ♗d4.

He would be safe after 31...♕e7 32 ♗xc5, for instance.

Luck played various roles in Caruana's career during this period. He was unlucky, for example, to be paired with a top-ten player, Peter Svidler, and be eliminated in the second round of the 2011 World Cup.

As Alexander Roshal, a legendary Russian magazine editor, put it, "The strong are lucky and the very strong are very lucky." Caruana was yet to be that strong.

12
The Surprisee

Thanks to Caruana's candor we know how often he was surprised after he sat down at the board. He admitted in his game notes when his pre-game analysis ended abruptly before his opponent's. Then he was not the one surprising his opponent. He was the surprisee. What he did in those situations is a clue to true talent.

The following game was played in another showcase of young players and for once he was facing someone younger than him, 17-year-old Parimarjan Negi.

Parimarjan Negi – Caruana
New Delhi 2010
Ruy Lopez, Anti-Marshall (C84)

1	e4	e5
2	♘f3	♘c6
3	♗b5	a6
4	♗a4	♘f6
5	0-0	♗e7
6	♖e1	b5
7	♗b3	0-0

When Black plays 7...0-0, rather than 7...d6, he is teasing.

He may answer 8 c3 with 8...d5, the Marshall Gambit. And maybe he won't.

Caruana did play the Marshall. But the earliest example in most databases is dated 2015.

8	a4	

Even Garry Kasparov, with his team of seconds and multiple computers, dodged the Marshall debate.

He "always avoided it as White and didn't play a single game with it [as Black] in his entire chess career," Ruslan Ponomariev wrote in *New In Chess Yearbook 133.*

8	...	b4
9	d4	

White's idea, also available in the immediate 8 d4 exd4 version, is that 9...exd4 10 e5! favors him.

9	...	d6

White benefits the most from a pawn on d4 in the Ruy Lopez

when he has played both c2-c3 and h2-h3. Here he hasn't.

Black would equalize after 10 c3 bxc3 and 11...♗g4.

And also after 10 h3 exd4! 11 ♘xd4 ♘a5 12 ♗a2 c5.

10   dxe5   dxe5

White still has a tiny advantage because of his control of the b3-f7 diagonal and his potential use of d5 as an outpost. But he must secure control of d5.

11   ♕xd8

The immediate 11 ♗g5? fails to 11...♕xd1 12 ♖xd1 ♘xe4.

11   ...   ♖xd8

12   ♗g5

This is a forgotten idea of the great Soviet player Yevgeny Vasiukov. Negi knew it because he had suffered twice previously, on the Black side.

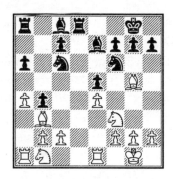

As Caruana studied a position he had never seen before, he worried about two White plans.

One is ♗xf6 followed by the pinning ♗d5.

The other is White pressure on the e5-pawn after ♘bd2-c4.

If he has to play ...♗d6, White damages his kingside pawns with ♗xf6.

12   ...   h6

Caruana considered 12...♖b8! so that his knight will not be pinned after 13 ♗xf6 ♗xf6 14 ♗d5. He would earn a substantial plus from 14...♘d4.

But he didn't like the looks of White's Plan B, 13 ♘bd2 and 14 ♘c4.

After the game he realized he would only be slightly worse after 13...h6 14 ♗e3 ♗d6 and 15 a5 ♘g4.

13   ♗xf6   gxf6!

Caruana would have no compensation for his bad f6-bishop after 13...♗xf6 14 ♗d5!.

For example, 14...♗b7 15 ♘bd2 ♘a5 16 ♗xb7 ♘xb7 17 ♘c4.

The Exchange sacrifice he uses in the game would not work in this sequence: 13...♗xf6 14 ♗d5! ♖d6 15 ♘bd2 ♗e6 16 ♘c4 ♖xd5 and now 17 exd5 ♗xd5 18 ♘cxe5!.

14 ♗d5! ♖d6

One of Vasiukov's games had gone 14...♗d7 15 ♘bd2 ♖ab8 16 ♘b3 with advantage to White.

Worse is 14...♗b7 15 ♘bd2 f5 in view of 16 ♗xc6 ♗xc6 17 exf5 and ♘e4.

15 ♘bd2

15 ... ♗e6!

16 ♘c4

White can decline the Exchange with 16 ♗xe6 and have reasonable winning chances after 16...♖xe6 17 ♖ad1 ♖d8 18 ♘c4.

Then his knights would land effectively on d5 and/or f5.

But not after 16...fxe6!, which is equal (17 ♘c4 ♖d7 18 ♖ad1 ♖ad8).

16 ... ♖xd5

17 exd5 ♗xd5

18 ♘e3

When Caruana chose 12...h6 he probably foresaw this position and noticed 18...♗xf3.

He would get a second pawn for the Exchange following 19 gxf3 ♘d4 20 ♔g2 ♔h7 and ...♖g8+.

But a key to playing an endgame an Exchange down is keeping control of the position. That is, minimizing enemy piece activity.

White's pieces would become the more active ones after 21 ♖ed1 ♖g8+ 22 ♔f1 ♘xf3? 23 ♘d5! and he would be close to winning.

18 ... ♗e6!

19 ♘h4

White could keep control with 19 ♖ad1 f5 and now 20 ♘d5, 20 b3 or 20 g3.

Caruana believed 19 g4 followed by ♘d2-e4 was better.

Then 19...h5! would allow the Black pawns to become a factor after 20 gxh5? f5 and ...e4.

But 20 h3! followed by ♔h2 and ♖g1 would be dangerous.

19   ...   ♗c5

20   ♘hf5

Negi sought a knight outpost at f5 instead. But Caruana felt a knight would "only look good" there.

20   ...   ♔h7!

Caruana patience.

He disdained 20...♘d4, which sets a simple trap: 21 ♘xh6+? ♔g7 costs material.

Also, 21 ♘xd4 ♗xd4 would nearly equalize chances (22 ♖ab1 ♗a2; 22 ♘d1 ♖d8).

But 21 ♘g3! would demonstrate that White's best knight outpost is on e4.

For example, 21...a5 22 ♘e4 ♗e7 23 c3!.

To reject 20...♘d4 21 ♘g3 Black would also have to see that White has only one dangerous reply to 21...f5.

Unfortunately, it is 22 ♘gxf5!.

Then 22...♗xf5 23 ♘xf5 ♘xf5 24 ♖xe5 is a lost ending.

Black can restore material equality after 23...♘xc2 24 ♖ec1 ♘xa1 25 ♖xc5 h5 26 ♖xe5 but his remaining pieces are much worse than White's.

21   c3!   bxc3

22   bxc3

White follows two basic rules for Exchange-down endgames:

The player with an extra rook (a) needs to open a file and (b) he would benefit from a trade of rooks (22...♖b8? 23 ♖ab1 or 22...♖d8? 23 ♖ad1).

22   ...   ♖g8

But there are other rules at work.

One pointed out by Boris Spassky is that knights are never weaker than when they protect one another.

White's knights lack offensive punch and are in danger of becoming liabilities.

23 ♔h1

He would still hold the reins after 23 ♖ad1!.

Instead, he looks for a way to anchor his f5-knight with g2-g4.

23 ... h5!

24 ♖ad1

Caruana believed a draw would be the natural result if White had gone ahead with 24 h3 and g2-g4.

24 ... ♔g6

25 ♘h4+ ♔h6

The knights cannot force a draw by repetition, e.g. 26 ♘hf5+? ♔g5!.

Then 27 ♘g3 f5 or 27 h4+? ♔g6 28 ♘g3 f5! favors Black.

26 g3 ♘e7!

27 ♖d2?

You can tell when you're losing control of the position: There are no particularly good moves.

This is a bad move. White protects the f2-pawn in anticipation of ...f5-f4. But he will now be unable to reply ♖b1 when Black seizes the b-file.

27 ... c6

28 ♘hg2 ♖b8!

Negi was getting into time trouble because he was trying to prove he still had an advantage.

29 ♖ed1? ♖b3

He is worse now. He should be thinking of defense, 30 ♖c2 ♖a3 31 ♖cc1 and then 31...♖xa4? 32 ♖a1!. A rook trade would still help White.

But Caruana would have plenty of useful waiting moves (31...♔g7, 31...♖a2) as well as 31...♘d5!.

30 ♖d8 ♖xc3

31 ♖a8 ♗b3

Under normal circumstances, White should be able to draw (32 ♖e1 ♗xa4 33 ♖xa6 ♗b3 34 ♖aa1! and ♖ec1).

But when players are short of time, Black will win this kind of position 80 percent of the time.

32	**♖a1**	**♗d4**
33	**♖e1**	**♗xa4**
34	**♖xa6**	**♗b3**
35	**♖a8**	**♗e6!**

The h5-pawn is irrelevant. After 36 ♖h8+ ♔g7 37 ♖xh5 White's rook would be exiled and Black can advance his c-pawn at will, 37...c5 and ...c4.

36	**h4?**	**♘g6**
37	**♖b1**	**f5!**
38	**♘d1**	**♖c2**
39	**♔g1**	**♖d2**
40	**♖a3**	**c5**

Black can also win with ...f4. But a Soviet-trained player was taught not to make irrevocable decisions just before the time control ends.

41 ♘e1 e4!

This ensures that ...c4 will be strong (not 41...c4? 42 ♘f3! ♖c2 43 ♘e1).

Black is winning.

42	**♘g2**	**c4**
43	**♘de3**	**♘e5**
44	**♖a6**	**♘f3+**
45	**♔f1**	**c3**
46	**♖c6**	**♔h7!**

This presents White with a choice of terrible moves, such as 47 ♖a1 ♗d7 48 ♖c7? ♗b5+ and mates.

It is not quite zugzwang because Black had a threat: 47...♖b2 48 ♖c1 ♗d7! and wins.

47	**♖c7**	**♗xe3**
48	**♘xe3**	**f4**
49	**gxf4**	**c2**
50	**White resigns.**	

In view of 50 ♖xc2 ♗h3+.

13
Point Getter

For his third Russian Team Championship, Caruana moved up to third board on the winning team. He was expected to produce points and was given White in eight of the ten rounds. He responded with six wins, four draws and a performance rating of 2862, by far the highest in an extremely strong tournament.

Caruana – Alexander Areshchenko
Russian Team Championship, Olginka 2011
Grünfeld Defense, Exchange Variation (D85)

1	d4	♘f6
2	c4	g6
3	♘c3	d5
4	cxd5	

Since becoming a master, the orthodox Exchange variation had become Caruana's favorite way to meet the Grünfeld.

4	...	♘xd5
5	e4	♘xc3
6	bxc3	♗g7
7	♘f3	

"But in this game I decided to try something different," he said afterwards. That is, not 7 ♗c4 c5 8 ♘e2.

7	...	c5

8	♗e3	♗g4
9	♖c1	

His opponent, a 24-year-old Ukrainian GM, must have known that Caruana had played a game a year before that went 9...0-0 10 d5 ♕a5 11 ♕d2 ♗xf3 12 gxf3 c4 with mutual chances.

9	...	♗xf3

But it was discovered that (9...0-0) 10 ♗e2! is stronger. So he reverted to an older idea, recently revived.

10	gxf3	

Previous games continued 10 ♕xf3 cxd4 11 cxd4 so that 11...♗xd4 12 ♗xd4 ♕xd4 13 ♖c8+.

But after 10...0-0 White's queen is misplaced on f3. He may have nothing better than the rough equality of 11 ♕d1.

| 10 | ... | cxd4 |

| 11 | cxd4 | 0-0 |

Caruana finds himself in another unfamiliar position. He had a vague memory of this occurring in a recent game between Giri and Nepomniachtchi (Wijk aan Zee 2011).

What he recalled is Nepo played ...e6, after 12 f4, and got a solid middlegame.

The position after 11...0-0 is much older, having arisen in a Gligorić - Beliavsky game 31 years earlier.

That turned out well for White (12 ♗c4 ♕a5+ 13 ♔f1! ♘c6 14 d5 ♘e5 15 ♗b3). Black may

do better with 12...♘d7 and ...♘b6/...♖c8.

12 d5!

Caruana relied on logic. If ...e6 was good for Black in the Nepo game, this was the way to discourage it: 12...e6 13 dxe6 ♕xd1+ 14 ♖xd1 fxe6 15 ♗c4!, with advantage.

| 12 | ... | ♘d7 |

| 13 | ♗h3 |

Black has three basic sources of counterplay. Two of them involve his knight.

The first is 13...b5 followed by ...♘b6-c4.

If White counters with 14 f4 ♘b6 15 0-0 ♘c4 16 ♗d4 Black can reply 16...♗xd4 17 ♕xd4 e6!.

We'll see this idea later. When Black can justify ...e6 (18 dxe6?? ♕xd4) he should be in good shape.

The second plan is 13...b6 and ...♘c5.

Every Grünfeld player knows that Black's control of dark squares (after ♗xc5 here) is usually good compensation for a pawn.

More critical is 14 f4 ♘c5.

Then 15 f3? e5! and 15 ♗g2 e6 should be good for Black but the jury is out on 15 e5 (15...f6 16 f5!).

13 ... ♔h8

Instead, Black prepares ...f5. "Slow but nevertheless interesting," was Caruana's comment.

The immediate 13...f5 loses the f-pawn, 14 exf5 gxf5 15 ♖g1 ♔h8 16 ♖g5.

Caruana analyzed much further: 16...♘b6 17 ♗xf5 ♘xd5 18 ♗e4 is difficult for Black, he said.

Computers avoid all this when they claim 14 0-0 is simply good for White.

14 f4

If White discourages ...f5 with 14 ♖g1, Black can revert to Plan A, with 14...b5! and ...♘b6-c4.

White would still stand well once he secures his king (♔f1-g2). But ♖g1 would look stupid.

14 ... f5!

Now Plan A is too slow, 14...b5 15 ♕d3 a6 16 ♖c6!.

But Plan B is also poor, 14...b6 15 0-0 ♘c5 16 ♖c4 e6 17 d6.

15 e5

Caruana spent a lot of time on this move. He admitted afterward 15 exf5 gxf5 16 0-0 would have been a simple, no-risk path to a plus.

After 16...♘f6 or 16...♘b6 he could have continued 17 ♗g2 followed by ♕d3 and ♖fd1, for example, while Black has to hunt for counterplay.

15 ... g5!

Hypermodern openings get crushed when they don't take risks to dissolve the enemy center.

If Black tries to solve his problems with 15...♕a5+, then 16 ♔f1 g5 is better than the game.

However, 16 ♕d2! ♕xd2+ is a bad endgame for him regardless

of how White retakes. Black would be playing without his g7-bishop.

And after 16...♛b5 White might go for a kingside attack with 17 ♝f1 ♛a4 18 ♜c4 and h2-h4-h5.

16 ♜g1!

Caruana had to act before his center becomes fragile. For example, 16 e6 gxf4 17 ♝xf4 ♞f6 18 ♝g2 ♛a5+ and now 19 ♛d2 ♛b5!.

But 16 fxg5 was a good alternative.

After 16...f4 17 ♝d4 ♞xe5 18 ♝c3 White can castle and avoid ...♛xd5.

16 ... gxf4

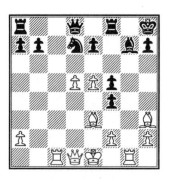

17 ♜xg7!

This is why Caruana spent a lot of time on 15 e5. But how does a master even consider a sacrifice like this?

One way is to look at the natural 17 ♝xf4 and realize 17...♞xe5

would be refuted by 18 ♜xg7! ♚xg7 19 ♝xe5+.

Once you see that, you examine 17...♝xe5. It seems to lose to a simple pin, 18 ♝xe5+ ♞xe5 19 ♛d4 ♛d6 20 f4.

However, this overlooks an equally simple tactic, the 20...♛b4+! 21 ♛xb4 ♞d3+ fork.

Before you abandon 17 ♝xf4 you try to find compensation for your lost pawn in 18 ♝h6.

But there are too many risky variables, such as a Black Exchange sacrifice, after 18...♛b6 19 ♝xf8 ♜xf8.

Nevertheless, there is something about the position in the diagram that suggests White can use his bishops to exploit Black's at-risk king. A grandmaster keeps looking.

17 ... ♚xg7

If you play over the game with a computer, it may quickly declare a draw - by perpetual check after 17...fxe3.

It can see 18 ♜xh7+ ♚xh7 19 ♛h5+ and then 19...♚g8 20 ♛g6+ ♚h8.

When it looks for something better than additional queen checks, it points out how White would lose after 21 ♜c4? ♛a5+! 22 ♚f1 e2+! 23 ♚xe2 ♛xa2+.

The machine would be guilty of the same impatience as a human who stops calculating in the previous diagram after looking at 17 ♗xf4?.

Give the engine more time and it sees the mate after 21 ♔e2!.

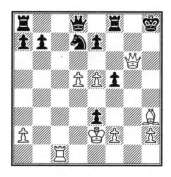

When computers have second thoughts

White clears the way for a rook check on g1 while avoiding ...♕a5+.

Black also loses after 21...♘f6 22 exf6 or 21...♘xe5 22 ♕h6+ ♔g8 23 ♖g1+ ♘g4 24 ♗xg4.

18   ♗xf4

Caruana couldn't calculate every scenario because his king is also insecure.

But tactics tend to flow in favor of one player or the other.

A master senses when they are running in his favor, e.g. 18...♕a5+ 19 ♗d2 ♕xd5?? 20 ♗h6+ costs the queen.

Black should be able to defend, such as with 19...♕xa2 20 ♖c7 ♕a3. Or 20...♖ad8 21 ♗c3 ♖c8!, again with equal chances.

18   ...   ♔h8!

But Black can seize the initiative. For example, 19 ♗h6 ♖g8 would threaten ...♖g1+.

That wins time for 20 ♔f1 ♕b6!.

White can allow a trade of rooks, such as 19 ♕d2 ♖g8 20 ♗xf5 ♖g1+ 21 ♔e2 ♖xc1 22 ♕xc1.

His bishops and extra pawn keep matters in balance after 22...♘b6 23 d6 and perhaps after 23 e6 ♘xd5 24 ♗e5+.

19   ♔f1?

Caruana is also playing to win and this is a way to stop both ...♕a5+ and ...♖g8-g1+.

He may have gotten the idea for his move after considering 19 ♕d3 ♕a5+ 20 ♔f1.

Then 20...♕xa2 21 e6! is good for him.

But 20...♘c5 favors Black (21 ♕d4 ♕a6+).

103

19 ... 🜚c8!

Caruana's last move indicated his willingness to play 19...♘b6 20 d6 or 19...♕a5 20 e6 ♘f6 21 ♗e5.

But 19...🜚c8! is based on principles – trading rooks is helpful when you are the Exchange ahead – and tactics.

After 20 🜚xc8 ♕xc8 Black threatens ...♕c4+ and ...♕xf4.

20 🜚xc8

One Black rook would get into the game after 20 🜚b1 🜚c4, if not two, 21 ♗h6? 🜚g8, when Black is much better.

20 ... ♕xc8

The proud White center would be collapsing after 21 ♕d3 e6! 22 dxe6 ♘c5.

21 ♕d4!

Played with the expectation of 21...♕c5 22 ♕xc5 ♘xc5 23 ♗g5!.

Then 23...🜚e8 24 ♗xf5 gives White enough compensation to draw.

Trickier is 23...e6 24 ♗e7 🜚c8 because 25 d6? ♔g7 is lost despite the protected passed d-pawn.

But 25 dxe6 and 26 ♗xf5 should draw. That's what Caruana was looking for now, a draw.

21 ... b6?

This threatens ...♕a6+/...♕xa2.

But like 21...♕e8 (and ...♕b5+) 22 e6+! it is far too slow.

Best was 21...♕c2!, not just to win the a2-pawn but to prepare ...♘c5-d3 and protect his f5-pawn.

To save himself, White would need to safely push a center pawn.

He would be lost after 22 d6 e6! because he had no further threats.

After the game Caruana wasn't sure if 22 e6+ ♘f6 23 d6 was good enough.

Computers give 23...♕b1+ 24 ♔g2 🜚g8+ 25 ♗g3 ♕e4+! 26 ♕xe4 ♘xe4 as lost but 25 ♔f3! as drawable.

They prefer 24...exd6 25 ♗xd6 🜚g8+ and 26...♔g7 – although only a Lasker plays chess like that.

22 e6+! ♘f6

23 ♗xf5

Only White has winning chances now. A trade of queens, 23...♕c5 24 ♕xc5 bxc5, would leave Black on the verge of zugzwang.

Then 25 d6 exd6 26 ♗xd6 ♖e8 27 ♗e5 ♔g7 and White's king will win the c-pawn and eventually outduel the rook.

23	...	♕a6+
24	♗d3	♕xa2

Black may have been counting on 25 d6 ♕xe6! (26 dxe7 ♖e8 or 26 ♗c4 ♕h3+).

25 ♗e5!

He is lost because of mating threats such as ♕h4xh7 as well as a prepared push of the d-pawn.

25	...	♕b3
26	♔e2	♕a2+
27	♔e1!	

So that 27...♕a5+ 28 ♔d1 and Black cannot meet the threat of 29 d6.

27	...	♔g8
28	♕h4	♕a5+
29	♔e2	

The safest king square is d1. How does he get it there without allowing checks at b3 or b1?

29	...	♕a2+
30	♔e1	♕a5+
31	♔d1!	

Now 31...♕xd5 32 ♕g5+ and 33 ♗xf6+.

31 ... ♕a3

The fastest win is 32 ♕g3+ ♔h8 33 ♕h3! with mate to follow.

32	♕g5+	♔h8
33	♕f5	♕a4+
34	♔e2	♕h4

This defense of h7 would have been forbidden by ♕h3. But even in time pressure Caruana can win with the idea he has been trying to execute since the opening.

35	d6!	exd6
36	e7	resigns.

14
Since Greco

"I never lived in Italy," said Caruana, the most famous Italian player since Gioachino Greco of the 1600s. During Fabiano's European years, he played relatively rarely in his ancestral home, compared with Hungary and Spain. He did enter Italy's marquee event, the annual Christmastime tournament at Reggio Emilia, on three occasions. But he never won it. The closest he came was tying for second and winning impressive games like this. His opponent had broken 2700 in 2010 and was higher rated than many of his young Russian rivals, including Ian Nepomniachtchi, until just before this game.

Nikita Vitiugov – Caruana
Reggio Emilia 2011-2
Trompowsky Attack (A45)

1	d4	♘f6
2	♗g5	

Grandmasters vary widely in meeting the Trompowsky Attack. Many of Caruana's rivals preferred the sharper 2...c5 and 2...♘e4 or the more solid 2...d5.

2	...	e6

This move was a favorite of Vladimir Chuchelov, who had become his trainer a year before this game.

The most popular reply, 3 e4, leads to the double-edged 3...h6 4 ♗xf6, since 4 ♗h4 g5 is an unsound gambit.

3	♘d2	h6
4	♗h4	c5

Now 5 e3 transposes into a Torre Attack hybrid (1 d4 ♘f6 2 ♘f3 e6 3 ♗g5).

5	e4	

Vitiugov was one of the first to try this gambit. He gets excellent compensation for a pawn after 5...cxd4 6 e5 g5 7 ♗g3 ♘d5 8 h4.

Two of Vitiugov's quick scalps went 8...gxh4 9 ♖xh4 ♘c6 10 ♘gf3 d6 11 ♗b5! with a burgeoning advantage.

106

5 ... d5!

Caruana offers to play a kind of offbeat French Defense, with 6 exd5 exd5 or 6...♛xd5.

6 e5

Instead, 6 dxc5 and 6...♝xc5 7 e5! is promising for White. But 6...♞c6 is safe enough.

6 ... g5

Now 7 exf6? gxh4 is much better for Black in view of his two bishops and probable extra pawn after ...♛xf6.

7 ♝g3 ♞fd7

8 h4!

White's opening demands a kingside target. He would be worse after 8 c3? ♞c6 or 8...♛b6.

Black has two standard ways of avoiding 9 hxg5 ♛xg5 10 ♞gf3.

One is to hunker down, 8...♜g8, and allow 9 hxg5 hxg5 10 ♛g4.

The other is 8...gxh4. Then 9 ♝xh4 ♝e7? 10 ♛g4 concedes too much.

Better is 9...♛b6, when White can continue in gambit style, 10 c4!?.

8 ... g4!?

An innovation? There are so many correspondence games that elude databases that it was hard to tell.

Caruana's move advertises his intent to solidify his kingside with 9...h5!.

That would be so good positionally that White needs to find a good reason not to play 9 ♛xg4.

Play could continue 9...♞c6 10 ♞gf3 ♛b6 and then 11 0-0-0 c4 would threaten 12...c3. It all but forces White into a sound piece sacrifice, 12 ♞xc4! dxc4 13 ♝xc4.

There is also 10...h5 11 ♛f4 cxd4 when White has one good move, 12 ♝b5!. But it is more than enough for the advantage.

So we are left with a mystery. We don't know what Caruana (and Chuchelov) had in mind after 9 ♛xg4.

And we can't tell what others think because 8 h4 has virtually disappeared from master practice.

9 dxc5

Instead, Vitiugov goes for quick piece play.

This recalls an anti-theory variation of the French Defense

that begins with the provocative 1 e4 e6 2 ♘f3 d5 3 ♘c3 and then 3...♘f6 4 e5 ♘fd7 5 d4 c5 6 dxc5 followed by ♗f4 and ♗d3.

Vitiugov's position looks like an improved version of that variation. White gets his rapid development *and* Black has to deal with his kingside weakness.

9 ... h5

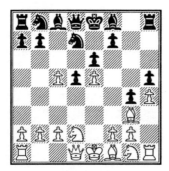

10 ♗b5

A year later at the Tal Memorial blitz tournament, Hikaru Nakamura challenged Caruana with 10 ♘e2.

He accepted the invitation to eliminate what was left of the White center, 10...♘c6 11 ♘f4 ♘dxe5.

Caruana was better, 12 ♘b3 ♗d7 13 c3, until tactics began to dominate, 13...♕f6 14 ♗b5! a6 15 ♗a4 ♗h6 16 ♘d3.

10 ... ♘c6

11 ♘e2

Vitiugov adopts the same attitude as Nakamura: He dares Caruana to target the e5-pawn.

11 ... ♘xc5

Dare refused: After 11...♗g7 12 c4! the center is opening.

Black cannot castle following 12...♘dxe5 13 0-0 in view of ♘f4xh5.

His king would be relatively safe on f8. But the position begins to look like a bad French Defense after 13...♔f8 14 cxd5 exd5 15 ♘b3, for example.

12 0-0 a6

13 ♗xc6+ bxc6

14 c4!

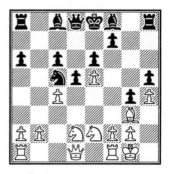

White prepares to open the c-file after ♕c2 or ♖c1.

Black can stop that with 14...d4?.

But this is a positional blunder, punishable by 15 b4! and ♘e4.

14 ... a5!

This stops White's other plan, pushing b2-b4 and occupying a5 or c5 with a knight.

It would have worked after 14...♗b7 15 b4 ♘d7 (15...♘d3 16 ♕b3) 16 ♖b1 ♗e7 17 ♘b3!.

Then 17...♔f8 18 ♘a5 or 17...♖c8 18 ♘c5 favors White.

Black cannot safely win a pawn (17...♗xb4 18 cxd5 cxd5 19 ♘bd4 or 17...♗xh4 18 ♘c5! ♗c8 19 ♗xh4 ♕xh4 20 ♕a4).

15	♘d4	♕b6
16	♕c2	

Remarkably, Black can afford to retreat his only developed minor piece in order to threaten ...♕xd4.

16	...	♘d7

White's d4-knight does not have a means of support (17 ♘2b3? a4!) or an appealing retreat (17 ♘e2 ♗a6).

17	♕d3	

Because of the gross disparity in development, a master in White's chair would start running his sacrificial motor.

For example, 17 cxd5 ♕xd4 18 dxe6 looks good.

Black's best response would be the unclear 18...♘c5! 19 exf7+ ♔xf7 20 ♖ad1.

But 17 cxd5? would help Black after 17...cxd5!. The pawn swap makes ...♗a6 stronger.

And the endgame after 18 ♕a4 ♕b4 or 18 ♕c6 ♕xc6 19 ♘xc6 ♗b7 favors Black.

17	...	♗a6

Now 18 b3 would support the c4-pawn and deny ...♕xb2.

But in the foreseeable future, only Black pieces would easily improve.

For example, 18...♗e7 19 ♖ac1 ♘f8!, followed by ...♖d8 and/or ...♘g6, is definitely in Black's ballpark.

If Vitiugov was going to try to break the bad trend, now was the time.

18 ♘xe6! fxe6

19 ♕g6+ ♚d8

After 19...♚e7? Black would be inviting ♗f4-g5+.

20 ♕xe6

White visualized this position and two promising plans when he chose 18 ♘xe6.

One is to prepare e5-e6. The other is to open the center with cxd5/♖fd1.

The first plan wins after 20...♖h6? 21 ♕f7 d4? 22 e6.

The second would win after 20...♚c8? 21 cxd5!.

For instance, 21...♗xf1 22 dxc6 or 21...cxd5 22 ♖ac1+ ♚d8 23 ♕xd5.

20 ... ♗e7!

This gives White a lot more to think about than 20...d4.

Now 21 cxd5 cxd5 22 ♕xd5 ♗b7 leads to a counter-attack

(23 ♕f7 ♕c6 24 f3 ♘xe5!) or an unfavorable endgame.

21 ♖fd1 d4

Now 22 ♕f5 would threaten 23 e6.

White would have four pawns for his sacrificed knight after 22...♖f8 23 ♕xh5 c5 24 ♕xg4.

But Black would have the upper hand after 24...♗c8 puts e5-e6 on the back burner.

Caruana would also have stingier defenses such as 22...♖a7 and 23 e6 ♖f8 24 ♕xh5 ♘f6, again with good winning chances.

Vitiugov faces the second critical moment of the game.

Like the situation after 17...♗a6, he can see how his position can deteriorate (22...c5!).

22 c5?

This additional sacrifice checks off so many boxes it deserved a better fate.

It stops ...c5, clears c4 for a knight and would open a file for his rooks after 22...♕b5? 23 ♘b3.

An endgame, 22...♕xc5 23 ♘b3 ♕d5 24 ♘xd4!, would be quite playable, 24...♕xe6 25 ♘xe6+ ♚c8 26 ♘d4 c5 27 ♖ac1.

And he would be free to gobble up kingside pawns after 22...♗xc5 23 ♘b3 (threat of ♖ac1/♘xc5) ♖f8 24 ♕g6.

22	...	♘xc5
23	♕f7	

White banked on 24 e6 followed, for example, by 25 ♕g7!.

Black can stop 24 e6 with 23...♗c8.

But that loses quickly to 24 ♘c4 ♕b5 25 ♖xd4+.

23	...	♖a7!

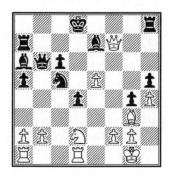

By protecting his e7-bishop, Black provides the escape ...♚c8.

He would be winning after 24 e6 ♚c8 25 ♗e5 ♖d8 26 ♕xh5

because he can take the initiative with 26...♗e2 27 ♖e1 d3, for example.

24	♖ac1	♖d7
25	e6	♖d5

Now his h5-pawn is rock-solid and he is ready for ...♘d3/...♖f8.

26	♘c4	♗xc4
27	♖xc4	♖f8
28	♕g6	♘b7!

The knight heads to f5 where it can capture on h4 or g3 (after 29 b3 ♘d6 30 ♖a4? ♘f5, for example).

29	♕e4	

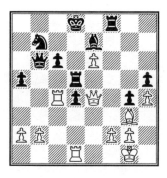

29	...	♘d6!

White might still have carried off a swindle after 29...♗f6?? 30 e7+! ♗xe7 31 ♖4xd4.

Caruana's move gives back a pawn so that his bishop will have a permanent target at f2.

30	&xd6	&xd6
31	&cxd4	&xd4
32	&xd4+	&c8

The rest is fairly routine provided (a) Black offers to trade heavy pieces and (b) he does not allow &xh5.

33	g3	&c5
34	&d2	&b7
35	&d7+	&b6
36	&e2	&d8

Now 37 &d2 &xd7 38 &xd7 &d6, as in the game, or 38 exd7 &c7.

37	&xd8	&xd8
38	&d2	&e7
39	a3	&e5
40	&d7	&d6
41	&e8	&xe6

White resigned after a few last spasms:

42 b4 axb4 43 axb4 &e5 44 &f1 &d6 45 &d8+ &c7 46 &d2 &d6 47 White resigns.

Fabiano's defensive skill was impressive in other games as well. Two years later Hikaru Nakamura said the new generation of grandmasters handled difficult positions better than their great predecessors. When a strong opponent amassed strong attacking or positional pluses, they didn't collapse. Training with computers had helped them defend better. "The resistance that the younger players, myself, Carlsen, Caruana also, put up is very different from the past, when it was easier to convert these kinds of advantages," he said in *New In Chess*.

15
Mozart or Salieri

Despite his successes by age 19, more doubts were expressed about Fabiano's future than almost any other young grandmaster. When he finished next to last at Biel 2011, the tournament winner, Magnus Carlsen, watched him play. "This guy is not going to be a threat" in the near future, he concluded. Russian GMs were also skeptical. "I would say that Magnus' future doesn't look promising," Evgeny Sveshnikov said. Sergey Shipov agreed. In some games he looked like a "nervous schoolboy instead of a grandmaster of class," he wrote.

Caruana was being contrasted with a rapidly improving rival two years younger than him. Anish Kumar Giri was born in St. Petersburg and grew up as another of the dozens of moderately talented Russian adolescents. When his family prepared to move to the Netherlands in early 2008 – an upheaval similar to what the Caruanas had endured – Russan chess authorities made little effort to convince Anish to stay. He was no Ian Nepomniachtchi, who outrated him by 300 points.

But, like Caruana, Giri quickly made GM norms in Europe. He was described as "the world's most promising junior" when he faced Fabiano at Wijk aan Zee 2012. The magazine 64 predicted that when the two met, "it will be understandable who plays the role of Mozart and who is Salieri." Knowledgeable readers knew Antonio Salieri as a once-exalted composer who was eclipsed by the younger Mozart. Like Salieri, Caruana "may write remarkable music and even achieve great successes," the magazine said. "But the sympathy of the public unavoidably lies" with Giri.

Caruana – Anish Giri
Wijk aan Zee 2012
Slav Defense,
Chebanenko Variation (D11)

1	d4	d5
2	c4	c6
3	♘f3	♘f6
4	e3	a6

Black's last move prepares to solidify his queenside with ...b5 before he decides what to do with his problem piece, his c8-bishop.

5   ♘c3   b5

A main line of this variation runs 6 b3 ♗g4. With his queenside somewhat compromised, White is unlikely to mount a kingside attack as in Game 11, such as after 7 h3 ♗xf3 8 ♕xf3 e6.

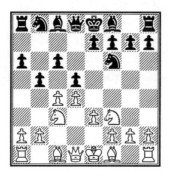

6   c5

In Siegbert Tarrasch's day this would have been ridiculed as a beginner's error.

White is ahead in development. Why not build on that lead with 7 cxd5 cxd5 and 8 ♗d3 ?

But an advantage in time quickly dissipates if it cannot be turned into threats. This is what happens after, say, 8...e6 9 0-0 ♗b7, when Black is equal.

6   ...   g6

7   ♘e5   ♗g7

Caruana had played 8 ♗e2 against Peter Svidler three years before and got a nice game from 8...0-0 9 0-0 ♗e6 10 f4 ♘e4 11 a4!.

8   f4

But, he admitted in *New In Chess*, "To be honest, I couldn't remember much about this variation during the game."

What he recalled is Black often meets an early ♘e5 with ...♘fd7! so he can trade knights.

Caruana wanted to answer ...♘fd7 with ♘d3! – and be sure Black could not reply with the thematic ...e5!.

8   ...   a5

This is another mystery move Tarrasch might have condemned as a waste of time.

But 8...♘bd7? simply drops a pawn (9 ♘xc6).

Black could prepare it with 8...♕c7 9 ♗e2 ♘bd7.

Then a trade of knight, such as 10 0-0 0-0 11 ♗d2 ♘xe5 12 fxe5 ♘d7, would turn out to be too loosening after 13 e4!.

114

9 ♗e2 ♛c7

The point of 8...a5 was to discourage a White plan of b2-b4/a2-a4!.

He should not play ...b4 unprovoked because White can open the queenside with ♘a4 and a2-a3!.

10 0-0

Now 10...♗e6 11 ♗d2 ♘bd7 would be solid.

But Black would be headed for a lifeless middlegame after 12 ♗f3 0-0 13 ♗e1 and ♗h4.

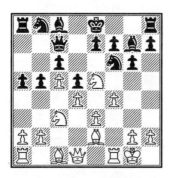

10 ... h5!

Pushing this rook pawn makes more sense than pushing the other:

Black's c8-bishop has one ideal square, f5. If it goes there after castling, g2-g4! is a good response. But after 10...h5, g2-g4 is off the table.

This is a common priyome, or strategic idea, in other openings.

Kasparov – Anand, World Championship match 1996, 14th game went 1 e4 d5 2 exd5 ♛xd5 3 ♘c3 ♛a5 4 d4 ♘f6 5 ♘f3 c6 6 ♘e5 ♗e6 7 ♗d3 ♘bd7 8 f4 g6 9 0-0 ♗g7 10 ♔h1 ♗f5 11 ♗c4 e6 12 ♗e2.

Grandmaster commentators were still criticizing Black's play when his 12...h5! revealed that he was, if anything, slightly better.

11 h3 ♗f5

12 ♗d2 ♘bd7

13 ♗f3

Caruana's original intention was to retreat his knight to d3 whenever Black played a knight to d7.

But Giri's clever play on the wings meant he had little to fear after 13 ♘d3 ♘e4 (14 ♘xe4 dxe4 and 15...a4).

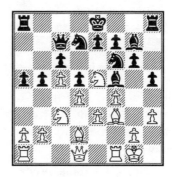

13 ... h4

A trade of at least one pair of minor pieces helps Black because he is constricted.

He would be secure after 13...♘e4 14 ♘xe4 dxe4! and

15 ♗e2 a4 16 ♘xd7 ♗xd7 and …f5, for example.

It takes some calculation to appreciate that 14 ♗xe4 would lose a pawn (14…dxe4 15 ♕c2) – and more calculation to realize 16 ♘xe4 would get White into an uncomfortable pin.

But how can Black afford another pawn move like 13…h4 ?

The answer is he stopped a good White maneuver, ♗e1 and ♗h4.

By discouraging White's best plans (b2-b4, ♗e1-h4) Giri can wait for Caruana to find another.

14 ♕e1!

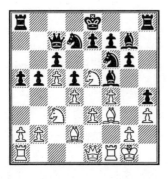

Black's last move more or less commits his king to the center because …0-0? will doom the h4-pawn.

Therefore, Caruana prepares to open the center with 15 e4!. On e1 his queen also watches both rook-pawns.

14 ... ♘e4

If Black secures greater control of e4 with 14…b4 15 ♘a4, he

hands White a line-opening plan, a2-a3!.

Play could go 15…♘xe5 16 fxe5 ♘e4 17 ♗xe4!. Then 17…♗xe4 18 ♘b6 and 19 a3! with a solid positional plus.

15 ♘xe4 dxe4!

The more natural 15…♗xe4 runs into problems after 16 ♗xe4 dxe4 17 ♘xd7.

For instance, 17…♕xd7 18 ♗xa5 or 17…♔xd7 18 f5.

If Black tries to finesse his way out, with 16…♘xe5, both 17 ♗xd5 and 17 fxe5 dxe4 18 ♕b1 and ♕xe4 are bad for him.

16 ♗e2

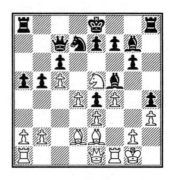

Despite the moves that would have scandalized Tarrasch, Black would stand remarkably well after 16…♘xe5 17 fxe5 f6.

That seems to doom the h-pawn after 18 exf6 exf6 19 ♖f4.

But 18…♗xf6! is excellent for Black.

Then he can castle kingside safely and bid for advantage with ...e5!.

Caruana intended to avoid this with 17 dxe5, rather than 17 fxe5.

His bad bishop would get some scope after 17...f6 18 exf6 ♗xf6 19 ♗c3.

But with ...♔f7, Black is solid.

That is perhaps the most striking feature of the game. Instead of the massacre that follows, Black was on the cusp of equality.

16 ... f6?

This advance, without ...♘xe5, has been in the back of both players' mind since 7 ♘e5.

Of course, it is weakening. But 17 ♘xd7 ♗xd7 would allow Black to seal the center with ...f5!.

Then his light-squared bishop would be bad. But so is White's dark-squared bishop.

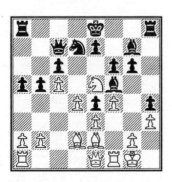

17 ♗xa5!

This sacrifice suggests itself because White will get three passed queenside pawns for his bishop.

17 ... ♖xa5?

Giri overlooked the sacrifice.

But what cost him the game was failing to see how he could activate his pieces after 17...♕xa5!.

Then 18 ♘xc6? ♕xe1 19 ♖fxe1 ♘b8! preserves the critical b5-pawn (20 ♗xb5? ♗d7!).

Instead, White should get a third pawn for his bishop with 18 ♕xa5 ♖xa5 19 ♘xc6 ♖a8 20 ♗xb5.

The outcome of the game would depend on whether he is allowed time to advance his passed a- and b-pawns.

Black might defend after the remarkable 20...e5!.

Then 21 a4 exf4 22 exf4 (22 ♖xf4? ♗h6) ♗e6! followed by ...♔f7 and ...f5.

18 ♘xc6 ♖a8

Quite lost is 18...♕xc6 19 ♕xa5 and 20 ♗xb5, when White has a rook and three pawns for two minor pieces that play badly in this pawn structure.

19 ♗xb5

19 .... ♗e6

In contrast with the note to 17...♖xa5, here 19...e5? is clearly bad (20 a4 exf4 21 exf4 ♗e6?? 22 ♕xe4).

20 a4 f5

If Giri blockades the center, 20...♔f7 21 ♕d1 ♗d5, Caruana would enjoy the rest of the afternoon pushing his queenside pawns to victory.

For instance, 22 ♘b4 e6 23 ♘xd5 exd5 24 b4 f5 25 a5 would be followed by ♕a4 and ♗xd7 or ♗c6/b4-b5.

21 ♕d2

Caruana has a backup winning plan of pushing the d4-pawn. Another way of doing this is 21 ♘e5, threatening 22 d5!.

21 ... ♗f6

22 d5! ♗f7

23 ♖ac1

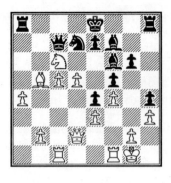

23 ... ♔f8

After 23...0-0 White has a choice of bulking up (24 ♖fd1 or 24 b4) or calculating 24 d6 exd6 25 cxd6 ♕-moves 26 ♘e7+!, which also wins.

24 b4 ♕c8

25 d6! exd6

26 cxd6 ♕e8

Caruana could win with second- or even fourth-best moves. Here 27 ♘e5, 27 a5 or 27 ♘d4 followed by ♖c7 would also do the job.

27 ♘e7 ♗e6

28 ♖c7 ♖h7

29 ♘d5

There was a clever finish in 29 ♗xd7 ♗xd7 30 ♖xd7 ♕xd7 31 ♕d5!.

This threatens mate on g8 as well as ♕xa8+.

29 ... ♗d8

30 ♖b7 ♖c8

31 a5

Caruana preferred what he called "the sadistic approach," the advance of the a-pawn.

31 ... ♔g7

32 a6 ♔h6

33 a7

Black is so tied up by the pins on the seventh rank and the b5-e8 diagonal that he will also lose kingside pawns.

33 ... ♕f8

34 ♘e7 ♘b6

35 ♕f2 ♖f7

36 ♕xh4+ ♔g7

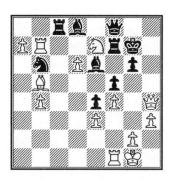

Caruana does not criticize opponents for refusing to resign in hopeless positions. Instead, he wrote, "He decided to play on to the end of the time control."

37 ♕g5 ♗d5

38 ♕xg6+ ♔h8

39 ♕h5+ ♔g7

40 ♘xf5+ ♔g8

41 ♘e7+ resigns.

Black loses more material (41...♗xe7 42 ♖xb6 or 42 dxe7 first).

16
Little Moves

Heading to his first Category 22 tournament was an unwanted adventure for Fabiano. He missed his flight from Zürich to Moscow, went to Frankfurt to make a connection, lost his luggage and finally arrived in the Russian capital at 3 a.m. on the day of the opening blitz tournament. He finished last in the blitz. He felt exhausted when he lost his first game of the Tal Memorial and had to defend a 107-move draw in the second.

But by tournament's end, he had won three games, all with White, including this.

Caruana – Vladimir Kramnik
Tal Memorial, Moscow 2012
Scotch Game (C45)

1	e4	e5
2	♘f3	♘c6
3	d4	

This was the first time Caruana played the Scotch Game. He said he didn't want "to bash my head against the Berlin Wall yet again."

Kramnik had revived the Berlin in winning the 2000 world championship match. He admitted he was secretly pleased when opponents avoided 3 ♗b5 against him. They were admitting they could not find an engine-vetted improvement for White. "Many are accustomed to analyzing by first pressing keys," Kramnik wrote in *New In Chess*. "But the Berlin is a variation in which the computer is practically helpless."

3	...	exd4
4	♘xd4	♘f6

This variation, in place of Kramnik's previous favorite 4...♗c5, is one that an opponent could prepare well with a computer.

5	♘xc6	bxc6
6	e5	♛e7
7	♛e2	♘d5
8	c4	♗a6

The reason is that White has many possible paths and they call for unusual moves.

You would not normally consider, for example, 9 b3, 9 ♛e4 and 9 h4, unless an omniscient machine told you they were good.

9	♘d2	g6
10	♘f3	♝g7

Before the game, Caruana looked at 10...♛b4+ 11 ♔d1, which leads to a double-edged position after 11...♜b8 12 ♛c2 ♘e7.

Or 11...♘b6 12 b3 ♝g7 13 ♛d2 followed by ♝b2 and ♔c2. He said this kind of position corresponded with his mood.

11	♝g5

If White can get past the tactical problems, his advantage in space will render him better chances than Black, as 11...♛c5 12 ♛d2 ♘b6 13 b4 would.

11	...	f6

Caruana was surprised by this reply. Instead, he analyzed 11...♛b4+ twelve moves into the future:

A recent game had gone 12 ♛d2 ♛xd2+ 13 ♝xd2 and then a pawn sacrifice, 13...♘b6 14 b3 d6 15 0-0-0.

Then came 15...dxe5 16 ♘xe5 ♝xe5 17 ♜e1 ♘d7 18 f4.

That was promising. But he carried his analysis further until he concluded White would have the edge after 18...f6 19 fxe5 ♘xe5 20 ♝c3 0-0 21 ♝e2 ♜fe8 22 ♝xe5! fxe5 23 ♝f3.

Of course, analysis this extensive is more of a fantasy than a preparation for reality.

But it's a confidence builder, the kind that helps before you sit down opposite a former world champion.

12	exf6	♛xe2+
13	♝xe2	♘xf6
14	0-0-0	

If White castles kingside, Black has easy equality (14 0-0 ♘e4).

It is more important for White's king to protect the pawn at b2.

14	...	0-0-0
15	♝e3	

This was the first original move and far from an obvious one. But it makes sense:

Black has only one real weakness, the a7-pawn. White has one, too, at f2.

Black would have equalized after 15 ♜he1 ♜de8! 16 ♘d4 ♘e4, for example.

15	...	♜de8

16	♗d3	d6

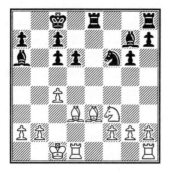

Now 17 ♗xa7? c5! would recall Bobby Fischer's loss of a trapped bishop in the first game of the 1972 world championship match.

Like Fischer's blunder, this was more complex than it seemed: 18 b4 ♗b7 19 bxc5 ♗xf3 20 gxf3 ♔b7 and Black slowly wins.

17 c5!

Black could claim an advantage, due to superior pawn structure, if he got to play 17...c5!.

17	...	♗xd3

18	♜xd3	

But the structure would slightly favor White after 18...d5? 19 ♗d4.

Instead, Kramnik makes his first major decision of the game.

18	...	♘d5

In retrospect, 18...♘e4! would have made the next hour less stressful for him.

If White then tries to preserve his pawn on c5, he can become overextended, 19 b4 ♜hf8 20 ♜a3? ♗c3, threatening ...♗xb4.

Instead, White can head to a balanced position with 19 cxd6 cxd6 and 20 ♜e1 or 20 ♘d2 (20...♘xd2 21 ♔xd2 ♗xb2? 22 ♜xd6).

19	cxd6	cxd6

20	♗xa7!	

This capture wasn't possible in the 18...♘e4 lines because the bishop would still be trapped by ...c5 and ...♘xf2 is threatened.

The position defies long-term calculation. Caruana did not think he was better and, like most everyone who followed the game, relied on general impressions.

Those impressions say Black will have compensation in his well-placed knight and rooks.

Yet within a half dozen moves Black's compensation ebbs away. Is this because of errors too subtle to be detected? Or is it because

Caruana's "little moves" are better than they seem?

20 ... ♔c7

This prepares 21...♖a8. So would 20...♔d7 but it is hard for Black to have faith in 21 ♖b3 ♖a8 22 ♖b7+ ♘c7 23 ♗b6 ♖fc8.

However, 21...♔c7, instead of 21...♖a8, revives his prospects for a strong ...♖a8, ...c5 or ...♖e2.

Black would hold after 22 ♗d4 ♗xd4 23 ♘xd4 ♖hf8 24 f3 ♘f4, for example.

21 ♗e3

This stops ...♘f4 and asks a question:

If Black doesn't change the basic framework of the position with ...♘xe3, which player could improve his chances more?

The answer is White. After 21...♖hf8 22 ♖hd1, for example, he can arrange his forces better with a2-a3, ♔c2 and perhaps b2-b4 and ♔b3.

Black does not have quiet moves that are as helpful as these.

21 ... ♖a8

So, let's consider 21...♘xe3 22 fxe3 d5, with the idea of doubling rooks on the e-file.

White would still be a pawn ahead after, say, 23 a3 ♖e4 24 ♖f1 ♖he8 25 ♘d2 (25...♖xe3? 26 ♖f7+).

But he has no obvious way to improve after 25...♖4e7 26 ♖f3 ♗h6.

Seeing this is a form of calculation that is much more difficult than announcing mate in eight.

Black also has alternatives that were worth a deep look, such as 21...♖b8.

Then 22 ♗d4 ♘f4 or 22 b3 ♘b4 or 22 ♖d2 ♘xe3 23 fxe3 ♖he8.

One gets the impression that Kramnik felt his position was so solid he didn't have to work that hard.

22   a3   ♖a4

And here 22...♖hb8! was the forcing way to go.

White can play 23 ♗d4 ♘f4 24 ♖e3! but 24...♗xd4 25 ♘xd4 ♘xg2 26 ♖e7+ ♔b6 is nothing much (27 ♖xh7 ♖f8).

23   ♖e1!

Kramnik threatened ...♖c4+.

For example, 23 ♖hd1 ♖c4+ 24 ♔b1 ♖b8! with a potential fork on c3 after 25 ♗d4 ♗xd4.

23   ...   ♖f8?

Caruana's 23 ♖e1! was another "little move" with a subliminal tactic.

After 23...♖g4 24 ♗d2! ♖xg2? 25 ♖xd5! and ♖e7+ he would get two minor pieces for a rook.

That might win after 25...♗xb2+ 26 ♔xb2 cxd5 27 ♗e3 and ♘d4/♖c1+.

If Black sidesteps this with 24...♔d7, White would consolidate with 25 ♖b3 ♗f6 26 g3.

Then his extra pawn looms larger than it did three moves ago.

24   ♘g5!

"Consolidate" is one of the (many) chess terms that has no exact definition.

Here White can consolidate if he uses his own threats (♘e6+) to sharply reduce Black's chances for counterplay.

24   ...   ♖e8

25   ♗b6+!   ♔d7

26   ♖xe8   ♔xe8

27   ♗e3

More consolidation: Caruana's king is safe and Kramnik lacks a target (27...♖g4 28 g3).

A swap of a pair or two of the remaining minor pieces would help White (27...♘xe3 28 ♖xe3+ ♔d7 29 g3 ♗h6 30 h4).

27   ...   ♔d7

28   ♖b3

Other good little moves were 28 g3 and 28 ♗d2.

But not 28 ♘xh7? ♖h4, when Black's rook suddenly become an equalizing force.

| 28 | ... | ♔c8 |

Or 28...♘xe3 28 ♖b7+ ♔c8 29 ♖xg7 ♘xg2 30 ♖xh7 and White can make slow progress (30...♖f4 31 ♖f7).

29	♗d2	h5
30	♘f7	♔c7
31	♖g3	♘e7
32	b4	

This shuts out the rook and threatens to grab another pawn after 33 ♗f4!.

| 32 | ... | ♔d7 |
| 33 | ♖d3 | |

Caruana was running short on time as he calculated his way through sidelines such as 33...♘f5 34 ♗f4 ♗d4 35 ♘xd6 or 34...d5 35 ♘e5+.

| 33 | ... | d5 |
| 34 | ♔c2 | |

He also avoided risky options, such as 34 ♗c3.

It would shorten matters after 34...♖xa3? 35 ♗xg7 ♖xd3 36 ♘e5+.

But 34...♗xc3 35 ♖xc3 c5! gets messy (36 ♖xc5 ♖xa3 and 36 bxc5 ♘c6 followed by ...d4).

| 34 | ... | ♘f5 |
| 35 | ♗c3 | |

Now this move works better, e.g. 35...♗xc3 36 ♖xc3 c5 37 ♔b3.

But even this required extensive calculation, of 35...♖xa3 36 ♗xg7 ♖xd3 37 ♔xd3 ♘xg7.

He had to be confident that 38 ♘e5+ and ♘xg6 is an easily winning knight endgame. It is.

| 35 | ... | d4 |

36 ♔b3

There were still some noisy tactics to put on mute, such as 36 ♗b2 ♗f6 and ...♔e6.

Or 36 ♗d2 ♔e6 37 ♘g5+ ♔d5.

36 ... ♖a8

37 ♘g5! ♔d6

Black would stay in the game because of his well-placed pieces after 38 ♘f3 c5 (39 bxc5+ ♔xc5 40 ♗b4+ ♔d5).

38 f3?

With more clock time, Caruana could have calculated 38 ♔c4 ♖xa3! 39 ♗xd4! and be certain about 39...♖xd3 40 ♗c5+ and ♔xd3.

That is getting close to what masters call "a technical win," meaning a position that can be shepherded to victory with more routine moves.

38 ... ♔d5

39 ♘e4

Caruana made his 38th move to protect his knight (and because he had only seconds left to reach move 40). Ironically, that poor move won the game because it prompted:

39 ... ♘e3??

40 ♖xe3! resigns.

After the game the players discovered 39...♖xa3+!!.

The key point is 40 ♔xa3 ♔c4 makes Black's passed pawn good enough to draw (41 ♖d1 dxc3).

Also, his far-superior king position would equalize after 41 ♖xd4+ ♗xd4 42 ♗xd4 ♔xd4.

The improbable finish, coming after Caruana's equally unlikely save of a lost position with Teimour Radjabov, put Caruana in first place on the eve of the last round.

"However, I wasn't quite up to the challenge," he wrote and lost to Levon Aronian "without a fight." He had to settle for a tie for second place, behind Magnus Carlsen — who was beginning to take him very seriously.

17
Minister of Defense

Sergey Karjakin's title as youngest-ever grandmaster was temporary and bound to be taken from him by a future junior. But "Minister of Defense" stuck with him. He earned it by becoming one of the hardest players in the world to defeat. His assets included a remarkable ability to deal with stress. This allowed him to outperform expectations in World Cups and, unfortunately for Caruana, the 2016 Candidates tournament. But when they met four years earlier, Karjakin still had some holes in his positional understanding:

Sergey Karjakin – Caruana
São Paolo 2012
Ruy Lopez,
Neo-Arkhangel Variation (C78)

1	e4	e5
2	♘f3	♘c6
3	♗b5	a6
4	♗a4	♘f6
5	0-0	b5
6	♗b3	

Soviet-era players had worked out a system of aggressively placing the Black bishops, 6...♗b7 7 ♖e1 ♗c5, with hints of queenside castling.

It was dubbed the Arkhangel Variation. Ambitious players liked Black's prospects after 8 c3 d6 9 d4 ♗b6.

But 6...♗b7 has a subtle defect and it wasn't well appreciated until the turn of the century.

That bishop will be somewhat misplaced if White keeps his e4-pawn solidly protected with 7 d3.

Then the position takes on the character of a good version of an anti-Marshall variation.

6 ... ♗c5

This is the Neo-Arkhangel, a transpositional trick based on waiting for White to commit his d-pawn. Caruana had used it since the 2009 World Cup.

7	c3	d6

8	d4	♝b6

With the d-pawn on d4, Black can undermine it with …♝g4! and threaten …exd4.

9   ♝e3

Karjakin adopts a small-chess policy of solidifying his center until Black makes some commitments of his own.

There is no threat to his e-pawn (9…♞xe4?? 10 ♝d5).

9   …   0-0

Karjakin had previously shown how 9…♝g4 10 ♞bd2 0-0 would provide him with a promising middlegame after 11 h3 ♝h5 12 ♝g5 (12…exd4 13 ♝d5!).

This points to another drawback of the Arkhangel: Black's other bishop could also turn out to be misplaced. He cannot easily break the pin on his f6-knight with …♝e7.

10   ♞bd2

Caruana had played this position more than any other top player, usually continuing 10…h6 followed by …♖e8.

10   …   ♝b7

This return to the old Arkhangel approach makes sense because ♝e3 interferes with the ♖e1's defense of the e4-pawn.

11   ♖e1

Black can live with the doubled-pawn structure of 11 d5 ♞e7 12 ♝xb6 cxb6 because of his better remaining bishop and kingside prospects (…♞g6, …h6, …♞h7-g5,…♝c8 and …f5).

11   …   exd4

Now 12 ♞xd4 ♞e5! is at least equal for Black because of …♞xe4, …♞fg4 or …♞d3.

12   cxd4   ♞b4

White's e4-pawn is threatened. He would lose coordination of his pieces after 13 e5 dxe5 14 dxe5 ♝xe3 15 ♖xe3 ♞fd5.

Also he would lose control of the center after 13 d5 ♘d3 14 ♖e2 ♖e8 or 14...c6!. That is better than 14...♘xb2 15 ♕c2.

13   ♕e2

"The critical move," Caruana said, without mentioning it was an innovation, at least at the GM level.

After 13 ♕b1 he would likely have replied 13...c5, with play as in the game, 14 a3 ♘c6 15 d5 ♘e7.

Then Karjakin's only chance for advantage would lie in getting his queen into the game from b1.

13   ...   c5

Karjakin's move offered a sacrifice, 13...♘xe4 14 ♘xe4 ♗xe4 15 ♗d2!.

That would force 15...♗xf3 because 15...♗d3? 16 ♕d1 costs material.

White would have some compensation after 16 ♕xf3 c5 17 ♕g3 or 16...a5 17 a3.

14   a3   ♘c6

15   d5

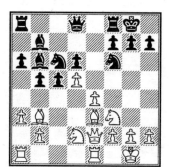

A premise of the Arkhangel is that Black's minor pieces perform well if the center is opened.

This is verified by 15 dxc5 dxc5 16 ♖ad1 ♕c7 and 16 e5 ♘g4 17 ♗g5 ♘d4! (or 17 ♗f4? c4!).

15   ...   ♘e7

When White closes the center in a Ruy Lopez, a standard plan is to attack the b5-pawn with a2-a4.

But here Black's queenside would be secure after 16...c4! 17 ♗c2 ♖e8 and ...♘g6.

16   h3

White should not allow 16...♘g4 17 ♗f4? c4, striking at f2.

16   ...   ♖e8

17   ♗c2   ♘g6

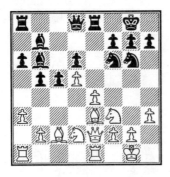

18　b3

After the game Karjakin's caution was widely criticized. He stopped ...c4 but surrendered control of c3.

Caruana expected 18 a4. Then 18...b4? is a positional blunder that rules out ...c4.

Correct is 18...c4!. White would not be ready for 19 ♘d4? because of 19...♘xd5! 20 exd5 ♗xd4.

Karjakin would likely have admitted that his queen is misplaced and tried 19 ♕d1 or 19 ♕f1.

Then chances would be roughly equal, e.g. 19 ♕d1 ♗xe3 20 ♖xe3 ♕c7 (so that 21 b3? c3!).

18　...　♗a5!

Now 19 a4 ♗c3! 20 ♖ac1 b4! 21 a4 a5 is similar to the game.

19　♖ab1

"I should have played something like 19 ♕d3," Karjakin said after the game.

That would stop ...♗c3 but also prepares the clever sacrifice 20 b4! cxb4 21 a4!.

Then 21...bxa4 22 ♖xa4 gives him queenside play that is well worth a pawn.

The reason ♕d3 fits in with this is he could meet 21...b3 with 22 ♕xb3!.

19　...　♗c3

20　♖ec1

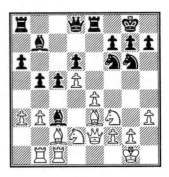

Caruana had already scored a victory "at home." He had spent only 11 minutes so far, compared with 45 for Karjakin.

20　...　b4!

We don't know which recapture he intended after 21 axb4. But 21...♗xb4 and ...a5 would establish a solid queenside blockade and free him to exert pressure on the e4-pawn.

21　a4?　a5

22　♗d3　h6

Black's last move is patient and a hint of how he can improve his position with other quiet moves.

Karjakin cannot. For example, 23 ♗c2? ♗a6 24 ♗d3? ♗xd3 25 ♕xd3 rids White of his worst minor piece.

But it condemns the e4-pawn to 25...♖a7 and ...♖ae7...♘xe4.

23 ♕d1?

In the post mortem, Karjakin called this "a horrible move."

Caruana generously said 23 ♕f1 "would be objectively equal."

But he added, "I like my game."

After 23 ♕f1 ♘e5 24 ♘xe5 ♖xe5 he would have a promising Exchange sacrifice, 25 ♘c4 ♖xe4! 26 ♗xe4 ♘xe4. Then the d5-pawn would drop, providing enough material "comp."

But Black can also edge towards a winning position just by doubling rooks on the e-file, e.g.

23 ♕f1 ♖e7 24 ♖c2 ♕c7 25 ♖d1 ♖ae8.

For example, 26 ♘b1? ♘xe4 27 ♗xe4 ♖xe4 28 ♘xc3 bxc3 29 ♖xc3 ♘e7! and ...♘xd5.

23 ... ♗a6!

A trade of bishops would still cost White the e-pawn.

24 ♗c2 ♖a7

Karjakin said in his calculations, he "completely forgot" what would happen if he lost control of the e2-a6 diagonal. He was soon in bad time pressure.

25 ♔h2 ♖ae7

Things are so bad for White that Caruana suggested the waiting move 26 ♔g1 now.

Black can then profit by a trade of knights, 26...♘e5.

This threatens 27...♘xf3+ 28 ♘xf3 ♘xe4 and 28 ♕xf3 ♘xd5! 29 exd5 ♖xe3 30 fxe3 ♗xd2.

131

White cannot keep making passive moves, as 27 ♘e1 ♛b6 28 ♔h2 ♝d4! indicates.

The d-pawn would become a terror after 29 ♝xd4 cxd4 and 30...d3.

26 g4

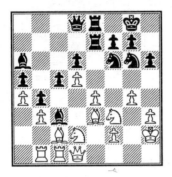

This desperate weakening begs for a flashy refutation.

One attempt is 26...♝xd2 27 ♘xd2 ♞xd5! so that 28 exd5 ♜xe3! 29 fxe3 ♜xe3 creates a winning attack (...♜e2+ and/or ...♛h4).

But a quiet alternative such as 26...♛d7 and ...h5 should also win.

Caruana thought for seven minutes and chose door number three.

26	...	♞xe4!
27	♘xe4	♜xe4
28	♝xe4	♜xe4

Black might pick up the d5-pawn when he wants (...♝b7 and ...♞e7).

But the game seemed certain to end quicker and more tactically, such as after 29 ♔g2 ♝e2! (30 ♛xe2 ♞f4+).

There are also winning sacrifices of the second Exchange after 29 ♘d2 (or 29 ♘g1) ♜xe3! 30 fxe3 ♛e7 and ...♛e5+.

29 ♛c2

The minister of defense looked at his own Exchange sacrifice, 29 ♜xc3 bxc3 30 ♛c2.

Black could win slowly in various ways, such as 30...♜b4 31 ♛xc3 ♛a8 and ...♝b7xd5.

But more fitting, as Caruana pointed out, was 30...♞e5 so that 31 ♛xe4 ♝d3.

The opposite-colored bishop position of 31 ♘xe5 ♜xe5 32 ♛xc3 ♜xd5 and ...♜d3 is dead lost.

29 ...   ♛e7

30   ♖g1

White could offer the Exchange another way, 30 ♖e1, with a threat of 31 ♗g5!.

But after 30...♗xe1 31 ♖xe1 ♛e8 Black wins by taking the d5-pawn or pushing his c-pawn.

Aside from the trap, there was another reason to try 30 ♖e1. It would have avoided another Black Exchange sacrifice.

30	**...**	**♖xe3!**
31	**fxe3**	**♛xe3**
32	**♖bf1**	**♗e2!**

The attacked knight cannot move because of ...♗e5+.

33   ♛f5

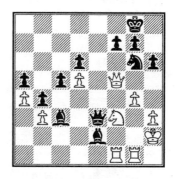

33   ...   ♗d3

You rarely see two bishops dominate two rooks so greatly in a middlegame. A bit faster is 33...♞h4! 34 ♞xh4 ♗e5+.

34	**♛d7**	**♗e5+**
35	**♔h1**	**♗e4!**
36	**♛e8+**	**♞f8**

Now, for example, 37 ♖g2 ♗xf3 38 ♖xf3 ♛xf3 and ...♛xh3+ is decisive, so White resigned.

18
Grand Slam

This game, like the last, was played at the end of an annual tournament series called the Grand Slam. It was an attempt, similar to the World Cup of 1988-89 and the Grand Chess Tour begun in 2015, to create a cycle of events like the annual tours by top golfers and tennis players. Top finishers in the Grand Slam advanced to a final tournament with a big-bucks payoff.

But organizing difficulties plagued the Grand Slam. The 2012 series was the last. It ended with a two-continent tournament. The first half was held in São Paulo, Brazil and the second in Bilbao, Spain. The following game was played in the next-to-last round when Caruana was tied with Magnus Carlsen for first place.

Caruana – Levon Aronian
São Paulo 2012
Ruy Lopez,
Anti-Marshall Variation (C88)

1	e4	e5
2	♘f3	♘c6
3	♗b5	a6
4	♗a4	♘f6
5	0-0	♗e7
6	♖e1	b5
7	♗b3	0-0
8	d3	

When Caruana allowed the Marshall Gambit, 8 c3 d5 9 exd5 ♘xd5 10 ♘xe5 ♘xe5 11 ♖xe5 c6, he often had to settle for a small-chess edge.

Against Aronian at Zürich 2014, for example, he went into the very drawish 12 d3 ♗d6 13 ♖e1 ♗f5 14 ♕f3 ♕h4 15 g3 ♕h3 16 ♗e3 ♗xd3 17 ♘d2.

| 8 | ... | d6 |
| 9 | a4 | ♗d7 |

This is already a rare position (more common are 9...b4 and 9...♗b7).

134

On d7, Black's bishop would help him equalize more easily after 10 ♘c3 ♘a5! 11 ♗a2 b4 and ...c5.

10   c3

Caruana transposes into a minimalist sub-variation that is more commonly reached with an early d2-d3. For instance, 6 d3 b5 7 ♗b3 d6 8 a4 ♗d7 9 c3 0-0 10 ♖e1.

10	...	♘a5
11	♗c2	c5
12	♘bd2	♖e8
13	d4	

This looks like a position that has been played a gazillion times. But it hasn't. White usually plays his pawn to d4 in one move, after investing a tempo in h2-h3.

The difference means Black could equalize without difficulty after 13...cxd4 14 cxd4 ♘c6 (14 ♘f1 ♗g4).

13	...	exd4

Aronian, a very aggressive player, wants a more unbalanced middlegame.

14	cxd4	♗g4
15	h3	♗h5

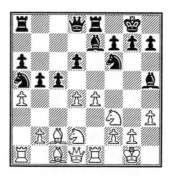

Members of Caruana's generation grew up with computers and Kasparov games. Many of them had little interest in games played before 1990.

Hikaru Nakamura called the classic books "a waste of time" and complained to his father, "Why do I have to study dead people?"

Caruana studied them. He understood how White can benefit from d4-d5 in this pawn structure, as Bobby Fischer had in a celebrated game with Viktor Korchnoi.

16   d5

But in another textbook game (Tal – Panno, Portorož 1958), White scored with the alternative plan, e4-e5.

Here 16 c5! dxe5 17 dxe5 opens the b1-h7 diagonal. This does a better job than 16 d5 of exploiting the diversion of Black's bishop to h5.

Black cannot protect his knight after 17...♘d5 18 ♗e4! with ...♗e6.

Also unfavorable for him is 17...♘d7 18 axb5 axb5 19 ♗e4.

16 ... ♕c8

One of the ideas behind 16 d5 was to bury the Black bishop with 17 g4 and 18 ♘h4, as in a classic Capablanca game.

Aronian planned to meet 17 g4 with 17...♗xg4 18 hxg4 ♕xg4+ with good compensation.

17 ♘f1 ♗d8?

Another idea embedded in 16...♕c8 is to transfer this bishop to b6.

It also uncovers the e-file for 18...♗xf3 19 ♕xf3 ♘xd5.

18 g4

The 18...♘xg4 19 hxg4 ♕xg4+ sacrifice doesn't work when White can block with 19 ♘g3 ♕xf3 20 ♘xh5!.

But 18 ♘g3 was stronger, since 18...♗xf3 19 ♕xf3 ♘xd5 20 e5! exposes Black's undermanned kingside, a la Tal.

For example, 20...♘b4 21 e6! ♖xe6 22 ♖xe6 fxe6 (22...♕xe6 23 ♕xa8) 23 ♕h5! and wins (23...g6 24 ♗xg6).

Black can avoid this with 18...♗g6 (instead of 18...♗xf3).

But then 19 ♘h4 and ♘gf5 puts him virtually a tempo behind the game.

18 ... ♗g6

19 ♘g3

Now 19...♗b6 20 ♘h4 c4 21 ♘gf5 makes it difficult to defend the d6-pawn.

19 ... b4!

Black's best bet is to push his queenside pawns to the sixth rank.

White would have been faster on the kingside after 19...♘d7 20 h4 and 21 h5 (or 20 g5 first).

20 ♘h4

"As usual, most natural is best," Caruana said of 20 ♗f4!.

Earlier, Black intended to meet an attack on the d6-pawn with …♘c4.

But here 20 ♗f4! ♘c4 21 ♕d3! would be too strong.

For instance, 21…♘xb2 22 ♕b3 wins material.

Or 21…♘e5 22 ♗xe5! dxe5 23 ♘d2 and ♘c4/♗b3 with a clear-cut positional edge.

20 … b3

Both players were crunching long variations.

Caruana had chosen 20 ♘h4 after calculating far into the future of 20…c4 20 ♘hf5.

He saw 21…b3 22 ♗b1 ♗b6 and then 23 ♘xd6? ♕c5.

He also liked this sequence because of a fantasy variation that goes 23 ♕f3 ♕c5 24 ♗f4! (24 ♗e3? ♕b4).

Then 24…c3 25 ♗xd6! cxb2 26 ♗xc5 bxa1(♕) 27 ♗xb6 wins.

The immediate 20…♘xg4 doesn't work after 21 ♘xg6, with play like the game (not 21 hxg4? ♗xh4).

21 ♗b1

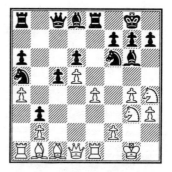

Now 21…c4 22 ♘hf5 c3 looks more dangerous than in the last note because of 23 ♘xd6 c2.

Caruana correctly evaluated 24 ♗xc2 bxc2 25 ♕d3 as favoring him solidly (25…♕c5 26 ♘xe8 ♘xe8 27 ♖e2!).

But he might have saved himself some serious clock time by recognizing how 22 ♗d2! would have ended his …c3 worries at little cost.

21 … ♘xg4

A desperation/best try in a worsening position.

22 ♘xg6!

Here 22 ♘hf5 would have favored White in every scenario -- except 22…♘e5!.

137

Then 23 ♘xd6? ♕xh3 24 ♘xe8 ♝h4! wins for Black (25 ♝f4 ♝xg3 26 fxg3 ♝h5).

22 ... ♘xf2!

Now 23 ♔xf2 fxg6! 24 ♔g2 ♝f6 didn't "look like a great deal of fun to me," Caruana said.

Thanks to the insertion of 20...b3 21 ♝b1, White's queenside is problematic after 25 ♕g4? ♕xg4 26 hxg4 c4!.

Black is not worse then because he has ...c4-c3 coming (27 ♘e2 ♖ab8).

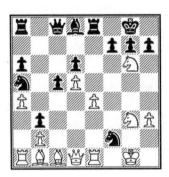

23 ♘e7+!

This zwischenzug denies Black ...fxg6. It is vital because now (a) Black will lack an open f-file for his attack and (b) White can pound g7 with ♘f5.

23 ... ♖xe7?

Aronian wanted to get his rook in play via e5.

He felt 23...♝xe7 24 ♔xf2 was slow.

He was right about 24...♕xh3?, for example, because of 25 ♖h1 ♕-moves 26 ♕h5 and wins (26...h6 27 ♝xh6, or 27 ♘f5 first).

But he didn't fully appreciate how he could have handled the position in a positional manner with 24...♝f6.

For example, 25 ♔g2 c4 26 ♖f1 ♝e5.

This avoids two sacrifices, 27 ♖xf6! gxf6 28 ♝h6 and 27 e5! ♝xe5? 28 ♝xh7+!.

White could slowly consolidate with, for instance, 27 ♕e2 and ♝f4.

But 23...♖xe7? is fatal.

24 ♔xf2 ♖e5

25 ♔g2

Black still wasn't threatening 25...♕xh3 because White's attack would be winning after 26 ♖h1! ♕d7 27 ♘f5 (27...g6? 28 ♕g4).

But there is a subtext to 25 ♔g2.

Aronian was tempting Caruana to play the more aggressive ♝f4.

But after 25...♝f6! 26 ♝xe5? ♝xe5 the situation is wildly unbalanced.

Even though a rook down, Black has real winning chances because of 27...♕xh3 or 27...♝xb2.

25	...	c4
26	♘f5	

The Karpov way of winning is 26 ♗d2 and ♗c3, when Black's counterchances vanish.

Caruana makes the outcome *look* uncertain by going for mate.

26	...	♗f6

27	♕f3	

27	...	c3!

All of a sudden Black appears to be back in the game. He threatens 28...c2 as well as 28...cxb2 29 ♗xb2 ♖xf5! and ...♗xb2.

White's edge would disappear after 28 bxc3 ♖xf5! – and he would even be in trouble after 28 ♕xc3? ♕xc3 29 bxc3 ♖xf5 and ...♗xc3.

28	♘h6+!	♚h8!?

29	♗d3	

Unnecessarily messy is 29 ♘xf7+ ♚g8 30 ♘xe5 ♗xe5.

After 29 ♗d3 the bishop cannot be trapped by ...c2. This gains time for 30 ♘g4 or...

29	...	♖e7

30	e5!	

Black's pieces would be neutralized after 30...dxe5 31 ♕e4 g6 32 ♖f1.

30	...	♗xe5

Caruana said there were many ways to win but did not elaborate. This was actually a remarkable comment for what he didn't say.

Another GM would have consulted his machine and pointed out 31 ♖xe5! dxe5 32 ♕e4.

Then 32...g6 33 ♗g5! or 32...f5 33 ♘xf5 wins.

31	♕e4	g6

32	♕h4!	

Now the threat of ♖xe5/♕f6 mate finishes matters.

For instance, 32...♕f8 33 ♖xe5! ♖xe5 34 ♕f6+ ♕g7 35 ♘xf7+ ♔g8 36 ♕xg7+ and ♘xe5.

| 32 | ... | f6 |

33	♖xe5!	dxe5
34	♕xf6+	♖g7
35	♕xe5	

Materially, Black is not far behind. But White can win easily once he gets his c1-bishop to the long diagonal.

For example, 35...♘c4 36 ♕xc3 ♘d6 37 ♕e5 ♕d7 38 ♗d2 and ♗c3.

| 35 | ... | ♕e8 |
| 36 | ♕xc3 | |

Black could resign, since 37 ♕xa5 as well as 37 ♗f4/♗e5 and 37 ♗g5/♗f6 are threatened.

36	...	♖c8
37	♕xa5	♖e7
38	♗g5	♖e2+
39	♔g1	resigns.

As a result of this game, Caruana tied for first place with Carlsen. The overall winner had to be chosen in a speed playoff. The chess world was just beginning to realize that Carlsen was invincible in rapid chess tiebreaks and he proved it here. Nevertheless, São Paolo/Bilbao was another Caruana breakthrough. His performance rating was 2892. From now on he was recognized as one of the world's best players.

19
Anti-Caruana

To appreciate Caruana's self-deprecating demeanor, it is worth a look at the anti-Caruana of annotators. Peter Leko's notes are often laden with breathless hype. Commenting on this game in New In Chess he ended no less than 23 sentences with exclamation points. "When I found this brilliant idea I was ready to go for it!" he wrote about his 29th move. Nevertheless, his move analysis is excellent and this remarkable game deserved that level of attention.

Peter Leko – Caruana
Dortmund 2012
*French Defense, Winawer
Variation (C18)*

1	e4	e6
2	d4	d5
3	♘c3	♗b4

Caruana "comes up with a new opening for each game!" Leko wrote.

The Winawer Variation was an acquired taste for Fabiano but also a comfortable fit. It was the sharpest French and the most susceptible to pre-game preparation.

4	e5	c5
5	a3	♗xc3+
6	bxc3	♘e7
7	♕g4	

"Surprise or not, I decided to play the most challenging move!" Leko wrote.

7	...	cxd4

When Caruana first played the Winawer in Europe he chose 7...♕c7.

That transposes into the game but allows White some extra options, such as 8 ♗d3.

The capture on d4 is more forcing, since 8 cxd4 ♕c7 is at least equal for Black (9 ♘e2 ♕xc2 or 9 ♗d2 ♕xc2 10 ♕xg7 ♖g8 11 ♕h7 ♘bc6).

8	♕xg7	♖g8
9	♕xh7	♕c7
10	♘e2	

Winawer players, a breed almost as fanatic as Najdorf Variation addicts, had concluded decades ago White can allow ...dxc3 in many subvariations but rarely ...♕c3+.

10	...	♘bc6

11   f4

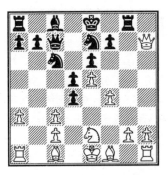

11   ...   dxc3

One of Caruana's 2005 games illustrated why it is fun to play Black in this variation:

His built up a lead in development, 11...♗d7 12 ♕d3 dxc3 13 ♘xc3 a6 14 ♖b1 ♘a5, while White advanced his kingside pawns, 15 h4 ♘c4 16 ♖h3 0-0-0 17 h5 ♘f5.

Development mattered more after the bishop-liberating ...d4 push, 18 ♕f3? ♗c6 19 ♕e2 ♘g3 20 ♕d3 ♘xf1 21 ♔xf1 d4!.

Caruana won after 22 ♘e4 ♖g4! 23 ♘g3 ♗b5 (versus Bruned, Collado Villalba 2005).

He could have finished faster with 23...♘e3+! 24 ♗xe3 dxe3 25 ♕xe3 ♗xg2+! 26 ♔xg2 ♕xc2+.

12   ♕d3   d4

Not just his bishop but also Black's queen seeks compensating play on the a8-h1 diagonal.

13   ♘xd4   ♘xd4

14   ♕xd4   ♗d7

For example, the natural 15 ♖b1 can lead to 15...♘f5! 16 ♕f2 ♕c6 and ...♕e4+.

Masters have drawn games by repetition after 17 ♖g1 ♕e4+ 18 ♕e2 ♕d4 19 ♕f2 ♕e4+. Some may even have been real games.

15   ♖g1

By protecting his g2-pawn White prepares to develop his f1-bishop and to stop ...♘f5 with g2-g4.

If White withdraws his queen first, 15 ♕f2 ♗c6 16 ♖g1, Black can threaten mate on d1 after 16...♖d8 17 g4 ♕d7 (18 ♗d3? ♗e4!).

15   ...   ♘f5

16   ♕f2

We are following a simple plot. If White is allowed to play g2-g4 he should be better. For example, 16...♕a5? (or 16...♗c6) 17 g4!.

Black's task is to keep finding tactical ways to distract him.

16 ...   ♕c6

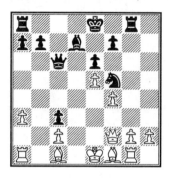

For instance, 17 g4 ♕e4+! and 18 ♗e2? ♘d4!.

Or 18 ♕e2 ♕a4 with the idea of ...♘d4.

17   ♗d3   ♕d5

This is still book. For the first time in six moves there is sharp disagreement about the best continuation.

Some masters vote for 18 ♗e3.

A crucial continuation runs 18...♘xe3 19 ♕xe3 ♖xg2 20 ♖xg2 ♕xg2 21 ♗e4 ♕xh2 22 0-0-0!.

This says something about how extensive Winawer Variation analysis can be.

18   ♖b1

And so does this: Theory says the next four, strange-looking moves are virtually forced.

18   ...   ♗c6

19   ♖b3   0-0-0

20   ♖xc3   ♔b8

21   g4   ♘d4

Now that he's gotten in g2-g4, White needs to fully consolidate to make his two extra pawns decisive.

22   ♖g3

He would be on the road to victory after ♗e3!, e.g. 22...♕a2 23 ♗e3! ♕a1+ 25 ♔d2.

22   ...   ♕h1+

Black's pieces are at the apex of activity but there is nothing for him in 22...♘f3+? 23 ♔d1.

23   ♗f1

The position becomes easier to play if each player asks what his opponent is threatening.

Here White again threatens 24 ♗e3 because 24...♘f3+? would lose to 25 ♖xf3 ♗xf3 26 ♗xa7+! and ♖xf3.

23 ... b6!

Leko wondered how much time humans would have needed, before computers, to realize "this is the best move!"

The main point of this innovation is simply that ♗e3 and ♗xa7+ is no longer possible. Black would win after 24 ♗e3? ♘f3+ 25 ♔e2 ♗b5+.

24 ♗b2

Caruana was readying counterplay on the d-file, with 24...♖d7 and 25...♖gd8.

But Leko's reply allows him to answer 24...♖d7? with 25 ♖cd3!.

His bishops could eventually overpower the Black rooks

following 25...♘xc2+ 26 ♕xc2 ♗b5 27 ♕e2.

This was the first point in the game when Caruana engaged in a big think.

After the tempting 24...♖xg4 25 ♖xg4 ♘f3+ White has only one way to avoid losing.

But it wins easily, 26 ♖xf3 ♗xf3 27 ♕g1! – 27...♖d1+ 28 ♔f2 ♖d2+ 29 ♔e3!.

24 ... ♗e4!

Black stops ♖cd3 and revives the idea of doubling rooks on the d-file.

Both players were considering the possible endgames in which White holds two extra pawns for the Exchange.

One occurs after 25 h3 ♖d7 26 ♖g1.

That forces 26...♘f3+ 27 ♖xf3 ♕xf3 28 ♕xf3 ♗xf3 29 ♗d3!, when White holds the high cards.

But it's a different story if Black plays 25...♖h8 instead of 25...♖d7.

Then 26 ♖g1 ♘f3+ 27 ♖xf3 ♕xf3 28 ♕xf3 ♗xf3 29 ♗d3? allows 29...♖xh3.

Black is also better after 29 ♖g3 ♖d1+ 30 ♔f2 ♗d5 because his rooks are active.

25 a4!

"I was very happy to find this idea!" Leko wrote.

He had a new way of meeting the doubling-rooks threat – 25...♖d7 26 ♗a3! and 27 ♗d6+.

"I was curious to see what Black would do!" Leko added.

25   ...   ♖d5

26   ♗a3

26   ...   ♖c8!

A trade of the c3-rook will renew the ...♘xc2+ threat.

27   ♗d6+   ♔b7

28   ♖xc8

The game could have ended soon after 28...♔xc8 29 ♖c3+.

Black must then avoid mates — 29...♔d8?? 30 ♕h4+ and 29...♔b7 30 a5! ♘f3+? 31 ♕xf3! ♗xf3? 32 a6+.

Instead, 29...♔d7! leads to two perpetual check finishes.

One is simple, 30 ♖c7+ ♔e8 31 ♖c8+ ♔d7 32 ♖c7+ ♔e8.

The other is not: 30 ♕h4 ♘xc2+! (30...♘f3+? 31 ♖xf3 and ♕e7+) 31 ♖xc2! ♖d1+! 32 ♔xd1 ♕xf1+ 33 ♔d2 ♕d3+ 34 ♔e1 ♕xc2 or 34...♕e3+.

28   ...   ♘f3+

Leko: "At first I did not even know what to think of this move!"

Was Caruana playing for a win? Or did he overlook the perpetual checks after 28...♔xc8/29...♔d7?

29   ♔e2!

A perpetual is still there after 29 ♖xf3 ♗xf3 30 ♖c7+ ♔a8 31 ♖c8+ or 30 ♖b8+ ♔c6 31 ♖c8+.

Or, if White wants to get fancy, 30 ♕xf3! ♕xf3 31 ♖c7+.

29   ...   ♖d2+

30   ♔e3

Black is mated if he takes the queen – 30...♖xf2 31 ♖b8+ ♔c6 32 ♗b5+ ♔d5 33 c4 mate.

30 ... ♚xc8

The mystery of Caruana's 28th move can be answered here: He was playing for a win.

After 31 ♗e2 he could have studied the position and chosen between 31...♕c1 and 31...♖xc2.

The capture provides some winning possibilities, 31...♖xc2 32 ♖xf3! ♗b7! with a threat of ...♕c1 +.

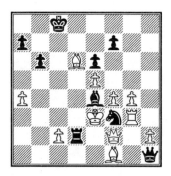

31 ♖g1

Leko was impressed with himself:

"I even do not know how to assess this move! It is one of the most spectacular moves I have ever made," he wrote.

"And once I had spotted it, I could not resist!...I did not even look for alternatives!"

He should have. The simple 31 ♗a6+ wins.

Then 32 ♕f1! would force Black to trade queens or give up his army (32...♕xh2 33 ♖h3!).

So the proper annotation is 28...♘f3+?? and 31 ♖g1??, as cruel as that may seem.

31 ... ♘xg1

32 ♚xd2

"Leko is really good at calculating lines," Garry Kasparov said on the first version of his Web site in 2000. But here the Hungarian misses a second probable win with ♗a6+.

White would be at least one pawn ahead after the dust settles from 32 ♗a6+ ♗b7 33 ♗xb7+ ♚xb7 24 ♚xd2

Or 32...♚d7 33 ♗b5+ with the idea of 33...♚c8 34 ♕xd2! (34...♕f3+ 35 ♚d4).

32 ... ♘f3+

With both players in time pressure, White could answer pass moves (33...♚b7) with ♚c3-b2 and then figure out how to win in the second time control.

33 ♚c3 ♘xh2

34 ♗e2 ♕a1+

35 ♔d2 ♛h1!

Repeating the position pushes the onus back to White.

There were blunders (36 ♛h4?? ♞f3+) to dodge.

But there were also traps to set such as 36 a5 bxa5?? 37 ♝a6+ and mates.

Then 36...♞f3+ 37 ♔e3 ♞e1 38 ♝f1! discoordinates Black's pieces (38...♞xc2+ 39 ♔d2 and wins).

White retains some winning chances after 36...♔b7 37 f5!.

36 ♛g3? ♞f1+!

37 ♝xf1 ♛xf1

Now it's the old story of the bishops of opposite color in an endgame.

Leko realized too late there was no mate on the dark squares. Black's king can escape to light squares (38 ♛c3+ ♔b7 39 ♛c7+ ♔a6).

38 ♛e3 ♛g2+

39 ♛e2 ♛xe2+

40 ♔xe2 ♝xc2

41 a5 bxa5

42 ♔d2 ♝g6

As Caruana played his move, the arbiters gestured "we had provided enough entertainment and could agree to a draw!" Leko wrote. He is the anti-Caruana in another way. As of 2021, he had beaten Caruana four times, drew seven and never lost.

20
Reserve Candidate

When FIDE regained undisputed control over the World Championship title in 2006, it widened the path to the championship match. More avenues to the Candidates tournament were opened up. Players could qualify for it due to a high rating. This was Magnus Carlsen's route to the title in 2013.

FIDE also created a new class of qualification tournaments, dubbed the Grand Prix. Caruana performed as his rating indicated he would in the 2013 Grand Prix cycle. A tie for second place at Thessaloniki 2013 helped earn him third place in the final cycle standings.

But only two players qualified for the 2014 Candidates tournament. He became the reserve Candidate, in case someone dropped out before it began. But no one did.

Here is his brightest game from the Macedonian tournament.

Caruana – Vasily Ivanchuk
Grand Prix, Thessaloniki 2013
Ruy Lopez,
Steinitz Defense Deferred (C76)

1	e4	e5
2	♘f3	♘c6
3	♗b5	a6
4	♗a4	d6
5	c3	

Caruana experimented with the Fischer favorite 5 0-0 before settling on 5 c3. The theory of 5 c3 is less volatile and the middlegame positions require more accurate defense from Black.

5	...	g6
6	d4	♗d7
7	0-0	♗g7

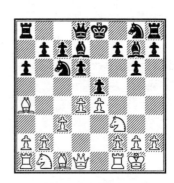

White's next major decision is what to do with the center.

He can (a) leave it intact, (b) open it with dxe5 or (c) close it with d4-d5.

In Fischer's era, the debate centered on (b) and (c). In his influential opening manual, Paul Keres said both 8 dxe5 and 8 d5 favored White.

As examples, he gave 8 dxe5 dxe5 9 ♗g5 and 8 d5 ♘ce7 9 ♗xd7+ ♕xd7 10 c4 ♘f6 11 ♘c3 0-0 12 c5.

8   h3

But the modern tendency is to wait for Black to commit his KN.

After 8...♘f6 White may play 9 ♖e1 followed by the usual ♘bd2-f1-g3 maneuver that is mildly favorable in so many Lopez variations.

On the other hand, after 8...♘ge7 White can opt for 9 ♗e3 followed by dxe5/...dxe5 and ♗c5. Then the e7-knight is something of a bone in Black's throat.

8   ...   h6

Black can wait, too. But 8 h3 was more useful to White than ...h6 is to Black because White can play ♗e3 without concern about ...♘g4xe3.

9   ♗e3   ♘ge7

10   ♘bd2   0-0

When Black puts his knight on f6, he hopes for pressure on the e4-pawn after ...♖e8 and ...exd4.

With his knight on e7, the e4-pawn is secure and Black would have a difficult middlegame following, say, 11 ♖e1 ♖e8 12 ♗c2.

11   dxe5

But he could get counterplay from 11 ♖e1 exd4 12 cxd4 f5!, with a threat to trap the e3-bishop with ...f4.

11   ...   dxe5

In principle, a trade of knights after 11...♘xe5 should help Black.

But 12 ♘xe5 dxe5 13 ♘f3 ♘c6? permits White to seize the initiative with 14 ♕d2 ♔h7 15 ♖fd1.

He would also be a mite better after 13...♗xa4 14 ♕xa4 ♕e8 15 ♕b3.

Or after 14... ♘c6 15 ♖ad1 ♕e7 16 ♖d5!.

12   ♗c5   ♖e8

13   ♖e1

A previous generation of 1 e4 players felt this pawn structure was too symmetrical to achieve a significant White advantage.

But Caruana grew up in the era of "small chess," when a tiny edge was good enough. He felt having a better-placed bishop (♗c5 versus ...♗g7) was reason to be optimistic.

13 ... b6

14 ♗a3 ♘a7

This knight retreat prepares to ease Black's congestion with 15...♘b5!.

Stopping it with 15 c4? would allow Ivanchuk to solve the problem of what to do with the other knight (15...♘ec6! and ...♘d4 with advantage to Black)

15 ♗xd7 ♕xd7

16 ♘c4

Surrendering control of the open file is too great a cost, 16...♕xd1 17 ♖axd1 ♘b5 18 ♗xe7 ♖xe7 19 ♖d5! and later ♖ed1.

Black should insert 17...♘ec6! before ...♘b5.

For example, 18 ♖d7 ♘b5 19 ♖ed1 ♖ad8 is virtually equal.

16 ... ♕e6

Ivanchuk had reason to play more aggressively. He had won his first four decisive games with Caruana.

As Black at Biel 2009, he scored one of his greatest victories:

1 d4 d6 2 e4 ♘f6 3 ♘c3 g6 4 ♗e3 ♗g7 5 ♕d2 c6 6 ♗h6 ♗xh6 7 ♕xh6 ♕a5 8 ♗d3 c5 9 ♘ge2 ♘c6 10 d5 ♘e5 11 ♗b5+ ♔d8! 12 ♘g3 c4! 13 h3 a6 14 f4 ♘f3+! 15 gxf3 axb5 16 0-0 b4 17 ♘ce2 ♕c5+ 18 ♔g2 ♗d7 19 c3 bxc3 20 ♘xc3 b5 21 a3 ♔c7 22 ♖ad1 ♖hg8 23 e5 ♘h5 24 ♖fe1 g5!! 25 exd6+ exd6 26 ♘xh5 ♖g6 27 ♘e4 ♖xh6 28 ♘xc5 dxc5 29 ♘g3 gxf4 and wins.

17 ♘e3 ♘b5

Now 17...♘ec6 would allow 18 ♘d5! with an evident White plus.

Black can make ...♘b5 and ...♘xa3 more of a threat by ruling out ♗xe7 with 17...c5.

But this makes his slightly bad bishop worse. This would become more of a factor after 18 b3 ♘b5 19 ♗b2.

18 ♗xe7 ♖xe7

19 ♕a4

Like Ivanchuk, Caruana has become more ambitious since 16 ♘c4.

He could have virtually forced a superior endgame with 19 ♕d5 or 19 ♕b3.

19   ...   ♘d6

But with queens on, the a6-pawn and c6-square are more vulnerable and he has the prospect of ♘d5 and ♖ad1.

For instance, 19...♖d7 20 ♖ad1 ♖ad8? 21 ♕xa6.

20   ♕c6!

20   ...   ♖c8

Your computer may tell you Ivanchuk should have played 20...♖d8 21 ♘d5 ♖ed7 so that ...♘xe4 is possible.

He does achieve counterplay after 22 ♘xc7 ♕c4 23 ♕xc4 ♘xc4.

But White has an extra pawn, 24 ♘d5 ♘xb2 25 ♘xb6.

21   ♖ad1

Doubling on the d-file (22 ♖d2, 23 ♖ed1) will be stronger now with queens on the board.

21   ...   ♔h7

Black wants to play ...♘e8 but the immediate 21...♘e8?? would lose to 22 ♘d5! because 22...♕xc6 23 ♘xe7 is check.

Or 22...♖d7 23 ♕xe6 fxe6 24 ♘xb6! ♖xd1 25 ♘xc8.

22   ♖d2   ♘e8

Of course, not 22...♕xa2 23 ♖xd6.

But how does White play for a win now?

He would trap his rook after 23 ♕xe6 ♖xe6 24 ♖d7? ♘f6! 25 ♖xf7 ♔g8.

Caruana makes another decision that initially stumps computers.

23   ♕b7   ♘d6

This tournament was conducted under the "Sofia rules." Offering a draw was illegal.

151

But draws could come about by a repetition of moves. Ivanchuk was hinting at a handshake here – such as after 24 ♕c6 ♘e8 25 ♕b7 ♘d6.

White must avoid 24 ♕xa6? ♘xe4, when he is worse.

The only alternative seems to be 24 ♕d5.

Then Black can sit on the position (24...♖ee8) or push White pieces back following 24...♕xd5 25 ♘xd5 ♖e6 and ...b5/...c6.

24 ♖xd6!

Bobby Fischer didn't make a speculative sacrifice – as opposed to a riskless sacrificial combination – until just before he was US Champion. Today's grandmasters do it much earlier.

24 ... cxd6

A simple way of judging an Exchange sacrifice is to look at the rooks of the player who accepts it. If they are active – if they can move easily on ranks and control distant squares – the sacrifice may be dubious.

That would be the case after 25 ♕xb6? ♕xa2.

Black would be the one with a serious advantage after 26 ♕xd6? ♖b7 27 ♘d1 ♕a5 28 b4 ♕b5 and ...♖d7, for example.

25 ♕xa6!

On the other hand, if those rooks are slightly passive, as they would be after 25...♖b8 26 ♘d5 ♖eb7 27 a4, the sacrifice is probably valid.

25 ... ♖cc7

After the game, annotators tried to get Black's rooks significant scope with ...f5.

Then the course of the game depends on whether White can maintain control of open lines. He would after 25...f5 26 ♘d2 ♖f8 27 ♘d5, for example.

26 ♘d5 ♖a7

But the rooks do get to roam after 27 ♕xb6? ♖eb7 28 ♕e3 ♖xa2 29 b4 f5!, with equal chances.

27 ♕b5 ♖eb7

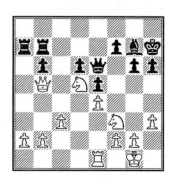

The position has stabilized. That is another way of saying the tactics step aside and let planning take over.

White can visualize a long-term plan:

He can (a) erect a protective wall of queenside pawns, such as with a2-a4 and b2-b3.

Then he will be ready (b) to trade queens.

That makes it safe for (c) his king to approach the queenside.

Unless Black's king can also run to that wing, White will then (d) pick off the b6-pawn.

That should set the stage for (e) a queening march of the White a- or b-pawn.

28   a4

Black's plans are of poorer quality. One is the passive 28...♗f6 29 ♘d2 ♗d8, to defend the b6-pawn.

White can go after the d6-pawn, after the solidifying ♘c4 and b2-b3, and then ♕c6 or ♘b4/♖d1.

28   ...   f5

Black's active plans are limited to trading queens and shooting for ...f5.

Endgames will be very difficult because White can quickly form an impregnable pawn phalanx.

For example, 28...♕d7 29 ♘d2 ♕xb5 (not 29...♖xa4? 30 ♕xd7 ♖xd7 31 ♘xb6) 30 axb5 and ♘c4.

29   ♘d2

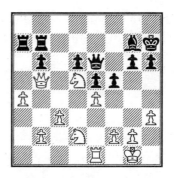

29   ...   ♗f6

Ivanchuk could see 29...fxe4 and 30 ♘xe4? ♖a5!.

But 29...fxe4 would turn out to be a strategic error after 30 c4!.

Once White adds a second centralized knight (♘xe4) to his assets, he could take the proper precautions (f2-f3, b2-b3) before picking off a second extra pawn.

30   ♕e8!   ♗e7

Of course, 30...♕xe8?? 31 ♘xf6+.

More tenacious was 30...♕f7. But Ivanchuk was apparently trying to exploit Caruana's time pressure.

The control was two hours for 40 moves -- with no Fischer-clock increments until move 60.

The absence of the usual 30-second increment complicated Caruana's usual routine of selecting a move.

"It's not so easy to know when you have to think and when you have to play quickly," he explained.

31 c4 ♕g8

32 ♕c6!

As in Games 9 and 12, White needs to maintain control by stifling counterplay. After 32 ♕xg8+? ♔xg8 Black can activate his bishop (...♗g5) and his king (...♔f7).

32 ... ♕d8

33 b3 ♕d7!

Proper desperation. Ivanchuk gives up a pawn that was doomed anyway. To accept it, Caruana has to trade one of his knights for the bad bishop.

34 ♕xd7 ♖xd7

35 ♘xb6 ♖db7

36 ♘c8! ♖a6

37 ♘xe7 ♖xe7

Annotators might dismiss the rest of the game as "a matter of

technique" or, in today's GM jargon, "a technical win."

True, there is little to calculate, at least immediately. But where do White's pieces belong? Specifically:

Should he start by shifting his king to c3 via e2 and d3?

Or is posting his rook on d5 a more immediate concern?

Does he need to play f2-f3?

Can he allow Black to sacrifice the Exchange back with ...♖b7, ...♖ab6 and ...♖xb3?

38 ♖e3! ♔g7

39 ♖d3 ♖b7

40 ♔f1

Those questions used to be answered during adjournment analysis, when a player could seal his 41st move.

But adjournments had died out when Caruana was learning how a knight moves. He had to find the right answers over the board, in a second time control (20 moves in an hour).

40 ... ♖ab6

41 ♔e2 ♔f6

Returning the Exchange, 41...fxe4 42 ♖d5! ♖xb3 43 ♘xb3 ♖xb3, is hopeless after 44 ♖xd6 ♖a3 45 ♖a6.

Or 44...♖b4 45 a5 ♖xc4 46 a6 ♖a4 47 g4.

42	♔d1	♔e6
43	♔c2	h5
44	f3	

This neutralizes ...fxe4 and prepares winning plans such as ♔c3 and a trade of rooks, ♖d5-b5.

Black has one active response, ...♔f6-g5-f4-g3xg2.

44	...	♔f6
45	♔c3	♖a6
46	♖d5	♔g5!

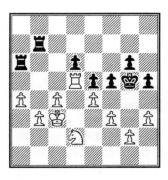

For the first time in more than a dozen moves Caruana has to really calculate.

Should he ignore Black's king raid? Or analyze 47 g3 h4 to a conclusion?

47   a5!

The right answer is: ignore.

The win would be endangered after (47 g3 h4!) 48 f4+ ♔f6! 49 gxh4 exf4, for instance.

And maybe after 48 gxh4+ ♔xh4 49 a5 fxe4 50 ♘xe4 ♖f7 and 50 fxe4 ♔xh3.

47	...	♔f4
48	b4	♔g3
49	♘b3!	♔xg2
50	b5	

Caruana could disregard the right half of the board because he can win on the left with the unstoppable ♖xd6, a5-a6, ♘c5 and b5-b6.

50	...	♖a8
51	♖xd6	♔xf3
52	a6	♖g7
53	♘c5	fxe4
54	b6	e3
55	♖f6+	resigns.

Looking back, Caruana's Exchange sacrifice did not gain a major edge by force. It was based on playability. He sensed it would be very difficult for Black to find the right defensive moves after 24 ♖xd6!. "I just couldn't resist," Caruana said.

21
Trivia Question

Has there ever been a world champion who failed to win a tournament game from a reigning world champion? This question sounds simple. But the word "reigning" is the key. José Capablanca won 19 tournament games from Emanuel Lasker, Alexander Alekhine and Max Euwe. But he never did it when they held the title.

Today there is much more competitive chess. Beating the champion is not nearly as remarkable a feat. Fabiano Caruana has notched more than 20 such wins against reigning champs. He did it for the first time in 2013, and in a "classical" game, during the reign of Viswanathan Anand.

Viswanathan Anand – Caruana
Tal Memorial, Moscow 2013
Ruy Lopez,
Anti-Marshall Variation (C84)

1	e4	e5
2	♘f3	♘c6
3	♗b5	a6
4	♗a4	♘f6
5	0-0	♗e7
6	♖e1	b5
7	♗b3	0-0
8	h3	

The Marshall Gambit lacks bite after 8 h3 because there is no target to attack at h2.

Black would have little compensation after 8...d5? 9 exd5 ♘xd5 10 ♘xe5 ♘xe5 11 ♖xe5 c6 12 d3 ♗d6 13 ♖e1 ♕h4 14 ♕f3, for example.

8	...	♗b7
9	d3	

But with his bishop on b7, there is a potential target at g2.

This is shown by 9 c3 d5! 10 exd5? ♘xd5 11 ♘xe5 ♘xe5 12 ♖xe5 ♘f4! and wins (13 f3 ♘d3 or 13...♗d6).

White should decline the pawn with 10 d3. But then c2-c3 is not particularly useful and Black is at least equal after 10...dxe4 11 dxe4 ♕xd1 12 ♗xd1 ♖fd8.

9	...	d5

If Black settles for the 9...d6 pawn structure, White can claim a

156

moral victory: He has delayed the common neutralizing trade, ...♝e6xb3.

10 exd5

White's only chance for an ambitious middlegame is to make the e5-pawn an enduring target.

He would have no attractive plan after, for example, 10 ♘bd2 dxe4 11 dxe4 ♝c5 or 10 ♘c3 dxe4 11 ♘xe4 ♘xe4 12 dxe4 ♕xd1.

10 ... ♘xd5

11 ♘bd2

Black has such an easy game now that 11 ♘xe5 later became more of a test of this variation. He would have some compensation after 11...♘d4.

11 ... f6

12 c3

This move was considered an innovation.

Instead of alternatives (12 a3, 12 a4, 12 ♘e4), Anand wants to exploit ...f6 with d3-d4.

Then ...exd4/cxd4 would expose a hole at e6.

12 ... ♚h8

"As usual, I probably made the wrong choice," Caruana wrote about this move. He apparently debated with himself about 12...♘a5 13 ♝c2 c5.

Then the consistent 14 d4 cxd4 15 cxd4 can get surprisingly double-edged after 15...♕c7 16 dxe5? ♖ad8!.

White would be way behind in development and facing danger from ...♘f4, ...♘b4 or ...♝c5.

But 16 ♘h4! with the idea of ♘f5 or ♝f5/♕h5 would give him immediate threats.

Black should settle for the less ambitious 14...exd4 15 cxd4 ♖e8, with equal chances.

By getting his king off the a2-g8 diagonal with 12...♚h8, Black was ready for 13 d4 exd4 14 cxd4 f5!, with good play.

157

13   ♗c2

Anand opens the way for ♘b3 so he might recapture on d4 with pieces, not a pawn, after d3-d4/ ...exd4.

13   ...   ♛d7

Caruana could have anticipated that plan with 13...b4, threatening ...bxc3.

Then 14 ♘e4? bxc3 15 bxc3 f5 is bad.

He would have a superior pawn structure after 14 c4 ♘f4 15 ♘b3 ♘e6! because of ...♛d7/...♖ad8 or ...a5-a4.

A master would recognize that White should change the structure – and a master would also be able to calculate 16 d4! to a safe harbor.

Chances would be balanced after 16...♘exd4 17 ♘fxd4 ♘xd4 18 ♘xd4 exd4 19 ♛h5! because that forces 19...d3 20 ♗xd3! ♛xd3 21 ♖xe7.

14   ♘b3   a5

Another good structure for Black would arise after 15 d4 a4! and 16 ♘c5 ♗xc5 17 dxc5.

Then he enjoys simple, centralized play with 17...♖fd8 with ideas such as ...♘ce7-g6 and ...♘df4.

15   a4!   bxa4

Now 15...b4? 16 c4 is poor because Black loses control of d4.

He would be distinctly worse after 16...♘f4? 17 ♗xd4 exd4 18 d4 followed by ♗e4 or d4-d5.

Better is 16...♘b6. But 17 c5 and 18 d4 would open the center favorably.

For example, 17...♘d5 18 d4 exd4 19 ♘fxd4 ♘xd4 20 ♘xd4! (20...♗xc5? 21 ♗f5 and ♘e6).

16   ♖xa4   ♘cb4!

Caruana chose the right move for the wrong reason.

He looked at 16...♘b6 and gave up on it after seeing 17 ♖h4! and 17...f5 18 ♘g5 because of what he called "a tremendous attack."

But the attack looks unimpressive after 18...h6 (19 ♕h5 ♕e8).

However, computers jump at the chance to point out 18 d4!, instead of 18 ♘g5?.

Then 18...♗xh4 19 ♘xh4 gives White ample compensation from 20 ♘c5 or 20 ♕h5.

Worse is 18...exd4 19 ♗g5! and 18...e4 19 ♘c5 ♗xc5 20 ♘g5!.

When Houdini showed Caruana 18 d4 after the game, he said he would trust its conclusion "since I don't understand much in this position."

17   ♖xa5

White's compensation would be slim after 17 cxb4? ♕xa4 18 ♘xa5 ♕xb4.

17   ...   ♘xc2

The d3-pawn will be a target after this. But another benefit is below the radar:

Without a light-squared bishop, White no longer has tactics based on d3-d4 and ♘h4/♕h5.

"I was happy my king would finally feel secure," Caruana said.

18   ♕xc2   ♘b6

But White's king is not secure because g2 could become a target after 18...g5 followed by 19...g4 or 19...♘f4, for example.

19   ♖xa8   ♖xa8

20   ♘bd2

Let's take a closer look at Black's compensation.

The pressure on d3 can't be exploited immediately by 20...♖d8 21 d4!.

Or by 20...c5 21 ♘e4 ♖d8 22 ♗e3 and 22...♕xd3 23 ♕xd3 ♖xd3 24 ♗xc5.

Black can afford to be patient. With 20...c5 21 ♘e4 ♘d5 he can slowly improve his pieces (...♗f8, ...♘c7-e6, ...♖d8), with excellent winning chances.

20   ...   g5!

But his "comp" is more visible now, since 21 d4 or 21 ♘e4 would be answered by 21...g4!.

White can quickly find himself lost, e.g. 21 d4 g4! 22 hxg4 ♕xg4 23 dxe5?? ♖g8.

Better is 23 ♘e4 ♖g8 24 ♘g3. Black could then choose between regaining his pawn, 24...♗xf3, or going for a knockout with 24...h5.

159

Chances remain fairly even in either case. But 24...h5 can get exciting after the sacrifice 25 ♘xe5! fxe5 26 ♖xe5.

Then it would be Black's turn to find a defense, 26...♗g5!.

A draw by repetition would be an honorable end of the game, 27 ♗xg5 ♖xg5 28 ♖e8+ ♖g8! 29 ♖e5! ♖g5 30 ♖e8+.

21   ♘h2   ♖d8!

22   d4!

One of the unappreciated skills in chess is navigating a deteriorating position towards a draw.

After 21 ♘h2 Anand committed himself to giving back a pawn. But how he gives it back matters.

He might have been able to hold the ending after 22 ♘c4 ♕xd3 23 ♕xd3 ♖xd3.

But after 24 ♘xb6 cxb6 25 ♗e3 b5 his restricted minor pieces would probably require him to

find several "only" moves in a lengthy ending.

22   ...   exd4

A practical benefit of 22 d4 is Caruana might have been tempted by 22...♕c6 because he saw the trick 23 ♘df3 ♖xd4! (24 ♘xd4? ♕xg2 mate).

Or 23 ♕e4 ♕xe4 24 ♘xe4 exd4 and then 25 ♘xg5? fxg5 26 ♖xe7 dxc3 and ...♖d1+.

But 25 ♘g3 would lead to a somewhat better endgame than in the game.

23   cxd4

Now Black gets nothing from 23...♗f8 24 ♘e4 or 24 ♘g4.

He can grab the d-pawn with 23...♘d5 24 ♘e4 ♘b4 25 ♕b3 ♕xd4.

But that creates tactical nightmares after 26 ♕f7!, e.g. 26...♘d5? 27 ♘f3 or 26...♘c6 27 ♗d2 and ♗c3.

23   ...   ♗b4!

This regains the pawn safely. But it will take at least one bad move or several minor errors by the world champion to beat him.

For example, 24 ♘hf3?? loses quickly, 24...♗xf3 25 gxf3 ♘d5 and ...♘f4/...♕xh3.

24 ♖e2

This is the first minor mistake. To get out of the pin, the rook should take some risk on d1 or even f1.

For instance, 24 ♘g4 ♘d5 25 ♖f1 h5 26 ♘e3 ♘f4 27 ♘e4.

24	...	♕xd4
25	♘df1?	

This is consistent with the hunker-down approach of his last move.

But after 25 ♕xc7 it would be very difficult for Black to prevail in an endgame without a queenable queenside pawn.

Instead, he would have to use his tactical pressure, such as 25...♕d5 26 ♘hf3 ♘a4.

There is no obvious way to crack 27 ♕c2 ♘c5 28 ♖e3 – or even 27 ♖e7 ♗xe7 28 ♕xe7.

Caruana gave 26...♘a8 (instead of 26...♘a4) and then 27 ♕c2 ♖c8 28 ♕d1. Nothing would be certain except that he would have continuing pressure.

25	...	♕c5

Computers like the paradoxical 25...♕d5 26 ♘e3 ♕d6 – because they can immediately see what humans don't, the rook-trapping threat of ...♗a6!.

26	♕xc5	♗xc5
27	♖c2	♗d6
28	♘g4	♔g7

Black can improve slowly but steadily (...♔g6 and ...f5-f4).

29	♗d2	♔g6
30	♘ge3	f5

This is the "hemming-in" process that worked so well in games when Steinitz and Tarrasch held the two bishops. It is the knights that get hemmed in, e.g. 31...f4 32 ♘g4? h5.

31	♘c4	♘xc4
32	♖xc4	♖a8

Black should avoid swapping rooks until he is certain about the resulting minor piece ending.

Black would probably be winning after 33...♖a1 34 ♖c1 ♖xc1 35 ♗xc1 f4 but he could not be sure about the prospects for ...♔f5-e4-d3.

33	♖c1	f4
34	♗c3	h5
35	♘d2	♗d5

36   f3?

The minor errors are adding up. This discourages ...g4 but surrenders control of e3.

After a pass such as 36 ♔f1 or 36 ♖e1, Black can make incremental improvements, such as ...♖a4, ...c6 and ...♔f5.

But it is far from clear that he could then win with ...g4 or a trade of bishops.

36	...	♗c5+
37	♔f1	♗e3
38	♔e2?	

The last miscue. Anand should have passed with the only piece that can move freely, 38 ♖d1 and 38...♖e8 39 ♖a1, for example.

38   ...   ♗c4+!

He may have overlooked 39 ♔d1 ♗f1! so that 40 ♘xf1 ♗xc1 41 ♔xc1 ♖a1+ and ...♖xf1 wins.

39	♔e1	♖e8

Just when it seemed White had run out of playable moves, Caruana suddenly saw a good one, 40 ♗e5!.

Then 40...♖xe5? 41 ♖xc4 leaves White with a powerful knight outpost at e4 and a likely draw.

But Black's bishops are so strong that he would have had good winning chances if he kept them, after 40...♗b5 41 ♗xc7 ♔f5, for example.

In fact, there is a study-like win in 41...♖e7!.

The White bishop is trapped on an open board and threatened by 42...♗b6+.

For instance, 42 ♗d8 ♗xd2+ 43 ♔xd2 ♖d7+.

40   ♔d1   ♗xd2

Now 41 ♗xd2 loses to 41...♗b3+.

41   ♔xd2   ♖e2+

42   ♔d1   ♖xg2

Black can win the other two kingside pawns as well.

43   ♗d4   ♗e2+

44   ♔e1   ♗xf3

45   ♖xc7   ♖e2+

46   ♔f1   ♖h2

Each of the Black pawns might queen now.

But the g-pawn has the best chance, e.g. 47 b4 ♖xh3 48 b5 ♖h1+ 49 ♔f2 g4 50 b6 ♖d1 51 ♗c5 ♖d2+ and ...g3.

47   ♖g7+   ♔f5

48   White resigns.

Answer to the trivia question: Only two world champions never won a tournament game from a reigning champion, Capablanca and Bobby Fischer.

163

22
Overrated

A universal epithet in chess is "overrated." It existed long before Arpad Elo began work on his rating system. In 1933, for example, writer Irving Chernev described Paul Morphy as "perhaps the most overrated" player in history.

"Overrated" is frequently used by weekend tournament players to deride their opponents. Grandmasters, at least most of them, are above that. But they occasionally describe a game as receiving more attention than it deserved. Anish Giri began his review of the games of Wijk aan Zee 2014 by telling New In Chess readers that Caruana's first-round victory was "overrated."

He was right. The over-the-top praise by on-line commentators had made it appear more impressive than it deserved. Caruana was the first to agree.

Caruana – Boris Gelfand
Wijk aan Zee 2014
Sicilian Defense,
Najdorf Variation (B90)

1	e4	c5
2	♘f3	d6
3	d4	cxd4
4	♘xd4	♘f6
5	♘c3	a6

Gelfand had been playing the Sicilian's Sveshnikov Variation. But he turned to the Najdorf Variation because of "my recent results," Caruana wrote.

He was alluding to his last five decisive Najdorfs – all won by

Black. No elite grandmaster in recent memory had been so unsuccessful as White against a single opening variation.

| 6 | f3 | e5 |
| 7 | ♘b3 | ♗e6 |

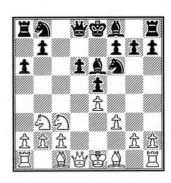

One of those losses – to Gelfand – had followed a main line, 8 ♗e3

♗e7 9 ♕d2 0-0 10 0-0-0 ♘bd7, and now 11 g4 b5 12 g5 b4 13 ♘e2 ♘e8.

Caruana emerged with an edge after the relatively new idea, 14 f4 a5 15 f5 a4 16 fxe6 axb3 17 cxb3! and 17...fxe6 18 ♗h3 followed by ♗xe6+ (or 18...♘c7 19 ♔b1).

8   ♗e3

Games like that reinforced the idea that ...0-0 in this variation prematurely provides White with a target.

But if Black develops 9...♗e7 10 ♕d2 ♘bd7, then 11 g4! poses a traffic problem.

He doesn't have time to clear a retreat square at d7 for his KN with 11...b5 and 12...♘b6 because of 12 g5!.

8   ...   h5

This violates a beginners' rule: "Don't play where you are weaker," Gelfand said, meaning the kingside.

"However, it has the right to exist," he added.

By virtually precluding g2-g4, Black forces White to look for a good Plan B.

Mere development doesn't create a plan. After 9 ♕d2 ♘bd7 10 0-0-0 ♖c8 11 ♔b1 ♗e7 White hasn't chosen one – but Black can (...b5, ...♘b6-c4).

9   ♘d5

This threatens 10 ♗b6.

If White delays his Plan B, with 9 ♕d2 ♘bd7 10 ♘d5, Black gets good play from 10...♘xd5 11 exd5 ♗f5.

9   ...   ♗xd5

But after 9...♘xd5 10 exd5 ♗f5 White could trade bishops, 11 ♗d3 ♗xd3 12 ♕xd3, without spending a tempo on ♕d2.

Then he can castle queenside and wait for a chance to exploit ...h5 in the middlegame.

10   exd5   ♘bd7

Instead, Gelfand leaves Caruana with a slightly bad light-squared bishop. Black can try to make it worse by attacking the d5-pawn and prompting c2-c4.

11   ♕d2   g6

Black no longer fears queenside castling by White, e.g. 11...♗e7 12 0-0-0 ♖c8 13 ♔b1 ♘b6=.

With 11...g6 he stops ♗d3-f5 but also prepares counterplay on dark squares, ...♗g7 and ...e4!/ ...♘e5.

12 ♗e2 ♗g7

Caruana and Gelfand had an encore when they repeated these moves later this year in the Petrosian Memorial.

Caruana tried to speed his queenside play with 13 ♘a5 ♛c7 14 c4.

But Gelfand was ready for 14...e4!.

Then 15 f4? ♘g4! would have favored him, e.g. 16 ♗xg4 hxg4 and ...f5.

Caruana made a positionally sound decision to maintain a pawn on f3 with 15 0-0 gxf3 16 gxf3 (not 16 ♖xf3? ♘e4).

However, Gelfand equalized with an Exchange sacrifice, 16...0-0 17 b4 ♖fe8 18 ♖ac1 ♖xe3 19 ♛xe3 ♗e8, and drew.

13 0-0

White's Plan B calls for c2-c4, ♖ac1 and c4-c5, perhaps with ♘a5/b2-b4 inserted.

It is so simple that the world's top-10 players debated whether it paid for Black to stop it at the cost of weakening the light squares.

For example, 13...a5 stops ♘a5 and b2-b4.

But 14 a4 0-0 15 ♗b5 ♛c7 16 c4 favored White in Carlsen – Vachier-Lagrave, Biel 2018.

13 ... 0-0

Gelfand relies on his dark-square strategem: 14 c4 e4! would again be annoying because of ...exf3/...♘e5.

He would be willing to meet 15 f4 ♘g4 16 ♗xg4 hxg4 17 f5 ♘e5 with its threat of ...♘xc4.

14 ♖ac1

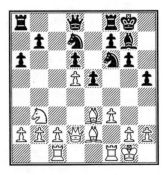

After the game, Caruana believed this position had not been played before, except in correspondence games.

Yet Anish Giri said *his* database showed it had occurred in 786 games.

Its popularity lies in its waiting-move quality.

This is shown by 14...e4 15 f4 ♘g4 16 ♗xg4 hxg4 17 f5!.

Then 17...♘e5 would not threaten a pawn on c4. White would have the upper hand after 18 ♗h6 ♘c4 19 ♕f4, for example.

And he would have enough comp for a pawn after 17...♗xb2 18 ♖b1 ♗-moves 19 ♘d4.

14 ... b6!?

This game convinced masters to play 14 ♘a5 when White still has the opportunity.

Among the sophisticated differences is that (14 ♖ac1) ♕c7 15 c4 allows White to meet 15...e4 16 f4 ♘g4 17 ♗xg4 hxg4 with 18 f5 ♘e5? 19 f6!.

15 h3

The last few notes showed how important a timely ...♘g4 is. Caruana's move stopped that and was an apparent innovation.

But why wasn't 14 h3 played a move ago?

Giri said it had – and 14...h4 had been the reply in a staggering "243 engine games."

Black then got good compensation for a pawn after 15 ♗g5 ♕c7 16 ♗xh4 ♘b6.

15 ... ♖e8

Black burned the ...h4 bridge a move ago – 15 h3 h4? 16 ♗g5 would just drop a pawn without the recourse of ...♘b6.

16 g4?

Caruana passes up 16 c4 for something more robust.

He wasn't concerned about 16 c4 e4? because 17 f4! is finally strong.

However, 16...a5 and ...♘c5 would have slowed him on the queenside.

How slow? Well, some computers recommend 17 ♘a1 followed by ♘c2-a3-b5. That's not much even if Black allows it to happen.

16 ... hxg4

Caruana's last move gained space and opened his playbook for a Plan C.

For example, 16...♕e7 might be answered by 17 g5 ♘h7 18 c3 followed by ♗d3, ♖ce1 and eventually f3-f4.

17 hxg4

By exchanging h-pawns, Black enabled himself to meet g4-g5 with ...♘h5 and...♘f4, even if it means risking a pawn.

"They asked me what I intended to do on 17...♘c5 18 ♘xc5 bxc5," Caruana wrote in *64*. His answer was 19 ♔g2 and 19...♕d7 20 ♔g3.

This is far from an advantage but at least it would be a plan — a Plan D, such as ♖h1 and ♗h6.

17 ... ♘h7?

Caruana pointed out how 17...b5! would have revived the forgotten ...♘b6xd5 counterplay.

Black is then better, as indicated by 18 c4 bxc4 19 ♗xc4 e4 and 20 f4? ♘xg4 or 20 g5 ♘h5 21 f4 ♘g3.

A key point is that 18 ♘a5 permits 18...♘xd5!.

For example, 19 ♕xd5 ♕xa5. Or 19 ♘b7 ♕c7 20 ♕xd5 ♘f6

21 ♕xd6 ♕xb7, with a Black advantage.

18 g5!

This snuffs out the intended ...♗f6-g5!.

And one more time 18...e4 would be met by 19 f4!.

Then 19...♗xb2 20 ♖b1 ♗g7 21 ♘d4! is more than sufficient compensation for a pawn.

18 ... f5

This (and 18...f6) was Black's only source of counterplay.

If he had passed, such as with 18...♕c8 and 19...♕b7, White can begin a strong kingside shift with 19 c3, 20 ♖f2 and ♖h2.

"From here on in, Fabiano played a great game," Giri said.

19 gxf6 ♗xf6

Black's kingside is more vulnerable after 19...♘dxf6 20 ♖f2! and ♗d3/♖g2.

168

20 ♖f2

Gelfand's hope was that a trade of bishops would allow him a dark-square blockade, e.g. 20 c3? ♗g5! 21 ♗d3 ♕f6.

20	...	♗g5
21	♖g2	♗xe3+
22	♕xe3	

But he is fatally weak on light squares, in particular g6 and h7, e.g. 22...g5 23 ♗d3 ♖e7 24 ♗f5 or 24 ♔f2/25 ♖h1.

| 22 | ... | ♘df8 |
| 23 | ♗d3 | ♖a7 |

Gelfand can bear the loss of a pawn (24 ♗xg6 ♘xg6 25 ♖xg6+ ♖g7) for a smidgeon of safety.

Caruana had intended 24 ♘a5 (24...bxa5 25 ♕xa7).

But he concluded 24...♖g7 25 ♘c6 ♕h4 would be getting unclear.

24 ♖f1

This move impressed the day's tournament commentator, Yasser Seirawan.

White can answer 24...♘f6 with 25 f4!.

However, what no one seemed to notice until after the game was that 24 ♕h6! followed by ♗xg6, ♘d2-e4 or ♔f2/♖h1 would be devastating.

For instance, 24...♖g7 25 ♔f2 ♕f6 26 ♘d2 ♕f4 27 ♕xf4 and 28 ♘e4 ♖d8 29 ♖dg1.

24 ... ♖f7

Black was concerned about 25 f4 but could have put up more resistance with 24...♖g7.

| 25 | ♕h6 | ♔h8 |
| 26 | ♘d2! | ♖f4 |

Gelfand found a way to set traps (27 ♗xg6 ♖f6!) and delay ♘g5 (27 ♘e4 ♖h4).

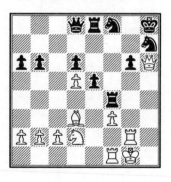

27 ♖g4

A curious decision considering that Black was in time pressure.

Caruana allowed him to play quick, easy moves, 27...♖xg4+ 28 fxg4 and 28...♕g5 29 ♕xg5 ♘xg5.

Then the endgame would be winnable after 30 ♘c4!.

His GM rivals would more likely have gone for a kingside wipeout with 27 ♖h2 followed by ♘e4, ♔f2 and ♖fh1.

| 27 | ... | b5 |

| 28 | ♘e4! | ♘d7? |

Gelfand said he lost "in part due to his strong play, in part due to my poor form."

It was too late for 28...♖xg4+ 29 fxg4 because of ♘f6 or ♖f7.

For example, 29...♕e7 30 ♘xd6! ♕xd6 31 ♖f7.

A tougher defense is 29...♔g8 30 ♘f6+ ♘xf6 31 ♗xg6! and then 31...♕e7 32 ♕g5! ♕g7 33 ♖xf6 ♖e7 34 ♖xd6.

Or 31...♖e7 32 ♖xf6 ♖g7 33 ♖xd6! (33...♕xd6 34 ♗h7+ and ♕xd6).

| 29 | ♖xg6 | ♖g8 |

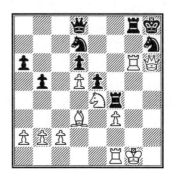

| 30 | ♘g5! | resigns. |

When journalists around the world voted for the Chess Oscar of 2013, they placed Gelfand and Caruana number four and five, after Magnus Carlsen, Vladimir Kramnik and Levon Aronian. Fabiano's credentials included winning major tournaments at Zürich and Bucharest, sharing first at the Paris Grand Prix and placing second at Baden-Baden.

23
Fox versus Hedgehog

"The fox knows many things," the poetic parable says. "The hedgehog knows one big thing." There are many philosophic interpretations of this – none having anything to do with the Hedgehog pawn formation.

Chessplayers can identify the fox as an opponent who plays almost every opening (Carlsen, Nakamura and, to a lesser degree, Caruana). A hedgehog is someone who devoutly adopts a single major opening whenever he has the chance. What is the proper way for a fox to play a hedgehog? Should he avoid his "big" opening? This game provides an answer.

Caruana – Teimour Radjabov
Gashimov Memorial,
Shamkir 2014
*King's Indian Defense,
Classical Variation (E92)*

1	d4	♘f6
2	c4	g6
3	♘c3	♗g7

Even before the retirement of Garry Kasparov, Radjabov was the world's foremost King's Indian advocate. His victims included veterans (Ivanchuk, Gelfand, four times each) as well as youngsters such as Carlsen, Nakamura and – in 2021 – Caruana.

4	e4	d6
5	♘f3	0-0
6	♗e2	e5
7	♗e3	

Caruana could have been discouraged by Radjabov's much greater experience, even with this variation.

No one has played this position more in international tournament games – 29 times, according to one on-line database, 365chess.com.

But a fox can see a benefit. Those games provide a wealth of insight into a hedgehog's thinking.

7	...	♘g4

It was discovered back in the 1960s that 7...♘c6? – the main line move after 7 0-0 – is a grave error.

White can launch a queenside initiative before Black has a kingside target, 8 d5 ♘e7 9 ♘d2! ♘e8 10 c5, for example.

8	♗g5	f6

Black takes what White gave him with 7 ♗e3 – a way to harass the bishop.

9 ♗h4 ♘c6

This was a minor surprise. More often Radjabov played 9...g5 10 ♗g3 ♘h6, with the idea of ...g4.

10 d5 ♘e7

11 ♘d2

As a fox, Caruana played the KID on occasion as Black. He later adopted 11...h5.

He was distinctly worse against Wesley So at the 2019 Norway blitz tournament after 12 0-0 ♘h6 13 f3 ♘f7 14 ♗f2 c5 15 dxc6 bxc6 16 b4!.

11 ... f5

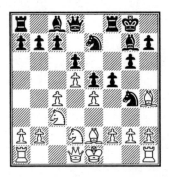

This is a natural King's Indian move but somewhat rare here. It prepares to put pressure on the center with ...♘f6 and goads White into resolving the center tension.

12 ♗xg4 fxg4

The drawback to Black's 11th move is that the center is static. It cannot be changed by ...fxe4. This may deprive his minor pieces of good squares.

13 ♗g5!

But his bishop would have had one after ...♗h6. So would his knight after 13 0-0? h6! followed by ...g5/...♘g6-f4.

13 ... h6

14 ♗e3

White heads for a middlegame in which his queenside attack, with c4-c5, will be more dangerous than Black's kingside attack, e.g. 14...g5 15 b4 ♘g6 16 c5 ♘f4 17 0-0 h5 18 ♘c4.

14 ... c5

When he examined Radjabov's games beforehand, Caruana could not have expected to play this exact position.

But he knew Radjabov liked to blockade the queenside with ...c5.

This pawn structure has puzzled 1 d4 players for more than 80 years. Should White take en passant?

Or should he attack the c5-pawn with b2-b4?

And if he does attack it, should he prepare with 罝b1? Or with a2-a3 so he can recapture with a pawn after b2-b4/...cxb4 ?

Experience in similar positions indicates the 15 罝b1 plan is best.

After 15...g5 16 b4, for instance, White would have the better of 16...b6 17 bxc5 bxc5 or 16...cxb4 17 罝xb4 b6 18 a4.

15 dxc6   bxc6

16 b4

This seeks to win pawn control of d5. It's a standard *priyome* and Caruana must have examined how Radjabov responded to it in the similar positions.

For instance, the Azeri GM had varied earlier with 11...包h6 12 f3 c5 and then faced 13 dxc6! bxc6 14 b4.

He was worse even though he was able to push in the center, 14...奧e6 15 b5 d5 16 包b3 (16...dxc4 17 包c5).

This was valuable insight even though...

16 ...   d5

...Radjabov innovated, diverging from the book-backed 16...奧e6.

17 exd5

Caruana could see how 17 奧c5? d4! can turn out badly for White.

Nor is 17 cxd5 cxd5 18 奧c5 d4 or 18 豐b3 奧e6 promising.

17 ...   cxd5

18 奧c5!

An irony of Hypermodern openings: If White dissolves part of his pawn center, the Black pawns that replace them can turn out to be over-extended.

White threatens 19 cxd5 (19...包xd5 20 奧xf8).

If Black freezes the center with 18...d4, his minor pieces are worse than White's because e4 is free (19 包de4).

If the center opens, 18...dxc4 19 包xc4 奧e6, his bishops can show what they can do. For example, 20 豐xd8 罝fxd8 21 奧xe7 罝dc8, with advantage.

White's knights can limit them with 19 ♘de4, instead of 19 ♘xc4.

Then 19...♕c7? 20 ♘d5! wins.

But for the first time in the game – and certainly not the last – Black could make a promising Exchange sacrifice, 19....♕xd1+ 20 ♖xd1 ♘c6! 21 ♗xf8 ♗xf8.

18 ... e4!

This is the first move that occurs to a true KID believer. Black opens the diagonal of his most trusted piece, with a ...♗xc3 threat.

Now 19 ♘xd5 ♘xd5 20 cxd5 ♖f5! and ...♖xd5 favors Black.

19 ♗xe7

Caruana accepts the challenge, which means *he* will probably have to offer the Exchange.

Analyzing this kind of position with a computer is more confusing than normal.

Engines tend to discount sacrifices, such as 19 ♖c1 e3! and then 20 fxe3 ♗e6 21 cxd5 ♘xd5 22 ♗xd5 ♕xd5 23 ♗xf8 ♖xf8.

Garry Kasparov explained the proper use of the computer in such situations: You need to know when to turn it on. And you need to know when to turn it off.

19 ... ♕xe7

20 ♘xd5 ♕f7

Black also has some comp after 20...♕e5 or 20...♕g5 followed by ...♗e6 and ...♖ad8.

By threatening mate on f2, he wins time to accept the Exchange.

21 0-0 ♗xa1

22 ♕xa1

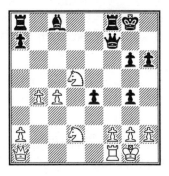

One of the overworked clichés of annotators is "dynamic equality."

Masters use it to explain why chances are equal in a complex, even chaotic, position.

But there is little that is dynamic here. Neither side has immediate threats. There are few pawn pushes to consider.

A better explanation is: Material is roughly equal but White has an easier time finding good moves.

22 ... ♗f5

What about endgames?

After 22...♕g7 23 ♕xg7+ ♔xg7 Black would be in no

danger because he can eliminate one of the knights.

For example, 24 ♘xe4 ♝b7 25 ♘c5 ♝xd5 26 cxd5 ♖f6!.

White should stay in a middlegame with 24 ♕c1 and 24...♝e6 25 ♘e3!.

The d5-outpost looks like the basis of his compensation. But his knights belong on dark squares, where they can't be easily attacked, until he is stronger.

23 ♘e3 ♖ad8

David Navara expressed the philosophy of modern grandmasters when he commented about one of his middlegame positions against Caruana.

His computer said the position was equal "whereas I would prefer White."

He added, "Those two statements are not contradictory." Many masters would say the same

of other positions. This is true here and remains true for nearly 20 more moves.

24 ♘b3 ♝e6!

Black has no major targets to attack except the c4-pawn – and the c4-square.

The square's significance is illustrated by 25 c5?.

Then 25...♝xb3 26 axb3 ♕xb3 27 ♘xg4 keeps the balance.

But 25...♝c4! would force 26 ♘xc4 ♕xc4.

Black's queen activity gives him very good winning chances, 27 ♕c1 ♕e2! (28 ♕xh6? ♕xf2+ and mates).

25 ♕c1 h5

26 ♘c5

White can improve his chances with a gauged push of the queenside pawns. Black's more static position is a difficult one for a KID player.

175

Radjabov does not like to pass or play prophylactically (26...♕e7).

26 ... ♖d4!

27 ♕c3

He is looking for a way to give back the Exchange, such as 27...♖fd8 28 ♘d5! ♖xc4 29 ♕xc4 ♗xd5.

But White would be moderately superior after 30 ♕d4. He can steadily improve, with ♖d1 and a2-a4. His knight cannot be attacked and f2 is well protected.

The endgame of 30...♕g7 31 ♖d1 ♕xd4 32 ♖xd4 may be winnable.

Radjabov probably rejected 28...♖4xd5 29 cxd5 ♗xd5 30 ♖d1 for the same reason.

However, 29...♗f5! and a capture on d5 with the queen or rook should equalize.

Then you can forget about what Capablanca said about how a ♕+♘-vs.-♕+♗ endgame favors the guy with the knight.

Black would not be worse after 30 ♖d1 ♖xd5 31 ♖xd5 ♕xd5.

But if Capa were Black he would love to play the ♗-vs.-♘ endgame after 32 ♕b3 ♕xb3 33 ♘xb3 ♗e6.

27 ... ♖xc4

This looks strong, since 28 ♘xc4? ♗xc4 would win.

28 ♕b2! ♖xc5

29 bxc5 ♗xa2

30 g3 ♗e6

31 ♖a1 ♔h7

32 ♖a4

White still has more incremental moves to make than Black, e.g. 32...♖c8 33 ♕a3 ♖c7 34 ♖a6.

But he will not make significant progress until he can use his knight better, 34...♕e7 35 ♖d6 ♖d7=.

32 ... ♕g7!

Simpler is an impregnable fortress: 32 ♕xg7+ ♔xg7 33 ♖xa7+ ♔f6.

For instance, 34 ♔f1 ♔e5 35 ♖c7 ♖c8.

33	♕d2	♖f7
34	c6	♕e5
35	♖a5	

Caruana's best chance lies in tying Black's heavy pieces to the c-pawn, looking for an opportunity to use his knight, ideally on d5, and eyeing a trade of rooks with ♖b7.

35	...	♕c7
36	♕c3	♕d6
37	♖b5!	

Now 38 ♖b7 ♖xb7? 39 cxb7 ♕b6 40 ♕c8! is a winning threat.

Black would not be lost after 38...♔g8 39 ♖xf7 ♔xf7 40 c7 ♗c8 41 ♕h8 – but getting close.

37	...	♗c8!

He can allow the knight in, 38 ♘d5, and then defend with 38...♖f5 39 ♕d4 a6 or 39...♖f7.

There are also surprising resources, such as 39...e3!.

Then 40 ♕xa7+ ♔g8 would cost White his knight.

A perpetual check is the best he can get after 40 fxe3 ♕a3.

38	♕c2	a6
39	♖d5	♕f6
40	c7!	

A clever try on the final move of the time control:

For 20 moves, Black has been relying on threats to capture on f2 (or to push ...e3 as in the last note).

But now he should threaten the c7-pawn instead, such as with 40...♕g7!.

For example, 41 ♕xe4 ♕a1+ 42 ♔g2 ♕c3!.

Even 43 ♖xh5+ ♔g7 is acceptable (44 ♕e5+ ♕xe5 45 ♖xe5 ♖xc7).

40 ... ♖f8?

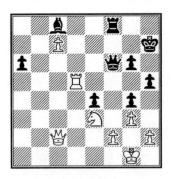

41 ♕d2!

A devastating "little" move. Black cannot stop ♖d8.

41 ... ♕f7

42 ♖d8! ♔g8

Computers want to win with 43 ♘d5 ♗b7 44 ♕b2 and then 44...♕xd5 45 ♕b6.

43 ♕d5

No human would choose that when this is available, e.g. 43...♕xd5 44 ♘xd5 and 45 ♘b6.

Also lost is 43...♗e6 44 ♖xf8+ ♔xf8 45 c8(♕)+ ♗xc8 46 ♕c5+.

43 ... ♔g7

44 ♕d4+ ♔h6

45 ♘c4! ♗e6

46 ♕c5!

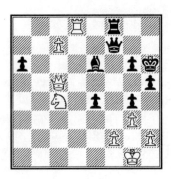

This wins a piece. **Black resigned** after 46...♖g8 47 c8(♕) ♗xc8 48 ♖xc8 ♖xc8 49 ♕xc8 ♕d5 50 ♘e3 ♕d3 51 ♕h8+ ♔g5 52 ♕f8!

In view of the ♕f4 mate threat.

Playing long games had become a trademark of Caruana. In this year he had more than 60 tournament games in major events that lasted 50 or more moves.

This was a hallmark of his generation. Magnus Carlsen, Hikaru Nakamura and Sergey Karjakin played a comparable amount of 50+ move games in 2014. Endurance had become a required asset in the modern grandmaster's skill set.

24
Rehabilitated

Caruana fans, the Fabianistas, were beginning to appreciate he was a streak player. He was capable of a series of great successes only to follow them with dismal reverses. When 2014 began, a widespread view was that his rapid progress was over. "Perhaps he has reached his ceiling or grown lazy," the Russian magazine 64 wrote. Evgeny Sveshnikov said Caruana did not take a studious approach to the game, like Garry Kasparov or Lev Polugaevsky. He was like other young players: "They just play chess."

Caruana did not seem like the same player who had won Dortmund 2012. In the same elite tournament, one year later, he finished a poor =5th place. "We weren't even certain that he would be invited again," said his trainer, Vladimir Chuchelov. He assured the German organizers "we would be rehabilitated if they gave us one more chance." Caruana used his chance to create one of the finest games in recent memory.

Caruana – Ruslan Ponomariev
Dortmund 2014
Petroff Defense,
Nimzovich Variation (C42)

1	e4	e5
2	♘f3	♘f6
3	♘xe5	d6
4	♘f3	♘xe4
5	♘c3	

This move was virtually forgotten until brought into fashion by, among others, Sergey Karjakin.

5	...	♘xc3

Annotators explained the popularity of 5 ♘c3 by saying that modern GMs had made a major discovery: White can quickly castle queenside after 6 dxc3 and continue ♗e3/♕d2.

But this is exactly what Aron Nimzovich did before World War I, when he debated the merits of 5 ♘c3 in games with Petroff pioneer Frank Marshall.

6	dxc3	

What White gets as compensation for the doubled pawns is more

179

space, control of the half-open d-file and support for knight outposts at d4 and d5.

6	...	♝e7
7	♝e3	♞c6
8	♕d2	

These two players reached this position a year before, at the Kings tournament in Bazna. Then Ponomariev played 8...0-0 9 0-0-0 ♞e5.

This entails some dangers for both sides. After 10 ♞d4? Black can get a rapid attack with 10...c5! 11 ♞b5 ♝e6.

Instead, 10 h4 and 10 ♔b1 are common. Experience has shown that inflicting a second pair of doubled pawns, 10...♞xf3 11 gxf3, would help Black win an endgame – but this is risky in a middlegame after ♖g1/♝d4.

Instead, Caruana chose 10 ♞xe5 dxe5 11 ♝d3, and enjoyed a brief initiative before he drew.

8	...	♝e6

This became the primary response to White's ♝e3/♕d2 system. Black's king may be safer after ...0-0-0, depending on White's next few moves.

9	0-0-0	♕d7

But 9...♝xa2 isn't quite sound, 10 b3 a5 11 ♔b2 a4 12 ♖a1 or even 12 ♔xa2 axb3+ 13 ♔xb3.

Caruana engaged in a waiting game with Hou Yifan at Wijk aan Zee 2016 after 10 h4 h6 11 a3.

He was waiting for 11...0-0?, which allows a winning sacrifice, 12 ♝xh6! gxh6 13 ♕xh6.

For example, 13...♝f5 14 ♝c4! ♖fd8 15 ♖h3! and ♖g3+ or 15...♝xh3 16 gxh3 and ♖g1+ wins.

Caruana was also waiting for 11...0-0-0 because 12 ♞d4 ♞xd4 13 ♝xd4 would threaten the pawns at a7 and g7.

Hou Yifan's solution was a waiting move, 11...♖g8!. It protects g7 and permits queenside castling.

She stood well in the ensuing middlegame, 12 ♘d4 ♘xd4 13 ♕xd4 c5! 14 ♕f4 d5.

10   ♔b1   ♗f6

"Pono" recognized the dangers of 10...0-0-0 11 ♗b5!.

But after 10...♗f6 he could break the 11 ♗b5 pin with 11...a6 12 ♗a4 b5 13 ♗b3 ♗xb3 and 14...0-0.

In addition, 11 ♘d4 ♘xd4 12 ♗xd4 ♗xd4 and 13...0-0! is a manageable disadvantage for Black.

11   h3

The subtle nature of these positions is shown by 11 h4, with the idea of 12 ♘g5.

Then 11...h6 12 ♘d4 ♘xd4 13 ♗xd4 ♗xd4 14 ♕xd4 0-0 looks like the 11 ♘d4 variation in the last note.

But ...h6 makes a crucial difference.

White can try to open a kingside file with 15 ♖g1 and 16 g4!.

Caruana had demonstrated this against Konstantin Landa at Reggio Emilia 2010, when he won neatly, 15 ♖g1 ♖ae8 16 g4! ♕c6 17 ♗g2 ♕a6 18 b3 ♗d7? 19 g5! h5 20 g6 ♖e7? 21 ♗d5! ♗e6 22 ♖de1 c5 23 ♕d1! ♖fe8 24 ♕xh5 fxg6 25 ♖xe6 resigns (25...gxh5 27 ♖xe7+ and mates, or 25...♖xe6 26 ♕xg6).

11   ...   h6

This makes ...0-0 too perilous. But White would have a ready-made attack after 11...0-0 12 g4! and 13 g5.

12   b3

In addition to reinforcing his king position, this move makes c3-c4 an attractive way to discourage ...d5.

12   ...   a6

13   g4   0-0-0

Now 14 ♘d4 lacks bite in view of 14...♗d5.

14   ♗g2

Caruana expected 14...♔b8 and intended 15 ♘g1! and ♘e2.

Then he could grab space with f2-f4-f5 or plant his knight on f4.

But Black should be near equality after 15...d5 16 f4 g6 and a timely ...h5.

181

14 ... g5?

Pono stops g4-g5 and provides counterplay after 15 ♘g1 h5 or 15 c4 d5!.

But he also creates significant weaknesses, on f6, g7 and h6.

15 ♘d4! ♘xd4

For example, 15...♘e5 can be answered by 16 f4! gxf4 17 ♗xf4.

The threat of ♗xh6 could lead to 17...h5 18 g5 or 17...♗g7 18 ♖hf1, with long-term White pressure.

He would also be able to tease the queenside with a mate threat of ♕e3-e4xb7.

16 cxd4

The f6-bishop became a somewhat bad piece after 14...g5. Therefore White avoids 16 ♗xd4 ♗xd4 17 ♕xd4 ♔b8.

Then 18 f4 can be neutralized by 18...gxf4 19 ♕xf4 f5 or just 18...f5.

That's a basic theme of the middlegame that follows: Both sides have kingside targets. White has to be concerned about pawn exchanges after ...f5 and ...h5.

16 ... d5

Black needed to stop d4-d5.

His problems would mount on both wings after 16...c6 17 f4! and then 17...gxf4 18 ♗xf4 h5 19 g5 ♗g7 20 d5! cxd5 21 ♗xd5.

For instance, 21...♗xh3 22 ♕b4 ♗g4 23 ♗xd6!.

Then the threat of ♕c5+ leads to 23...♕b5 24 ♕f4 ♗xd1 25 ♖xd1 followed by 26 ♗xf7 or 26 a4! ♕d7 27 ♕c4+.

17 f4! gxf4

18 ♗xf4 h5

If Black defends his h6-pawn with 18...♗g7, White could make progress by doubling rooks on the e-file and trading bishops with ♗e5.

Black's best defense would be to insert ...h5 at some point, leading to the same kind of position that occurs in the game.

19 g5 ♗g7

Black will need counterplay from ...f6 or ...h4 to survive.

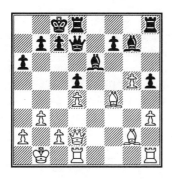

20   ♖de1

Caruana has made very few – and very good – irrevocable decisions, such as 15 ♘d4! and 17 f4!.

He can enhance his chances further by doubling rooks and trading bishops.

But he may have done better with another can't-take-back move, 20 h4. This stops ...h4 and prepares ♖de1, ♖hf1 and ♗e5.

For instance, 20 h4 f6 21 g6 tests Black's defensive skill more than in the game, e.g. 21...♗g4 22 ♖df1 and 23 ♗f3.

20   ...   h4!

21   ♗e5   ♖dg8

22   ♕f4   ♕d8

Pono waits for a moment, coming soon, when Caruana cannot improve his position without burning bridges.

23   ♗f1!   ♔b8

24   ♗d3

White threatens 25 g6 fxg6? 26 ♗xg7 and ♖xe6.

24   ...   ♗c8!

Caruana was surprised because he had discounted this move because of 25 ♕xf7 ♗xe5 26 dxe5.

Then 26...♖xg5 27 e6! or 26...♕xg5 27 ♕xd5 looked good.

And he had seen 26...♖f8 would allow a promising queen sacrifice 27 e6 ♖xf7 28 exf7.

The pair of passed pawns could win after 29 g6.

Wonderful... except Black can insert 27...♕xg5! and hold easily.

25   ♔b2   ♗xe5

26   ♖xe5   ♖g7

Thanks to 20...h4, Black can keep pressure on the h3- and g5-pawns.

White could rid himself of one weakness with 27 ♖f1 ♗xh3 28 ♖h1 ♗e6 29 ♖xh4.

But Black would be rock solid after 29...♖hg8.

27 a4!

Caruana tries to prompt an irrevocable step from Black.

If Pono passes with 27...♔a8, White could threaten the under-defended c7-pawn with 28 ♖he1 and ♖e7.

For instance, 28...♗xh3 29 ♖e7 and then 29...♔b8 30 g6! is strong.

27 ... a5

The a5-pawn can be protected by ...b6.

28 ♔a2 ♔a7

Both sides have opportunities to offer a trade of one pair of kingside pawns.

But which pair?

After 28...♖hg8 29 ♕xh4 ♖xg5, Black has to deal with a passed White h-pawn.

That looms larger in a middlegame (30 ♖xg5 ♖xg5 31 ♕f4 and 32 h4).

Or in an endgame (30...♕xg5 31 ♕xg5 ♖xg5 32 h4 ♖h5 33 ♗e2).

This is hardly conclusive. But Pono didn't want to make such a commitment while he can pass with his king.

29 ♕d2

White will need a tactic to win. One of the ideas he can work with is ♕f6.

But 29 ♕f6? ♕xf6 30 gxf6 ♖g3! throws away his edge.

29 ... ♔b8

So would 30 ♕xa5? ♖xg5.

30 ♕f4 ♔a7

31 ♖he1!

Out of constructive passes, Caruana takes the plunge. He threatens 32 ♖e7!.

31   ...   ♗xh3

We saw a position similar to 31...♔b8 32 ♖e7 ♗xh3 33 g6 in the note to 27 a4.

Black could build a possible fortress with 33...♖xg6! 34 ♗xg6 fxg6.

Then comes 35 ♖g7! ♕d6! 36 ♕xd6 cxd6 37 ♖xg6 ♗f5 38 ♖xd6 ♗e4! and 39...h3.

But simpler and better is 33 ♖1e5 and 34 ♖xf7.

A key line is 33 ♖1e5 ♗c8 34 ♖xf7 ♖xf7 35 ♕xf7 h3.

Then 36 g6? h2! ends in a drawish pawn race.

But 36 ♖xd5 leads to a trade of queens and 38 g6!, with a possible win.

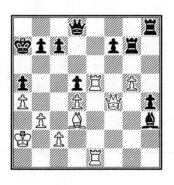

32   ♖h1

Not 32 ♖e7 ♕d6!, when another fortress can form after 33 ♕xd6 cxd6 34 g6 ♖xg6!.

32   ...   ♗c8

White has been saving ♕f6 for the right moment. It would come with 32...♕d7? 33 ♕f6! because 33...♖hg8 34 ♖e7! and wins.

33   ♖xh4

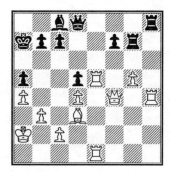

So we end up with the trade of h-pawns after all.

Is this position different from, say, the sequence in the note to 26...♖g7 ?

Yes, Black could avoid a trade of rooks then.

But here, with the Black king on a7 and the a5-pawn undefended, White could meet 33...♖hg8 with 34 ♖h7!.

For instance, 34...♖xg5 35 ♖xg5 ♕xg5 36 ♕xc7!.

Or 35...♖xg5 36 ♖xf7 c6? 37 ♖f8.

33	...	♖xh4

34	♕xh4

The passive defense 34...♖g8 35 ♕f4 ♖g7 would lose to 36 ♕f6! ♕xf6 37 gxf6 ♖g4 38 ♖xd5.

There is also potential for zugzwang after 34...♚b8 35 ♕f4.

For example, 35...♚a7 36 ♕f6!.

Or 35...♕d6 36 ♕f3! ♗e6? 37 ♕f6! ♖g8 38 ♗h7 ♖e8 39 g6!.

34	...	b6?

Black was left with a choice of pawn moves and picked the wrong one.

He would hold after 34...c6!.

Then 35 ♕f4 ♗h3 foils the queen-trading plan (36 ♕f6 ♕xf6 37 gxf6 ♖g3).

35	♕h6

Now 35...♕f8 36 ♕f6! and ♖e7.

35	...	♖g8

Caruana saw how 36 ♕f6 would likely draw after 36...♕xf6 37 gxf6 ♗e6!, e.g. 38 ♗f5 ♗xf5 39 ♖xf5 ♖g6!.

36	♕c6!

While his opponent was thinking, Caruana spotted a stunning way the game could end.

He didn't expect it to happen. But he made a mental note to show it to Ponomariev after the game.

He was prepared, instead, to win a long endgame after 36...♖xg5 37 ♖xg5 ♕xg5 38 ♕xc7+ ♗b7 39 ♕xf7.

36	...	♗e6

This is the best square for the bishop if queens are traded, as we saw in the note to 35...♖g8.

In contrast, 36...♗b7 37 ♕f6! ♕xf6 38 gxf6 is lost.

Then Black's bishop arrives at e6 too late, 38...♗c8 39 ♖e7 ♗e6 40 ♖xc7+ ♔b8 41 ♖e7.

37 g6

There would have been a nice finish after 37...♖f8 38 g7 ♖g8 and now 39 ♖g5!! followed by ♗h7xg8.

This is based on 39...♕xg5 40 ♕xc7+ ♔a8 41 ♗b5! and the threat of ♗c6 mate.

37 ... ♖g7

"When he played this move, I became very excited," Caruana recalled in *New In Chess*. The mating finish he had seen a move earlier was becoming a reality.

He said he "could hardly believe his good fortune" when Ponomariev "fell into it."

38 gxf7 ♗xf7

"Now comes a double deflection," he wrote.

He could have added "which belongs in every tactics textbook."

39 ♖e7! ♕xe7

40 ♗a6! ♔xa6

"Seeing that mate was inevitable, Ruslan, as a gentleman, allowed it to be played on the board," said Chuchelov.

41 ♕a8 mate

You may never know when you are about to play a really good game. Sometimes you don't know that you are playing a great game *while* you are playing it. Caruana is one of the few players who described afterwards when a spectacular finish came to him. (He did it again in Game 32.)

25
The Streak

When Caruana began his first Sinquefield Cup by winning game after game it was a sensation. Had anyone ever done anything like that before? Well, Wilhelm Steinitz won 25 consecutive games, in tournament and matches spread over nine years. Bobby Fischer scored 20 victories in a row during his 1970-71 run-up to the world championship.

But Steinitz and Fischer played several much weaker opponents during their string. Caruana's victims were all in the world's top ten. The only thing close to his achievement was Reuben Fine's six wins against world-class opponents at the start of AVRO 1938. But this was interrupted when José Capablanca swindled him into a draw. Caruana's streak was unique. It began with this game.

Veselin Topalov – Caruana
Sinquefield Cup, St. Louis 2014
English Opening,
Symmetrical Variation (A35)

1	♘f3	♘f6
2	c4	c5
3	♘c3	♘c6
4	g3	d5
5	cxd5	♘xd5
6	♗g2	♘c7

The knight retreat was made famous by Akiba Rubinstein and Mikhail Botvinnik and has become almost automatic in master games.

Black wants to prevent d2-d4 and enjoy a substantial advantage in operating room after ...e5.

7	0-0

White has two primary ways to challenge that space edge, with the flanking pawn breaks b2-b4 and f2-f4.

Two months before the Sinquefield Cup, Caruana went for the b2-b4 break with White, against Karjakin.

But he got little after 7...g6 8 h4 h6 9 d3 ♗g7 10 0-0 ♗d7.

7	...	e5

As Black, Caruana had faced the f2-f4 plan two years before, in a

Swiss team championship game that went 8 d3 ♗e7 9 ♘d2 ♗d7 10 ♘c4 f6 11 f4.

Then 11...exf4? 12 ♗xf4 ♘e6 13 ♘d6+ is quite poor.

Caruana followed book, 11...b5! 12 ♘e3 exf4, and equalized after 13 ♖xf4 0-0 14 ♘ed5 ♗d6.

8   a3

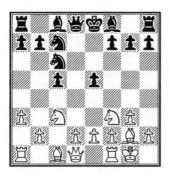

This move, dating back to Vasya Pirc and Anatoly Ufimtsev, became topical in the 21st century.

It is partly based on a tactical trick, 8...♗e7 9 b4! and then 9...cxb4 10 axb4 ♗xb4 11 ♘xe5!.

White favorably regains his piece after 11...♘xe5 12 ♕a4+ ♘c6 13 ♗xc6+ bxc6 14 ♕xb4.

Black can ignore 9 b4. But having achieved a strategic break, White would stand well after, for instance, 9...0-0 10 bxc5 or 10 b5 ♘d4 11 ♘xe5.

8   ...   ♖b8!

9   d3

The 9 b4 trick no longer works because the b8-rook protects the b4-bishop after 9...cxb4 10 axb4 ♗xb4 11 ♘xe5 ♘xe5 12 ♕a4+ ♘c6 13 ♗xc6+ bxc6.

9   ...   ♗e7

10   ♗e3

Topalov goes for a quick attack on c5 with pieces.

10   ...   0-0

11   ♖c1   ♗d7

The bishop looks awkward on d7 but there is a tactical explanation.

If Black defends the c5-pawn with ...b6, his c6-knight is unprotected.

For example, 11...f6 12 ♘e4 b6.

White gains a small plus from 13 b4 in view of 13...cxb4? 14 ♖xc6.

12   ♘d2

Both players were up to date on the latest theory.

Previously, 12 ♘e4 b6 13 b4 looked promising.

The key point is 13...cxb4 14 axb4 ♗xb4 allows a sound gambit, 15 d4! exd4 16 ♘xd4.

But one month before this game, Black equalized easily with 14...♘b5! and ...♘bd4 (Nisipeanu – Nagy, Pardubice 2014).

Therefore, Topalov switched to the other flanking idea, f2-f4.

12 ... ♘d4

It could not be thwarted, e.g. 12...b6 13 ♘c4 f6 14 f4 or 13...b5 14 ♗xc6 ♗xc6 15 ♘xe5.

13 ♘c4

But the immediate 13 f4 exf4! illustrates the problems with it.

Then 14 gxf4 ♗g4 exposes e2 to danger (15 ♘c4 ♘ce6).

Better is 14 ♗xf4 but 14...♘de6! 15 ♗e3 ♗f6 is also excellent for Black.

13 ... f6

14 f4 exf4

15 ♗xf4

As in the last note, 15 gxf4 ♗g4, allows Black to improve his position with simple moves (...♕d7/...b5 and putting rooks on the open files).

15 ... ♘de6

But 15...♗g4 was not as effective now because White has a g-pawn to drive the bishop back, 16 h3 ♗h5 17 g4.

16 ♗d2

The position is so balanced it was inevitable computers would recommend ways to repeat moves, such as 16...♘d4 17 ♗f4 ♘de6 18 ♗d2.

16 ... b6

This illustrates a shortcoming of what the Hypermodern masters preached in the 1920s.

They did not believe that putting pawns in the center was bad.

Rather, they felt that 1 e4 and 1 d4 were *premature* because they provided Black with a target.

They preferred 1 ♘f3 and 1 c4 so they could safely occupy the center with pieces or pawns in the middlegame.

In the diagram, we see how a Hypermodern opening preserved White's central pawns. But they are more liability than asset.

He would like to plant a knight on d5 anchored by the e-pawn. However, 17 e4 ♗c6 would threaten his newly weak d3-pawn.

If he plays ♘d5 without pawn support, 17 ♘e3 ♘d4 18 ♘cd5 ♘xd5 19 ♘xd5, he would be worse because his e-pawn is weak, 19...♗g4!.

17 g4

Topalov felt he had an advantage. After two minutes' thought, he opted for a plan that would confirm this.

He prepared a maneuver of the d2-bishop to its best diagonal, h2-b8.

Unlike after 15 ♗xf4 ♘de6, the bishop would be safe on g3.

17 ... ♗e8

He may have been thinking of a pawn sacrifice, 17...♘d4 18 e3 ♘c6 19 d4 and then 19...cxd4 20 exd4 ♘xd4 21 ♗f4.

18 ♗e1

Black is tempted to throw in 18...♕d4+ 19 e3 (else ...♕xg4) ♕d7 so that the d3-pawn is terminally backward.

But then Topalov would have a more promising pawn sacrifice than in the previous note – 20 ♗g3! ♖d8 21 ♕f3 ♕xd3 21 b3 with tactics based on ♕b7!.

18 ... b5

In the post-mortem, Caruana said he wasn't "really playing for an advantage" until move 23.

But this is certainly a bid for more than the equality he could claim after the routine 18...♕d7 and 19...♖d8.

19 ♘e3

Earlier ...b5 was hazardous in view of ♘a5.

But here 19 ♘a5 ♕d4+ costs a pawn with little hope of compensation.

19 ... ♗d6!

191

Both players have good diagonals for their king bishop. The huge difference is Black's has a target at h2.

Nevertheless, play would be roughly balanced after 20 ♘e4 ♗e5 21 b4! cxb4 22 axb4 ♘f4, for example.

20 ♘cd5?

Topalov mistakenly thought trading a pair of knights would open up chances for his bishop on the e4-g8 diagonal and for his remaining knight, on f5.

But it is Black's d6-bishop that is benefitting the most.

For instance, 20...♗c6 21 ♘xf6+? ♖xf6 22 ♗xc6 and now 22...♗xh2+ 23 ♔xh2 ♕d6+ is good.

But 22...♗f4! 23 ♗f2 ♘d4 is close to a win.

20 ... ♘xd5

21 ♗xd5

Black would be clearly superior after 21 ♘xd5 ♗c6 22 e4 ♗xd5 23 exd5 ♘d4 and ...f5.

21 ... ♗f7

22 ♘f5 ♗e5

Black's advantage is manifest. He threatens 23...♗xb2 and prepares ...♘d4.

23 ♕d2?

"I failed to find the moment when I should switch to playing for a draw," Topalov said after the game. This seemed like the best moment.

For example, 23 ♗c3 ♗xc3 24 bxc3 would eliminate Black's best minor piece and deny him ...♘d4.

Then 24...g6! 25 ♘e3 ♕d6 26 ♕e1 and ♕f2 may be defensible.

23 ... ♘d4!

The trade of another pair of minor pieces will reveal a pawn structure that is pockmarked with White weaknesses (h2, g4 and soon on d3).

Caruana said he was surprised to discover he "had an enormous advantage almost out of nowhere."

24   ♗xf7+

The last good defensive stab was probably 24 e3 ♗xd5 25 exd4.

Topalov would get some piece activity for his lost pawn after 25...cxd4 26 ♖c5 and ♗g3.

24   ...   ♖xf7

He would have none after 25 ♘xd4 ♕xd4+.

25   ♖d1   ♘xf5

26   gxf5   ♕d4+

27   ♗f2   ♕g4+

Black's advantage dwindles after 27...♕xb2? 28 ♕xb2 ♗xb2 29 ♗xc5.

28   ♔h1

It would all but disappear after 28...♕xf5? 29 ♗xc5.

And attacking h2 with 28...♕h3 29 ♗g1 is not impressive.

Caruana seeks a third weakness.

28   ...   c4!

He needed only about a minute for this, probably because he had seen how strong it was at least two moves earlier.

It will expose either the d3-pawn (29 e4 ♖d7) or the b2-pawn (after dxc4/...bxc4). It also takes ♗xc5 off the table.

29   ♕c2

The win would become elementary after 29 d4 ♕e4+ 30 ♔g1 ♖d7.

29   ...   ♖e8!

Now if Black gets to play ...♕xf5, the reply ♗xa7 will not attack the b8-rook.

193

But there is a more important point: Black sets up ...♖xe2.

He threatens, for example, 30...♕h5 31 ♗g1 ♗xh2! 32 ♗xh2 ♖xe2 and wins.

30 dxc4

White was lost in the longer run after 30 ♖g1 ♕xf5 31 ♗g3 ♗xg3 32 ♖xg3 ♖d7.

39 ... ♕h5!

Not 30...bxc4? 31 ♖g1, when White is alive.

31 h4 ♕g4

32 ♕d3

White cannot allow 32...♕h3+.

He would be mated after 32 ♖d3 ♕e4+ 33 ♔g1 bxc4 34 ♖d2? ♕g4+.

32 ... bxc4

The endgame would be a routine win, 33 ♕f3 ♕xf3+ 34 exf3 ♗xb2 and ...c3.

33 ♕e3 ♖fe7

34 b3 ♗b2

35 White resigns.

The c-pawn again wins after 35 ♕g3 ♕xg3 and 36...c3.

26
A Second Among Equals

International chess looked like a monarchy during the reign of Garry Kasparov. After he lost the championship title, there came an interregnum. It was a period of "first among equals," when the world champion seemed to be the best player in title only.

Furthermore, the identity of the equals changed every year or two. As 2012 began, former champ Vladimir Kramnik acknowledged that Magnus Carlsen was marginally ahead of him and two others, Levon Aronian and Vishy Anand. (Anand was the reigning world champion.)

What happened in the next two years was the margin separating Carlsen from the pack grew substantially. At the same time, a new group formed. Each could be considered "second among equals." The 2014 Sinquefield Cup left no doubt that Caruana had become a member of the club.

Magnus Carlsen – Caruana
Sinquefield Cup, St. Louis 2014
Bishop's Opening (C24)

1	e4	e5
2	♗c4	

This is the first Bishop's Opening played by Carlsen that you will find in many databases.

2	...	♘f6
3	d3	c6
4	♘f3	d5
5	♗b3	♗b4+

Elite players meet so often that they have theoretical rematches. After all, there are just so many good openings worth playing.

When Carlsen and Caruana repeated these moves at Stavanger 2018, the world champion varied with 6 ♗d2.

Caruana achieved easy equality after 6...♗xd2+ 7 ♕xd2 a5 and then 8 c3 ♘bd7 9 exd5 cxd5.

Caruana also uses the Bishop's Opening as White because, well, there are just so many good openings worth playing.

When he had to deal with 6...♗xd2+ 7 ♕xd2 a5 his novel solution was 8 ♘c3.

This looks modest but it was an offer of the bishop, 8...d4 9 ♘e2 so that 9...a4 10 ♗xf7+! ♔xf7 11 ♘xe5+.

6	c3	♗d6

The point of Black's fifth move was to prompt c2-c3 so that a knight on c3 cannot exert pressure on the center.

In contrast, the immediate 5...♗d6 can lead to 6 exd5 cxd5 or 6 ♘c3, as in Game 4.

7	♗g5

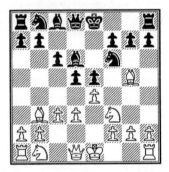

A base strategy for White is to force a change in the pawn structure, with ...dxe4 or ...d4.

Since ♘c3 is no longer possible, Carlsen's pinning move is his most ambitious option.

7	...	dxe4
8	dxe4	

Carlsen has a predilection for ♗g5 in 1 e4 e5 openings, according to Anish Giri.

Giri indicated this is often an error.

8	...	h6

Caruana points out one reason why it can be.

After 9 ♗e3 White's pieces get into a traffic jam, following 9...♕e7 10 0-0 0-0 11 ♘bd2 ♘g4! and ...♘xe3.

9	♗h4	♕e7

Black threatens 10...g5 11 ♗g3 ♘xe4 and also hints at queenside castling, along with ...♘bd7-f8-g6.

10	♘bd2	♘bd7

Caruana couldn't understand why Carlsen was playing quickly. His moves didn't even hint at an advantage, e.g. 11 0-0 ♗c7 and 12...♘c5.

11	♗g3	♗c7
12	0-0	

If Carlsen had entertained thoughts of queenside castling earlier they would be dispelled by 12 ♕e2 ♘h5.

Black would be comfortably superior after 13 0-0-0? ♘c5 14 ♗c2 a5.

12	...	♘h5!

On-line spectators may have been confused by Carlsen's earlier play. But now they knew he had botched it.

Black will enjoy a two-bishop advantage after, for example, 13 ♘c4 ♘xg3 14 hxg3 ♘f6 15 ♕e2 0-0.

Caruana suspected Carlsen had miscalculated, thinking 12...♘h5 would lose a pawn after 13 ♘xe5 and ♕xh5.

This overlooks a common tactic in similar positions – 13...♘xe5 14 ♕xh5 ♗g4! and wins (15 ♕h4 g5 or 15 ♗xf7+ ♔f8).

13 h3?

Since ...♘xg3 is coming, Carlsen hit upon the idea of recapturing with the f-pawn so that f7 becomes a target.

But there was a better way, 13 ♘h4! and then 13...♘xg3 14 fxg3.

Once Black avoids 14...0-0? 15 ♘g6 he would be positionally better (14...♘f6 15 h3 ♗d7 or 15...♗e6) but not as well off as in the game.

13 ... ♘xg3

14 fxg3

Having "the two bishops" is a distinct – but potential – advantage.

Caruana could have waited for his Bs to appreciate slowly, after 14...0-0 (15 ♘h4 ♕g5).

This was Anatoly Karpov's instructive policy in a game that began with a very different opening, 1 d4 ♘f6 2 c4 e6 3 ♘f3 b6 4 ♗f4 ♗b7 5 e3 ♗e7 6 ♘c3 ♘h5 7 ♗g3 d6 8 ♗d3 ♘d7 9 0-0 g6.

His opponent, Boris Spassky, hoped for play on the f-file after 10 h3 ♘xg3 11 fxg3.

Karpov responded cautiously, 11...0-0 12 ♖c1 ♗f6 13 ♖c2 ♗g7 14 ♖cf2 ♕e7.

The game progressed slowly, 15 ♔h2 a6 16 ♕e2 ♖ae8 17 ♗b1 c6 18 a3 f5, and only became a positional wipeout after 19 e4 c5 20 exf5 exf5 21 ♕xe7 ♖xe7 (Montreal 1979).

14 ... ♘c5!

"I was already playing for the maximum," Caruana said.

197

He admitted afterward that making this move quickly was "a bit careless" because he knew Carlsen would probably sacrifice.

15 ♗xf7+!

The best practical choice. White has no tactical chances to compensate him after 15 ♘h4 ♘xb3 16 axb3 g6.

Or after 15 ♗c2 0-0 16 ♕e2 a5 17 a4 b6 and ...♗a6.

15 ... ♔xf7

Carlsen's sacrifice "may not have been totally correct," Caruana told Slate.com. "But it turned the game into a very complicated one, almost immediately."

At first, he had the easier decisions to make: Not 15...♕xf7?? 16 ♘xe5 because of 16...♕e6 17 ♕h5+ and wins.

16 ♘xe5+

Since this game was quickly analyzed the world over, Magnus fans asked their computers to find improvements for White.

They found 16 ♘h4+ ♔g8 17 ♘g6 so that 17...♕g5 leads to 18 ♖f8+ ♔h7 19 ♖xh8+ ♔xg6.

This resembles what could have happened in the game. But in the 16 ♘h4+ version there is a Black pawn still on e5 – and the difference makes 20 ♕f1! strong.

White would threaten 21 ♘f3 and 22 ♘h4+.

He would be holding after 20...♕xd2 21 ♖xc8! because of the threat of ♕f5 mate.

But in the game – with the e5-pawn gone from the board -- this would fail because of 21...♕e3+! 22 ♔h2 ♕xg3+ or 22 ♔h1 ♘xe4.

It was a brilliant discovery but...

Instead of 17...♕g5? Black could give up his queen with 17...♕d6 or 17...♕d8 and 18 ♖f8+ ♕xf8 19 ♘xf8 ♔xf8 with good winning chances.

If the e5-pawn was gone, this fails to 20 ♕h5! and ♕xc5+ or ♖f1+.

16 ... ♔g8

17 ♘g6 ♕g5!

18 ♖f8+ ♔h7

Caruana expected 19 ♖xh8+ ♔xg6 20 ♘f3 and then 20...♕xg3 21 ♕c2.

Then White would threaten 22 ℤxc8! ℤxc8 23 e5+ and wins.

But Caruana had foreseen how 21...♗g4!! 22 ℤxa8? ♗xf3 wins for him.

As often happens in deep-dive calculation, the key idea (...♗g4!) stayed with him.

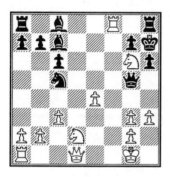

19   ♘xh8!

"A big shock for me," Caruana said. He thought 28 minutes.

It was well spent because there are at least five tempting responses.

The first, 19...♕xg3, is met by 20 ♘f1 when White's king is safe and chances are suddenly in balance.

Candidate number two is 19...♗xh3. It virtually forces 20 ℤxa8.

Then 20...♕xg3?? 21 ♕f3 sputters to a loss.

Black must take a perpetual check instead with 20...♕e3+!

21 ♔f1 ♗xg2+! 22 ♔xg2 ♕xg3+ 23 ♔f1 ♕h3+.

Candidate number three, 19...♘d7, was more devious.

The rook would drop after 20 ℤe8 ♘f6 21 ℤf8?? ♕c5+ and ...♕xf8.

But 20 ℤf7, among others, gets sticky after 20...♕xg3 21 e5! opens the diagonal leading to Black's king.

What might have been

Black is not winning after 21...♔xh8 22 ♘f3 ♘xe5 23 ℤf8+ ♔h7 24 ♘xe5 and ♕c2+.

19   ...   ♗g4!

199

Caruana had noticed the forcing nature of ...♗g4 when calculating 19 ♖xh8+.

It could be used in a different sequence, 19...♕e3+! 20 ♔h1 ♗g4!.

This looked good even though he would be two pawns down after 21 ♕xg4 ♖xf8 22 ♘g6 ♖f7.

For example, 23 ♘f3? ♘xe4 or 23 ♘f1 ♕g5.

Is this better than what happens in the game?

That isn't clear even years after the game. One benefit of the immediate 19...♗g4! is that 20 ♕xg4? ♕xg4 21 hxg4 ♖xf8 is an easy win.

20   ♕f1

20   ...   ♘d3

Caruana counted on winning because he threatens 21...♕e3+ 22 ♔h1 ♕xg3.

He didn't need to examine 20...♗e2 because 21 ♕f5+ ♕xf5

22 ♖xf5 conjured up images of a Carlsen swindle (22...♔h8? 23 ♔f2 ♗a6 24 ♖xc5 ♗b6 25 b4).

But 22...♗b6! provides good winning chances, e.g. 23 ♔h2 ♖xh8 24 ♖e1 ♗a6 25 b3 ♖d8.

21   ♕xd3

Not mentioned in the players' post-mortem analysis were two superior defenses. One is 21 ♔h1 so that there is no check on the b6-g1 diagonal.

Then a magical-Magnus escape is possible, such as 21...♕e3? 22 ♘g6! ♔xg6? 23 ♕f7+ ♔h7 24 ♕g8+ ♔g6 25 ♕f7+ with perpetual check.

But Black would have another favorable pieces-vs.-rook endgame after 21...♖xf8! 22 ♕xf8 ♗e2 23 ♕f5+.

When he analyzed the game in *New In Chess*, Caruana pointed out another defensive try, 21 ♘g6.

That transposes into the 21 ♔h1 perpetual check line after 21...♕e3+ 22 ♔h1 ♔xg6? 23 ♕f7+.

This would have forced Caruana to search for a win after 22...♕xg3 23 e5!.

He admitted that with "accurate" moves, Carlsen would probably have held a draw, with 23...♖xf8 24 ♘xf8+ ♔g8 25 ♘g6 ♘f2+ 26 ♔g1 ♘xh3+ 27 ♔h1.

21 ... ♖xf8

22 hxg4 ♕xg4?

Despite all the deserved attention to this game, this move has evaded criticism.

More accurate is 22...♔xh8! since White would have nothing better than transposing into the game with 23 ♘f3 ♕xg4.

For example, 23 ♘b3? fails to 23...♗b6+ 24 ♘d4 c5.

23 ♘f3?

The difference is 23 ♘b3! allows White to resist with ♖f1.

For instance, 23...♗b6+ 24 ♘d4 c5 25 ♖f1 ♖xf1+ 26 ♔xf1 cxd4 27 ♘f7!.

23 ... ♕xg3

Carlsen still had a few tactical torches to juggle. The best is making the e-pawn a queenable weapon.

The right way was 24 ♘f7! ♖xf7 25 e5+ so that 25...♔h8? 26 e6! ♖e7 27 ♖e1 with a likely draw.

Better is 25...g6 or 25...♕g6. But Carlsen has drawn positions that were much worse than that.

24 e5+?

"He makes mistakes, he's just human," Caruana said after he beat Carlsen earlier in 2014 at the Gashimov Memorial. "He makes fewer mistakes, but he makes them."

24 ... ♔xh8

25 e6 ♗b6+

26 ♔h1

26 ... ♕g4!

The weakness of the e6-pawn, combined with his superior minor piece, is enough to win.

He can also use the threat of a mating net. For example, 27 e7 ♖e8 28 ♖e1 ♕h5+ 29 ♘h2 ♗c7 and now 30 ♕h3? ♖xe7! 31 ♕xh5 ♖xe1+.

Or 30 g3 ♕f7 31 ♕d7 ♗xg3 and 31 ♕e3 ♕d5+.

27   ♕d6

Caruana called this "a great move" and it cost him 12 minutes to find a flaw.

He wouldn't have taken more than a few seconds to find 27 ♖e1? ♖xf3 28 ♕xf3 ♕h4+ and ...♕xe1+ mates

27   ...   ♖d8!

There was no more than perpetual check after 27...♖xf3 28 gxf3 or a mildly favorable ending after 27...♕h5+ 28 ♕h2.

Also, it would have been difficult to untangle after 27...♔g8 28 e7 ♖e8 29 ♖e1.

28   ♕e5   ♖d5!

The rook is more valuable as an attacker (...♖h5+) than as a means of stopping the e-pawn.

29   ♕b8+   ♔h7

30   e7   ♕h5+

31   ♘h2?

Carlsen "probably hallucinated something," Caruana wrote.

Yes, in two ways. First, he expected 31...♖e5 32 g4!.

31   ...   ♖d1+

Second, he saw this possibility in his earlier calculations but forgot about it when he saw how 31 ♕h2 ♕e8 would threaten ...♖h5 and win the e-pawn.

32   ♖xd1   ♕xd1+

33   ♘f1   ♕xf1+

34   ♔h2   ♕g1+

35   White resigns.

"It turns out that I was better prepared for the complications," Caruana told Slate.com. "I outplayed him."

27
Home Work

Vladimir Chuchelov attributed much of Fabiano's historic streak to home preparation. "Three games were essentially won in the opening," his second said. He cited Caruana's games with White against Maxime Vachier-Lagrave, Veselin Topalov and Levon Aronian. But what exactly does winning a game at home mean? There are several answers.

For example, his second-round game with MVL began:

1 e4 c6 2 d4 d5 3 e5 ♗f5 4 ♘f3 e6 5 ♗e2 c5 6 ♗e3 ♕b6 7 ♘c3 ♘c6 8 0-0 ♕xb2 9 ♕e1 cxd4 10 ♗xd4 ♘xd4 11 ♘xd4 ♗b4 12 ♘db5 ♗a5 13 ♖b1 ♕xc2 14 ♖c1 ♕b2 15 g4 ♗g6 16 f4 ♗e4 17 ♖f2.

Black "was unlucky," Caruana said. He had prepared these moves months before, for another opponent, but didn't get to use them.

When MVL chose **17...♘h6,** he remembered that his analysis had concluded 17...♔f8 was

necessary. He found the refutation, **18 ♗d3 ♕b4 19 ♖b1 ♕c5** *and then* **20 ♘xe4! dxe4 21 ♕xa5.** *In effect, it took less than half an hour of clock time to win.*

Four rounds later, Veselin Topalov was also unlucky. He also went into an opening Caruana had prepared for a different opponent. Caruana made his moves at blitz speed, including his novelty at move 13. Topalov was unnerved, moved quickly and was soon lost.

Caruana's innovations were far from crushing. White's advantage in the MVL game would have been minimal after 17...♔f8 and he would have had no more than equality if Topalov had found the proper 15th move. Caruana's victory in the third game was built on a much more sophisticated basis.

203

Caruana – Levon Aronian
Sinquefield Cup, St. Louis 2014
Ruy Lopez,
Anti-Marshall Variation (C84)

1	e4	e5
2	♘f3	♘c6
3	♗b5	a6
4	♗a4	♘f6
5	0-0	♗e7
6	d3	

The first rule-of-Ruy says that when White defends his e-pawn he is threatening ♗xc6 and ♘xe5. That is when Black most often plays ...b5.

6	...	b5

But here a valid alternative is 6...d6, as in Game 60.

7	♗b3	0-0
8	♘c3	d6

The second Ruy rule: When Black defends his e-pawn, he makes a positional threat to gain the two bishops with ...♘a5xb3.

The usual White response after 7...d6 is to create an escape route for his bishop at c2 with 8 c3.

9	a3	

But with his knight on c3, this move became a focus of attention. White gets little from 9 ♘d5 ♘a5!.

9	...	♘a5

Aronian later became the world's leading proponent of 9...♗g4 followed by ...♘d4. He drew fairly easily with Caruana at London 2017 after 10 ♗e3 ♘d4 11 ♗xd4 exd4.

10	♗a2	♗e6

But Aronian was also the most experienced GM on the Black side of this position. His opponents had limited success with 11 b4 ♗xa2 12 ♖xa2 ♘c6.

11	♗xe6	

This challenges the conventional wisdom that says ♗xe6 is harmless in various narratives of the Giuoco Piano and Ruy Lopez.

White cannot occupy d5 with a knight after ...fxe6, while Black opens lines for his f8-rook and potentially the queen (...♛e8).

11	...	fxe6
12	b4	♘c6
13	♗d2	

White's options include ♘e2 followed by either c2-c4 or a2-a4.

But if he removes his knight from the queenside, he hands Black another source of counterplay, ...a5.

For instance, 13 ♘e2 d5 14 ♘g3 a5 is something White should avoid.

The pawn structure created by 11 ♗xe6 gave Black a choice of four basic policies:

(a) *Leaving the pawn structure intact.* He could pursue a kingside plan such as 13...♕e8 and ...♘h5/ ...♕g6.

(b) *Change it by trading knights with 13...♘d4.* His pieces would be freed a bit by 13...♘d4 14 ♘xd4 exd4 15 ♘e2 c5. This would expose his queenside to greater pressure after 16 a4 and ♕b1-b3.

(c) *Attack the queenside.* Thanks to 13 ♗d2, White can respond to 13...♕d7 14 ♘e2 a5 with 15 c3. Then Black can add 15...d5 into the mix, with uncertain prospects.

13 ... d5

Aronian chooses (d), *Gain space with this move,* followed by ...♕d6 or ...♗d6 and potentially ...d4/...a5.

14 ♖e1

White will avoid exd5 because it undoubles the Black pawns.

Black will be reluctant to make his doubleton permanent with ...dxe4.

Of course, tactics would make either of these irrevocable steps favorable.

With his rook on e1, White may be able to win the e5-pawn after exd5.

14 ... ♕d6

But the most likely change in the structure is ....d4. It can help Black on either wing.

For example, 14...d4 15 ♘e2 ♗d6 16 ♘g3? ♕e7 allows him to go for 17...a5.

Or he can take aim at the kingside with ...♘d7 and ...♖f6, or even a ...♖xf3 sacrifice.

But the structure would not be not finished changing after ...d4. With 16 c3!, instead of 16 ♘g3?, White would get favorable play on the c-file.

15 ♘a2

Caruana's pre-game preparation was built on this strange move.

It is not a tactical TN as in the MVL and Topalov games. It is partly strategic – eyeing a ♘c1-b3 maneuver – and prophylactic. It anticipates ...d4 as well as ...♘d7 followed by ...♘d4!.

15 ... ♘d7

Black might be over-extended on the queenside if he jumps into 15...a5 16 ♘c3! and 16...axb4 17 ♘xb5.

In the background are White's latent tactics directed at the e5-pawn.

For example, 16...♖fb8 17 exd5! exd5 18 bxa5 ♖xa5 19 ♘xe5!.

Then 19...♘xe5 20 ♗f4 ♘fd7 21 d4.

16 ♕e2

This kind of position rewards patience.

Forcing matters, such as with 16...♗f6 17 c4?, would turn out badly after 17...dxc4 18 dxc4 ♘d4!, when Black stands splendidly.

16 ... d4

By sealing the center Black ends tactics based on exd5/♘xe5. He frees his d7-knight for queenside duty (...♘b6-a4) and also makes ...a5 more viable.

17 ♖eb1!

Caruana keeps his other rook at a1 in case the a-file is opened.

After 17 ♖ab1 ♖fb8 and 18...a5 Black would have the upper hand following 19 bxa5 ♘xa5 or 19...♕xa3.

17 ... ♘b6

In the post-mortem, both players indicated Black must have missed a major improvement.

At first Caruana felt 17...a5 was a possibility.

For example, 18 bxa5 ♘xa5 19 ♖xb5 ♕xa3.

But later he concluded 20 ♕d1, with its threat of 21 ♘b4, would be quite good for White.

18 ♘c1 ♘a4
19 ♘b3

The Black knight on a4 is more imposing than the White knight on b3. Yet after the game, it seemed clear White was slowly winning.

One reason is the possibility of ♘a5!, followed by an exchange of knights, would allow ♘xe5.

19 ... ♖f7

Aronian's post-game candidates for improvement included 19...♘c3.

He said 20 ♗xc3 dxc3 21 ♕e3 ♖ad8 "looked very exciting to me" (21 ♕e1 ♘d4).

Some computers prefer 21 ♖d1, to threaten 22 d4.

After 21...♘d4 22 ♘fxd4 exd4 23 e5 ♕d5 they slightly favor the good knight over the bad bishop.

Instead, he misjudged how a shift of his rooks would improve his chances for a later ...♘c3.

20 ♖c1 ♖d8

21 ♘g5 ♖f6

"Unpleasant" is a term Caruana often uses in his annotations. He means a position that is not provably inferior but would be unless some "best" moves are played.

In his *New In Chess* notes he said 21...♗xg5 22 ♗xg5 ♖df8 23 ♖f1 would be "unpleasant" for Black.

White can prepare c2-c3 and ♗d2 and ♖ac1. Or he could go for a kingside try of g2-g3, ♔g2 and h2-h4-h5.

22 ♕h5

22 ... h6?

"Definitely a mistake," Caruana said immediately after the game (but not in his published notes).

He had looked at 22...♖h6 during the game and believed 23 ♕f7+ ♔h8 24 ♕f3 was somewhat favorable.

Computers recommend 24 h4 instead, because of 24...♗xg5 25 hxg5 ♖f8 26 ♕xf8+ ♕xf8

207

27 gxh6. But 24...♕d7, threatening
...♖f8, is not as clear.

23	♘f3	♖df8
24	♖f1	♖8f7
25	♖ae1	♗f8

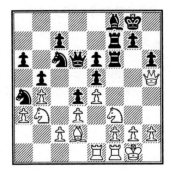

26 h3!

White's queen has a powerful
post on h5 and long-term pressure
on the e5-pawn.

But ♘h2-g4! is the immediate
threat.

It would likely be enough to win
after, say, 26...♗e7 27 ♘h2 ♔h7
28 ♘g4.

A key point is that 28...♖f5!
29 exf5 ♖xf5 30 ♕e8 ♖f8 does
not trap the queen because of
31 ♘f6+! (31...♗xf6 32 ♕h5).

26	...	g6
27	♕h4	♕e7

Now 28 ♘h2 ♖xf2! would
waste White's superiority.

28 ♕g3

He returns to the tactical idea
that has been dormant for more
than a dozen moves – a trade of
knights (♘a5) to win the e5-pawn.

28	...	♗g7

Aronian is relying on tactics
now. For example, 29 ♘xe5?
♘xe5 30 ♖xe5 ♖xf2, when the
queen is attacked.

He also thought he might
sacrifice an Exchange to blockade
the kingside, such as with 29 ♘h2
♔h7 30 ♘g4 ♖f4 31 ♗xf4 exf4
32 ♕f3 e5.

To win, White would need to
open the position for his rooks,
such as by a well-prepared g2-g3
or c2-c3, perhaps after a trade of
knights.

But Caruana found a much
simpler idea.

29	♘a5	♘xa5
30	♘xe5!	

Another version of the Exchange sacrifice is 30 bxa5 ♖xf3! 31 gxf3 ♔h7.

White would be much better but his advantage can slip away after 32 f4 exf4 33 ♗xf4 e5 and ...♗f6, for example.

30 ... ♘b7

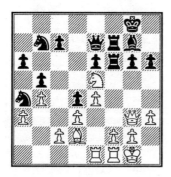

The first line that many computers spit out is 31 ♘xf7? ♕xf7.

But that leaves White without a clear-cut plan.

31 ♘xg6

Caruana's idea is simply to push his kingside pawns.

This works after 31...♕e8 32 e5 or 31...♖xg6 32 ♕xg6 ♕f6 33 ♕g4.

"This sacrifice was a no-brainer," he wrote.

That doesn't mean he knew he had a forced win. Rather, he knew it would be very difficult for Aronian to defend.

31 ... ♕d8

32 e5

A tad better than 32 ♘e5 (32...♖f8 33 ♘g4).

32 ... ♖f5

33 f4

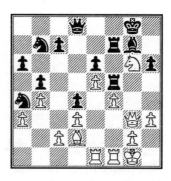

33 ... c5

In the post-mortem, Caruana said it was finally time for 33...♘c3.

Winning would be harder if he gave up his bishop, 34 ♗xc3, or allowed an Exchange sacrifice (34 ♘h4 ♖h5 35 ♘f3 ♖hf5 36 ♕f2 ♖xf4, for example).

34 ♘h4 ♖h5

35 ♘f3

The clumsy h5-rook is threatened by ♕g6.

35 ... ♔h7?

Aronian, still believing he had drawing chances in the post-mortem, said 35...♕e8 would be "very unclear."

But 36 bxc5 and 37 ♘xd4 (or 36 ♕g4 first) are virtually winning.

36	♕g4!	♖hf5
37	♘h4	♔h8
38	♘xf5	♖xf5
39	♕g6	

44	f7	♖e7
45	♖f6!	♘b6
46	♗xh6	♘d7
47	♖ef1!	cxb4

Of course, 47...♘xf6 48 ♗xf8 ♖xf7 49 ♖xf6.

48	axb4	♗xh6
49	♖xh6+	♔g7
50	♖h5	resigns.

In view of 50...♘d8 51 ♖g5+ ♔f8 52 ♖g8 mate or 51...♔h6 52 f8(♕)+ ♘xf8 53 ♖g8.

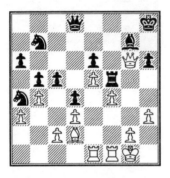

There is no defense to 40 g4 and 41 f5.

39	...	♕e7
40	g4	♖f8
41	f5	♕e8

The endgame is quite lost, but so was 41...exf5 42 ♖xf5 or 42 ♗xh6 or 42 gxf5.

| 42 | ♕xe8 | ♖xe8 |
| 43 | f6 | ♗f8 |

White has a variety of winning plans and chooses to win the h6-pawn and invade with rooks.

When Deadspin asked Caruana in 2018 to name the best game of his career, he replied: "That's a tough question. There are a lot of games which I've really enjoyed." But he only cited this game. "I was really proud of that game."

28
New/Old Rival

One round after that, Caruana faced his oldest rival – although Hikaru Nakamura would not admit they had become rivals. When they first met, in New York tournaments, "Naka" was a grandmaster rated 400 points above Caruana. Here is one of their first games.

Caruana – Hikaru Nakamura, New York Masters, May 2004
1 e4 c5 2 ♘f3 d6 3 d4 cxd4 4 ♕xd4 a6 5 ♗e3 ♘c6 6 ♕b6!? ♕xb6 7 ♗xb6 ♘f6 8 ♘c3 e6 9 0-0-0 ♗e7 10 h3 0-0 11 ♗c4 ♗d7 12 ♖he1 ♖fc8 13 ♗b3 ♗e8! (with the idea of 14...♘d7 15 ♗e3 b5) 14 ♘a4 ♘b4 15 ♔b1 d5! 16 ♗d4? ♗xa4 17 ♗xa4 ♘xe4 and Black won.

But when Fabiano broke 2600 in early 2008, Nakamura was less than 100 points ahead of him. The gap had virtually disappeared in the next four years. Theirs was the closest rivalry among US players since Bobby Fischer challenged Samuel Reshevsky nearly 60 years before.

Hikaru Nakamura – Caruana
Sinquefield Cup, St. Louis 2014
Slav Defense (D14)

1	d4	d5
2	c4	c6
3	♘f3	♘f6
4	♘bd2	

Question: Is this move –

(a) a way to avoid the main lines of 4 ♘c3 dxc4 and 4...e6?

(b) a bit of transpositional trickery?

(c) or a suggestion that White's knight is misplaced on c3 in a Slav Defense?

The best answer is (d) – all of the above.

White would sidestep the Meran Variation and a lot of other book-filling analysis after 4...e6 5 e3 ♘bd7 6 ♗d3.

His knight is often misplaced on c3 but would stand well after 4...dxc4 5 ♘xc4.

Black can get in trouble quickly -- 5...♗f5 6 ♕b3 ♕c8 (6...♕c7 7 ♗f4!) and now 7 ♘g5 threatens 8 ♘xf7! ♔xf7? 9 ♘d6+ as well as 8 ♘e5.

4   ...   ♗f5

The most evident drawback to 4 ♘bd2 is White's lack of pressure on d5.

This allows Black to develop his c8-bishop without incurring the problems that 4 ♘c3 ♗f5 does (after 5 cxd5 cxd6 ♕b3!).

5   ♘h4

But ...♗f5 also has a drawback. The bishop cannot easily avoid capture.

It can retreat, 5...♗c8!?. Then 6 e3 e6 7 ♘hf3! ♘bd7 transposes into a Semi-Slav line that has been out of fashion since Mikhail Tchigorin's heyday.

There have even been draws after 6 ♘hf3 ♗f5 7 ♘h4 ♗c8.

5   ...   ♗e4

6   f3   ♗g6

This is considered Black's best way of meeting 5 ♘h4.

The extra move f2-f3 (compared with 5...♗g6) is usually more loosening than useful.

In contrast, 5...♗g4 6 h3 ♗h5 7 g4! is helpful after 7...♗g6 8 ♘xg6 and 9 ♗g2.

7   e3   e6

8   g3

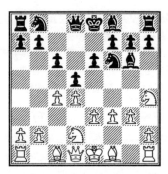

Another difference: The addition of f2-f3 means ♘xg6/ ...hxg6 will give Black tactical chances directed at g3 and h2.

After 8 ♘xg6 hxg6 9 ♕c2? Black can even play 9...♘h5 and threaten 10...♘g3!. White's best defense then is the feeble 10 ♖g1.

8   ...   ♗e7

9   a3   ♘bd7

Now 10 ♗g2? ♗d3! would expose White's ♘h4 plan as a flop.

Nakamura intended 8 g3 primarily as a means of safeguarding his kingside, not necessarily to prepare ♗g2.

10   cxd5

This asks Black to choose between 10...cxd5 – when he would seek middlegame play from ...e5 – and 10...exd5, when he would be seeking it from ...c5.

Note that Nakamura waited, with the useful 9 a3, for Black to commit one of his pieces, before cxd5.

If Naka had played 9 cxd5, Caruana would know that 9...cxd5! is best because then he can develop his b8-knight on the superior c6-square.

10 ...   cxd5

There is nothing wrong with 10...exd5. Then 11 ♘xg6 and 12 ♗g2 is a dead-even way to approach the middlegame.

11   ♘xg6   hxg6

12   ♗d3

With his bishop on d3 there are chances for a kingside attack, after 12...0-0 13 f4 and the advance of the g- or h-pawn.

If Black had recaptured 10...exd5, he would generate serious counterplay from 13...c5!.

12 ...   e5!

13   0-0

Note that 13 dxe5 ♘xe5 14 ♗b5+ ♘c6 is splendid for Black.

But 14...♔f8 is even better. Black's h8-rook is already well developed thanks to 11...hxg6. And his king would be quite safe on f8.

A Black advantage would become evident after, for example, 15 0-0 ♕b6 16 ♕e2 d4 17 exd4 ♕xd4+ 19 ♔-moves a6!.

13 ...   0-0

There was no benefit for either player to end the center tension.

After 13...exd4? 14 exd4 White can continue smoothly with f3-f4 and ♘f3-e5, for example.

By keeping the tension with 13...0-0, Black could meet 14 f4 with 14...e4! 15 ♗e2 ♖c8 and potentially ...♘b6-c4.

14   ♕b3!

If White ends the tension, 14 dxe5 ♘xe5 15 ♘b3, he gets a knight outpost on d4.

But 15...♖c8 16 ♘d4 ♗c5 and ...♕b6/...♖fe8 is an easier position for Black to play than White.

14 ...   ♕c8

This move looks routine. But it cost Black 28 minutes, his longest think of the game. Why?

For a calculator like Caruana, the answer likely lies in 14...a6.

It would not be hard to evaluate 15...b5! followed by ...♕b6 as good for him.

But he would have to foresee whether 15 ♕xb7 ♗c5 or 15...exd4 16 exd4 ♗c5 was playable.

Both are, e.g. 15...♗c5 16 dxc5? ♘xc5 17 ♕b4 ♘xd3 with the advantage, or 16 b4 ♗b6.

15 ♘b1!

He may have preferred 14...♕c8 because he expected to get an edge with ...♗d8-b6!.

But 15 ♘b1! allows White to pressure d5, e.g. 15...♗d8 16 ♘c3.

15 ...   exd4

White would have the easier middlegame after 15...e4? 16 fxe4 dxe4 17 ♗c2 and ♘c3.

16 exd4   ♘b8

Or after 16...a6 17 ♘c3 ♕c6 18 ♗g5 and ♖ac1.

17 ♘c3   ♘c6

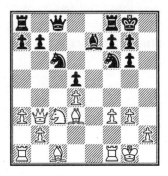

A roughly balanced middlegame begins.

White has the two bishops. But the "two bees" have an inherent disadvantage that you learn when you are a beginner and soon forget.

Unlike other pairs of minor pieces, they cannot attack or protect the same square.

Here the square that matters is d4. Black can attack the d-pawn with all three of his minor pieces. White can defend it with two.

18 ♗e3

White could resolve that problem by 18 ♘xd5 ♘xd5 19 ♕xd5.

Then 19...♖d8 20 ♕a2! is fine for him in view of the 21 ♗xg6 threat.

But 19...♞xd4!, based on 20 ♕xd4?? ♝c5, is stronger because Black's main threat is a kingside attack after 20...♖d8 and 21...♕h3!.

His position is preferable after 20 ♔g2 ♖d8 21 ♕a2 ♕c6 (22 ♝e4 ♕a6).

18 ... ♕d7

19 ♖ad1

Black's next decision is how to develop his rooks.

A stereotypical plan would be 19...♖ae8 and ...♝d8-b6, perhaps with ...♖e7 and ...♖fe8.

But Black will have no point of penetration for his rooks after ♝f2. Moreover, White can counter the bishop maneuver with ♞a4!.

19 ... ♖fd8

20 ♖fe1 ♞e8!

Instead, Black places a priority on reorganizing his minor pieces, with ...♞c7-e6 and ...♝f6.

There was no danger in 21 ♞a4 now because Black can afford the weakening 21...b6.

Then 22 ♝b5 or 22 ♝a6 can be met by ...♞c7.

21 ♝f2 ♞c7

The b7-pawn is untouchable (22 ♕xb7?? ♖ab8).

22 ♝f1 ♝f6

White is poised to meet ...♞e6 with ♝h3.

23 ♕a2?

Instead of shooting for b2-b4 with this move, he might have gone for 23 h4 with ♔h2 and ♝h3 to come.

23 ... g5!

Caruana discourages h2-h4 and f3-f4 and weighs an attack on the h-file with rooks after ...g6 and ...♔g7.

24 b4 g6

25 ♕d2 ♔g7

Black can meet 26 ♗e3 ♘e6 27 ♗h3 with 27...♘cxd4! because of ...♘xf3+.

26 b5   ♘e7

Earlier, Black might have been happy to cement this knight on c4 (26...♘a5).

But now ...♘e7 is stronger because it is part of a powerful ...♘f5/...♘e6 plan.

27 ♗e3

Nakamura has to choose between trading off his better bishop or taking the radical step of g3-g4.

27 ...   ♘e6

28 ♗h3

After 28 g4 Black could double on the c-file. But 28 ♗h3 was based on a bad idea.

28 ...   ♘f5

29 ♗xf5   gxf5

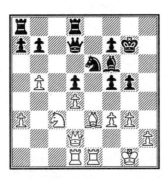

Black eyes ...f4!.

For example, 30 ♕d3 f4 31 ♗f2 fxg3 32 hxg3 ♖h8! is strong and 31 gxf4? gxf4 32 ♗f2 ♘g5 is winning.

30 f4?

Witnesses said Nakamura took six seconds to choose this.

It is the kind the bullet-chess king would ordinarily reject as positionally dreadful.

Instead, 30 ♘e2! would have been good preparation for ♕d3.

He would still be in trouble after 30...♕xb5 31 ♕c2! or 30...♖h8 31 ♕d3 ♘c7 32 ♘c3 but hardly lost.

30 ...   g4!

31 ♕d3   ♖ac8

32 ♖c1   ♖c4

Now on 33 ♕xf5 ♘xd4 Black would be winning with ...♘b3 or ...♘f3+ after a trade of queens.

33 ♘e2   ♘c7

34 ♘c3

Naka fans had been hoping for a liquidation to an endgame in which a Black error or two would spoil the win.

That might happen, for instance, after 34 ♖xc4 dxc4 35 ♕xc4

♘xb5 36 a4 ♘xd4 37 ♘xd4 ♗xd4
38 ♗xd4+ ♕xd4 39 ♕xd4+ ♖xd4
40 a5 followed by ♖b1 or ♖e5.

But this is wishful calculating.
Black can keep wood on with
36...♘d6 and penetrate on the
c- or e-file.

A sample line is 37 ♕b3 ♖c8
38 ♖c1 ♖e8! 39 ♖c2 ♕e7 40 ♗f2
♕e4 and White is on the cusp of
zugzwang.

| 34 | ... | ♖c8 |

35   h3!

Naka knows when to go
desperate. Without this, Black
would have won with ...♘e8 and
....♗d8-a5 or ...♘d6-e4.

35	...	gxh3
36	♔h2	♘xb5
37	♘xb5	♕xb5
38	♔xh3	

Nakamura prepares ♕xf5. The
immediate 38 ♕xf5? gets mated
after 38...♕b2+ 39 ♔xh3 ♖h8+
40 ♔g4 ♕g2!.

38	...	♕d7
39	♔g2	b5
40	♖b1	a6

Computers have the luxury of
pointing out how 40...♖c2+
41 ♗d2 ♖8c4 wins the d4-pawn.

But on the final move of a time
control it was not worth the drama
of trying 42 ♖e2 ♗xd4 43 ♖h1
and 44 g4.

| 41 | ♖bc1 | ♕e6 |

At move 40 Caruana received
30 more minutes for the rest of
the game, with a 30-second
increment.

He would have had less to think
about after 41...♖8c6! followed
by ...♕c8 or ...♕e6.

| 42 | ♗f2! | ♖xc1 |

The queen-for-two-rooks swap
wins.

But 42...♕e4+! was a slightly
better version (43 ♖xe4 fxe4 and
...♖xc1).

And 42...♕d7 was a conservative
winning alternative.

Caruana had spent five minutes
each on his last two moves.

| 43 | ♖xe6 | fxe6 |
| 44 | g4! | |

44 ...   fxg4?

"I felt that I had complicated the win quite a lot," Caruana admitted after the game – particularly when he realized he overlooked 44...♗h4! (45 ♗xh4 ♖8c3).

45   ♕e2   ♔f7

46   ♕d3

Caruana had nine minutes left to find a way to safeguard his king and was soon in another time scramble.

Neither 46...♖g8 47 f5! nor 46...g3 47 ♕h7+ ♔f8 48 ♔xg3 looked convincing.

46   ...   ♖1c2

47   ♕h7+   ♔e8

48   f5?

Streaks in sports are often extended thanks to what is remembered as accidents. This is one.

White would most likely have drawn after 48 ♔f1!.

For example, 48...♖8c3 makes 49 f5! playable (49...♖f3

50 ♕g8+ ♔d7 51 ♕xe6+ and ♕xf6).

48   ...   ♗xd4!

49   ♕g6+   ♔d8

50   ♕xe6

There were no more good checks. Caruana had only two minutes left. But with the increment he slowly shifted his king to queenside safety:

50...♖xf2+ 51 ♔g3 ♖c3+ 52 ♔xg4 ♖g2+ 53 ♔f4 ♖f2+ 54 ♔g4 ♔c7! 55 ♕e7+ ♔b6 56 ♕d8+ ♖c7 57 ♕xd5 ♗c5 58 ♕d8 ♔b7 59 f6 ♗xa3 60 ♕d5+ ♔b6 61 ♕d8 ♗c5 62 ♕b8+ ♖b7 63 ♕d8+ ♔a7 64 ♕d5 ♗b6 65 ♔g5 ♖c7 66 ♔g6 b4 67 ♕e6 ♗d4 68 White resigns.

Caruana's final score was 8½-1½ and a 3103 performance. Garry Kasparov's best-ever performance was 2881 and Anatoly Karpov's was 2899, according to Chessmetrics.

29
Energy Crisis

The reserve Candidate of the previous Grand Prix cycle tried again. He began with two consecutive GP tournaments, at Baku and Tashkent, separated by only one week. In its report on Baku, New In Chess called Caruana "the man who is most often named as Magnus Carlsen's next challenger."

But after leading for much of the Azeri tournament, Caruana ran short of energy. He needed at least one win in the final two rounds to protect his chances of reaching the 2016 Candidates tournament. Here is his next-to-last round.

Dominguez – Caruana
FIDE Grand Prix, Baku 2014
English Opening,
Symmetrical Variation (A36)

1	c4	c5
2	g3	g6
3	♗g2	♗g7
4	♘c3	♘c6
5	♖b1	

The Symmetrical Variation of the English often becomes a race to see who gets to push his b-pawn first.

This led to truly symmetrical middlegames in the 1970s after 5...♖b8 6 a3 a6 7 b4 cxb4 8 axb4 b5 9 cxb5 axb5 and even 10 ♘f3 ♘f6 11 0-0 0-0.

5	...	b6!?

In reversed form, 5 b3 and 6 ♗b2 was a favorite of Vasily Smyslov, who was seeking a trade of dark-squared bishops. It infrequently got him an opening advantage, just a playable middlegame.

In Caruana's version, Black will play ...d6, so that b2-b4xc5 is fairly harmless after ...dxc5.

6	a3	♗b7
7	b4	d6

8   ♗b2   e6

In the few previous GM games with Black's setup, Vladimir Lazarev of France preferred 8...♕d7 and ...♘e5 in order to trade the light squared bishops.

9   ♘b5   ♗xb2

10   ♖xb2

White's ninth move prepared d2-d4. But now we see the b5-knight is awkwardly placed: He has to calculate the consequences of ...a6 from now on.

10   ...   ♘ge7

It is remarkable how much trouble White can get into after ten moves of a "symmetrical variation." For instance, 11 ♘f3? ♘e5!.

After 12 d3 ♘xf3+ 13 ♗xf3 ♗xf3 14 exf3 Black will eventually sink his remaining knight onto d4.

Instead, White can prepare ♘f3 with 11 d3.

Then Black's options include 11...cxb4 12 axb4 d5! with a better endgame in sight after 13...dxc4 14 dxc4 ♕xd1+.

11   e3?

White's KN is not particularly well placed after 11 ♘h3. But Caruana felt it would lead to equal chances.

Besides 11...0-0, he would have the trick 11...♘a5 (12 bxa5 ♗xg2).

After a swap of bishops, 12 ♗xb7 ♘xb7 13 0-0 0-0 he can play for an advantage with 14 ♘f4 d5!.

Or after 14 d4 a6 15 ♘c3 cxb4 16 axb4 ♕c7 and 16 ♖xb4 ♘c6.

11   ...   0-0

Castling is a natural principled move you can play without calculating.

But Caruana began to crunch variations that might exploit the undefended g2 bishop.

He looked at 11...a6 12 ♘c3 ♘xb4 13 ♗xb7 and then 13...♘d3+ 14 ♔e2 ♘xb2 15 ♕b3 ♘xc4.

He saw that 16 ♗xa8? ♕xa8 was splendid for him (17 ♘f3 ♕xf3+! 18 ♔xf3 ♘xd2+).

But he gave up on the line when he concluded 16 ♕xc4 favors White after 16...d5 17 ♕d3.

220

He underestimated 17...♖a7 18 ♗xa6 0-0, or just 16...b5.

12   ♘f3

Black could still use diagonal tactics after 12 ♘e2?? ♘xb4! – because 13 ♗xb7 ♘d3+ 14 ♔f1 ♘xb2 15 ♕b3 a6 still works.

12   ...   ♘e5

13   d3   ♗xf3!

A decision nearly as counter-intuitive as Caruana's ...♗xc3 against Radoslaw Wojtaszek at Wijk aan Zee 2021. The logic is clearer this time:

Black should be better. But 13...♘xf3+ 14 ♗xf3 ♗xf3 15 ♕xf3 d5 16 0-0 is nothing much.

He needs a target to prove his superiority. The c4-pawn stands out.

14   ♗xf3   d5

Now 15 cxd5 ♘xd5! favors Black because of ...a6!.

15   ♗e2

The designated target would be exploited by 15 0-0 a6 16 ♘c3 dxc4!.

Then 17 ♗xa8 ♘xd3! gives Black two nice extra queenside pawns for the Exchange, after 18 ♖d2 ♕xa8 19 bxc5 ♘xc5, for example.

15   ...   d4

Another move that surprises.

Caruana considered 15...a6 16 ♘c3 d4 favorable. But he didn't see a clear path of progress after 17 ♘e4.

Better is 15...a6 16 ♘c3 cxb4! because White's queenside pawns are vulnerable in the endgame of 17 axb4 dxc4 18 dxc4 ♕xd1+.

16   exd4   cxd4

Black threatens to trap the knight with 17...a6.

White cannot afford more weaknesses, such as 17 f4, because 17...a6 16 fxe5 axb5 sets up ...♘f5-e3.

17	a4	a6
18	♘a3	a5!

It is not visible yet but the pawn structure will resemble a reversed Modern Benoni Defense. His move secures an outpost at c5, e.g. 19 b5 ♛d6 and ...♘d7-c5.

19	0-0?	axb4
20	♖xb4	♛d6

The queen is so well placed here that White's failure to rule it out with 19 ♘b5! was cited as one of the factors in his defeat.

21 ♘c2!

Black was readying pressure against the a4-pawn (21...♖a6 and 22...♖fa8).

White can offset that with counter-pressure against the d4- and b6-pawns: 22 ♛a1 ♘7c6 23 ♖b3 ♖fa8 24 ♖a3 and 25 ♖b1.

21	...	♘d7

Caruana felt his position would be strategically won if he could play ...♘c5 unmolested.

22	♛a1	e5
23	f4!	

Caruana called this the most difficult position in the game for him. His method of move selection is revealing:

First, he naturally looked at forcing moves, such as 23...♘c6 24 ♖b5 ♘c5.

Then 25 ♖xb6 seemed good for White (25...♘xa4? 26 ♖xc6 ♛xc6 27 ♗f3).

But he looked further and saw 25...e4! 26 ♘b4 ♘xa4! would give him good winning chances.

Then he considered 25 fxe5, instead of 25 ♖xb6. He saw White would be safe after 25...♛xe5 26 ♗f3 ♖xa4 27 ♛d1.

His calculation led him to the positional conclusion. Maintaining a pawn on e5 was vital.

23	...	f6!

24 ♜b5   ♞c5

The a-pawn is doomed on a4 (25 ♜b4 ♜fb8 and ...♞c6).

This means a4-a5 is necessary, now or after 25 fxe5.

White may hold if he liquidates the queenside – and all four rooks, such as with 25 a5! bxa5 26 fxe5 fxe5 27 ♜xa5 ♜xa5.

For example, 28 ♜xf8+ ♔xf8 29 ♕xa5 e4 30 ♞e1!.

25 fxe5   fxe5

White can transpose into that position after 26 a5! ♜xa5 27 ♜xf8+ ♔xf8 28 ♜xa5 bxa5 29 ♕xa5 e4 30 ♞e1 e.g. 30...e3 31 ♕a8+.

26 ♜xf8+?

This leads to play similar to the last note but amounts to an indirect swap of his f1-rook for the a8-rook. That would help White – if there were no kingside tactics.

26 ...   ♜xf8

But there are tactics coming, such as ...♞f5 followed by ...e4 and ...♞xg3!.

27 a5?   bxa5

There are also f-file tactics, 28 ♕a3? ♕f6 and ...♕f2+ will mate.

28 ♕xa5   ♞c6

29 ♕e1   e4!

Black's main idea is ...♞e5 and ...exd3.

If White overprotects d3 with 30 ♕d1 ♞e5 31 ♞e1, Black penetrates on the f-file, 31...♕f6!.

A cute finish would be 32 ♜xc5 ♕f2+ 33 ♔h1 ♞g4!.

Then 34 ♞g2 ♕f6 sets up ...♞f2+ and wins after 35 ♕e1 ♞f2+ 36 ♔g1 ♞h3+ 37 ♔h1 exd3 38 ♝xd3? ♞f2+ and ...♞xd3.

30 ♞b4   ♞e5!

Much better than 30...♘xb4 31 ♕xb4 ♕f6 in view of 32 ♕xc5!.

Technical problems remain after 32...♕f2+ 33 ♔h1 ♕xe2 34 ♕d5+.

Or after 33...♕e1+ 34 ♔g2 ♕xe2+ 35 ♔h3.

31   dxe4

Instead, 31 ♕d1 would be the same position as in the note to 29...e4 but with White's knight on b4, rather than e1.

The difference means 31...♕f6 32 ♖xc5 ♕f2+ 33 ♔h1 ♘g4?? fails to 34 ♗xg4.

But 33...♘f3! works instead – 34 ♗xf3 exf3 35 ♕g1 ♕e2! and ...f2.

31   ...   d3!

32   ♗d1   ♕d4+

Now on 33 ♔h1 d2 34 ♕e2 Black could win with 34...♘xe4 as in the game.

But 34...♘f3! and the threat of ...♕g1 mate is faster.

33   ♔g2   d2

34   ♕e2   ♘xe4

35   White resigns.

Caruana went on to share first place in Baku with Boris Gelfand. But being in the lead for so long carries an emotional and physical cost, as another of the players, Dmitri Andreikin, said. The strain is much less for a player who knows early on that he has no chance of finishing at the top of the crosstable.

When most of the Baku players moved on to the second Grand Prix tournament, at Tashkent, Gelfand played listlessly and finished last. Andreikin, who was next to last at Baku, played with energy and won.

And Caruana? He went from a plus-two score in Baku to plus-one in Tashkent. That was good enough for first place in the Grand Prix standing. But not enough to make reaching the 2016 Candidates a certainty.

30
Bumpy Ride

It became certain after the final Grand Prix tournament of the cycle, held in FIDE's tournament-site-of-last-resort, Khanty Mansiysk. Caruana won three and drew three of his first six games and secured first place in the overall Grand Prix standings. But his qualification was not that smooth, as flawed games often make it appear. Case in point:

Caruana –
Evgeny Tomashevsky
Khanty-Mansiysk 2015
Slav Defense,
Chebanenko Variation (D15)

1	d4	d5
2	c4	c6
3	♘f3	♘f6
4	♘c3	a6
5	a4	

Back in the 1990s Alexander Beliavsky began experimenting with this way of discouraging ...b5. It's a fairly innocuous move but it opens an analytical debate:

Who benefits from the addition of the a-pawn moves?

Another way of asking the question is: Can either side transpose into a more familiar Slav Defense line in which the addition of a2-a4 and ...a6 helps him?

For example, can Black play 5...♗f5, a move that is dubious a move earlier?

The answer is, "No." Even with the a-pawns advanced, 6 ♕b3! is still a strong reply.

5	...	e6

Let's try another question: What about 5...dxc4, the move that characterizes the Czech Variation?

The Czech runs 4...dxc4 5 a4! and then 5...♗f5 6 e3 e6 7 ♗xc4, with a marginal White edge, as countless games have shown.

But with the a-pawns advanced, we get a Czech line in which Black chose the fairly useless move 5...a6?.

6 ♗f4

Caruana points out another benefit of his move order. If the a-pawns had not moved, 5 ♗f4? is dubious because of 5...dxc4! and ...b5 or ...♘d5.

But in our game, 6 ♗f4 works well because 6...dxc4 7 e3 b5 8 axb5 regains the pawn.

6 ... a5

Now we see a reason why the advanced a-pawns help Black.

Both sides created holes. Black's last move makes sure he can plant a knight or bishop on the hole at b4.

He also ruled out the cramping a4-a5 which could have allowed White to exploit the hole at b6.

7 e3 ♗e7

8 g4

The principled moves 8 ♗d3 and 8 ♘e5 are objectively better. But the "bayonet gambit" move g2-g4 had a powerful allure in

many similar positions in the last 30 years.

It works when Black has left his g7 pawn unprotected: 8...♘xg4 9 ♜g1 favors White after 9...♘h6 10 ♜xg7 ♘f5 11 ♜g1.

8 ... ♘a6

9 g5

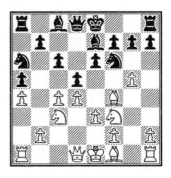

9 ... ♘d7?

The knight is poorly placed but has no escape from the edge of the board after 9...♘h5.

Play could continue 10 ♗e5 ♘b4 11 ♗e2 0-0 12 ♜g1. Black will probably have to brave the consequences of ...f6!.

10 h4 ♘b4

11 ♗e2 b6

The usual antidote to ♗f4 in a Queen's Gambit Declined is ...c5. But here that would allow a problematic ♘b5 and ♗c7 or ♘c7.

12 h5

White is "playing without an opponent" on the kingside. If Black castles, he faces the prospect of a killing ♕b1! and g5-g6.

And 12...♗a6 13 cxd5 ♗xe2 14 ♕xe2 and 15 0-0-0 would only help White.

12 ... ♗b7

13 cxd5!

This averts 13...c5!, which would have given Black a playable game.

13 ... exd5

White would enjoy a queenside initiative after 12...cxd5 13 ♘b5 ♖c8 14 ♖c1.

Or 12...♘xd5 13 ♘xd5 exd5, when Black has traded off his best piece.

14 ♕d2

Computers want White to play ♔f1 here and in various scenarios. It's not a bad move but queenside castling makes more sense, e.g. 14...♘f8 15 0-0-0 ♘e6 16 g6 ♘xf4 17 exf4.

14 ... f5

15 gxf6

But here 15 ♔f1 and ♔g2 is a good alternative. White can then play on the queenside with ♘a2xb4 and ♖hc1.

15 ... ♗xf6

Black had better defensive chances after 15...♘xf6 and 16...♘e4.

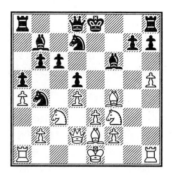

16 h6

This induces a weakness on f6. But g7 would be more vulnerable after 16 e4! 0-0 17 e5 ♗e7 18 0-0-0 b5 19 ♖dg1!.

16 ... g6

17 e4 dxe4?

This should have lost the game. Black's counterattack would have balanced chances after 17...0-0 18 e5 ♗e7 19 0-0-0? b5!.

18 ♘xe4 0-0

19 0-0-0?

This makes it a game again. Black has so many holes that 19 ♗c4+ ♔h8 20 0-0! would have made ♘fg5-e6 hard to meet.

19 ... ♘d5?

It was easy to dismiss 19...b5! with a quick look at 20 ♘d6 and ♘xb7.

White would dominate the key files after 20...♗a6 21 ♔b1 bxa4 22 ♗xa6 ♖xa6 23 ♕e2 and ♖he1/♖c1.

But both players overlooked 20...♘b6!.

Then 21 ♘xb7? ♕d5! threatens to win with 22...♕a2 or 22...♘c4, and should equalize.

20	♗g3	♗a6
21	♗xa6	♖xa6
22	♖he1	♖a8
23	♔b1	♗e7
24	♕d3!	

This anticipates ...♗b4 and clears the decks for two plans. Both call for a favorable trade of knights.

One is ♘e5!/...♘xe5/dxe5. The other is ♖c1/♘c3!. Black no longer has queenside counterplay.

24	...	♖f5
25	♘e5!	♕c8
26	♘c3	♘xc3+
27	♕xc3	♘xe5
28	♕b3+	♖f7

Black's vulnerability to last-rank mates becomes a factor after 28...♘f7 29 ♖xe7 ♖d5 30 ♖de1! ♕f5+ 31 ♔a1.

29	dxe5!	♕f5+
30	♔a2	♗b4
31	e6	♖e7

32 ♗h4!

The e-pawn wins after 32...♗xe1 33 ♗xe7 ♗xf2? 34 ♗d8!.

32	...	♖ee8

33	e7+	♕f7

If 33...♔h8 White wins by getting his queen or bishop onto the mating diagonal running from c3 to h8.

For example, 34 ♕c4 c5 35 ♖e3 or 35 ♖e4 prepares ♗g3-e5+.

34	♖e6!	b5

35	♖d8	bxa4

36	♕e3	

The decisive threat is 37 ♔a1! and 38 ♖xa8.

36	...	♗xe7

37	♖xa8	♖xa8

38	♗xe7	♖e8

39	♔a1	a3

40	bxa3	♕f5

41	♕c3	resigns.

Fabiano's rating had reached the world number two spot in late 2014 and remained there until mid-2015 when he dipped below 2800. His rating did not surge again until mid-2018 when he reoccupied second place and closed in on Magnus Carlsen.

31
Three Phases

A world champion must be beaten in all three phases of a game, the old saying goes. He should be surprised in the opening, eclipsed in the middlegame and ground down in the endgame. You can find evidence of this in the championship years of Alexander Alekhine, for example.

But those games are rare. When a champion, even a former champ, loses nowadays, the scorecard looks like that of a tennis match. A player wins one set, but loses the next. Advantages are secured, then dissipate. Superior defensive skill turns a winnable position into a drawable one. Neither player passes the 100 percent purity test of computers.

In this game former champion Vladimir Kramnik badly errs in the opening. Caruana obtains a winning advantage. But he fails to find the killing moves. Inexact follow-ups bleed his advantage until it is almost dry. He has to beat Kramnik all over again. And he does.

Vladimir Kramnik – Caruana
Dortmund 2015
Neo-Grünfeld Defense (D78)

1	♘f3	d5
2	g3	g6
3	♗g2	♗g7
4	d4	♘f6
5	0-0	0-0
6	c4	c6

Bobby Fischer shocked an earlier generation of masters by claiming Black can be better in purely symmetrical positions, such as 7 cxd5 cxd5 because of 8 ♘c3 ♘e4!.

7	♘bd2	a5
8	b3	a4

Fischer's claim was laughed at. But the unbalancing power of ...♘e4 slowly caught on.

Black can claim at least a small edge after 9 b4 ♘e4!.

For example, 10 ♘xe4? dxe4 11 ♘g5 ♕xd4 and 11 ♘e5? f6.

Also 10 e3 ♗g4 and 10 ♗b2? a3 11 ♗c1 ♘xd2 followed by 12...dxc4.

9   ♗a3

Caruana admitted that his knowledge of this line was based on a single game (Radjabov-Carlsen), which he remembered from Wijk aan Zee 2012.

Magnus equalized after 9 ♗b2 ♗f5 10 ♘e5 ♘bd7 11 ♘xd7.

9   ...   axb3

After Kramnik ruled out ...a3 with his last move, there was no compelling reason to delay this swap.

Yet Caruana took 20 minutes to innovate with this move, rather than the book 9...♖e8 and 9...♗f5.

10   axb3   ♗f5

Now 11 ♘e5 ♘e4! is quite equal, e.g. 12 ♘xe4 dxe4! rather than 12...♗xe4 14 ♗h3.

One can imagine Caruana calculating 12...dxe4 13 g4 ♗c8!?

and then 14 ♗xe4 f6 15 ♘xg6? hxg6 16 ♗xg6 f5! until he was convinced he would be much better.

11   ♘h4   ♗e6

He expected 12 e3 because he felt 12...♘bd7 13 f4 and 14 f5 would be problematic.

But White's queenside is the more vulnerable wing after 13...♘b6.

Black would have a clear advantage following 14 cxd5? ♘bxd5 and a lesser one after 14 f5 ♗d7 or 14 c5 ♘bd7 15 f5 ♗xf5 16 ♘xf5 gxf5 17 ♖xf5 e6.

12   ♖e1

Kramnik chose this after his first big think. He aims for 13 e4.

Instead, 12 ♕c2 ♘a6 13 e4? just drops a pawn after 13...dxe4 14 ♘xe4 ♘xe4 and 15...♕xd4.

12   ...   ♘e4!

231

A trade of knights improves Black's position in many closed openings. Here 13 e3 ♘xd2 14 ♕xd2 ♘d7 is roughly equal (15 ♕c2 ♘b6 16 c5? ♘d7).

13 ♗xe4

Three months earlier, Kramnik had lost to Caruana, again with White, when a slow-developing positional struggle suddenly exploded in his face.

He was evidently disappointed to find that 13 ♘xe4 dxe4 would force him into a dead-even endgame after 14 ♗xe4 ♕xd4.

He invested 20 minutes on this move and made his next moves fairly quickly.

13 ... dxe4

14 ♘xe4

There didn't seem any reason to reconsider this because 14 e3 f5 and 14 ♗b2 ♖xa1 15 ♕xa1 f5 were so obviously dangerous.

14 ... ♕xd4

15 ♕c2?

But it was time to rethink his 13th move calculation.

He can bail out with 15 ♕xd4 and then 15...♗xd4 16 ♗b2 ♖xa1 17 ♗xa1.

That endgame is roughly balanced – unless Black keeps his two-bishop edge, with 17...♗b6!.

15 ... ♗f5!

Clearly inferior to this are 15...♕xa1?? 16 ♖xa1 ♗xa1 17 ♗xe7 and 15...♕d8 (or 15...♖e8) 16 ♗b2.

16 ♘xf5

Kramnik must have overlooked 16 ♗c5 ♕e5! (17 ♖xa8 ♗xe4) – or 16...♕xe4 17 ♕xe4 ♖xa1!.

16 ... gxf5

After only one real error, a former world champion is in deep trouble as White (17 ♘c5 ♖xa3 18 ♖xa3 ♕xc5).

17 ♘g5!

Kramnik needs to find ways for Caruana to go wrong. There were none in 17 ♘d2 ♛c3! (18 ♛xf5 ♛xd2 or 18 ♛a2 ♛a5).

17 ... ♛g4!

Caruana passes the first middlegame test by rejecting 17...h6? 18 ♗b2! ♛xb2 19 ♛xf5 hxg5 20 ♖xa8, when White has some drawing chances.

18 f4! ♗xa1

19 ♖xa1

White is losing but not yet lost. To win Black needs to play moves at least as good as White from now until an endgame.

Here 19...c5! and ...♘c6 would have been a big step.

19 ... h6

20 ♘f3

There was no reason to bluff with 20 h3!??.

That would succeed after 20...♛xg3+ 21 ♔h1 ♘d7? 22 ♖g1, for example.

But Black can call the bluff in various ways and simplest is 21...hxg5 22 ♛xf5 ♛xf4.

20 ... ♘d7?

Caruana (and numerous machines) said 20...♛g7 would have allowed him to centralize the queen and win after 21 ♖a2 ♛f6 and ...♛e6-e4.

He may have feared ♘e5 at some point but 22 ♘e5 ♘d7! 23 ♘xd7 ♛d4+ and ...♛xd7 becomes child's play.

21 ♖d1!

Finding a good move, even at the elite GM level, is often just a matter of looking for an unprotected enemy piece you can attack.

21 ... ♖xa3

22 ♖xd7

White eyes ♛b2 and ♘e5.

For example, 22...e6? 23 ♛b2 should draw (23...♖fa8? 24 ♖xf7! or 23...♖aa8 24 ♘e5).

22 ... ♛h3!

233

Caruana realized he must use his extra Exchange for attack and look for tricks.

For example, 22...♖fa8 23 ♖xb7 e5!! is a wonderful shot.

Then 24 ♘xe5 ♕h3 or 24 fxe5 ♖a2 25 ♕d3 ♕e4! wins.

However, if White plays 23 ♔g2! instead, his king is safe and he is nearly equal (23...♖a2 24 ♕d1).

23 ♕c3

Black's winning chances soar once a rook lands on the last rank.

He would win after 23 ♖xe7? ♖a1+ 24 ♔f2 ♕f1+ 25 ♔e3 ♖c1! 26 ♕xf5 ♖c3+ 27 ♔d4 ♕a1, for example.

Kramnik's move tries to delay ...♖a1(+). A good alternative is 23 ♕d1 so that he can force a trade of rooks with ♖d8+.

But Black would still have winning chances after 23...♖fa8 24 ♖d8+ ♔h7 25 ♖xa8 ♖xa8 26 ♔f2 ♖a3.

23 ... e6?

Caruana spent six of his remaining 15 minutes here. His move pushes the game into the "three outcomes" category: Black can lose as well as win or draw.

The right way was 23...♖fa8! with good winning chances after, for example, 24 ♔f2 ♖a1 25 ♖d8+ ♖xd8 26 ♕xa1 f6.

Caruana calculated 23...♖fa8! 24 ♖xe7 ♖a1+ 25 ♔f2 instead and concluded White was safe.

Only later did he find 25...♖f1+ 26 ♔e3 ♕g2! and then 27 ♕f6.

What might have been

It seems Black has to conjure up a perpetual check.

There is a clever one in 27...♕f2+ 28 ♔d3 ♖d1+! 29 ♔c2 ♖c1+!.

Then:

(a) 30 ♔xc1? ♕f1+ 31 ♔b2 ♕a1+ or 31 ♔c2 ♖a2+ wins the queen.

234

(b) 30 ♔b2?? ♖a2+! mates (31 ♔xa2 ♕a7+!).

(c) and 30 ♔d2! would miraculously draw after 30...♖a2+ 31 ♔d3! ♖d1+ 32 ♔c3.

However, Black has a forced win in the diagram.

Caruana pointed out 27...♖xf3+!, instead of 27...♕f2+.

The main line runs 28 exf3 ♕g1+ 29 ♔d3 ♕d1+! 30 ♔e3 ♕e1+ 31 ♔d3 ♖d8+.

24   ♖xb7   ♖fa8

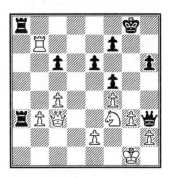

25   ♔f2

Kramnik could force matters with 25 ♕f6 ♖a1+ 26 ♔f2 and give Caruana an opportunity to force a draw with queen checks at f1 and c1.

But 25 ♔f2 is practical. White has real winning chances.

25   ...   ♖a1

For example, Black could err by trying to try to get his queen onto the long a1-h8 diagonal.

He would be worse after 25...♕h5 26 h4! or 25...♕g4? 26 ♖xf7! (26...♔xf7 27 ♘e5+).

26   ♔e3

Kramnik has outplayed Caruana in the game's second phase. But unless someone blunders, a draw is likely, either by repetition of position or perpetual check.

A trade of rooks, such as 26...♖1a7 27 ♖xa7 and ♕b4, is also even.

It is hard to see how queens could be swapped, but if they were, White would have good chances of winning the c6- or f7-pawn.

26   ...   ♖f1!

But if you look for White's weakest point, you see the b3-pawn but also the one at e2.

Black has ways of attacking it after ...♖f1 followed by ...♕g2 and either ...♖f2 or ...♕f2+.

27   ♕f6   ♖f8

235

White's pieces seem as well placed as they can be. If he tries to win with 28 ♖c7 then after 28...♕g2 29 ♖xc6?? would free Black from fear of ♕xf7+. He would win with 29...♖b8! and ...♖xb3+. Or 30 b4 ♖a8! and ...♖a3+.

28   ♖d7

There was one piece that could be significantly improved, his king.

After 28 ♔d4! there is a real winning plan of ♔c5! and ♔xc6.

The king can even go in the other direction and help mate – *a la* Short – Timman, Tilburg 1991 – after 28...♕g2 29 ♕xh6 ♕f2+?? 30 ♔e5 ♕xe2+ 31 ♔f6!.

28   ...   ♖b1

29   ♖b7   c5!

A draw is still the most likely result. But with ♔d4 off the table, it is getting harder for White to play accurate moves.

He hasn't been able to move his knight because of ...♕xh2.

A queen trade is now very bad, e.g. 30 ♕h4? ♕xh4 31 ♘xh4 ♖a8 32 ♘f3 ♖a3 or 32 ♖b5 ♖a2 and ...♖bb2.

30   ♖b5   ♖f1!

It may look like Black is repeating the position. But 31 ♖b7, for example, would lose after 31...♕g2! because of 32 ♕xh6 ♕f2+ and ...♖d8+.

31   ♘d2?

The only way to assure a draw was 31 ♖xc5!.

Kramnik must have seen 31...♕g2 32 ♕xh6 ♕f2+ 33 ♔d2 ♕xc5 34 ♕g5+ is perpetual check.

But he likely rejected this line in view of 33...♖d8+.

This is the beginning of the third and fatal phase of the game. White overlooked 34 ♖d5! and draws after 34...exd5 35 ♕g5+.

31   ...   ♖c1!

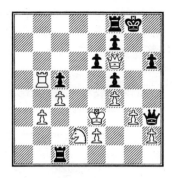

32 ♕b2

Black's main threat was ...♕xh2.

He would deliver mate after 32 ♘f3 ♕f1 (eyeing ...♖c2) 33 ♕xh6? ♖c3+!.

32 ... ♖d1

Once the White pieces pulled back from their optimal squares, Black progress was inevitable.

For example, 33 ♘f3 ♕g2 34 ♕e5 ♖b1! 35 ♖b8 ♖xb8 36 ♕xb8+ ♔h7 is slowly lost.

33 ♕c2 ♖h1

34 ♘f3 ♕g2

White's chief drawing resources, such as ♕xh6/♕g5+, are long gone.

The entrance of Black's other rook would decide after 35 ♕d3 ♖f1! and ...♖a8.

35 ♕c3 ♖f1

36 ♕f6 ♖f2!

The weakest point falls (37 ♕b2 ♖xf3+ 38 exf3 ♕xb2).

37 ♔d3 ♖xe2

38 ♘g5 ♖d2+

39 White resigns.

Kramnik only lost five games as Black in 2015 – three of them to Caruana.

32
"My Ortueta-Sanz"

Today's world-class players are typically well connected to their fans by social media. Caruana is not. His Web site, caruanachess.com, was launched in 2015 and quickly became dormant. He has tens of thousands of Instagram followers but rarely posts. He hired a company to handle his social media but gave up on it. His smartphone broke during the 2018 Candidates tournament – and being out of the loop helped him win, he said. In some years, he has gone months without tweeting. But he had something to say after this game.

Liviu-Dieter Nisipeanu –
Caruana
Dortmund 2015
Evans Gambit (C52)

1	e4	e5
2	♘f3	♘c6
3	♗c4	♗c5
4	b4	

This was played in the last round, when Caruana led an eight-player field that included Vladimir Kramnik, Wesley So and Ian Nepomniachtchi. The only one close to him was GM Liviu-Dieter Nisipeanu, barely in the world's top 100, who trailed Caruana by a half point.

4	...	♗xb4
5	c3	♗a5
6	d4	

"Modern opening analysis has completely defanged" the Evans Gambit, Caruana wrote.

This doesn't mean 4 b4 is refuted, but rather that it can no longer be counted on for an initiative.

6	...	d6

There is still quite a variety of options for both sides. For instance, the old-school 6...exd4 was revived by Michael Adams at Wijk aan Zee 2001 to beat Alexander Morozevich after 7 0-0 ♘ge7.

238

7 ♕b3 ♛d7

Black's defense against ♗xf7+ looks artificial.

But by ruling out checks on the a4-e8 line, it makes ...♗b6/...♞a5 an attack-killing finesse.

White would be worse after 8 0-0 ♗b6! 9 dxe5? ♞a5!, for example.

8 dxe5

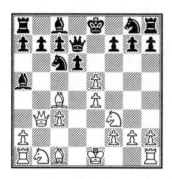

8 ... ♗b6!

When Caruana annotated this game he said 9 ♞bd2 dxe5 favors Black.

He was quickly challenged by a 14-year-old master, Ruifeng Li, who tried 10 ♗b5 f6 11 ♞c4 in the 2015 Millionaires Open.

They drew after 11...♞ge7 (11...♛f7!?) 12 0-0 ♛e6 13 ♕a4.

9 a4

This has a more immediate point, 9...dxe5 10 a5! ♗c5 11 a6.

Then 11...bxa6 12 ♕a4 brings back 19th century style tactics such as 12...♞f6 13 ♗xf7+.

For instance, 13...♛xf7 14 ♕xc6+ or 13...♚xf7 14 ♕c4+ and ♕xc5.

9 ... ♞a5

Grabbing the two-bishop advantage this way is why 9 0-0 and 9 ♗a3 are also played infrequently.

10 ♕a2 ♞xc4

11 ♕xc4 ♞e7

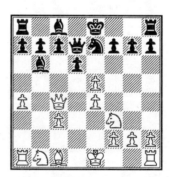

12 ♗a3

At the previous London Classic, Hikaru Nakamura tested Vishy Anand with 12 exd6.

There was nothing wrong with 12...♕xd6 and 13 a5 ♗c5 14 ♗a3 ♗xa3.

Anand preferred 12...cxd6 and drew following 13 0-0 0-0 14 ♕d3 ♘g6.

12 ... 0-0

White's last move was new and we don't know what he had planned after 12...d5, 12...♘g6 or even 12...♕g4, the moves recommended by computers.

After 12...d5 13 exd5 ♕xd5, for example, he can quickly lose if avoids an engame, 14 ♕h4? ♘g6 15 ♕g3 ♕e4+!.

Or 15 ♕b4 c5 16 ♕b2 ♘f4 17 0-0 ♗h3! and Black wins.

13 0-0

This has seemed like an Armageddon game since 4 b4, with White striving to avoid equal-looking positions. Under Armageddon rules, a draw is the equivalent of a Black victory.

13 ... ♖e8

This move foresees a trade of his targeted d6-pawn for the e4-pawn, resulting in an endgame of little risk. Since a draw would clinch first prize for Caruana, that is a more-than-acceptable outcome of the opening.

He briefly considered going for a big middlegame edge, with 13...♘g6 14 exd6 cxd6 – so that 15 ♖d1 ♕g4! would threaten 16...♘f4.

Then 16 ♗xd6 ♘h4! (17 ♘xh4 ♕xd1+) wins.

He stopped calculating when he saw 16 h3! – and didn't notice how 16....♘e5! leads to another favorable endgame (17 hxg4 ♘xc4).

14 exd6

Caruana would have been more or less forced to seize the attack after 14 ♖d1? ♘g6 15 exd6 ♘f4.

14 ... cxd6

15 ♖d1 ♕c6!

This forces White to choose between a poor endgame...

16 ♘bd2 ♝e6

17 ♛xc6

… and the stakes-raising 17 ♛d3.

That move threatens to win a pawn, 18 ♝xd6 ♖ad8 19 e5, or obtain good play with 18 ♘d4 ♝xd4 19 cxd4.

But Black could minimize his own risk by liquidating, 17...d5, or counterattacking, 17...♘g6! 18 ♛xd6 ♛xc3 and ...♖ad8.

17 … ♘xc6

18 ♝xd6 ♖ad8

With two bishops and better pawns, Black is likely to regain his pawn and then play for an endgame squeeze. A dramatic finish hardly seemed likely.

19 ♝b4

If you are still in the Armageddon mind-set, you might as well stay optimistic with 19 e5 and c3-c4-c5 or ♘e4.

White would not be losing after 19...♝a5 20 ♘d4 ♝xc3 21 ♘xc6!, for example.

19 … ♖d3

Since at least move 12, Caruana has played solid moves when more adventurous alternatives were available.

Here the more ambitious policy is to insert 19...a5 20 ♝a3 before 20...♖d3.

But then the b6-bishop is unprotected. Before Black can play ...♖xc3 safely, White will equalize with 21 ♖ab1 or 21 ♖db1.

And if you've seen this game before, you know Black's a-pawn has a different destiny.

20 a5?

The practical try is 20 ♘f1, whether playing to win or draw.

It sets a trap, 20...♖xd1 21 ♖xd1 ♝b3 22 ♖a1 ♖xe4? loses to a ♘d2 fork.

After 22 ♖a1 Black may have nothing better than the fairly equal 22...♗c2 23 e5 ♘xe5 24 ♘xe5 ♖xe5 25 a5 and ♘e3.

20 ... ♗c7

21 ♘f1

Black threatened the paralyzing pin 21...♖ed8.

Thanks to White's last move, the a5- and b7-pawns are weaker. That makes 22 ♖db1 preferable.

21 ... ♖xd1

22 ♖xd1

22 ... ♘xa5

If Black was merely playing to draw, 22...♗xa5? 23 ♗xa5 ♘xa5 24 ♖a1 ♘c6 26 ♘d4! would be safe enough.

23 ♘d4!

Black's bishop would become a major player after 23 ♖a1 ♘c6 24 ♘d4 ♘xb4.

It would win after 25 cxb4? ♗e5.

It would play a leading role in the grindable endgame of 25 ♘xe6 ♖xe6 26 cxb4 ♗b6.

23 ... ♘c4!

White would have good drawing chances after 23...♘c6 24 ♘xe6 or 23...♗d7 24 ♖a1.

24 ♘xe6

It would begin to look like a textbook endgame, reminiscent of a Capablanca victory, after 24 ♘d2 ♘xd2 25 ♖xd2 a5 26 ♗a3 ♗c4.

24 ... ♖xe6

Capablanca might have been horrified by the computer suggestion of 24...fxe6 25 ♗c5.

25 ♖d7

25 ... ♖c6

This game illustrates how the stars can align. A brilliancy may come about from simple, solid moves.

If Caruana were seeking a quick, impressive finish he would have gone for the fancy 25...♝b6 26 ♖xb7 h5!.

That averts a last-rank mate and would win the e4-pawn after 27 ♘g3? h4.

The game could proceed 27 g3 ♖xe4 28 ♖b8+ ♔h7 29 ♖c8 ♘b2 and ...♘d3, with a high probability for a Black win.

26   ♘g3   g6

Everything is in place for a ho-hum march of the a-pawn.

Black would win after 27 ♔f1 a5 28 ♝e7 a4 29 ♔e2 a3.

27   ♘e2

Many computers initally evaluate the position as equal. They see 27...a5 28 ♘d4 ♖a6 29 ♖xc7.

27   ...   a5

Caruana recalled how he got up from the board after satisfying himself that he was winning.

He saw 28 ♝e7 a4 29 ♘d4 and then 29...♘b6! or 29...♘e5!.

That forces 30 ♘xc6 ♘xd7 followed by 31 ♘b4 f6 and ...♔f7 and the eventual advance of the hero a-pawn.

28   ♘d4?

"When I came back to the board and saw his reply, I couldn't believe my luck in being able to end the tournament in such style," he wrote in *New In Chess*.

28   ...   axb4!

Now computers quickly see the finish they didn't after 26...g6.

29   ♘xc6   b3

Black wins a piece after 30 ♘b4 b2 31 ♖d1 ♘a3!.

30   ♖xc7   ♘d6!

31   White resigns.

Final position

The b-pawn queens.

Note that ...♘d6 is a star move in other finishes. For example, 30 ♘a7.

Then 30...b2 31 ♖d1 ♘a3 gets slightly complicated after 32 ♘b5! ♘xb5 33 ♖b1 ♘xc3 34 ♖xb2.

But 30...♘d6! makes it easier (31 ♖xc7 b2 or 31 ♘b5! ♘xb5 32 ♖d2 ♘xc3 33 ♖b2 ♘xe4 34 ♖xb3 ♘c5).

After the game, Caruana tweeted, "This was my Ortueta – Sanz."

This went over the heads of many of his followers. It referred to a classic combination with the same basic material:

Ortueta – Sanz,
Madrid 1933

Position after 31 ♘a4

Black won with **31...♖xb2! 32 ♘xb2 c3 33 ♖xb6** and now **33...c4! 34 ♖b4 a5!**. **White resigned** because the c-pawn queens.

The finish has fascinated players of all strengths and many called it the game that made the greatest impression on him. Tigran Petrosian recalled how, when he first saw Ortueta – Sanz in a book, "I couldn't believe two extra White pieces could not overcome the doubled pawns of the opponent. I remembered this ending my entire life." Will Nisipeanu – Caruana inspire 21st century players in the same way?

33
Bidding to Better Bobby

Bobby Fischer maintained a phantom presence in US chess long after he played his final game. Amateurs grew up on his games. Caruana said when he played in American tournaments before leaving for Europe, "in a way, he was always there."

Fischer was there, indirectly, in his earliest lessons. His teacher Bruce Pandolfini based some of Fabiano's study on examples from Soviet texts written by I. O. Lipnitsky and Georgy Lisitsyn and a Polish book on rook endgames. Pandolfini showed the books to him because they had once been Fischer's own copies. "I did that deliberately since Fabiano seemed to be inspired by Bobby," he said.

Fabiano grew up in the post-Fischer era when talented American youngsters were regularly compared with Fischer by US mass media. "Is He the Next Bobby Fischer?" a Wall Street Journal headline in 1991 asked, above a profile of Jorge Zamora. The New York Times, in 2005, and National Public Radio, in 2012, called Hikaru Nakamura the next Fischer. Caruana would have been subjected to the same burdensome comparison if he had not left for Europe just as he was becoming a master.

As he edged closer to the world championship, he was inevitably asked if he was motivated by Bobby. "I'd say the one player who has always blown me away and inspired me has been Bobby Fischer," Caruana told Britain's Guardian newspaper.

In the following game he discovered the same opening nuances that Bobby had.

Caruana – Wei Yi
Wijk aan Zee 2016
Ruy Lopez, Open Defense (C83)

1	e4	e5
2	♘f3	♘c6
3	♗b5	a6
4	♗a4	♘f6
5	0-0	♘xe4

The Open Defense of the Lopez bears a resemblance to the Berlin Defense (3...♘f6 4 0-0 ♘xe4).

Like the Berlin, it has had widely fluctuating appearances at the elite level.

The Open was at the height of fashion as the 20th century began, then fell in and out of popularity several times. As the 21st century began, it had dropped behind 5...b5 as the role of prime alternative to 5...♗e7.

6	d4	b5
7	♗b3	d5
8	dxe5	♗e6
9	c3	♗e7

The usual move is 10 ♘bd2. Wei Yi had had some success meeting it with the double-edged 10...♘c5 11 ♗c2 d4.

Caruana knew that line – because he had played it when he adopted the Open Defense as Black.

10   ♗c2

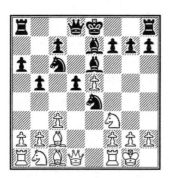

This is different because on 10...♘c5 White has 11 ♘d4!.

When White can play this thematic move safely in an Open Defense, he usually he earns a positional edge.

After 11...♘xd4? 12 cxd4 his center is solid and the backward c7-pawn is a textbook middlegame target.

Different positional pluses emerge after 11...♕d7 12 ♘xe6 ♘xe6 13 f4 and 12...♕xe6 13 b4.

10   ...   ♗g4

But is the sacrifice 10 ♘d4 ♘xe5 sound? Bobby Fischer must have answered "Yes" when he played 10 ♗c2 in 1966.

White would have good "comp" after 11 ♖e1 ♘c4 12 b3 and 11...♘g6 12 f4.

And 11 f4! is even stronger.

11   h3

Wei Yi plunged into 42 minutes' thought. The position was unfamiliar because he had fallen for a transpositional trick.

He could have played 10...0-0 and reached a major line of the Open Defense after 11 ♘bd2.

But he didn't want to play that line. He was hoping to play 10 ♘bd2 ♘c5 11 ♗c2 d4!.

Of course, he saw 11...♗e6? would concede the loss of two tempi with his bishop.

He discovered 11...♗xf3 would be strongly answered by 12 gxf3! ♘-moves 13 f4.

For example, 12...♘c5 13 f4 ♕d7 14 ♕f3 and ♖d1 would virtually doom the d5-pawn, following b2-b4 and ♗b3, as Caruana pointed out.

11 ... ♗h5

Black calculated that 12 ♗b3 ♘xe5 would be fine for him.

For example, 13 ♗xd5 ♗xf3 14 gxf3 ♘xf3+ 15 ♔h1 ♕d6 threatens ...♕h2 mate.

Or defend 13 ♕xd5 ♘xf3+ 14 gxf3 with 14...♘f6 15 ♕c6+ ♘d7 16 ♖d1 ♖b8! and ...♖b6.

12 g4

Fischer evidently came to the same conclusions when he played this at the 1966 Olympiad.

12 ... ♗g6

Bobby continued 13 ♗b3 and won the d5-pawn. His opponent, Fridrik Olafsson, got plenty of comp after 13...♘a5 14 ♗xd5 c6!.

Olafsson could also have played 13...♘c5 14 ♗xd5 ♕d7 or 14 ♕xd5 ♘a5! with excellent chances.

Therefore, Fischer's 11 h3 seemed to lack bite.

13 ♘d4!?

Caruana was trying to improve on Fischer by clearing the way for a kingside pawn advance beginning with f2-f4!.

The test of 13 ♘d4 seems to be 13...♘xe5.

But the rough material equality of 14 f4 ♘g3 15 fxe5 ♘xf1 16 ♔xf1 doesn't quite make up for the superiority of White's minor pieces.

13 ... ♕d7?

But the real test was 13...♘xd4!. White would be lost after14 ♕xd4 ♗c5 (15 ♕d1 ♕h4).

Two months after this game, in the Women's World Championship, challenger Maria Muzychuk played 13...♘xd4! and nearly beat Hou Yifan after 14 cxd4 h5!.

A key variation is 15 f4 hxg4 16 f5 ♖xh3, when 17 fxg6?? ♖g3+ would win after 18 ♔h2 ♗d6 or 18...♗g5.

Hou luckily drew after 15 f3 ♘g3 16 ♖f2 when Black's attack petered out to a perpetual check.

So why did Caruana allow this possibility?

In the post-mortem, he said he looked at 13...♘xd4 14 cxd4 h5 "a couple of weeks ago" but didn't say what he found.

14   f4

We can guess that his computer-assisted prep concluded 14...h5 15 f5 hxg4 is harmless after 16 fxg6.

White would be winning after 16...♖xh3 17 ♗xe4 dxe4 18 gxf7+ and 19 e6!.

14   ...   ♘xd4

Black should be trading bishops, with 14...♘g3 15 ♖f3 ♗xc2.

White may be a shade better after 16 ♕xc2 ♘e4 17 ♗e3 but it's a dim shade.

White can avoid this at his peril, by 15 f5? ♘xf1 16 ♕xf1 ♗c5 or 16 ♔xf1 ♘xe5, with advantage to Black.

Or 16 fxg6 when opening the f-file, 16...fxg6!, will favor Black after he castles queenside and puts a rook on f8

15   cxd4

Now 15...h5 16 f5 hxg4 fails: 17 ♗xe4! dxe4 18 fxg6 ♖xh3 19 gxf7+ and 20 ♘c3.

15   ...   f5

16   ♗e3

Despite all the move-order ingenuity and missed tactical prospects, the position has stabilized. The pawn structure is White's only real advantage.

In *Chess Life*, Caruana was quoted as saying he considered 16 exf6 ♗xf6 17 f5 ♗f7.

But his structural edge would be loosening and "the knight on e4 is very hard to get rid of."

16   ...   0-0

Black's king would be secure after 16...h5 17 g5 0-0.

But White would have queenside prospects with ♘c3/♗b3/a2-a4.

17 ♘c3

Although the knight is his best piece, 17...♘xc3 18 bxc3 c5 is a way for Black to avoid being slowly squeezed.

There are complications after 19 dxc5 ♖ac8 20 ♗b3.

But Caruana indicated he would settle for 19 a4.

For example, 19...♖ac8 20 axb5 axb5 21 ♖a6.

Or 19...cxd4 22 ♗xd4! b4 23 cxb4 and ♗b3.

17 ... c6

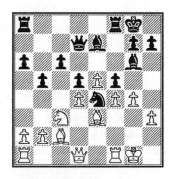

18 ♗xe4!

Also good was 18 ♘xe4! (18...fxe4? 19 f5).

White would enjoy a sizable edge after 18 ♘xe4 dxe4 19 ♗b3+ ♔h8 20 d5 cxd5 21 ♕xd5.

A reason to prefer 18 ♗xe4 is that in the last variation Black can stop d4-d5 with 19...♗f7 20 ♗xf7+ ♖xf7 and ...♕d5.

18 ... dxe4

19 d5!

So that 19...cxd5 20 ♕xd5+ ♕xd5 21 ♘xd5 ♗d8 becomes a winning bind after 22 ♗c5 ♖e8 23 ♘e3.

This may be easier to win than grabbing the Exchange with 22 e6 ♖e8 23 e7 ♗xe7 24 ♘c7.

19 ... b4

20 dxc6 ♕xd1

This drives White's knight back, compared with 20...♕xc6 21 ♕d5+ ♕xd5 22 ♘xd5.

Then 22...♗h4 23 ♘xb4? ♖ab8 and ...♖xb2 would get Black play.

But White can nurture his edge slowly, with 23 ♖fd1 and ♖ac1, with a likely win.

21 ♘xd1 ♖fd8

Black would stand well if he could recapture the c6-pawn. But he can't, 21...♖ac8 22 ♖c1 ♗e8 23 c7 or 22...♗d8 23 ♘f2.

22 ♖c1 ♖d3

23 ♗c5

Caruana goes for the knockout with his passed pawns (23...♗xc5+ 24 ♖xc5 and 25 e6).

The consolidating 23 ♖e1 and ♘f2 would have won without much effort.

23	...	♝d8

24	e6	♜c8

Black could safely resign after 24...♜xh3 25 gxf5 ♝xf5 26 e7 or 24...fxg4 25 ♞f2!.

25	e7	♝a5

26	gxf5	

Caruana had initially calculated 26...♝xf5 27 ♞e3 ♝xh3 28 ♜fe1.

But then he saw 28...b3! does the refuting (...♝xe1).

However, 28 ♜f2 is good enough to win after 28...♚f7 29 ♞c4!.

26	...	♝e8

27	♞f2	♜d5

28	♞xe4	

Now 28...♜xc6 29 ♜fd1 ♜xf5 30 ♜d8 is lost.

28	...	♝xc6

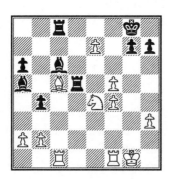

29	♝xb4!	♝xb4

30	♜xc6!	

Queening combinations are a natural way to end the game, e.g. 30...♜xc6 31 e8(♛)+.

Or 30...♜b8 31 ♜b6! ♜b5 32 ♜xb5 axb5 33 f6! with ♜d1-d8+ to come.

30	...	♜e8

31	f6	♜d4

32	♜e6	resigns.

Let's scroll back to move 10.

Two world champions, Capablanca and Karpov, had passed up 10...♞c5 and then 11 ♞d4!.

But it was used by David Bronstein to crush Paul Keres, after 11...♞xe5? 12 f4! ♞c4 13 ♞c6 ♛d7 14 ♞xe7 ♛xe7 15 b3! and ♝a3.

Their game was a state secret – literally. It was played in a confidential Soviet training camp for the USSR Olympiad team. The players were under strict orders not to disclose the moves of the training games.

The attempted improvement, 10...♝g4 11 h3, was discovered by Fischer. And then Caruana tried to improve on Fischer with Bronstein's idea in a different form, 13 ♞d4!?.

34
Attack, Defense and Wilhelm Steinitz

When Fabiano was seven and eight he went over many Fischer games, from My 60 Memorable Games, with Pandolfini. He eventually studied Botvinnik's One Hundred Selected Games and Soviet Chess Championship, 1941, Nimzovich's My System and Chess Praxis and Reinfeld's The Immortal Games of Capablanca, among others. Fischer and Capablanca games were favorites.

But when they started, "we concentrated on short chess games that emphasized basic principles of development and attack. Several Morphy games, some Steinitz..." Pandolfini recalled.

When Steinitz was young he played dashing gambit-chess. Later he set down guidelines for successful attack and defense that are still respected today. This game and Game 35 show how modern players tweaked Steinitz's theory.

Caruana – Hikaru Nakamura
Candidates tournament,
Moscow 2016
Ruy Lopez, Berlin Defense (C65)

1	e4	e5
2	♘f3	♘c6
3	♗b5	♘f6
4	d3	♗c5

5	♗xc6	

The 21st century has been a continuous struggle to find the elusive plan that ensures at least promising prospects against the Berlin Defense.

Caruana and his colleagues investigated a wide variety of fifth moves, including 5 c3, 5 ♘bd2, 5 ♘c3 and 5 0-0. None solved the puzzle.

The text has the benefit of clarifying the center pawn structure, since 5...bxc6? 6 ♘xe5 is an unsound pawn sacrifice.

5	...	dxc6

But 6 ♘xe5 allows 6...♕d4!, threatening ...♕xf2 mate as well as the knight.

6 ♘bd2

The position takes on the stolid character of a delayed exchange variation of the Ruy, such as 3...a6 4 ♗a4 ♘f6 5 0-0 ♗e7 6 ♗xc6 dxc6.

In the orthodox Exchange Variation, 3...a6 4 ♗xc6 dxc6, Black can defend his e5-pawn with ...f6. He equalizes after 5 ♘c3 f6!, for example.

6 ... 0-0

Since Black's knight stands in the way of ...f6, he temporarily relies on tactics, e.g. 7 ♘c4 ♖e8 8 ♘cxe5? ♖xe5! 9 ♘xe5 ♛d4.

7 ♛e2 ♖e8

8 ♘c4 ♘d7

But he needs a long-term defense of the pawn.

Steinitz's theory of defense, as interpreted by his successor Emanuel Lasker, held that the best way to meet a threat is the least costly way.

Giving up his two-bishop edge (8...♗g4 9 h3 ♗xf3) is more expensive than 8...♘d7, for example.

9 ♗d2 ♗d6

Why not the "cheapest" defense of the e5-pawn, ...f6 ?

The answer comes from another page of Steinitz's theory, dealing with attack:

An attack should not succeed without a weakness in the enemy camp, he said.

White would like to attack the Black king after ...0-0. But he cannot easily open a kingside file – unless ...f6 opens the way for g2-g4-g5xf6.

This reasoning was challenged in the 21st century when grandmasters tried to crush the Berlin by pushing White's kingside pawns anyway.

The position in the diagram arose twice in the same round at Wijk aan Zee 2015.

Caruana played 10 h4 against Sergey Karjakin while Wei Yi played the same move against David Navara.

Caruana and Karjakin played relatively quickly, 10...♘f8 11 h5 ♘e6 12 0-0-0 c5.

Wei Yi and Navara played slowly. They shot glances at the Caruana game as they took an hour to play 10...c5 11 h5 h6 12 0-0-0 on their own board.

The primary difference between the two games was ...h6.

It seems minor but it allowed Wei Yi to blast the Black kingside open, 12...♘b8 13 ♖dg1 ♘c6 14 g4! f6 15 g5!.

Then 15...hxg5 16 h6 – or, as the game went, 15...fxg5 16 ♘xg5! and wins.

The moral is that ...f6 and ...h6 made g4-g5 stronger. Steinitz could have told them that.

10   0-0-0   b5

Black has at least as much justification to attack the enemy king as White. The a2-pawn is unprotected and not easily defended.

11   ♘e3

The knight would be misplaced on a5 (11 ♘a5 c5! followed by ...♘f8-e6-d4).

11   ...   a5

Both players are attacking "and the only question is who will be first," Caruana wrote.

But he added that when he and his second analyzed similar positions the night before this game they found "White has many defensive resources."

In fact, it is not who attacks first but who defends better.

12   ♘f5

Poor defense makes the attack faster, 12...g6? 13 ♘h6+ followed by 14 h4! and 15 h5.

12   ...   a4

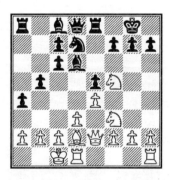

If White can sacrifice a pawn to open lines – as we saw in the Wei Yi game – so can Black.

For example, 13 g4 b4 14 ♔b1 b3 15 cxb3 axb3 16 axb3 ♘c5 and the b3-pawn will fall.

Worse is 14 ♖hg1? b3! 15 a3 bxc2 and …♗a6/…♘c5, when the d3-pawn is a new target.

If White accepts the pawn offer, 14 ♘xd6 cxd6 15 ♗xb4, Black gets ample compensation after 15… c5!.

For instance, 16 ♗c3 d5 17 exd5 ♘b6 or 16 ♗a3 ♘f8 and …♘e6-f4.

13   ♗g5!   f6

Black would slow his own attack significantly after 13…♘f6 and would probably have to play …h6 at some point.

14   ♗e3

At the cost of two bishop tempi Caruana created the kingside weakness he needed to open lines with g4-g5.

14   …   ♘c5

Five moves from now we will appreciate how 13 ♗g5! made sense and how 14…♘f8 would have defended the kingside better.

15   g4   ♗e6

16   ♔b1

But for the time being, Black's attack looks much more powerful.

For example, 16…♕d7 17 ♖hg1 ♕f7 threatens …♗xa2+.

Then 18 b3? axb3 19 cxb3 allows a sound piece sacrifice on b3 – of either piece.

For instance, 19…♗xb3 20 axb3 ♖a3 wins.

Instead of 18 b3?, White can defend a2 and delay …b4 with 18 a3.

But more in the spirit of an opposite-wing attack is 18 g5!.

Then 18…♗xa2+ 19 ♔a1 and 19…a3 20 b3 ♗xb3 21 gxf6! wins.

Caruana's calculating machine was running when he examined, instead, 18…♗xf5 19 exf5 a3! 20 b3 e4.

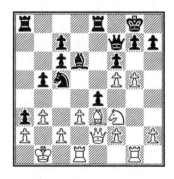

What might have been

With his king on b1, White cannot permit 21 dxe4? ♘xe4 because …♘c3 is check (22 ♕d3 c5! and …c4).

254

Caruana said 21 g6 hxg6 22 fxg6 ♕d5 would be "a complete mess of a game."

Computers allow us to clean up a mess. They suggest 23 ♘d4 exd3 24 ♕g4! to get the queen to h7.

For instance, 24...♖e4 25 ♕h3 ♖xd4 26 ♕h7+ ♔f8 27 ♕h8+ ♔e7!.

Machines then come to their favorite evaluation – 0.00 – after 28 ♕xg7+ ♔e6 29 ♕f7+ ♔e5 30 f4+ ♔e4.

Perpetual checks are likely after 31 ♗xd4 ♕xd4 32 cxd3+.

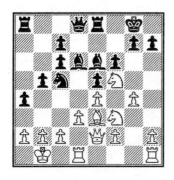

Back to reality:

16   ...   b4

Reversing the battery, 16...♗f7 17 ♖hg1 ♕d7 18 g5 ♕e6, is ineffective because ...♕xa2 is just a check, not a mate.

For example, 19 a3 ♕xa2+ 20 ♔c1 ♕a1+? 21 ♔d2 ♕xb2 22 gxf6 and White wins.

17   g5

17   ...   b3?

There was still life in the 17...a3 18 b3 ♗xf5 19 gxf5 e4 idea.

This time, after 20 dxe4 ♘xe4 21 ♕c4+ ♔h8, White can cope with the threatened knight check on c3 with 22 ♗d4.

Perhaps only a computer would be able to foresee that Black is quite safe after 22...♖a5! (23 gxf6 gxf6 24 ♕xc6 ♖xf5).

18   ♖hg1!

This nonchalance can come about from strong nerves and a process of elimination.

White can select this move by concluding he would lose if he captures twice on b3.

The fastest punishment of 18 cxb3 axb3 19 axb3? is 19...♕b8 with mating threats (20...♕xb3 and 21...♖a1+!).

Keeping the a-file partially closed, (18 cxb3 axb3) 19 a3, looks better.

But we can eliminate that when we see how 19...♗xf5 20 exf5 ♘a4 is bound to lead to a deadly sacrifice on a3 or b2.

Calculate long enough and the only candidate left is 18 ♖hg1!.

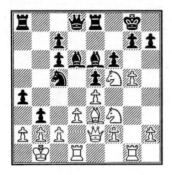

18   ...   bxa2+

White would win quickly after 18...dxc2+? 19 ♕xc2 in view of ♗xc5 or gxf6.

If Black goes on the defense, 18...g6, White can afford 19 cxb3 axb3 20 a3.

The difference between this scenario and the one we looked at a move ago (18 cxb3? axb3 19 a3) is that ♖hg1 made White's attack one move faster.

For example, he can ignore 20...♘a4 21 gxf6 ♗xa3 and win with 22 ♘h6+.

That is, 22...♔h8 23 ♘xe5! or 22...♔f8 23 ♘g5!.

19   ♔a1   ♗xf5?

Black's last chance to slow White's attack was 19...g6.

Then 20 gxf6 ♕xf6 21 ♗g5 ♕f8 22 ♘3h4, for example, is nearing a knockout. But it's not there yet.

20   exf5

20   ...   a3

White has positional as well as attacking methods to finish the game. After 20...♔h8, for example, he would have a big edge with 21 ♘d2 and ♘e4.

21   b3   ♘a6

22   c3

In *64* Caruana added a note that did not appear in his other comments.

He initially intended 22 d4 but wasn't confident about 22...e4 23 ♕c4+ ♔h8 24 gxf6 ♕xf6.

Later he concluded 25 ♘e5 was sufficient to win.

22   ...   ♗f8

23 ♘d2!   fxg5!

So that 24 ♘e4 ♕d5 and White's king suddenly becomes a factor again.

24 ♖xg5   ♘c5

25 ♖g3!

Intuition could tell Caruana that 25...♕xd3 26 ♕xd3 ♘xd3 should be won for him.

But it takes some calculation to see 27 ♘e4 ♘b2 28 ♖dg1 and ♗h6 is crushing.

25 ...   e4

26 ♗xc5   ♗xc5

Black could safely resign after 26...exd3 27 ♕g4. He is in desperation mode anyway.

27 ♘xe4   ♗d6

28 ♖h3   ♗e5

29 d4   ♗f6

30 ♖g1   ♖b8

31 ♔xa2

There was no reason to calculate 31 b4 ♗xd4 32 ♖d3!. Any safe move would have won.

31 ...   ♗h4

32 ♖g4   ♕d5

33 c4   resigns.

This victory came in Caruana's first game of the second half of the Candidates and gave him his first realistic chances of a first place finish.

Had he won his next-to-last round he would almost certainly have qualified to challenge Carlsen in the world championship match of 2016.

But he missed several chances in that game, lost the final round to Sergey Karjakin and had to wait three years.

Publicly, he took this in typical Caruana style: "Life is pretty long," he told *New In Chess*. "I will have more chances in the future."

35
Steinitz, Part II

We're going to step out of the chronology to look at a similar game with a very different moral. Caruana again attacks a Black kingside but it has not been compromised by ...f6. He succeeds after Black plays ...f6! unprovoked but fails to follow up with an attack-killing ...h6!. The game became a time-trouble battle of traps, counterattacks and clever tactics.

Caruana – Viswanathan Anand
London 2017
Ruy Lopez, Berlin Defense (C65)

1	e4	e5
2	♘f3	♘c6
3	♗b5	♘f6
4	d3	♗c5
5	♘c3	

Caruana tried this move twice against Alexander Grischuk in the Champions Showdown three months earlier. He lost both times. That was usually enough for him to abandon an opening move for good.

But he had tried 5 ♗xc6 dxc6 6 ♘bd2 against Anand in that tournament – also without success. He was willing to give 5 ♘c3 one last try.

5	...	0-0

One of the benefits of 5 ♘c3 is that 5...d6 allows White to win the two bishops with 6 ♘a4, as in a Vienna Game.

It's a small-chess advantage but something to play without risk.

6	♗xc6	dxc6

Berlin Defense theory offers another oddity here:

This position could have come about via a Four Knights Game, 1 e4 e5 2 ♘f3 ♘c6 3 ♘c3 ♘f6 4 ♗b5 and now 4...♗c5 5 ♗xc6 dxc6 6 d3 0-0.

But it almost never does – because 4...♗c5 and 6...0-0 are considered dubious.

Yet despite two dubious moves, his position is nearly equal.

7   h3

This is not just prophylaxis (7 0-0 ♗g4!) but a feint towards an attack with g2-g4.

Anand knew that was possible because one of Caruana's games with Grischuk earlier in 2017 had gone 7 ♘e2 ♖e8 8 h3 ♘d7 9 g4.

7   ...   ♘d7

8   ♗e3   ♗d6!

Black's loss of time is worthwhile to retain the two bishops as well as prepare ...c5 and ...♘b8-c6-d4.

Anand may have remembered a game Caruana played as Black, against Michael Adams two years before.

It went 9 ♕d2 c5! 10 0-0 ♘b8! 11 ♘h2 ♘c6 12 ♘e2 ♘d4 and he had equalized.

9   ♘e2

What Caruana may have remembered from that game is

that Adams's queen was awkwardly placed on d2. In this game he delays a decision about his queen.

9   ...   ♖e8

10   g4

This is the first new move and not one a computer will likely recommend to you.

10   ...   ♘c5

11   ♘g3   ♘e6

12   ♘f5

In fact, some engines urge ♔f1-g2 by White. To understand this variation, "it's a better idea to just turn the computer off," Caruana said.

12   ...   c5

If White plays 13 c3 to stop ...♘d4, Black can shoot for ...a5 and ...b5-b4.

Perhaps only AlphaZero would consider 14 ♕d2 and 0-0-0 then.

13   h4

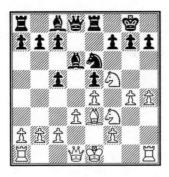

13   ...   a5

The consistent move is 13...♘d4.

But Caruana's delay in touching his queen makes 14 c3! ♘xf3+ 15 ♕xf3 effective.

Then nearly half of Black's 14 moves were spent on maneuvering a knight that he traded off.

A White attack could proceed unimpeded (15...♗e6 16 c4! and 17 g5).

But 14...♘xf5? 15 gxf5 would be worse because of the opened kingside lines.

For example, 15...♗f8 16 ♘g5 threatens 17 ♕h5.

Then 16...h6 17 ♘xf7! ♔xf7 18 ♕b3+ ♔f6 19 ♖g1 and the threat of ♗g5+! wins.

Or 16...♕f6 17 ♕h5 h6 18 ♖g1 since 18...hxg5? 19 hxg5 is suicide.

14   h5

Both players had been blitzing their moves up to now. Engines like Black's chances after 14...a4, the move Caruana expected.

14   ...   ♖a6

Surprised, he took 14 minutes to reply.

He has made too many committal moves to drastically change plans.

A positional recipe such as 15 a4 would be fine – if his g- and h-pawns were back on the second rank.

Caruana looked at 15 c3 ♘f4 and considered 16 ♗xf4 exf4 17 ♕d2 ♗e6 18 c4 too fuzzy to try.

15   ♕d2?   ♘d4!

Anand was waiting for this. His superiority would be clear after 16 ♘3xd4 cxd4 17 ♗g5 f6 18 ♗h4 ♗f8 and ...h6.

Then his doubled pawns would be corrected and his king is safe (19 g5? ♗xf5 20 exf5 ♕d5).

No better is 16 ♗xd4 cxd4 17 0-0-0 ♗b4 or 16 ♘3h4 ♗f8.

16 ♖h3 ♗f8

So far, Steinitz has been exonerated again.

Because Black hasn't weakened his king position, his winning chances would be obviously superior after 17 c3 ♘xf3+ 18 ♖xf3 ♗e6 19 g5? ♕d7 and ...♗xf5 or ...♖d8.

This sequence also shows how ...♖a6! was a fine defensive move – 20 g6 fxg6 21 hxg6 hxg6 22 ♘h4 ♗g4!.

17 0-0-0 ♗e6

18 ♔b1

Caruana mistakenly thought he was doing well and expected 18...♘xf3 19 ♖xf3 c4.

18 ... f6!

But now ♘g5 is ruled out, and the ...♕d7-f7 idea that might have arisen in the Nakamura game is a dangerous possibility.

White cannot exploit 18...f6 with 19 ♖g1 ♕d7 20 g5? because of 20...♗xf5 21 exf5 ♕xf5.

19 c3

He can, however, play 19 ♗xd4 cxd4 20 g5 but then he would suffer on the dark squares, 20...♗b4 21 ♕c1 ♖b6 (threat of ...♗a3) 22 b3 a4.

Caruana admitted he was "extremely unhappy with my position."

It was a reverse of this point, move 19, of the Nakamura game, when he wrote: "Now I was extremely happy with my position."

19 ... ♘xf3

20 ♖xf3

Steinitz's theory allowed for exceptions: There were times when pushing a pawn makes a castled king safe.

He would have approved of 20...h6!, sealing the kingside.

Then the outcome of the game would likely depend on whether Caruana could defend the queenside.

For example, 21 ♖g3 ♕d7 22 f4 exf4 23 ♗xf4 ♕f7! finally makes a2 a serious target.

Then 24 c4 b5! and 24 a3 b5 and ...b4! would look grim for White.

20 ... c4?

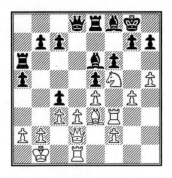

Anand had taken 14 minutes for 19...♘xf3 and immediately played 20...c4.

It made good positional sense, since 21 dxc4 ♗xf5! favors him after 22 gxf5 ♖d6.

This is based on a neat tactic, 22 ♕xd8 ♗xe4+ 23 ♔c1 ♖xd8 24 ♖xd8 ♗xf3 25 ♗c5 ♖d6! and his two bishops will outgun the White rook in the endgame.

21   ♕c2

He must have misjudged this as well as 21 g5 (21...♗f7 22 gxf6 ♗xh5 23 ♖g1!).

21   ...   cxd3

22   ♖xd3   ♕c8

Black will still be better if he can get in ...h6, ...b5 and/or ...♗c4.

23   g5!

It is easier to find moves, as Caruana put it, when your position is strategically dubious.

Then you can ignore the quiet candidate moves and look only for forcing lines.

23   ...   fxg5

Anand apparently decided against 23...♗f7 and ...♕e6 because 24 g6 or 24 gxf6 gets scary.

For instance, 24 g6 hxg6 25 hxg6 ♗xg6 26 ♖d1 and ♖g1.

24   ♗xg5   ♗f7

Anand's move prepares ...♕e6!.

But once again, 24...h6! was better.

After 25 ♗c1 ♗f7 Black's king is safe, the h5-pawn is weak and ...♕e6 is still coming.

25   h6   gxh6

Not 25...g6? 26 ♘e3, when ♕d1/♘d5! makes White suddenly superior.

26   ♗c1!

Played instantly. Caruana had seen how strong it was when he chose 25 h6.

262

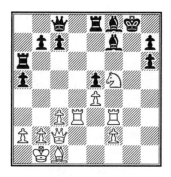

The bishop defends his king better on c1 compared with 26 ♗e3 ♕e6 27 b3 a4 28 c4 and then 28...axb3 29 axb3 ♖ea8 or 29...♕c6.

Also, on e3 the bishop would have gotten in the way of ♘e3-d5.

26	...	♕e6
27	b3	a4

Black should prepare this with 27...b5 because now White can play:

28	c4

Crisis over. Caruana understood he was no longer losing.

28	...	axb3
29	axb3	♕c6

In fact, 29...♖ea8 30 ♗b2! would favor him.

His king is the safer one and he would have 31 ♖d5 and 31 ♕d2/ 32 ♖d7 coming up.

30	♖g3+	♔h8

31	♖d1

Caruana met the ...♕xe4 threat with this, rather than with 31 f3, because he kept the option of ♗b2/f2-f4!.

31	...	b5

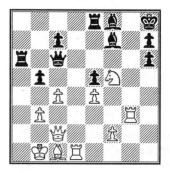

Now he had to consider 32 ♗b2 bxc4 and sort out 33 f4 ♗g6 and 33 ♖d8 (33...♖xd8?? 34 ♗xe5+ but 33...♖a5!).

32	c5

This has the benefit of setting traps. One is 32...♗xc5 33 ♗b2!.

Then 33...♗g6? 34 ♖c3 or 33...b4? 34 ♖d8! ♗d4 35 ♖xd4! loses.

Best is 33...♗d6! with a probably drawn endgame to follow 34 ♕xc6 ♖xc6.

32	...	b4

A draw was also likely after 32...♕xc5 33 ♕xc5 ♗xc5 34 ♖d7! (34...♗g6 35 ♗xh6 ♗f8).

33	♗b2

But Anand thought he was better in view of 33...♖a5 and ...♖xc5. He made two oversights.

33   ...   ♗g6?

He belatedly saw 33...♖a5 would be met by 34 ♖d8!.

Black would be mated after 34...♖xd8 35 ♗xe5+ and lose his queen after 34...♖xc5 35 ♗xe5+.

He would also be losing after 34...♖aa8 35 ♖xa8 ♕xa8 36 f4 and probably after 34...♕xc5 35 ♖xe8 ♗xe8 36 f4 as well.

The second error was failing to appreciate:

34   ♖d5!

Now 34...♗xf5 35 exf5?? ♕xd5 looks great. But White

would end the game with the zwischenzug 35 ♖xe5!.

34   ...   ♕b5

Also lost is 34...♕f6 35 f4. Anand is playing for swindles now (...♕f1+).

35   ♖g1   c6

36   ♖xe5   ♖xe5

37   ♗xe5+   ♔g8

Problemists may prefer 38 ♗b2 and ♕d2-d4.

38   ♗d4   ♔f7

39   ♘h4   resigns.

In the crunch stage, moves 32-35, Anand was outplayed.

At the highest level, the deciding factor in a game is rarely a matter knowledge or even skill. "It's a concentration thing," Caruana told fastcompany.com in 2021. "It's having the ability and the stamina to focus for a long period of time."

36
"Ultimate Opponent"

Garry Kasparov announced in 2005 he had retired from "professional chess." But he repeatedly returned to speed chess tournaments in the next decade, playing well over 100 games against elite grandmasters. Each time, his appearance was hyped as his return to chess.

This game was played in a speed tournament grandly titled "The Ultimate Blitz Challenge." Kasparov complained of making "multiple blunders in winning positions." He didn't get that chance this time.

Garry Kasparov – Caruana
St. Louis 2016
Scotch Game (C45)

1	e4	e5
2	♘f3	♘c6
3	d4	exd4
4	♘xd4	

No one did more to spur the revival of the Scotch than Kasparov, beginning with his 1990 world championship match with Anatoly Karpov.

4	...	♗c5
5	♗e3	

Caruana also adopted the Scotch as White. He usually preferred 5 ♘xc6 and then 5...♕f6 6 ♕d2 dxc6 7 ♘c3, as Kasparov had in his 1993 world championship blowout of Nigel Short.

5	...	♕f6
6	c3	♘ge7
7	♗c4	

The chief White advantage in the Scotch is control of greater space. He could enhance that with f2-f4.

7	...	0-0

Black can anticipate f2-f4 with well-timed attacks on the e4-pawn and/or ...d5.

For example, 7...♘e5 8 ♗e2 ♕g6 and then 9 ♗f3? d5 10 exd5 ♘d3+ .

8	0-0	

The standard line is 8...♗b6, protecting the bishop as well as the c7 square.

Black can get into early trouble after 8...♖e8? 9 ♘b5! and be lost after 9...♗xe3 10 fxe3.

8   ...   b6

Caruana tries a rare way of developing his QB.

Now 9 ♘a3, a good move after 8...♗b6, would allow 9...♗xa3 10 bxa3 ♗b7, with rough equality.

9   ♘c2   ♘e5

Another point to Black's eighth move is that 8...♗b6 9 ♘c2 ♘e5 would have offered White a small edge after 10 ♗b3 or 10 ♗e2.

But here 10 ♗b3? ♗a6! favors Black.

For years after Kasparov's withdrawal from the tournament circuit, rumors circulated about his secret computer files.

Until his calamitous Bucharest 2021 tournament, it was believed he was still years ahead of contemporary GMs because of opening discoveries he had never used.

However, this position seemed to catch him off guard.

10   ♗e2

He took more than a minute, a huge amount in a blitz game. Did he need that much time to remember that 10 ♗xc5 bxc5 and ...♖b8 was dubious? Or to recall his evaluation of 10 ♘d2 ♘xc4 11 ♘xc4 ♕e6 ?

10   ...   ♗b7

Caruana adopts a Hypermodern approach to a 19th century opening. He wants to provoke White's e- and f-pawns forward.

If White declines, such as with 11 ♘d2, Black can stop f2-f4 with 11...♘5g6

Then 12 f4? ♗xe3+ 13 ♘xe3 ♘xf4 drops a pawn and 12 ♗f3 ♘h4! is also poor.

11   f4

White can find himself dangerously behind in space after 11 ♗xc5 bxc5 12 ♘d2 d5.

For example, 13 exd5? ♘xd5 and ...♘f4/...♖ad8.

Or 13 f4 ♘5g6 14 e5 ♕b6.

11   ...   ♘5g6

12   e5

In a speed game, walking into a pin like 12...♕c6 13 ♗f3 ♘d5 is playing with fire.

But White has no better than a minimal edge after 14 ♗xc5 ♕xc5+ 15 ♕d4.

12   ...   ♕e6

Caruana hints that White's center is overextended (13...f6 or 13...d6). He had four minutes left, nearly twice as much time as Kasparov.

13   b4!

But true to style, Kasparov plays for more than the safety of 13 ♗f3.

Then 13...♗xf3 14 ♕xf3 ♗xe3+ 15 ♘xe3 ♘h4 followed by the blockading 16...♘hf5 and ...d6 should equalize.

13   ...   ♗xe3+

The sacrifice 13...♘h4 is dubious, 14 bxc5 ♘xg2 15 ♕d3 or 14...♗xg2 15 ♘d4.

14   ♘xe3

White threatens to win a piece with 15 f5 ♕xe5 16 ♘g4 ♕e4 17 ♗f3.

14   ...   ♘h4

Caruana matches Kasparov's aggression by playing for more than the equality of 14...♘f5 15 ♘xf5 ♕xf5.

15   ♗g4

A long-forgotten game, Armad – Arencibia, Capablanca Memorial 1991, had gone 15 ♕d3 d6 and chances were balanced after 16 ♗g4 ♕h6.

15   ...   f5

Equally good is 15...♕g6 so that 16...♘xg2 17 ♘xg2 ♗xg2 18 ♔xg2 h5 is threatened.

But in a speed game, a forcing move is always tempting (15...f5 16 exf6?? ♕xe3+).

16   ♗e2

White threatens to pin the queen with 17 ♗c4.

267

Black's long-term concern is White's superior pawn structure. He can no longer undermine it with ...f6.

Without a change in the structure, Black will be gradually pushed back.

For example, 16...d6 17 &c4 d5 18 &b3 &ad8? 19 g3! ♞4g6 20 ♞d2 and ♞f3.

16 ...   ♚h8!

But Black can change it with ...g5! and target g2 after opening the g-file.

For example, 17 ♞d2? g5! (18 fxg5? f4 and Black wins).

17 &c4?

Computers claim 17 g3 can lead to a repetition of moves, 17...♛c6 18 ♚f2! and then 18...♛h6 19 ♚g1.

Humans don't play blitz like that.

They prefer the craziness of 17...d6 (18 gxh4 ♛g6+) or 17...g5 18 gxh4 gxf4, when anything can happen.

17 ...   ♛g6?

Third best, after 17...d5 and 17...♛h6, because it blocks the g-pawn.

After 17...d5 18 &-moves g5! Black is for choice.

18 &f2   d6

The d-file will be opened by force, since 19 e6 d5 drops a pawn.

19 exd6   &ad8

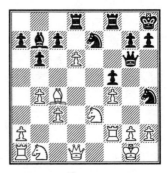

Magnus Carlsen said a "concrete player" like Caruana typically plays below his strength in speed chess because he doesn't have enough time to calculate as much as he needed.

This was also true of Kasparov. He needed more time to realize that after 20 ♞a3 &xd6 21 ♛f1! his knight would stand well following ♞b5.

20 d7   &c6

Now 21 &d2? ♞f3+ illustrates a new feature of the position. White is tactically vulnerable on g2 but also on f3.

268

21	♘d2	♖xd7

22	♕e2	

A Hypermodern strategy succeeds with a delayed occupation of a weakened center.

That would be the case after, for example, 22 ♕c2 ♖fd8 23 ♘df1 ♗e4 24 ♕b2 ♘c8 and ...♘d6.

22	...	♖e8!

You won't find it in many modern texts or web sites:

But a rook is usually well-placed on a file that is also occupied by the enemy queen.

It is ancient advice. The self-styled "Professor of Chess," J.H. Sarratt, wrote in 1821:

"Whenever your Adversary's Queen is on her King's second square, endeavor to move a rook on your King's square."

Even if there are pieces in between, "this is frequently good," he added. Here this is illustrated by 23...♘d5 or

23...♘xg2 24 ♘xg2 ♘d5 (25 ♕f3 ♘e3!).

23	♖e1	

Kasparov can meet 23...♘xg2? 24 ♘xg2 ♘d5?? with 25 ♕xe8+.

But choosing 23 ♖e1 over 23 ♘df1 left Kasparov with 16 seconds for the rest of the game.

23	...	♘c8!

The knight seeks e4 via d6.

Caruana spent 24 seconds of his remaining two minutes on it, probably considering 23...♘g8, with a similar idea (...♘f6-e4).

A difference between the two is 23...♘g8 24 ♗xg8, eliminating the knight.

But 24...♔xg8 25 ♘dc4 ♗b5 or 25 ♘df1 ♗xg2 would be headed to a loss.

24	g3	

Another difference is a swindle attempt.

White could have threatened a last rank mate with 24 ♘xf5 ♖xe2 25 ♖fxe2 and ♖e8+.

Caruana would still have winning chances after 25...♖d8 26 ♘xh4 ♕f6.

But if Kasparov had found 24 ♘xf5!, Caruana – with much more time – might have found the easier win after 25...♖e7!.

For example, 26 ♘xe7 ♘xe7 27 g3 ♘hf5.

24	...	♖de7
25	♘df1	♘d6

Everything is in order. Black threatens 26...♘e4 as well as 26...♘xc4 followed by ...♘f3+.

26	♗d3	♗e4

Now 27 ♗xe4 ♘xe4 and ...♘xf2 costs the Exchange. But it would take some accurate moves to untangle Black's pieces on the kingside.

27	♕d1	♗xd3
28	♕xd3	♘e4

The Exchange still falls (29 ♖fe2 ♘f3+).

The rest is explained by the clock. Caruana had nearly a minute left. Kasparov had only eight seconds.

29	♘d5?	♖d7

A bit quicker is 29...♘xg3 30 hxg3 ♖xe1.

30	♕c4	♘xf2
31	♖xe8+	♕xe8
32	♔xf2	♘g6
33	♘fe3	♕e6

The text will close the curtains after 34...♘e7 or 34...c6.

34	♕b3	c6!
35	**White resigns.**	

The finish was badly marred by the clock.

After 29 ♖ee2! White's position is defensible (29...♘xf2 30 ♖xf2 because Black cannot coordinate his pieces without losing material).

But Kasparov won his mini-match with Caruana 5-2. When he came out of retirement again in 2020, for a "Champions Showdown" in St. Louis, he lost to Caruana.

37
Strategically Won

In this game Caruana's position was "strategically won" after just 17 moves. There is no precise definition of the term. But it is widely understood as connoting a positional advantage great enough to be converted to victory without considerable effort.

But instead of cashing his trumps, including an extra pawn, in an endgame, Caruana continues an attack on the enemy king. He sacrificed one, then two pawns, set the stage for piece sacrifices and finished off with a textbook queen sack.

Caruana – Teimour Radjabov
Gashimov Memorial,
Shamkir 2016
Sicilian Defense,
Rossolimo Variation (B31)

1	e4	c5
2	♘f3	♘c6
3	♗b5	g6
4	♗xc6	

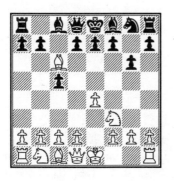

When 3 ♗b5 became recognized as the "Rossolimo Variation" – and not just "Another Crazy Idea of Nimzovich's" – this capture was considered premature.

But it suddenly became profound when Bobby Fischer adopted it in his 1992 rematch with Boris Spassky.

The reason is Black must make a defining decision about his pawn structure so early that White can select the best formation of his own pawns.

For instance, 4...bxc6 allows White to build a nice center with c2-c3 and d2-d4!.

4	...	dxc6

But now 5 c3? can be met by 5...♕d3!.

5	d3	

White is more or less free to complete a no-think development plan -- ♘c3, ♗e3, ♕d2 and probably h2-h3 at some point – before deciding where to castle (usually 0-0-0).

This would not work as well after 4...bxc6 because Black

can quickly use the half-open b-file.

For example, (4...bxc6) 5 d3 ♗g7 6 ♘c3 ♘f6 7 ♗e3 d6 8 ♕d2 ♖b8 9 0-0-0? ♕a5 and Black is threatening 10...♕b4!.

5	...	♗g7
6	h3	♘f6

Black often locks the center with ...e5, develops his knight on e7 – and then tries to figure out what to do with the knight.

By putting it on the flexible square f6, Black hasn't abandoned the ...e5 idea.

7   ♘c3

Magnus Carlsen used tactics to play it, with 7...b6 8 ♗e3 e5 against Caruana at Wijk aan Zee 2015.

Caruana figured out the tactic: 9 ♘xe5 would be met by 9...♘xe4.

He chose 9 0-0, kept a nice edge but eventually lost.

Grandmasters subsequently adopted Carlsen's 8...e5?. After all, he was the world champion.

Then they discovered 9 ♘xe5! ♘xe4 10 ♕f3! loses a pawn.

7   ...   0-0

That trick would work now after the commonly played 8 ♗e3 b6 9 ♕d2 e5 (10 ♘xe5? ♘xe4!).

Instead, White often continues 10 ♗h6.

After 10...♕d6 11 ♗xg7 ♔xg7 Black has good chances of equalizing with ...♘e8-c7-e6-d4, similar to Anand's maneuver in Game 35.

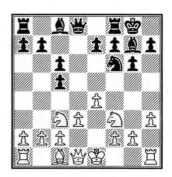

8   ♗f4

Caruana would have known that Radjabov had previously played 8...♘h5 9 ♗e3 b6 10 g4 ♘f6 – and that 10 e5! f5 11 exf6 would have been unpleasant for him.

8   ...   b6

272

This was a new move. The pawn blocks ...♕a5 but that's a minor concern for now.

9 ♕d2 ♖e8

10 0-0-0

Caruana will soon have to choose from among the various promising ideas -- ♗h6, ♗e5, ♘e5 and e4-e5.

Pushing his e-pawn is best when Black's knight cannot go to d5, such as after 10...♘d7.

10 ... a5

Now that White's king is committed, Black is justified in pushing queenside pawns. He might have started with 10...b5.

Then 11 ♘e5? ♕a5! works.

Black would be winning after 12 ♘xc6? ♕a6 13 ♘e5 b4.

Better is 11 ♕e3 with an unclear outlook after 11...♕b6 12 ♗h6 e5.

11 ♘e5

This is the first move of the game Caruana took time (14 minutes) to think about.

11 ... b5!

Black's attack is still worth much more than a pawn after 12 ♘xc6? ♕b6 13 ♘e5 a4.

12 ♕e3

Suddenly White has to play carefully to avoid getting the worst of it.

He wants to trade bishops but must avoid tricks such as 12 ♗h6? ♘xe4! when Black is solidly superior (13 ♘xe4 ♗xe5 14 ♘xc5 ♕d5).

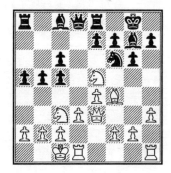

12 ... ♕b6

Black will be relying on two ideas in what turns out to be the critical stage of the game, the next half dozen moves.

One idea, as we'll see, is the attacking ...a4-a3. But he's not ready for it yet because 13 ♕xc5 was threatened.

The other idea is ...♘d7, to swap White's best piece.

Black may have talked himself out of 12...♘d7! because 13 ♘xd7 ♗xd7 or 13...♕xd7 allows White to play 14 e5! under good conditions.

However, if Black inserts 13...♗d4!, he would be at least equal. His c5-pawn would be secure and he has his own attack with ...a4/...♕a5 coming.

Also favorable to Black is 13 ♘g4 because of his other idea, 13...a4!, e.g. 14 e5 b4.

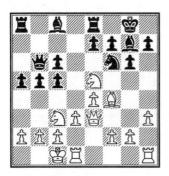

13   ♗h6   ♗h8

Retreating his bishop was probably Radjabov's intention since 9...♖e8 but he took nearly an hour over this and the next two moves.

If he speeds ahead with 13...♗xh6 14 ♕xh6 a4, he can open queenside lines.

But White's castled position is remarkably resilient. For example, 15 h4 b4 16 ♘e2 b3 and now

17 a3 bxc2 18 ♖d2! ♖b8? 19 ♖xc2 with a positional edge for White.

Engines also point out 15 ♘xf7! so that 15...♔xf7 16 e5.

Play could continue instead 15...b4! 16 ♘g5 bxc3 17 bxc3.

Those perpetual-check loving machines say they are done after 17...♕c7 18 ♘xh7! ♘xh7 19 ♕xg6+ ♔f8 20 ♕h6+. And so will we.

14   f4

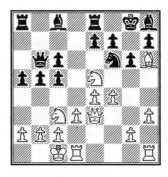

This is a wake-up call for Black. White prepares 15 f5 and 16 ♕g5.

Then it seems simple: White captures twice on g6 and mates.

14   ...   a4!

Radjabov finds a clever counterattack – 15 f5 ♘h5! threatens his e5-knight and allows him to win after 16 ♘f3?? a3!.

Instead, the 16 ♘xf7 sacrifice looks good (16...♔xf7 17 fxg6+ hxg6 18 ♖hf1+ ♔g8 19 ♕g5).

But it is refuted by 16...♗d4! (17 ♕g5 ♗f6 18 ♕e3 a3!).

15 ♖hf1!

This renews the threat of 16 f5.

Then 16...♘h5? is too slow, 17 fxg6 fxg6 18 ♘xg6!

Then 18...hxg6 19 ♕g5 ♔h7 20 ♖f7+ ♘g7 21 ♗xg7 ♗xg7 22 ♕e5.

Of the two ideas he's been counting on, 15...a3? now fails to 16 b3! because the queenside is more or less sealed.

But the other idea, 15...♘d7!, is viable because 16 ♘xd7 ♗xd7 opens the h8-bishop's diagonal and makes 17...a3! a threat.

Therefore, 17 e5! and 17... f5! are not only good but, in practical terms, virtually forced.

This is crucial because 18 exf6? exf6! turns the tables and favors Black.

Instead, White can keep the chances roughly balanced if he

targets g6 after 18 h4 or 18 g4 (18...fxg4? 19 f5).

For example, 18 h4 ♗e6 19 h5 b4 20 hxg6! hxg6 21 ♕g3 and 20...bxc3 21 gxh7+ ♔f7! 22 bxc3.

15 ... e6?

Faulty prophylaxis. This effectively takes f4-f5 off the table. But he lacks counterplay.

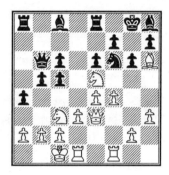

16 g4!

Now 16...♘d7 17 ♘xd7 ♗xd7 makes 18 e5! f5 19 exf6 strong since 19...exf6 is no longer legal. White's attack would roll on after 19...♗xf6 20 ♘e4.

16 ... a3?

Black would not be lost after 16...b4 17 ♘b1.

But getting close (17...b3 18 cxb3 axb3 19 a3 ♗a6 20 ♘d2 and ♘dc4).

17 b4!

White wins a pawn and effectively seals the queenside shut.

17	...	♘d7
18	♘xd7	♗xd7
19	e5	f5!

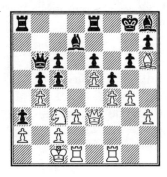

20 ♘e2!

White's last two moves excluded Black counterplay, such as 20 exf6 ♗xf6 21 ♘e4? ♗d4!.

His position is strategically won. He can win after offering an endgame with ♕xc5, any time he wants.

Instead, he goes for the kingside knockout.

20	...	♗g7
21	♗xg7	♔xg7

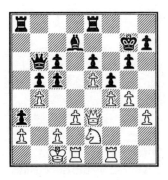

22	h4!	fxg4

Radjabov must have been tempted by 22...♕d8, which gets out of the pin and prepares ...♕xh4.

But 23 bxc5 ♕xh4? 24 g5! would have trapped his queen (♖h1).

23 h5!

This prepares 24 hxg6 hxg6 25 ♖h1 and 26 f5/♕h6+.

23	...	gxh5

Now both 24 ♖h1 and 24 f5 exf5 25 ♖h1 would win.

24 ♘g3

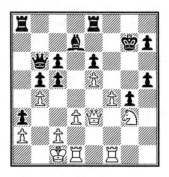

But putting his knight to work is natural. His basic plan is to get it to f6 and pound h7 with rooks.

24	...	♔h8
25	♘xh5	♖e7
26	♘f6	♗e8
27	f5!	

276

From now White has a choice of wins and this is faster than 27 ♖h1 ♗g6 28 ♖dg1 ♗f5 29 ♘xg4.

27 ... exf5

28 ♖xf5

But 28 ♖h1! and 29 ♕g5 or 29 ♕h6 would have all but forced mate.

28 ... ♕c7

29 ♖g5

29 ... ♖g7

Or 29...♗g6 30 ♖xg6! hxg6 31 ♖h1+.

30 ♖h1 ♗g6

31 ♖xg4

Black is finally freed from the pin on c5 and can play 31...cxb4. But the advancing e-pawn would be as decisive, after 32 e6, as in the game.

31 ... ♕f7

32 ♔b1

No reason to be fancy with 32 bxc5 ♕xa2 33 ♕h6!.

32 ... cxb4

33 ♕d4

Threatening, among others, 34 e6 ♕xe6 25 ♖xg6!.

33 ... ♗f5

34 e6!

It is mate after 34...♗xe6 35 ♖xh7+ ♖xh7 36 ♘xh7+ ♔xh7 37 ♕e4+ or after...

34 ... ♖xg4

35 exf7! ♖xd4

36 ♘e8! resigns.

38
Blitz Nemesis

Of all possible pairings, the most dangerous for Caruana was against Hikaru Nakamura at blitz. His fellow American held the world's number one blitz rating for years and it was nearly 200 points ahead of Caruana's.

During 2021 Naka was barely among the world's top 20 rated players in classical chess. But he continued to fatten his plus score against Caruana at blitz: It reached 27 victories, against nine losses and 15 draws.

The following game was played in another 2016 speed event in St. Louis, the Champions Showdown. It's a back-and-forth battle with numerous errors and fascinating ideas.

Hikaru Nakamura – Caruana
Champions Showdown (blitz),
St. Louis 2016
Slav Defense (D12)

1	d4	♘f6
2	c4	c6

Black's first two moves look like a transpositional finesse. But he will have nothing better next move than to transpose into a Slav Defense.

3	♘f3	d5
4	e3	♗f5
5	♘c3	e6
6	♘h4	♗e4
7	f3	♗g6

Two years before, Nakamura had played 8 g3 in a similar position during Caruana's seven-game win streak (Game 28). Here he adopts a more orthodox policy.

8	♕b3	♕c7
9	♘xg6	hxg6
10	♗d2	

The h-pawn is immune (10...♖xh2? 11 ♖xh2 ♕xh2 12 ♕xb7).

10	...	♗e7

Black could defer this move in favor of 10...♘bd7.

Then 11 0-0-0 dxc4! 12 ♗xc4 b5 13 ♗-moves a6 and ...c5 gives him a very nice game.

11	cxd5	cxd5

White has a more comfortable game after 11...exd5 12 e4 or 11...♘xd5 12 g3 and 13 e4.

278

12 0-0-0

His king is safer on the queenside – provided he turns the c-file friendly with ♔b1! and ♖c1.

12 ... ♘c6

13 ♔b1 a6

14 ♖c1

Now 14...b5? allows a sound piece sacrifice – either one – on b5.

That is, 15 ♘xb5! axb5 16 ♗xb5 or 15 ♗xb5! axb6 16 ♘xb5 ♕d7 17 ♖xc6! ♕xc6 18 ♖c1, with a big edge in either case.

So far, so book.

White's best middlegame plans lie on the kingside, such as g2-g4-g5, or in the center with a prepared push of the e-pawn.

It is easy to imagine a ferocious Nakamura attack after 14...0-0 15 ♕d1 b5 16 g4.

For example, 16...♖fc8 17 h4 and 18 h5 gxh5 19 g5!. His bishop will come to life at d3.

But 14...♔f8 has value because Black can play 15...♘a5 without worrying about 16 ♕a4+ b5? 17 ♘xb5. His KR stands well on the half-open h-file.

14 ... ♘d7

15 ♗d3 ♖c8

16 ♘e2!

White stops 16...♘a5 and prepares e3-e4/♗f4.

He also waits for 16...0-0 17 h4!, when he has the beginning of an h4-h5 initiative.

Relatively best is 16...♕b6 (17 ♕a4 ♕a7 or 17 ♕d1 ♗b4).

16 ... b5?

Objectively, this is awful. But speed chess has its own principles: "A minute in blitz is equal to a pawn," according to blitzmeister Maxim Dlugy.

If this is true, losing a pawn is worthwhile if it costs your opponent a minute.

This is heresy at classical chess. At a slower speed, 17 a4! would be punishing.

Black can either concede a pawn, such as 17...bxa4 18 ♕xa4 a5? 19 ♗xa5 or 19 ♗a6.

Or he can suffer following 18...♘db8 19 e4!.

17 e4?!

But 16...b5 could be considered a good blitz move because White wasn't willing to spend time calculating 17 a4!.

Instead, 17 e4 looked right because 17...dxe4? 18 ♗xe4 gets into an awful pin.

17 ... ♘b6

This is the only good reply but is sufficient for an advantage.

The prospect of ...♘c4! is so daunting that some computers recommend 18 ♗a5 and ♗xb6.

Machines don't get depressed defending an inferior bishops-of-opposite-color endgame such

as 18...♘xa5 19 ♖xc7 ♘xb3 20 ♖xc8+ ♘xc8 21 axb3.

18 exd5 exd5!

Better than 18...♘xd5 19 ♗e4! ♕d7 20 ♗xd5 with equality.

Now 19 ♕d1 ♘c4 20 ♗xc4, would favor Black no matter how he retakes (20...bxc4 and 21...♕b6, for example).

Swapping the other bishop, 19 ♗f4 ♗d6 20 ♗xd6 ♕xd6, is no better after ...♘c4.

19 ♘f4 ♕d6

20 ♘e2

Another blitz guideline that violates classical chess principles:

When you don't have any good moves, repeat the position. It's likely to be just as safe as it was.

White would be close to lost after 20 h3 ♘c4 21 ♗xc4? dxc4 22 ♕e3 0-0, followed by ...♗f6 or ...♗g5.

20	...	♘c4

| 21 | ♗f4 |

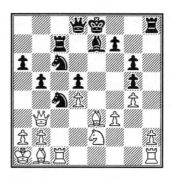

21	...	♕d7

You are a good tactician if you spotted 21...♕xf4 22 ♘xf4 ♘d2+.

You are a good calculator if you carried that further, to 23 ♔a1 ♘xb3+ 24 axb3 and saw that only 24...♗g5! favors Black. (25 ♖ce1+ ♔f8 26 ♘xd5 ♘xd4).

But you're a good practical player if you appreciate that his position is worth more than just a superior endgame.

22	g4	g5!
23	♗f5	♕d8
24	♗e3	

Nakamura is barely holding on. The knight fork on d2 would have cost material after 24 ♗xc8? gxf4.

24	...	♖c7
25	♔a1!	g6
26	♗b1	

Black cannot make further queenside progress (26...♘6a5 27 ♕d3 ♘xe3 28 ♕xe3 ♘c4 29 ♕f2).

The most fertile tactical ground is the e-file. Exploiting it best requires Black to vacate e8.

The king is safest after ...♔f8/...♗f6 and ...♖e7. But 26...0-0 and ...♗f6/...♖e8 is more ambitious.

26	...	♕d6?

This only hints at ...♖xh2. What he really wants is 27...♕e6!.

27	♗f2!

But Nakamura spots ♗g3! and begins one of his patented blitz comebacks.

27	...	♖c8
28	♗g3	♕d7
29	♕d3	

Given time (30 h3) White can equalize with 31 f4.

29	...	a5!

Caruana finds new queenside tactics: 30 h3 a4 31 f4 ♘6a5 with ideas such as 32...♖a8 and 33...♘b3+! 34 axb3 axb3+ and wins.

30 f4!

This tries to distract him with 30...♕xg4 31 f5!, when White has equalized (31...gxf5 32 ♕xf5 ♕xf5 33 ♗xf5).

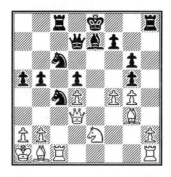

30 ... a4

Caruana sees a second mating pattern, after 31...♘b4 32 ♕f3 a3 32 b3.

He would win if he can open the long diagonal leading to the king.

There is even a smothered mate finish, 32...♘d2 33 ♖xc8+ ♕xc8 34 ♕f2? ♕c2! with a threat of 35...♕xb1+! 36 ♖xb1 ♘c2 mate.

31 fxg5?

Trying to maintain a slight time lead, Nakamura moved instantly. A draw would have been the most probable result of 31 f5!.

31 ... ♗xg5

32 ♘f4

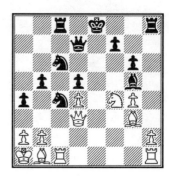

He may have seen fantasy finishes such as 32...0-0 33 h4! ♗xf4? 34 ♗xf4 ♕xg4 35 ♖dg1 ♕xf4? 36 ♖xg6+! and mates.

The forcing way to thwart that is 33...a3 34 b3 ♗f6!, using the mating pattern Caruana spotted earlier.

32 ... ♗f6

White's other hope was a knight sacrifice on g6.

It would work after 33 ♖ce1+ ♘e7? 34 ♘xg6!.

Or 33...♔f8? 34 ♘xg6+! fxg6 35 ♖hf1! with threats of ♖xf6+, ♗e5 and ♕xg6.

But the attack dies after 33...♔d8!.

33 ♘xg6

This held out hope for 33...fxg6? 34 ♕xg6+ ♕f7 35 ♖hf1! and White is saved.

| 33 | ... | ♗xd4 |

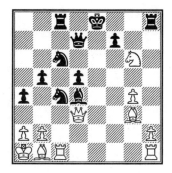

More accurate is 33...a3! because...

34   ♖ce1+?

White would not be losing after 34 ♖xc4!.

In fact, he would win after 34...bxc4 35 ♕e2+ ♔d8? (or 35...♘e7?) 36 ♗f5!.

The proper outcome of this wonderfully chaotic game is a draw after 35...♕e6 36 ♖e1! ♕xe2 37 ♖xe2+ ♔d8 38 ♘xh8.

34	...	♔d8
35	♕xd4!	♘xd4
36	♘xh8	

The queen sacrifice was the best (blitz) try in an otherwise hopeless position.

Black now can win with 36...a3!, or any of several defensive moves.

But he remembered one of his mating patterns.

36	...	♘b3+!
37	axb3	axb3
38	♗h4+	♔c7

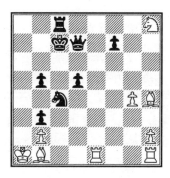

| 39 | ♗f5 | |

Of course, 39 ♖e7 ♖a8+ is lost.

But did you see that 40 ♗a2 ♘d2! is yet another mating pattern?

39	...	♘d2!
40	♖c1+	♔b6!
41	♗f2+	d4
42	**White resigns.**	

Either the rook or queen would have mated on the a-file

39
Cultural Divide

The ranking of the world's top players was overhauled during the first two decades of the 21th century. Two factors helped speed this. One of them was prevalence of computers for opening preparation. The other was the popularity of shorter time controls.

"The seven-hour control is quite boring for me, and almost all the young players of my age group prefer faster play," Sergey Karjakin said in 2007.

Garry Kasparov, who grew up on the format of forty moves in two and a half hours, deplored the change. "Now you do not need to have a deep understanding of chess in order to win," he said.

Kasparov and Karjakin were on opposite sides of a cultural divide. Kasparov's skill set included decades of experience. But there was so much information available via computers by 2010 that it compensated for a lack of experience, Vishy Anand said. Anand said members of the older generation – which included Anand – were at a disadvantage for a second reason: "Calculation is assuming a bigger and bigger role in chess these days. That favors the young by definition."

Anand was one of two world-class players who breached the divide and played nearly as well in 2016 as in 2006 (or 1996). The other was Vladimir Kramnik.

Caruana – Vladimir Kramnik
Leuven (Rapid) 2016
Ruy Lopez, Berlin Defense (C65)

1	e4	e5
2	♘f3	♘c6
3	♗b5	♘f6
4	d3	

Amateurs regularly avoid the Berlin endgame, 4 0-0 ♘xe4 5 d4 ♘d6 6 ♗xc6 dxc6 7 dxe5 ♘f5 8 ♕xd8+ ♚xd8, for the simple reason that it's an endgame. Grandmasters have other reasons. One is the Berlin's resistance to pre-game computer prep.

A rare case of Caruana winning the endgame against an elite

284

opponent was Caruana – Carlsen, Gashimov Memorial 2014.

It went 9 h3 h6 10 ♖d1+ ♔e8 11 ♘c3 ♗d7 12 ♗f4 ♖d8.

The string of routine moves was broken by 13 ♘e4!? ♗e7 14 g4! ♘h4 15 ♘xh4 ♗xh4 16 ♔g2. Caruana successfully mobilized his kingside pawns and won.

4	...	♗c5
5	c3	0-0
6	0-0	d6

Now that the e5-pawn is protected, Black can shift his knight from c6 to g6. This rules out ♗xc6 and enables him to punch back in the center with ...c6 and ...d5.

7 ♘bd2

White is not ready for 7 d4 ♗b6 because he has landed, a tempo down, in the Classical (3...♗c5) Variation of the Ruy.

This variation is under a cloud in its usual version. But with an extra tempo, Black would threaten 8...♘xe4 as well as 8....exd4 9 cxd4 ♗g4, undermining the d4-pawn.

There is nothing for White in 8 ♗xc6 bxc6 9 dxe5 dxe5 and he is significantly worse after 10 ♘xe5? ♗a6!.

7	...	♘e7
8	d4	exd4

Now this exchange is forced, as 8...♗b6 9 dxe5 costs a pawn.

9	cxd4	♗b6

Long after he resuscitated the Berlin Defense in the 2000 world championship match, Kramnik recalled the irony:

Garry Kasparov had a technological advantage in the match because of his state-of-the-art computers.

But he failed to press the advantage of being White because his machines told him 4 0-0 ♘xe4 was almost lost for Black.

"I think this was a trap Garry fell into," Kramnik told

The Perpetual Chess Podcast in 2021. "Computers were wrong."

Kasparov drew every 4 0-0 game, in fact all eight match games in which he was White, and lost his title.

10   ♖e1

In the decades after the match, younger players discovered ways to test the Berlin in 4 d3 variations.

Kramnik was able to keep up with them. He was one of the world's experts on the position after 9...♗b6.

When Caruana tried 10 b3 at Dortmund 2012, Kramnik equalized with 10...d5 11 e5 ♘e4 12 ♗d3 ♗f5.

10   ...   ♗g4

11   h3   ♗h5

And when Caruana was Black, he met Veselin Topalov's 12 ♕b3 with 12...d5 13 e5 ♘d7 and drew in the 2015 Sinquefield Cup.

12   a4   a6

13   ♗f1   ♘c6!

This was an improvement over 13...♖e8 14 a5! ♗a7 15 ♕b3, which gave White a nice space edge in Anand – Topalov, Moscow 2016.

Kramnik's move renews Black's pressure on d4. Now 14 g4? ♗g6

is better for him, e.g. 15 d5 ♘b4 or 15 e5 dxe5 16 dxe5 ♘e4.

14   a5!

He must have expected this because he took only seconds to decline the pawn offer.

White would get compensation after 14...♘xa5 15 d5, when he threatens to win the knight (16 b4).

Black must play 15...c5 and the position recalls a 19th century Evans Gambit. White would get ample play from 16 b3 followed by ♗b2, ♕c2, ♗d3 and perhaps ♘h4-f5.

The second way to accept the gambit is 14...♗xa5.

White's compensation is more visible after 15 g4 ♗g6 16 d5 because a knight move would lose the a5-bishop.

Instead, 16...♗xd2 17 ♘xd2 and 18 f4! is promising for White.

14   ...   ♗a7

White also has comp after the third option, 14...♗xd4 and 15 g4 g6 16 ♘xd4 ♘xd4 15 f4 ♗g6.

That leaves the fourth possibility, 14...♗xf3 15 ♘xf3 ♗xa5.

This is different from 14...♗xa5 because the e1-rook is attacked. Then 16 ♖e2 or 16 d5 ♗xe1 17 dxc6 are unclear.

15   ♖a4

Kramnik paused for the first time and thought for a minute and a half.

15   ...   h6

He might have been OK after 15...♘xd4 and the forcing line 16 ♖xd4! ♗xd4 17 g4 ♗xf2+ 18 ♔xf2 ♗g6.

But in a speed middlegame, two minor pieces are almost always going to matter more than a rook and two pawns.

This is particularly true when the rooks can't get into the game

yet (19 b4 ♖e8 20 ♗b2 ♘xe4 21 ♘xe4 ♗xe4 22 ♕d4).

16   ♕c2   ♖e8

17   ♗d3

We can safely declare Caruana the winner of the prep battle.

His pawn center is secure and he has ways to improve incrementally (b2-b3, ♗b2).

He doesn't need complications such as 17 ♗xa6 ♘xd4 18 ♘xd4 bxa6.

17   ...   ♗g6

18   b3   ♕d7

19   ♗b2

In a typical modern opening, the pawn structure allows White access, if not control, of his first four ranks.

Black is usually confined to his first three ranks. But that is sufficient for near-equality if he can find good squares for his heavy pieces.

We notice how difficult a Black position is when he can't find those good squares, for instance after 19...♖ad8 20 d5!.

Then 20...♘e7 21 ♗xf6 or 20...♘e5 21 ♘xe5 dxe5 22 ♘c4, confers a clear advantage on White.

19 ... ♘h5?

This is the first time in the game that Caruana did not reply instantly.

He had probably prepared to meet 19...d5! with 20 e5 ♗xd3 21 ♕xd3 ♘h5.

That new pawn structure favors White but not prohibitively so, after 22 ♕e3 ♘d8 and ...♘e6.

20 d5!

This stops Kramnik's intended 20...♘f4! 21 ♗f1 d5!, which would have favored him.

20 ... ♘e5

He had to give White a superior pawn structure or a space advantage, such as after 20...♘e7 21 ♘h4! ♘f4 22 ♕c3! f6 23 ♗f1, with a threat of ♕g3.

21 ♘xe5 dxe5

22 ♘f3

White has target pawns at b7, c7 and e5.

After 22...f6 23 ♖b4 ♖ab8 24 ♗c1 White would meet ...♘f4 with ♗xf4 and ♖c1, and begin harvesting pawns.

So, Kramnik gambles.

22 ... ♘f4

Caruana had to determine whether 23...♘xh3+ 24 gxh3+ ♕xh3 was a real threat and whether 23 ♗f1 ♘xd5 would endanger his advantage.

23 ♘xe5!

The answers are "maybe" and "no." Caruana found what should have been the winning move.

23 ... ♕d6

24 ♘g4

The right way was 24 ♕d2!.

He may have overlooked that 24...♖xe5 25 ♕xf4 ♖xd5? does not work because 26 exd5! protects his queen by the a4-rook.

Instead, Black can sacrifice the Exchange with 24...♘xh3+ 25 gxh3 ♖xe5 26 ♗xe5 ♕xe5.

Then ...♗c5-d6 would defend c7 and menace the kingside.

But 27 ♔g2 and f2-f4 wins.

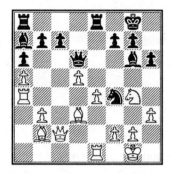

Caruana had his eyes on winning with a mate threat, 25 ♕c3! and 25...f6 26 e5!.

24 ...   ♘xd5?

Black had time for 24...h5!.

The key point is 25 ♕c3 f6 26 e5? then allows 26...♘xd3! 27 exd6 ♖xe1+ 28 ♔h2 hxg4 and Black has turned the tables.

Better is 25 ♘e3 and 25...♘xd3 26 ♕xd3 when White has to win the game all over again.

25 ♖d1!

But now 25...♘b4 26 ♕c3; 25...♘f6 26 e5 and 25...♘e7 26 ♕c3! f6 27 ♗c4+.

25 ...   ♘f4

26 ♕c3!   ♘e6

Or 26...♘h5 27 ♗e2! ♕f8 28 ♘xh6+.

27 ♗c2

White would have made the game much longer by 27 ♘xh6+ ♔h7 28 e5? ♕c5.

Or much shorter with 28 ♘f5!.

Then after 28...♕c5 29 ♕d2 both 30 ♖c4 and 30 ♗xg7! ♘xg7 31 ♕h6+ are threatened.

27 ...   ♕c5

28 ♖c4   ♕g5

29 ♖d5   ♕h4

Good enough to win is 30 ♖xc7!.

But after 30...♖ad8 White lacks a powerful follow-up (31 ♖xb7? ♗d4!).

30 ♔h2!

In a speed game, this is much stronger. Black has to see how 31 g3! and 31 f4!/32 f5 have become threats.

30 ...   c6

He didn't have enough time to realize 30...h5! 31 g3 ♕e7 32 ♘h6+ ♔h7 is not hopeless.

Black can hang on, for at least a while, after 33 ♘f5 ♕f8 34 f4 ♖ad8.

31	g3	♕e7
32	♘xh6+	♔h7
33	♘f5	

Now, however, 33...♕f8 is lost after 34 ♖d7 and ♖xb7.

33	...	cxd5
34	exd5!	

White also wins after 34 ♘xe7 dxc4 35 ♘xg6.

34	...	♕f6

But 34...♗xf5 35 ♗xf5+ and 36 dxe6 was resignable.

And 34...♕f8 leads to a massacre after 35 ♖h4+ ♔g8 36 ♘h6+ ♔h7 37 ♘xf7+ and ♗xg6.

Caruana paused here for nearly three of his remaining seven minutes.

The endgame of 35 ♕xf6 gxf6 36 ♖h4+ ♔g8 37 ♗xf6 ♘g7 38 ♗xg7 f6 39 ♗xf6 has to be winning. But there was better:

35	♖h4+	♔g8
36	♘h6+	♔f8
37	♗a3+	

When he chose his 35th move, Caruana saw the mating pattern of 37...♖e7 38 ♘f5!! and ♖h8.

37	...	♘c5
38	♗xc5+	♗xc5
39	♕xc5+	♕e7
40	♘f5!!	resigns.

Final position

A flawed game, but how many times is a former world champion mated in this elegant a manner?

40
Standard, Non-Standard

Masters know when to violate general principles. This is one of the fundamental reasons they are masters. They can recognize a counter-intuitive but good positional move as readily as amateurs spot basic mating patterns.

When Levon Aronian defeated Anish Giri at the 2015 Sinquefield Cup he gave credit to an unusual recapture, 16 exf3!. It doubled his f-pawns. But it gave him a better way to control the center, after f3-f4. Aronian called it a "standard, non-standard move."

Caruana demonstrated another unusual pawn capture in the following game. It was played in the last round, after he had drawn his first eight games. He was in danger of drawing all of his games, that is, "a Giri."

Caruana – Anish Giri
Sinquefield Cup, St. Louis 2016
Ruy Lopez, Open Defense (C81)

1	e4	e5
2	♘f3	♘c6
3	♗b5	a6
4	♗a4	♘f6
5	0-0	♘xe4

The Open Defense became a battleground for these two players in 2015.

At Wijk aan Zee, Giri was White and eventually drew a lost position.

Five months later, Giri was Black at the Gashimov Memorial

and drew an equal heavy-piece endgame.

6	d4	b5
7	♗b3	d5
8	dxe5	♗e6
9	♕e2	♘c5

Fashion follows computer function.

When the Howell (9 ♕e2) Variation first became popular, after World War II, the most popular version was 9...♗e7. This lasted for decades, with no major discoveries.

Then computers claimed 9...♘c5 would bring Black close to equality.

10 ⌶d1 ♘xb3

Now 11 axb3 opens half of the a-file for White's rook. The doubled b-pawns can help c2-c4 pound at the d5-pawn.

11 cxb3

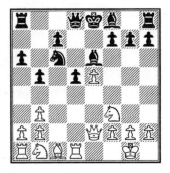

On-line commentators treated Caruana's last move as a bizarre novelty.

But more than 50 years ago the non-standard cxb3 was commonly praised.

It was played in this move order and in the related one, 9...♗e7 10 ⌶d1 ♘c5 and then 11 ♘c3 ♘xb3 12 cxb3!.

11 ... ♗e7

One of the benefits of cxb3 is that it makes it easier to occupy c5 with pieces.

For example, 11...♕d7 12 ♘c3 ♗c5 13 ♘e4 ♗b6 and now 14 ♗e3 ♗xe3? (14...d4!) 15 ♕xe3 favors White.

12 ♘c3 0-0

This position was once considered bad for Black because of a well-publicized miniature, Ivkov – Donner, Havana 1966. It went:

13 ♗e3 ♘a5 14 ⌶ac1 ♘b7? (14...c5) 15 ♘e4! ♗g4 16 h3 ♗xf3 17 ♕xf3 c6? 18 ♘g3 ⌶c8 19 ♘f5 g6? 20 ⌶xd5! ♕e8 21 ♗h6 resigns.

Yet the cxb3 idea was slowly forgotten.

13 ♗e3

If White had recaptured 11 axb3 and play continued as in the game, Black would be at least equal after 13...♘b4!.

He would prepare 14...c5 and be able to punish 14 ♘e4? with 14...♗f5!.

But in our game, 13...♘b4? just loses time after 14 a3!.

13 ... ♕d7!

Black doesn't need ...c5 to discourage White from occupying c5.

After 14 ♘e4? ♗g4! he would threaten 15 ...♘xe5.

Then 15 ♘c5 ♗xc5 16 ♗xc5 ♖fe8 reveals the e5-pawn to be fatally weak.

White's other natural plan, pressuring the d5-pawn, will be dead if Black can play 14...♘d8 and 15...c6.

White has another option, trading bishops so that he can occupy c5 with a knight following ♘e4.

But again there is a problem. Black would stand well after 14 ♗g5 ♖ad8 15 ♖ac1 ♖fe8 and ...d4.

14   h3

To sum up: In some positions Black wants to put his knight on d8 (and ...c6). In others he wants to play ...♖ad8 (and ...d4).

He can't do both. This is why 14 h3 – an innovation -- is a useful pass.

14   ...   ♖ad8

White would win the waiting game after 14...♘d8 15 ♘e4 and ♘c5!.

15   ♖d2!

Now that ...♘d8/...c6 is impossible, Caruana prepares 16 ♖ad1 and ♘xd5.

15   ...   f6

This move would have been better a move ago. But chances remain balanced.

So far, White hasn't paid a price for his doubled pawns.

But he would after 16 ♗f4? fxe5 17 ♘xe5 ♘xe5 18 ♗xe5 c5! and ....♕c6/...d4.

There is no real advantage in 16 exf6 ♗xf6, e.g. 17 ♖ad1 ♕f7 or 17 ♗g5 ♗xh3!.

16   ♖ad1!

Now 16...♗b4 17 exf6! would be a tactical problem (17...♖xf6? 18 ♗g5).

Or a positional one (17...gxf6 18 ♘d4).

16   ...   ♘xe5

Giri had to decide whether to offer a trade of knights or keep them on the board.

After 16...fxe5 17 ♘xd5 White threatens a discovered attack on the queen (18 ♘f6+ or 18 ♘b4).

It could lead to the same kind of rooks-versus-queen endgame as in the game, 17...♗xd5 18 ♖xd5 ♕xd5 19 ♖xd5 ♖xd5.

The Fischer rule

Many beginners' books say two rooks are equal to a queen. But Bobby Fischer indicated this was only true when there are no minor pieces.

What could be called Fischer's rule states:

The more minor pieces there are, the greater the queen's superiority.

This would be underlined here by 20 ♕c2! and ♕e4.

White has a significant advantage – not just because of the weak e5-pawn but because the queen may do greater damage with ♕g4-e6+!.

For example, 20...♘b4 21 ♕e4 c6 22 ♕g4 and 22...♔h8? 23 ♕e6 ♗f6.

Then the presence of an extra pair of minors is a boon to White after 24 ♗g5, 24 ♘g5 or 24 ♗d2 ♘xa2 25 ♕xc6.

17   ♘xe5   fxe5

18   ♘xd5

With knights off the board, Black can try 18...♗d6 without fear of ♘g5!.

But this presents White with another option, 19 ♗g5 ♖de8 20 ♘xc7! ♕xc7 21 ♖xd6.

Despite the bishops of opposite color, he would have reasonable winning chances after, say, 21...♕a5 22 a3 ♗xb3 23 ♖c1 and ♖c5.

18   ...   ♗xd5

19   ♖xd5

Now 19...♕e6 seems to lead to a fairly balanced queen-and-bishop endgame, 20 ♖xd8 ♖xd8 21 ♖xd8+ ♗xd8.

But 22 ♗d4 is somewhat unpleasant to defend.

For example, 22...♗f6 (22...e4 23 f3) 23 ♕e4! with prospects of ♕b7.

19   ...   ♕xd5?

But this is a fundamental error, violating Fischer's rule.

20 ♖xd5 ♖xd5

21 ♕c2

White has the greater winning chances because of his superior bishop and his queen's potential invasion of light squares (e4, c6, g4, f5 and e6).

If you don't believe this, set up this position on a computer with a slightly different pawn structure:

Shift the e5-pawn to f7. Then rearrange the Black queenside pawns so that they are on a7, b7 and c6.

Your machine will tell you Black has a powerful advantage.

But in our game it will say a White edge slowly intensifies.

21 ... c5

Black can safeguard his pieces better with 21...♗d6 22 ♕e4 c6.

But after 22 b4 White can pursue the same kingside pawn

advances of the game without queenside distraction.

22 g3 ♔h8

There is no bulletproof defensive formation on Black's kingside.

But 22...g6! appears better, e.g. 23 ♕e4 ♖fd8 24 h4 ♔g7.

23 h4!

Caruana violates Capablanca's rule by putting his pawns on the same-colored squares of his bishop. This benefits his king.

23 ... ♖fd8

Black would love to liquidate pawns. But 23...♖c8 (and ...c4) invites a light-square invasion, 24 ♕f5.

The game could end immediately, 24...♖c6?? 25 ♕f7! and wins with ♕xe7 or ♕e8+.

Or more slowly, 24...♖cd8 25 ♕e6 and ♕xa6.

24 ♕e4 h6

25 ♔g2 ♗f6

295

26 ♚h3

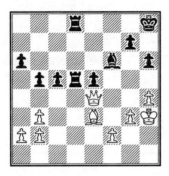

Black's pieces have no offensive power.

The rooks cannot double on the seventh rank, for example.

White has both tactical ideas (♕g6/♗xh6) and a strategic plan of pushing his g-pawn to g5, with king support.

26 ... h5!

Giri visualizes a fortress: 27 ♕g6 e4 28 ♕xe4 ♗xb2 and perhaps 29 ♕e6 ♗f6 30 ♕xa6 b4.

Then White has no easy way to create a passed pawn or use his king. Of course, Magnus said there's no such thing as an impregnable fortress...

27 a4!

Caruana wants to create a passed pawn while Black is running out of playable passes.

Now 27...♚g8 28 ♕f5 e4 29 ♕xe4 ♗xb2 and the fortress doesn't hold, 30 ♗g5!.

27 ... ♜d3

Semi-desperate since it abandons the h-pawn with check.

28 axb5 axb5

29 ♕g6 e4

30 ♕xh5+ ♚g8

31 ♕f5

White may need one of the queenside pawns (31...♜xb3?? 32 ♕e6+). Also winning was 31 ♕xc5.

With the fortress idea dead, Black's best bet for a draw is to trade bishops.

Now 32 ♕xc5 ♗d4! gets needlessly complicated (33 ♗xd4 ♜8xd4 34 ♕xb5 e3).

32 ♕xe4 c4

There was still a slim drawing chance after White trades his last queenside pawn.

33 bxc4 bxc4

| 34 | ♕xc4+ | ♖3d5 |

Subtract one of White's pawns and his simple win vanishes.

For instance, if the h4-pawn were gone, Black could defend with ...♔h8 and ...♗d4.

| 35 | g4! |

But now Black cannot stop White from pushing them to g5, h5 and f4, with the king advancing to g4.

| 35 | ... | ♔h8 |

| 36 | g5 | ♗d4 |

One of many winning scenarios runs 36...♔g8 37 h5 ♖d7 38 f4 ♖d8 39 ♔g4 ♖d7 40 ♗c5 ♖d8 41 ♗e7! ♖8d7 42 g6! and mates.

| 37 | ♗xd4 | ♖xd4 |
| 38 | ♕f7 |

The simplest win now is g5-g6 and getting the queen to h5 for ♕h7+.

| 38 | ... | ♖8d7 |

Thanks to his h-pawn, White's king can hide, e.g. 38...♖d3+ 39 ♔g4 ♖8d4+ 40 ♔h5.

| 39 | ♕e8+ | ♔h7 |
| 40 | ♕h5+ |

But not 40 g6+?? ♔h6 when the win is magically gone.

| 40 | ... | ♔g8 |

41	g6!	♖e4
42	♕h7+	♔f8
43	♕h8+	♔e7
44	♕xg7+	♔e6
45	♕h8	♖d3+
46	♔h2	resigns.

41
Square Grabbing

After a decade in Europe, Caruana returned to the United States. He was promised $200,000 a year to play for the US, according to the Italian chess federation, which lost his services. This became the rare chess story that gained traction with mainstream media. "The United States is buying up nerds!" the popular comedian Jon Stewart said on his widely watched "The Daily Show." Magnus Carlsen repeated the quip, tweeting "So they are indeed buying nerds!"

Caruana said he could not talk about the financial details. But he denied he had changed nationalities. "I had dual nationality from birth," he said. "I feel connected to both countries. I would like to represent both, but only one is possible... I feel very much an American, but I cherish my Italian roots."

In his first appearance on a US team, Caruana led the Americans into the last day of the 2016 Olympiad with a one-point lead over a surprising Ukraine squad. A victory by almost any margin in the final round seemed to guarantee the first gold medals for the US in 40 years.

But two of his teammates appeared to be in trouble as their match, against Canada, unfolded. Caruana adopted one of his most aggressive White openings and claimed an advantage in space by move eight. It grew with a series of square-grabbing moves.

Caruana – Evgeny Bareev
Olympiad, Baku, 2016
Caro-Kann Defense,
Advance Variation (B12)

1	e4	c6
2	d4	d5
3	e5	♗f5

4 ♘f3

The Advance Variation had been a Fabiano favorite for years, with 4 c4 and 4 h4 but also with the slow development scheme of ♘f3/♗e2 that was popularized circa 1990 by Nigel Short.

4	...	e6

5   ♗e2   ♘d7

Black's knight would be better placed on c6, as in the comparable e4-e5 variations of the French Defense.

But 5...c5 6 0-0 ♘c6 7 c3 leaves Black's other knight hunting for a good square.

6   0-0   ♗g6

This frees f5. Black would be in relatively good shape after, for instance, 7 ♘bd2 ♘h6 8 ♘b3 ♘f5 9 c3 ♗e7.

His counterplay would come from ...f6 and/or ...♖c8/...c5.

7   a4

With the center closed, White can't do much of a forcing nature. But with 8 a5 he can convert his advantage in time, that is, development, into an advantage in space.

7   ...   ♘e7

If Black stops that with 7...a5, it becomes much riskier to play ...c5 because of the hole at b5.

8   a5

Black's space problem worsens naturally after, say, 8...♘f5 9 c4 ♗e7 10 ♘c3 0-0.

A consequence of controlling much more space is that you can take liberties. White could safely play 11 g4! ♘h4 12 ♘xh4 ♗xh4 12 f4!, with a threat of f4-f5.

8   ...   a6

It is too late for 8...c5 because of the light-square weaknesses incurred by 9 a6.

For example, 9...b6? 10 ♗b5 ♘f5 11 c3 and ♕a4.

9   b4!

White's c1-bishop was somewhat bad after 3 e5 and was made worse by 8 a5. How does 9 b4 help him?

The answer is ...c5 has been all but ruled out and Black's pieces will be limited to his first three ranks for the forseeable future.

In contrast, White's b1-knight would have a bright future after ♘bd2-b3-c5!.

9 ... ♘f5

If Black contests the queenside, 9...b6 10 axb6 ♕xb6 11 c3 a5, he will be outgunned when 12 ♘bd2 threatens ♘b3xa5.

For example, 12...♕d8 13 bxa5 ♖xa5 14 ♗a3 ♘f5 15 ♗xf8 ♖xa1 16 ♕xa1 and ♕a6.

10 c3 f6!

Bareev, once an elite GM, had played infrequently since 2010.

But he knew enough about pawn structures to understand he would run out of useful moves soon after 10...♗e7 11 ♗f4 0-0 12 ♘bd2.

11 ♗f4 fxe5

Black can't separate his space problem from his tactical problems. For example, 11...♗e7? allows a strong 12 g4! ♘h6 13 exf6!.

12 dxe5

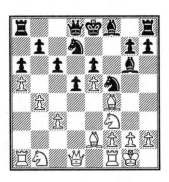

Yes, e5 would be a nice square for a White minor piece, 12 ♘xe5 ♘xe5 13 ♗xe5.

But exchanging pieces helps Black. He would reach a relatively safe middlegame following 13...♗d6.

After 12 dxe5 Black has to be concerned about g2-g4 followed by ♘d4 and ♘xe6.

12 ... ♗e7

13 g4!

Black would have escaped after 13 ♘bd2? 0-0 14 ♘b3 ♗h5, for instance.

13 ... ♘h4

Black ultimately loses because he won't be able to defend his knight on h4. But 13...♘h6 14 ♘d4 is as bad as it looks.

14 ♘d4 ♗f7

15 ♗g3

Now 15...0-0 16 f4 and f4-f5 is what Caruana has been playing for.

Black does not get enough counterplay after 16...c5 17 bxc5 ♘xc5 18 ♘d2 (if 18...♗g6 then 19 ♘2b3!).

15 ... h5?

Even strong grandmasters make errors of desperation when the alternatives appear so dismal.

The best chance for middlegame counterplay lay in 15...g5 so that after 16 ♗xh4 gxh4 17 f4 he can try to flee with ...♕c7 and ...0-0-0.

16 gxh5

Caruana said he was "pretty convinced I would win" now.

16 ... ♕c7

He was more certain after Bareev allowed his bishop to g4.

Black should have tried to blockade the kingside with 16...♘f5! 17 ♘xf5 gxf5 followed by ...♘f8-e6.

However, there were tactical obstacles, such as 18 ♖e1 ♘f8 19 ♕c2! ♕d7 20 ♘d2.

Then 20...♗xh5? 21 e6! ♘xe6 22 ♕xf5 loses.

17 ♗g4! ♖h6

18 f4

Given a free hand, Caruana will have a choice of winning by picking off the stranded h4-knight (♕e1 and ♗xh4) or by completing a strategic plan (f4-f5!).

18 ... c5

19 bxc5 ♕xc5

For example, 19...♘xc5 20 f5! ♘xf5 21 ♘xf5 exf5 22 e6 and wins.

20 ♔h1!

The immediate 20 ♕e1? would permit Black to get back into the game with 20...♗xh5.

With 20 ♔h1! White's unpinned d4-knight could meet ...♗xh5 with ♘xe6!.

20	...	0-0-0

21	♘d2	♖dh8

22	♕e1	

Now 22...♘f5 23 ♗xf5 exf5 24 e6 would be resignable...

22	...	♗xh5

23	♗xe6!	

...as is this position. White has a knockout plan of f4-f5 and ♖f4.

23	...	♗e8

24	f5	♗d8

25	♖f4!	g5

26	♖f2	

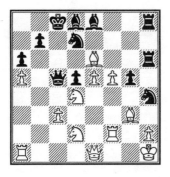

This last finesse frees White to advance both his f- and e-pawns.

26	...	♗c7

27	♕e3	♔b8

28	f6	♘f8

29	♗g4	♘hg6

30	♘2b3	♕a7

31	f7	resigns.

The US team ended the tournament in a tie with Ukraine in match points. Only hours later did they learn they had taken the gold medal on tie-breaking points.

Caruana's final score, 7-3, earned a bronze medal as the third best result on first board. In the previous Olympiad, Hikaru Nakamura had the 18th best result on first board and the US tied for 12th. The last time an American received any Olympiad medal on first board was when Bobby Fischer earned silver in 1970.

302

42
Going for the Kill

More and more in modern master chess, the player who gains an advantage faces a decision around moves 25 to 30. Should he seek – or allow – piece exchanges that lead to an endgame? And if so, which pieces? Which endgames?

Or should he press in the final moves of the first time control, at the risk that the tension in the position will peter out? Magnus Carlsen might handle the position in this game differently after move 24 because of the grindability of Black's potential endgame. Caruana opts, instead, for complications.

Arkadij Naiditsch – Caruana
Karlsruhe 2017
Vienna Game (C28)

1	e4	e5
2	♗c4	♘f6
3	d3	♘c6

This is a perfectly good alternative to the 3...c6 that we saw in Games 4 and 26. It offers White an opportunity to transpose into the Two Knights Defense with 4 ♘f3.

| 4 | ♘c3 | |

He chooses another opening, the Vienna Game.

| 4 | ... | ♘a5 |

And that's the name we'll stick with. After 4...♗c5 5 f4 we would have transposed once more, to a King's Gambit Declined.

| 5 | ♘ge2 | |

Bent Larsen did more than anyone to bring the Vienna Game out of mothballs.

During a Candidates match in 1965, he beat Lajos Portisch surprisingly easily after 5...♘xc4 6 dxc4.

With ...d5 virtually ruled out, Larsen carried out a simple development plan of 0-0, b2-b3, ♗b2 and ♘g3.

303

5	...	♝c5

6	0-0	0-0!

Caruana's delay in ...♘xc4 means White cannot fianchetto his other bishop because 7 b3? c6! would threaten 8...d5.

7	♘g3	h6

Now White's c1-bishop has no obvious future.

He would not be happy with two pairs of doubled pawns, 8 ♝e3? ♝xe3 9 fxe3 ♘xc4 10 dxc4.

8	h3	d6

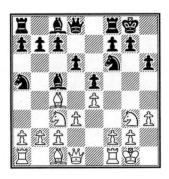

9	♝b3!

White's best chance for an advantage is ♘a4xc5.

For example, 9...♘xb3 10 axb3 ♝e6 10 ♘a4! is deceptively strong, e.g. 10...♝b6 11 ♘xb6 axb6 12 ♖xa8 ♛xa8 13 f4!.

9	...	c6

10	♘a4	♘xb3

11	axb3	♝b4

Similar is 11...♝b6 12 ♘xb6 ♛xb6 13 ♝e3 and 14 f4!.

12	♝d2

White apparently didn't want to play 12 c3 ♝a5 because his knight is stalemated and must find an answer to 13...b5.

12	...	♝xd2

13	♛xd2	d5

Now 14 f4 dxe4 15 fxc5 ♛d4+ 16 ♖f2 ♛xe5 is balanced.

A good alternative is 14 exd5 cxd5 15 f4 or 14...♘xd5 15 ♖fe1.

14	♛b4

Naiditsch looks instead to his left, with a threat, 15 ♘b6.

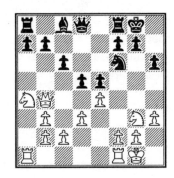

14	...	b6!

He overlooked this positional nicety based on a tactic, 15 ♘xb6? ♖b8!.

Caruana prepares to build a dark-square pawn mass.

This is more ambitious than the forcing 14...b5 15 ♘c5 a5 16 ♕c3 ♕c7 17 b4, when chances are roughly even.

15   ♘c3?

It wasn't too late for 15 exd5! ♘xd5 16 ♕e4 with rough equality.

15   ...   c5

16   ♕a3   d4

17   ♘ce2   a5!

White would have recovered if he had been allowed to play 18 b4! or 17...♕d6 18 f4.

18   f4   ♗e6

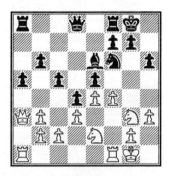

Because White's queen is offside and unable to defend the kingside, he should avoid 19 fxe5 ♘d7 and ...♘xe5/...♕g5/...h5-h4.

19   ♖ae1

For most of the remainder of the game Black retains the option of playing to win on the queenside.

After 19 f5? ♗d7 White would safeguard his king but dash prospects of his own kingside play.

Black could methodically prepare a queenside breakthrough (...♗c6, ...♕e7, ...b5 and ...a4!).

19   ...   exf4

20   ♘xf4

Caruana had easy decisions to make since 14...b6. But now he has to choose between a kingside plan or opening the a-file, after 20...♕c7 and ...♕e5/...♗d7/...a4.

20   ...   ♘d7

He opts for ...♘e5/...♕h4 or ...♕g5.

It he had tried to preserve his bishop, with 20...♗c8 and then ...♘d7, he would allow White's knights a free, equalizing ride to d5 and f5.

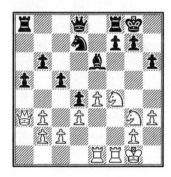

21   ♕a1

Another piece trade, 21 ♘xe6 fxe6, would magnify the difference between the queens and remaining knights (22 ♕a1 ♕g5 or 22 ♕a4 ♕c7).

If rooks also depart, after 22 ♖xf8+ ♕xf8 23 ♕a4 ♘e5, White has a lingering problem with his queenside pawns.

For example 24 ♖f1 ♕d6 25 ♕b5 ♕c6 26 ♕xc6 ♘xc6 and potentially ...♘b4xc2.

21	...	♕g5
22	♔h2	♘e5
23	♕d1	♖ae8

White's prodigal queen has returned and he is nearly equal.

But endgames, such as 24 ♕h5 ♘c6 25 ♕xg5 hxg5, would be difficult for him because of the chronic ...♘b4xc2 problem.

24   ♘ge2

We are approaching the point when Caruana has major decisions to make.

For example, he can decide to go for a kingside kill with 24...♗d7 and ...♗c6 followed by ...f5.

That requires calculating 25 ♘d5 and 25...♗c6! 26 ♘xb6 f5.

This would win after 27 ♕c1 ♕h4 28 ♕f4 ♕d8! followed by 29...♕xb6 or 29...fxe4.

24	...	♘g6

Instead, he quickly opted for ...♕e5.

Both players understood that 25 ♘xg6 fxg6! would allow Black excellent winning chances after ...♕e5+/...g5!.

25	♕c1	♕e5
26	♔g1	♘h4

Black has created a potential new way to win, a knight ending.

It could come about after 27 ♖f2 g5! 28 ♘xe6 fxe6.

The rooks are likely to depart, 29 ♖ef1 ♘g6 30 ♖xf8+ ♖xf8 31 ♖xf8+ ♔xf8.

Then a trade of queens is also probable (32 ♕e1 ♔e7 33 ♕f2 ♕f6 34 ♕xf6+), with good prospects for Black.

| 27 | g3 | ♘g6 |

| 28 | ♔g2 | ♛d6 |

Another option is a ♛+♗-vs.-♛+♘ endgame, 29 ♔h2 ♗d7 30 ♘xg6 fxg6 31 ♖xf8+ ♖xf8 32 ♖f1 g5! 33 ♖xf8+ ♔xf8, once again with plenty of ways the game can end 0-1.

| 29 | ♔h2 | |

Yet another possibility is a heavy piece endgame, after 29 ♘xe6 fxe6 30 ♘g1 ♘e5 31 ♘f3 ♘xf3 32 ♖xf3 ♖xf3 33 ♔xf3.

In heavy piece endings, priority No. 1 is king safety.

The ability to create/push a passed pawn is No.2

White's king is not in trouble in this scenario but Black can play for a win with 33...b5 and 34...a4.

| 29 | ... | ♘e5! |

| 30 | ♔g2! | |

Caruana was ready for ...♗d7-c6 and ...f5. So, why did White move his king onto the potentially toxic h1-a8 diagonal?

The answer is that after 30...♗d7 he can stifle ...f5 with 31 g4! ♗c6 32 ♘h5 and ♘eg3.

This would be impossible with his king on h2 because of ...g5.

| 30 | ... | f5! |

If Caruana didn't want one of the potential endgames, this was the best try. It would win after 31 exf5? ♗d5+ and ...♘f3(+).

| 31 | ♘xe6 | ♖xe6 |

| 32 | exf5 | |

The f-file would be disastrously opened after 32 ♘f4? ♖ef6.

| 32 | ... | ♛d5+ |

White played his next move instantly. He had to expect ...♘f3+.

33   ♔g1?

The difference between this and 33 ♔h2! seems obscure but it is decisive.

After 33 ♔h2 ♘f3+? Black's advantage is negligible, 34 ♖xf3 ♖xe2+ 35 ♖xe2 ♕xf3 36 ♕e1.

To play for a win he should delay the check with 33...♖ef6 and capture on f5, e.g. 34 ♘g1 ♖xf5 35 ♖xf5 ♖xf5.

But White can safely offer the Exchange with 34 g4! ♘f3+ 35 ♖xf3 ♕xf3 36 ♕f4!.

White's powerful knight and protected pawn is sufficient compensation after 36...♕xf4+ 37 ♘xf4 or 36...♕a8 37 ♘g3 ♖e8 38 ♘e4.

33   ...   ♖ef6

But now 34 g4 ♘f3+ 35 ♖xf3 ♕xf3 36 ♕f4 would lose the h-pawn.

Black wins after 36...♕xh3 37 ♘g3 g5! 38 ♕f3 h5! 39 gxh5 ♖xf5.

Tougher is 36 ♕g3 ♕xg3+ 37 ♘xg3. But 36...g6! would win eventually.

34   ♘f4   ♘f3+

35   ♔f2

Also lost is 35 ♔h1 ♕c6 36 ♖e4 ♘g5. There is one more point to appreciate.

35   ...   ♕xf5!

This is it: 36 ♖e2 can be met by 36...♘h2 37 ♖h1 ♕xh3.

36   ♔xf3   ♕xh3

37   ♖e4   g5

The rest is the usual inertia of time trouble, e.g. 38 ♖h1 ♖xf4+ 39 ♖xf4 ♖xf4+ 40 ♕xf4 ♕xh1+.

38   ♔e2   ♕xg3

39   ♖f3   ♕g4

40   ♕h1   ♖xf4

41   White resigns.

The control is over and 42 ♖xf4 ♖xf4 will be a lost pawn endgame after 43...♕xf3+.

43
Wounding

Had Naiditsch escaped in that game (after 33 ♔h2!), critics could blame Caruana for trying too hard to win a position that should have been treated more conservatively. The opposite critique can be made about the following game. He badly wounds White in the opening. But then he misses two powerful, if not decisive opportunities to kill.

However, he preserves the tactical tension in the position. The longer that tension remains, the more likely the better tactician prevails.

Georg Meier – Caruana
Karlsruhe 2018
Ruy Lopez, Exchange Variation
(C69)

1	e4	e5
2	♘f3	♘c6
3	♗b5	a6
4	♗xc6	dxc6
5	0-0	♕f6

The rare 5...♕f6 is attributed to Svetozar Gligorić and had been a Caruana favorite for years.

Like David Bronstein's 5...♕d6, it prepares queenside castling.

The Bronstein line is considered OK for Black after 6 d4 exd4 7 ♘xd4 ♗d7 and ...0-0-0 and less so after 6 ♘a3.

| 6 | d4 | |

But here 6 ♘a3? permits Black an easy game with 6...♗xa3 7 bxa3 ♗g4.

6	...	exd4
7	♗g5	♕d6
8	♘xd4	

Caruana had previously played 8...♗d7 9 ♘c3 ♘e7 and was ready to meet 10 ♕d2 or 10 f4 with 10...c5!.

White has an extra tempo (♗g5) compared with the Bronstein

variation. But it may help Black after:

8 ... ♗e7

For example, 9 ♗xe7 ♘xe7 10 ♘c3 ♗d7.

And then 11 ♕d2? c5! 12 ♘b3 ♕xd2 13 ♘xd2 0-0-0.

9 ♗e3

Caruana had played 9...♘f6 before.

His opponent, Arkadij Naiditsch, stopped ...♘g4 with 10 f3! and achieved a mild plus after 10...0-0 11 ♘d2 c5 12 ♘c4.

9 ... ♘h6

This move is superior because 10 f3 allows 10...f5!.

Then ...fxe4 would help Black.

But ...f4! is better because it would give him a very nice pawn structure, with a secure outpost on e5.

White cannot afford to trade his second bishop, 11 ♗xh6? ♕xh6

12 exf5 0-0 or 12 ♘xf5 ♗xf5 13 exf5 0-0 and ...♗d6, when he would be woefully weak on dark squares.

10 ♕d2

White is willing to play an endgame, 10...c5 11 ♘b3 ♕xd2 12 ♘1xd2, because Black is a move or two away from securing his queenside pawns.

For example, 12...b6 13 ♗f4! ♗d6? 14 ♗xd6 cxd6 15 ♘c4 wins a pawn.

10 ... g5!

This stops ♗f4 so 11...♘g4 and 12...♕xh2 mate is a threat.

It is tactically based on 11 ♗xg5? ♗xg5 12 ♕xg5 ♖g8 with advantage (13 ♕d2? ♗h3 or 13 ♕h4 ♕xd4 14 ♕xh6 ♕xb2).

11 ♘f3

White could have stopped 11...♘g4 with 11 h3 or 11 f3.

The former makes it easier for Black to try to open the kingside, e.g. 11...♖g8 12 ♘c3 ♗d7 13 ♖ad1 0-0-0 and ...♕g6/...f5.

On the other hand, 11 f3 makes 11...c5 stronger because 12 ♘f3 is not possible.

The endgame of 12 ♘b3 ♕xd2 13 ♘1xd2 b6 14 ♖ad1 f5 is nice for Black.

11 ... ♖g8

This was the first move Caruana thought about.

The 11...♕xd2 endgame would be fine for him. But he would prefer the 11...♖g8 12 ♕xd6 cxd6 version.

12 h4

White tries to exploit his only target (12...gxh4? 13 ♕xd6 and 14 ♗xh6). But he underestimated Black's reply.

12 ... ♕g6!

Your computer may initially scream "Error!" Let it calm down and realize the mistake was 12 h4?!.

13 hxg5

White drops a piece after 13 ♗xg5?? or 13 ♘xg5?? because of 13...f6.

13 ... ♘g4

14 ♘c3

Another trap is 14 ♗f4 h6 15 gxh6? ♘e5! or 15...♘h2!.

14 ... h6!

15 ♗f4

One of the paradoxes of opening preparation is that no matter how much you study a position at home, you may not understand it fully until your clock is ticking.

Caruana took 25 minutes here, his biggest think of the game.

15 ... ♗e6?

He didn't appreciate how strong 15...hxg5 16 ♗xc7 ♕h6 was.

Then on 17 ♖fd1 ♖h8 18 ♔f1 it was a better time for 18...♗e6 because it threatens 19...♕h1+ 20 ♔e2 ♗c4+.

311

16   ♗xc7!   ♖c8

White defends easily after 16...hxg5 17 ♘d4! and f2-f3.

17   ♗b6

The bishop keeps control of d8 and averts 17 ♗g3 ♖d8!.

This is important in view of 18 ♘d4? c5 and 18 ♕e2 hxg5 19 ♖fd1 ♕h6 and ...♖h8.

17   ...   hxg5

18   ♘e2!

The knight will stop ...♕h1 mate after ♘g3.

18   ...   c5

Caruana's advantage has slipped away. His pieces would not defend the e-file well after 18...♕xe4? 19 ♖fe1 and ♘g3.

19   ♘g3   ♖h8

Or the d-file after 19...♗c4? 20 ♖fd1! and ♕d7+.

20   ♖fd1   ♕h6

One of the points of 18...c5 was ...♖c6-d6.

But here 20...♖c6? 21 ♗d8! ♖d6 22 ♕c3 loses.

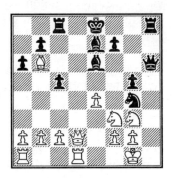

Nevertheless, Caruana's plan of mate on h-file is breathing again.

He threatens to win after 21...♘h2! and ...♘xf3+.

For example, 22 ♘e1 ♗g4! or 22 ♘e5 f6 23 ♘d3 ♘g4 and 23...♗d6.

Meier had 16 minutes left to reach move 40 and became desperate.

If he had safeguarded his bishop with 21 ♗a5 Black can build up with 21...♘h2 22 ♘e1 f6 and ...♔f7 with equal chances.

21   b4?

Machines point out the remarkable 21 a4 ♘h2 22 ♖a3!, so the rook can go to d3 for defense or counterattack.

For example, 22...♖c6 23 ♘e5 ♖xb6 26 ♖d3! and ♖d8+.

Another counter-attacking trick is 22...♗g4? 23 ♘e5! so that

23...♗xd1? 24 ♕d7+ or 23...♘f1 24 ♘xg4!.

The test of this ingenuity is 22...♘xf3+ 23 ♖xf3 ♕h2+ 24 ♔f1 ♗c4+ 25 ♖d3.

White will have compensation for the Exchange on light squares (♘f5).

But Black would have some winning chances after, say, 25...♖h6 26 a5 ♗xd3+ because 27 ♕xd3? ♖d6.

21   ...   cxb4

22   ♗d4   f6

23   c3

This was White's idea, to open lines, when he chose 21 b4.

23   ...   bxc3

Black's king will be not entirely secure for some time so Caruana should skirt past minefields like 23...♗c4 24 ♕c2 ♗d6 25 e5! ♗xe5? 26 ♕e4!.

24   ♗xc3

24   ...   ♔f7?

This is the kind of safety move you can play with little thought.

But it was the ideal moment for the idea Black has been saving, 24...♘h2!.

White must move his knight to avoid ...♘xf3+.

Then 25 ♘d4 allows the stunning 25...♘f1!

For example, 26 ♘xf1 ♕h1 mate or 26 ♔xf1 ♗c4+ 27 ♔e1 ♕h1+!.

White can try 25 ♘e1 instead. But 25...♗g4 does the job, e.g. 26 f3 ♖c4 and ...♗c5+.

25   ♖ac1!

Now 25...♘h2 doesn't work because of 26 ♘xg5+! (26...fxg5 27 ♗xh8).

25   ...   ♖c4

And neither 25...♗c5 26 ♗d4 nor 25...♖cd8 26 ♕b2 yields anything.

Caruana has lost his advantage on the board again.

26   ♗d4   b5

But he still has a big edge on the clock.

He spent most of his remaining 16 minutes here, apparently convincing himself he had no immediate tactics.

313

Instead, he secured his endgame assets (the two bishops, queenside majority).

27 ♕a5?

White has a variety of safe procedures, among them 27 ♖xc4 ♗xc4 28 ♕c2 with the idea of 29 e5 counterplay.

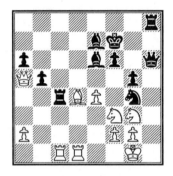

Instead, he plays for 27 ♖xc4 ♗xc4 28 ♕c7!.

Black can cover c7 with 27...♗d6. That also threatens ...♗xg3/...♕h1 mate.

White must reply 28 e5 and Black could choose between the slight advantages of 28...♗xe5 and 28...♘xe5.

27 ... ♘h2!

This is the move a professional likes to play.

If his opponent finds the best reply, 28 ♘e1!, he can repeat the position by force, 28...♘g4! 29 ♘f3.

Then he can go for 29...♗d6, the same line he would have gotten after 27...♗d6.

If he had more time after 28 ♘e1!, he could calculate 28...♖xc1 29 ♖xc1 ♗g4.

Then he has that surprise threat again, 30...♘f1! and wins.

White would have only one good defense but it was good enough, 30 ♖c7! so that 30...♘f1 31 ♖xe7+! ♚xe7 32 ♕c7+.

28 ♕xa6? ♘xf3+

29 gxf3

29 ... g4!

This threatens a rook (...♖xc1) as well as a mate (after ...gxf3).

And yet Black had two faster wins, beginning with 29...♕h2+! 30 ♔f1.

One is 30...♖hc8. White cannot allow ...♖c2 or ...♗c4+ (31 ♖xc4 ♗xc4+).

Also winning is 30...♖d8 because the bishop is threatened.

Then 31 ♗e3 ♖xc1 32 ♖xc1 allows mate after 32...♖d1+! 33 ♖xd1 ♗c4+.

30	f4!	♕xf4

31	♖xc4	

31	...	bxc4!

Previously ...♗xc4 was a key to mating scenarios.

But here it was more important to rule out ♘f5 and to create a threat to push the c-pawn.

The endgame would not be an easy win after 31...♗xc4 32 ♕b7! ♕h6 33 ♕xe7+ ♔xe7 34 ♘f5+.

32	♗e3	

White must have feared ...♕h6-h2+.

But 32 ♖b1 ♕h6? 33 ♖b7! counterattacks sufficiently to draw.

Black's only solid winning idea after 32 ♖b1 is one that had likely occurred to Caruana after 30...♕xf4, the rook sacrifice on g3.

32	...	♕f3!

There is no defense to 33...♖h3! now.

33	♖d6	

This is a good seconds-left bid to confuse Black. The attacked e6-bishop cannot move (33...♗c8? 34 ♕xc4+ and wins).

After 33...♗xd6 34 ♕xd6 White could set traps in the mutual remaining seconds.

33	...	♖h3!

34	♖xe6	♖xg3+

35	fxg3	♕xe3+

36	♔h2	♕f2+

37	♔h1	♕f1+

38	**White resigns.**	

It is mate after 38 ♔h2 ♕h3+ and ...♗c5.

In retrospect, the only way to keep the game going a while after 33...♖h3 was 34 ♗c5.

Then White is so tied up that 34...c3 and ...c2 is an easy way to win.

44

Avenged

Caruana won the US Championship in 2016 on his first attempt. It was a feat duplicated only by a select few (Bobby Fischer among them).

But he finished =3rd the next year, second in 2018 and =2nd in 2019. Like Pal Benko before him, he was finding greater success abroad than in his national championship.

He did avenge one of his 2017 losses, to Varuzhan Akobian, in the following sacrifice-packed game.

Caruana – Varuzhan Akobian
US Championship,
St. Louis 2018
*French Defense,
Steinitz Variation (C11)*

1	e4	e6
2	d4	d5
3	♘c3	♘f6
4	e5	

This had been a primary anti-French weapon of Caruana's for years.

4	...	♘fd7
5	f4	c5
6	♘f3	

Caruana's persistence is reflected in a running battle he had in this variation with Georg Meier.

They played it in three straight Dortmund tournaments, 2012-2014. They drew the first game.

6	...	♗e7

The second headed, after 6...♘c6 7 ♗e3 cxd4 8 ♘xd4 ♗c5, into the most topical variation of the day, 9 ♕d2 0-0 10 0-0-0 a6 11 ♕f2 ♗xd4! 12 ♗xd4 b5.

They continued to repeat book moves, 13 ♗e3 ♕a5 14 ♔b1 b4 15 ♘e2 ♕c7.

But after 16 ♘g3 a5 17 ♘h5 a4 Black's attack was faster. Caruana was lucky to draw.

A year later he tried one more time, with 16 ♘d4! instead of 16 ♘g3.

He came prepared with an unusual idea of creating bishops of opposite color, after 16...♘xd4 17 ♗xd4 a5 18 ♗b5.

This time his attack succeeded, following 18...♗a6 19 ♗xd7! ♕xd7 20 g4 and f4-f5.

7	♗e3	♘c6

8	♕d2	b6

Black chooses a logical yet very rare policy:

White often clarifies the center to gain access to d4 (8...a6 9 dxc5).

Black's 8...b6 discourages dxc5 because he can retake with the b-pawn.

He can also wait for White to commit his king, such as with 9 0-0-0 0-0 10 ♗d3? c4 11 ♗e2 b5! with a terrific attack (12 ♘xb5 ♖b8).

9	♗b5!

But there is a downside.

The key to Black's defense in a French is the e6-pawn. That makes f4-f5 a natural strategic goal of White.

After 9...♗b7 10 0-0-0 a6 his initiative accelerates, 11 ♗xc6 ♗xc6 12 f5!.

Then 12...exf5 drops the d-pawn (13 dxc5 and 14 ♘xd5) and reveals how far behind in development Black is.

9	...	♕c7

10	0-0-0

In an offbeat opening variation, even a natural move like 10 0-0-0 can be an innovation.

Previous experience showed how 10 0-0 would get play like the game, after 10...a6 11 ♗xc6 ♕xc6 12 f5.

Castling queenside means seeking Black counterplay from 10...f6? or 10...c4 is dubious in view of 11 f5!.

317

Clarifying the center with 10...cxd4 11 ♘xd4 would collapse the strong point at e6 after 11...♗b7? 12 ♗xc6! ♗xc6 13 f5.

Black would be nearly lost after, for example, 13...0-0 14 fxe6 ♘xe5 15 ♗f4.

Better is 11...♘xd4 12 ♗xd4 a6 and 13...b5 when White's advantage is fairly limited.

10 ... a6?

The main alternative is to complete development, 10...♗b7 11 ♔b1 0-0.

But again White's assault on e6 is fast, 12 g4 ♖ac8 13 ♖hf1 and f4-f5.

11 ♗xc6 ♕xc6

12 f5!

If Black tries to escape the center, with 12...♗b7 and 13...0-0-0, White stops him with 13 ♗g5!.

Then 13...♗xg5 14 ♕xg5 g6 is lost after 15 fxe6 fxe6 16 ♘e2 and

♘f4. Not much better is 15...♕xe6 16 ♖he1.

12 ... c4

Black already was seeing a limited number of desperate measures.

One is 12...0-0 with dreams of queenside attack after, say, 13 g4 b5.

Black can offer an Exchange sacrifice, 13 f6! gxf6 14 ♗h6 ♗b7 (Not 14...♖d8?? 15 ♕f4 and wins) 15 ♗xf8 ♗xf8.

However, 16 exf6 ♘xe5 17 ♘e5 doesn't offer much hope of survival, e.g. 17...♕c7 18 ♕g5+ ♗g7 19 ♖hf1.

Instead, Akobian places his remaining chips on his queenside pawns.

As it turns out, White could even allow Black to queen one of the pawns in two key variations.

13 f6!

Each of the natural candidates, 13 ♗g5, 13 fxe6, 13 g4 and 13 f6, keeps an advantage, of varying degrees.

The forcing moves have the most appeal. For example, 13 fxe6 fxe6 14 ♖hf1 and ♗g5 is quite good.

Less so is 13...♕xe6! 14 ♗g5 ♗b4.

13   ...   gxf6

14 exf6   ♗xf6

A knight on e5 would be so strong that it is easy to reject 14...♘xf6 15 ♘e5 ♕-moves 16 ♖hf1 and ♗g5.

But keeping the f-file closed with 14...♗d6 had some appeal (15 ♗f4 ♗b7).

Instead, White can play 15 ♗h6 and ♗g7, followed by picking off the h7-pawn with ♕h6 and/or ♘g5.

15 ♖hf1!

The f-file becomes toxic for Black after 15...♗e7 16 ♘e5 ♘xe5 17 dxe5.

Then White threatens 18 ♕f2 and ♕xf7+. The positional plan of ♗g5 and a trade of bishops is also powerful.

15   ...   b5

Another version is 15...♗b7 16 ♕f2, when White prepares both 17 ♘e5! and 17 ♗g5.

For example, 16...0-0-0 17 ♗g5 ♗xg5+ 18 ♘xg5 and ♘xf7.

Black might survive after 16...♗e7 17 ♘e5 ♘xe5 18 dxe5 0-0-0 19 ♗xb6 ♖df8. But he would need White's help.

16 ♕f2!

16   ...   b4

Now the engines point out the flashy 17 ♘e4! dxe4 18 ♘e5!.

That opens the d-file for 18...♗xe5 19 ♕xf7+ ♔d8 20 dxe5 and ♖d6!.

Not much better is 18...♕d5 19 ♘xd7 and ♕xf6.

319

17 ♘e2

But this also makes 18 ♘e5! strong.

Among the nice finishes is 17...♕c7 18 ♘e5 ♘xe5 19 ♕xf6 ♘g6 20 ♘f4!.

Then 20...♕e7 loses to 21 ♘xd5! (21...exd5 22 ♕c6+ or 21...♕xf6 22 ♘xf6+ and 23 d5!).

And 20...♖f8 sets the table for 21 ♘h5 and 22 ♗h6.

17 ... b3

18 ♘e5!

He can allow the b-pawn to promote, 18...bxa2 19 ♘xc6

a1(♕)+ 20 ♔d2 ♕a4 21 ♘e5! and wins.

Or 20...♕xb2 21 ♖b1 ♕a3 22 ♘e5!.

18 ... ♗xe5

Also lost was 18...♘xe5 19 ♕xf6 ♖f8 20 dxe5 bxa2 21 ♔d2 and ♗h6.

19 ♕xf7+ ♔d8

20 dxe5 bxa2

21 ♔d2

Now the threat is ♘d4 followed by ♘xc6+ or ♘xe6+.

21 ... ♖f8

22 ♕xh7 ♖xf1

23 ♖xf1

White can also allow Black to queen after 23...c3+ 24 ♘xc3!? d4 25 ♗xd4 ♕xg2+ 26 ♖f2 ♕xf2+ 27 ♗xf2 a1(♕) 28 ♕g8+ and ♕xe6.

23 ... d4!

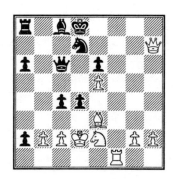

A nice trap: White might overlook 24 ♘xd4? c3+!, when he is no longer winning (25 bxc3 ♕xg2+ 26 ♖f2 ♕d5).

24	♕g8+	♔c7

25	♘xd4	♕d5

26	♕xe6!	

Almost all endgames are won for White, e.g. 26...♗b7 27 ♕xd5 ♗xd5 27 ♖a1.

Or 26...♕xe6 27 ♘xe6+ ♔c6 28 ♖a1 and ♖xa2.

26	...	♕a5+

27	c3	

The main point of 26 ♕xe6! is that 27...a1(♕) 28 ♖xa1 ♕xa1 presents White with a cute mate after 29 ♕d6+.

For example, 29...♔b7 30 ♕d5+!

(keeping c6 clear) ♔b8 31 ♘c6+ ♔b7 32 ♘d8+.

27	...	♘xe5

28	♖f7+!	♘xf7

The deadly ♗f4+ also appears after 28...♗d7 29 ♖xd7+ ♘xd7 30 ♗f4+.

Then 30...♔d8 31 ♘c6+ or 30...♔c8 31 ♕c6+.

29	♗f4+	

But not 29 ♕xf7+?? ♗d7 when White has no more than a draw (30 ♗f4+ ♔c8 or 30 ♘e6+ ♔c6).

29	...	♔b7

30	♕xf7+	resigns.

Black allowed mate rather than the hopeless 29...♘e5 30 ♗xe5+ ♕xe5 31 ♕xe5+ ♔d8 32 ♕d5+ ♔e8 33 ♘c2.

45
Caruana Gambits

Computers were once thought to sound the death knell for gambits. Engines routinely found refutations of pawn offers that were once considered sound. Analysis showed that compensation was often a chimera. Initiatives ground to a halt when met by proper defense.

What wasn't expected was the way computer-aided grandmaster prep would discover new gambits. We saw one of those ideas in Game 39 and we will see others in the pages that follow. Unexpectedly, a leader of the 21ˢᵗ century gambit revolution was Fabiano Luigi Caruana.

David Navara – Caruana
St. Louis Rapid & Blitz (Blitz)
2017
English Opening,
Caruana Variation (A20)

1	c4	e5
2	g3	♘f6
3	♗g2	

This move order often leads to 3...d5 4 cxd5 ♘xd5 5 ♘c3, a Reversed Sicilian Variation.

3	...	c6

This is very similar to a gambit identified with Paul Keres.

After the more common move order 1 c4 e5 2 ♘c3 ♘f6 3 g3, Keres tried 3...c6.

If an unwary opponent played the routine 4 ♗g2, he would continue 4...d5! 5 cxd5 cxd5 and then 6 ♕b3 ♘c6 7 ♘xd5 ♘d4!.

4	♘f3	

This attack on the e5-pawn is the primary way of testing the Keres Variation, because ...♘c6 is impossible.

But in Caruana's move order, 4 d4 is preferred, with roughly equal chances after 4...exd4 5 ♕xd4 d5 6 ♘f3 ♗e7.

4	...	e4

If Black plays 4...d6 he agrees to play a King's Indian (...g6) or Old Indian (...♗e7) Defense.

Instead, 4...e4 reminds us that the English is a Hypermodern opening. Black can occupy center squares with pawns. Will White be able to undermine them?

5	♘d4	

Yes, he can after 5...d5 6 cxd5 cxd5 7 d3!.

For example, 7...♗c5 8 ♘b3 ♗b6 9 0-0 and 10 ♘c3.

This has proven so effective that experience says Black should abandon his pawn center with 6...♕xd5! and drive White's knight out of the center.

Caruana has quite a different idea.

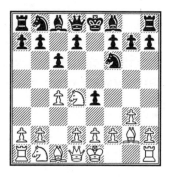

5   ...   ♕b6

This move violates general principles so much it shared the blame for Mikhail Tal's loss of his world championship title.

Tal introduced it in a similar position – 1 c4 e5 2 ♘c3 ♘f6 3 g3 c6 4 ♘f3 e4 5 ♘d4 d5 6 cxd5 ♕b6!?.

Then if White defends his knight with 7 e3, his light squares are seriously weakened by 7...cxd5 8 ♗g2 ♘c6 9 ♘xc6 bxc6 and ...♗a6!.

Tal's opponent, Mikhail Botvinnik, played 7 ♘b3 and won. Tal was soon an ex-champion and an early ...♕b6 was considered refuted.

6   ♘b3

Caruana's idea is very similar, after 6 e3 d5.

White's light squares become weak after 7 ♘c3 ♗g4 8 f3? exf3.

In fact, this happened in an Aronian – Caruana game that was played the same day as this Navara – Caruana game. Black won after 9 ♗xf3 ♗xf3 10 ♕xf3 dxc4.

6   ...   a5

This makes an inconvenient threat of 7...a4.

The knee-jerk response to a RP advance is a corresponding RP advance.

Who benefits more from the advanced a-pawns after 7 a4 ?

The probable answer is Black because, for example, he can occupy b4 with a minor piece.

He can continue gambit play with 7...d5 8 cxd5 ♘xd5! and 9 ♗xe4 ♗h3.

White will have a hard time completing development after 10 ♘c3 ♘a6, e.g. 11 ♘xd5 cxd5 12 ♗xd5 0-0-0 13 ♗f3 ♔b8.

7   d3

After 7 d4 Black would get a good game from 7...d5 (8 ♘c3 dxc4).

Better is 8 cxd5 cxd5. But the pawn structure favors Black because d2-d3 is ruled out.

7   ...   a4

Now 8 ♗e3?? c5 and White is lost (9 ♘3d2 ♕xb2).

8   ♘3d2

A new opening idea passes a test when other grandmasters adopt it.

Two years later in the Sinquefield Cup, Caruana tried 8...♗c5 9 0-0 e3 against Wesley So.

He got a fine game after 10 fxe3 ♗xe3+ 11 ♔h1 ♘g4 12 ♘e4 0-0.

This apparently impressed So because he adopted Caruana's opening.

He equalized as Black in the 2021 Paris blitz against Peter Svidler after 12 ♘c3 0-0! (rather than 12...♘f2+ 13 ♖xf2 ♗xf2 14 ♘de4 and ♘xa4).

8   ...   d5!

This is a promising gambit that Caruana had introduced to GM chess two months earlier, at another Paris blitz tournament.

Denying White 0-0 is worth a pawn, 9 dxe4 dxe4 10 ♘xe4 ♘xe4 11 ♗xe4 ♗h3!.

Caruana's opponent in Paris, Veselin Topalov, chose 10 e3, and Caruana got some light-square compensation after 10...♗g4 11 ♕c2 ♘bd7.

But 10...♘bd7 11 ♘c3 ♘c5 is simpler.

9   cxd5   exd3

Black needs to interpolate this capture because the pawn sacrifice is not sound with the c-pawn off the board.

That is, 9...cxd5 10 dxe4 dxe4 11 ♘xe4 ♘xe4 12 ♗xe4 ♗h3.

The difference is d5 is available for White's queen or knight.

For instance, 13 ♘c3 ♗c5 14 e3 ♘d7 15 ♘d5! ♕d6 16 ♘f4.

10   0-0!

White offers his own gambit but it cannot be accepted, 10...dxe2?? 11 ♕xe2+ ♗e7? 12 d6 or 11...♔d8 12 ♘c4 with a winning attack.

10   ...   cxd5

11   exd3

All of these moves had been played six days earlier at the Sinquefield Cup, in Svidler – Caruana.

Then Fabiano tried 11...♗e7 and was surprised by another White pawn offer, 12 ♘c3 ♕a5 13 ♖e1 ♘c6 14 b4!.

Svidler had evidently prepared 14...♘xb4? 15 ♖xe7+! ♔xe7 16 ♗a3!.

His attack would be too great after 16...♔d8 17 ♖b1 ♘c6 18 ♘b5.

Caruana equalized with difficulty after 14...axb3 15 ♗b2 ♕d8.

11   ...   ♘c6

12 ♘c3

Of all pawns, it is the one on a4 Black cannot afford to lose here.

He would land in a poor endgame after 12...♗e6 13 ♘xa4! ♕d4 14 ♘c3 ♕xd3 15 ♘b3 ♕xd1 16 ♖xd1.

12   ...   ♕a5!

And not 12...♗g4? 13 ♘xd5! ♘xd5 14 ♕xg4.

13   ♖e1+   ♗e7

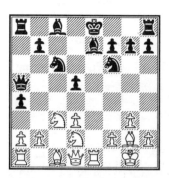

It looks like White should be able to do something with his lead in development. But as the Hypermoderns learned in the 1920s, if the enemy center remains unmolested, you can quickly find yourself worse.

Here, for example, 14 ♕f3? ♗e6 favors Black.

14 ♘f3   0-0

15 ♗d2   ♕a6

Time to evaluate.

White never got the pressure on the d5-pawn or the piece-play in the center he wanted in the opening.

Chances would be equal after 16 d4 ♗e6.

Then Black has tactics based on his a-pawn, e.g. 17 ♗f4 a3! 8 b3? ♗b4 or 18 bxa3 ♗xa3 and ...♖fc8.

Instead, White might try yet another pawn offer, 17 ♘g5 ♘xd4 (17...♗g4 18 ♕b1!) 18 ♗f4.

16   ♗g5   ♗e6

17   ♘e5?

Black's slight edge in space might have become more tangible after 17 a3 h6 or 17...♖fd8.

17   ...   ♘xe5

18   ♖xe5   h6!

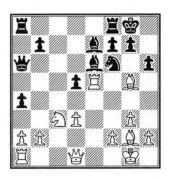

But now White's pieces find themselves in a traffic jam.

His rook would be trapped after 19 ♗e3 ♗d6.

His bishop is trapped after 19 ♗h4 g5 (although Black can get a riskless edge with 19...a3).

If 19 ♗d2, Black might spurn the pawn offer, 19...♕xd3, because 19...♗c5 and its threat of 20...♗xf2+ 21 ♔xf2 ♘g4+ is better.

The abject retreat 19 ♗c1 also allows Black a choice of favorable moves (19...d4, 19...♗g4, and 19...a3).

Finally, White can't afford to hand Black control of dark squares, 19 ♗xf6 ♗xf6 20 ♖-moves a3!).

19   ♗f4

Navara probably intended to sacrifice the Exchange, 19...♗d6 20 d4 ♗xe5 21 dxe5 ♘d7? 22 ♘xd5, with some comp.

19   ...   a3

Before deciding on ...♗d6 Caruana inflicts queenside damage.

White can't back out with 20 ♖e2 without incurring more problems after 20...d4 21 ♘e4 ♘d5.

20   ♖b1   ♗d6!

21   d4   ♖ac8

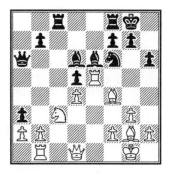

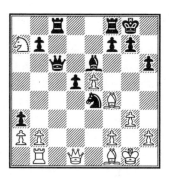

There may be better preparations for ...♗xe5 or ...bxa3.

But it was good speed-game technique to leave White with the difficult decisions.

If White retracts his Exchange offer, 22 ♖e3 ♗xf4 23 gxf4, Caruana could convert his positional edge with 23...♗f5! 24 ♗f1 ♕d6 25 ♗d3 ♗xd3 and 26...♕xf4.

22 ♗f1! ♕c6

23 ♘b5 ♗xe5

Now 23 ♗xe5 ♗f5 and 23 ♘a7 ♕c2 are resignable.

24 dxe5 ♘e4

25 ♘a7?

Lost in the long run is 25 ♘xa3 ♗f5 (26 ♖c1 ♕b6) or 25 ♘d4 ♕c7.

25 ... ♕c2!

White may have hoped for 25...♕b6? 26 ♗e3, when he can keep hoping.

26 ♘xc8

He would have needed a miracle after 26 ♗e2 ♖c5 or 26...♕xd1+ 27 ♗xd1 ♖c5.

26 ... ♕xf2+

27 ♔h1 ♖xc8

Black threatens mate after 28...♖c2. It would be over after 28 ♖c1 ♖xc1 and ...axb2.

28 ♕e2 ♖c2

29 ♕xf2 ♘xf2+

30 ♔g1 axb2

White waited to resign after...

31 ♗e3 ♗f5

32 ♗d4 ♘h3+

33 ♗xh3 ♖c1+

34 ♔f2 ♗xb1.

46
Move Five Innovation

At a session of Mikhail Botvinnik's celebrated school for talented youngsters, he asked each of the students how many games they played a year. Twelve-year-old Vladimir Kramnik said 30. Botvinnik was shocked. Too little, he said. Then 15-year-old Alexey Shirov said 115. Botvinnik shook his head. Too many.

But that was Botvinnik – and that was decades ago. Today, elite players have a much busier calendar. In 2018 Caruana played a staggering 222 games, including six major tournaments and one never-to-be-forgotten world championship match. Playing one tournament after another had its creative benefits, as he showed in this last-round game against his rival for first prize.

Nikita Vitiugov – Caruana
Baden-Baden 2018
Petroff Defense,
Modern Attack (C43)

1   e4   e5

2   ♘f3   ♘f6

"The Petroff is my most well-prepared opening," Caruana said after the 2018 Candidates tournament. Despite its drawish reputation, half of his six decisive games in the Berlin tournament were Petroffs.

3   d4

White's base strategy in most Petroff lines is to induce ...♘xe4 and then try to make the knight a liability, by threatening or undermining it.

A familiar version is 3 ♘xe5 d6 4 ♘f3 ♘xe4 5 d4 d5 6 ♗d3 followed by 7 0-0 and c2-c4.

Very similar is 3 d4 ♘xe4 4 ♗d3 d5 5 ♘xe5 followed by 0-0 and c2-c4.

3   ...   ♘xe4

4   dxe5

This move, a favorite of Ian Nepomniachtchi, was once considered a fundamental error that allowed Black easy equality.

4   ...   d5

5   ♘bd2

White seeks a knight trade (5...♘xd2 6 ♗xd2) that would give him a slight lead in development.

In Berlin, Caruana swapped knights and equalized soon after 6...♗e7 7 ♗d3 c5, against Alexander Grischuk.

Afterwards he wondered if there was a way to complicate in the diagram position below.

But neither 5...♘c5 6 ♘b3 nor 5...♗f5 6 ♘d4 look promising.

In the two weeks between the end of Berlin and the start of Baden-Baden he found that a sound innovation was still possible at move five.

5   ...   ♕d7!

If Black's queen were still on d8, the trade 6 ♘xe4 dxe4 would favor White after 7 ♕xd8+.

But here 7 ♕xd7+? ♘xd7 is at least equal for Black.

6   ♗d3

Of course, the queen looks stupid on d7. But if Black is allowed a few untroubled moves, it may stand well.

For example, 6 ♗e2 ♗e7 7 0-0 0-0 8 c4 ♖d8.

If there is a way to punish 5...♕d7 it may be 6 ♘xe4 dxe4 7 ♘d4, with the idea of sacrificing the e-pawn (e5-e6), followed by ♗c4.

For example, 7...♗c5 8 ♗e3 ♕e7? 9 e6!.

But Caruana returned to 5...♘xd2 after this game, and 5...♕d7 more or less disappeared from GM chess.

6   ...   ♘c5

7   ♗e2

This position could have arisen after 5...♘c5 6 ♗e2 with one less tempo for Black. But that tempo is ...♕d7. The next few moves are a debate over whether that move is useful or harmful.

7   ...   g6

There was nothing wrong with 7...♗e7. Caruana's move is more ambitious.

Black could manage his slight inferiority after, say, 8 0-0 ♗g7 9 c4 0-0 10 cxd5 ♕xd5 11 b3.

8 ♘b3!

The natural target for White in a Petroff is the e4-knight. Now it is the same knight on c5.

White would develop smoothly after 8...♘xb3? 9 axb3 and then 9...♗g7 10 0-0 0-0 11 ♗f4 ♘c6 12 ♕d2.

Then Black has nothing better than moving the misplaced queen, to e7, e6 or f5.

8 ... ♘e6!

On e6, Black's knight stops ♗f4 and provides some control of the key squares d4 and c5.

Too great an extravagance is 8...♘a4?. Then 9 ♕d4 threatens 10 e6, e.g. 9...♗g7 10 ♗h6! c5 11 e6! with advantage

9 ♗e3?

Logic says White has a lead in development and should enlarge it.

But logic also suggests that if Black can afford a tempo for 8...♘e6!, White can spend one to trade it off, with 9 ♘bd4 or 9 ♘g5.

For example, 9 ♘bd4 ♘xd4 10 ♘xd4 ♗g7 11 f4 would favor White.

Or 9...♗g7 10 ♘xe6 fxe6 11 h4! with a powerful attack after 11...0-0? 12 h5.

9 ... c5!

Here pawn structure trumps development.

After 10 0-0 White would be roughly four moves ahead in the traditional metric of getting the first-rank pieces off their original squares.

But White cannot do anything with his lead in development because the structure limits him.

In fact, if his b3-knight were back on b1 he could get the upper hand with 10 ♘c3!, e.g. 10... d4? 11 ♘e4.

330

But as it stands, Black will be better when he improves his position with …b6, …♗b7, …♗g7, …♘c6 and …0-0.

10 ♘g5!

White needs a target or two. The c5-pawn is the best candidate, so he trades off its best defender.

10 … b6

11 ♘xe6

He would get another target after 11…♕xe6? 12 ♗f3.

11 … fxe6

The structure is somewhat unfamiliar. But not to Caruana, who had sought it two weeks before in the Candidates tournament in Berlin.

His game with Grischuk began **1 e4 e5 2 ♘f3 ♘f6 3 d4 ♘xe4 4 dxe5 d5 5 ♘bd2 ♘xd2 6 ♗xd2 ♗e7 7 ♗d3 c5 8 c3 ♘c6 9 0-0 ♗g4 10 ♖e1 ♕d7 11 h3 ♗h5 12 ♗f4 ♕e6 13 a3 0-0 14 b4 h6 15 ♗g3 b6 16 ♘d4 ♗xd1 17 ♘xe6 fxe6 18 ♖axd1**.

White would have good play if 19 ♗a6! is allowed.

He would threaten ♗b7 but also forestall the favorable …a5!.

This would win time for f2-f4/♖f1 and f4-f5!.

Caruana reacted properly, **18…c4!**, and solidified his queenside, **19 ♗c2 b5** and …a6.

Then his strategic goal was …d4, which he carried out and won.

12 a4!

But until there is a very good reason Black should leave the structure intact.

If he anticipates 13 a5 with 12…a6 13 a5 c4?, White's knight lands on d4, with a considerable edge.

12 … ♗b7

13 0-0 ♘c6

Black will be tempted for several moves to open the long diagonal with tempo, …d4.

But granting access to c4 and e4 would ease White's game, e.g. 13...d4 14 ♗g5 ♗g7 15 f4 ♘c6 16 ♗b5 a6 17 ♗c4 followed by 18 a5, 18 ♕g4 or ♘d2-e4.

14 f4 ♗h6

15 a5

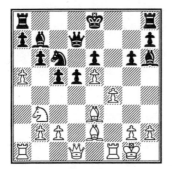

White's move has two goals – weakening the c5-b6-a7 chain and driving Black's b7-bishop off its diagonal (15...0-0 16 a6!).

To appreciate the much stronger 15 ♗b5! White had to see 15...a6 16 ♗e2!.

The point is ...a6 weakens the chain. It would crumble after 16...0-0? 17 a5! or 16...♘e7? 17 a5!, with a clear White edge.

He can even retreat the other bishop, 16...d4 17 ♗c1!, so that 17...a5 18 ♘d2! allows the knight to c4 or e4.

15 ... ♘e7!

Now 16 a6 ♗c6 or 16 axb6 axb6 17 ♖xa8+ ♗xa8 doesn't get White back to equality.

16 ♗g4!

If Black is allowed to catch up in development he may be ready for ...d4!.

One of many favorable sequences runs 16 c3 0-0 17 ♕d2 ♘f5 18 ♗f2 d4!.

The main tactic is 19 cxd4 ♗xf4! 20 ♕xf4 ♘xd4 (21 ♕e3 ♕d5! and wins).

16 ... d4!

White intended 16...♘f5 17 ♗xf5! exf5 18 c3 with a reasonable middlegame.

But he also had a drastic measure in mind, 16...0-0? 17 ♗xc5! bxc5 18 ♘xc5.

17 ♗c1 0-0

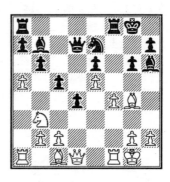

Black has a target, the f4-pawn, which he can threaten with ...♘d5.

White can anticipate that with 18 c4. Then he can threaten ♕d3-h3 followed by ♗xe6+ or ♕xh6.

Black has tactical defenses, such as 18 c4 ♖f7 19 ♕d3 ♖af8 20 ♕h3 ♘f5.

Then 21 ♗xf5? ♖xf5 22 ♕xh6 ♖h5 traps the queen.

But the main reason it is difficult to choose 18 c4 is it makes the passed d4-pawn a potentially winning asset in any endgame.

18	♕d3	♗d5!
19	♕h3	♗g7
20	♘d2	♘f5
21	c4	dxc3?

Caruana spent ten of his remaining 37 minutes on a minor positional error.

After 21...♗c6! he could aim for either...♖ab8/...b5 or ...♖ae8 and ...♘e3.

For example, 22 ♘f3 ♖ab8 23 axb6 axb6 24 b3 b5 with a growing advantage.

22	bxc3

White should not allow 22 ♕xc3 ♘d4!.

22	...	♖ad8
23	axb6	axb6
24	♖e1	

Now 24 ♗f3! followed by 25 ♗xd5 ♕xd5 26 ♕f3 held out good chances of equalizing.

24	...	b5!

25	♘e4

"The engines were screaming for 25...♗xe4!!" Peter Leko said.

It is based on the clumsiness of White's rook after 26 ♖xe4 h5.

For instance, 27 ♗f3? ♕d3 28 ♗b2 ♕c2 29 ♖e2 ♖d2 and wins.

Black's advantage is less impressive after 27 ♗xf5.

But it might be sufficient after 27...♕d1+ 28 ♔f2 ♖xf5 (29 ♕f3 ♕h1 and 29 ♖e1 ♕b3).

25	...	♕e7

Instead, Caruana prepares ...b4, to create a passed pawn.

26	♘g5	h6
27	♘f3	♗c6

He adds another winning idea, ...♖d3.

For example, 28 ♗a3 ♖d3 29 ♖fc1 ♗d5 and ...b4 or ...♘e3.

Or 28 ♘d2 c4 29 ♗e2? ♕c5+ and wins (30 ♔h1 ♕f2 or 30 ♔f1 ♘e3+).

28	♗xf5	gxf5
29	♗e3	♖d3
30	♖ac1	♖a8!
31	♕h4	

There was nothing to be done about ...♖a3xc3.

31	...	♕xh4
32	♘xh4	c4

The Black pawns cannot be blockaded, as 33 ♗d4 b4! 34 cxb4? ♖xd4 and 33 ♗c5 ♗f8 demonstrate.

33	♔f2	♗f8
34	♘f3	♗d5

Quiz time: Try to find the "Black to play and win" after 34...♗xf3 35 ♔xf3 ♗c5 36 ♖e2.

35	♘d4	♗c5
36	♘xf5?	

This loses quickly, as does 36 ♘xb5 ♖a2+.

36	...	♗a3!
37	♘xh6+	♔g7
38	f5!	

A final trap: Black wins material with 38...♖xe3 39 ♔xe3 ♗xc1+ 40 ♖xc1 ♔xh6.

But 41 g4! ♔g5 42 f6 ♔xg4 43 ♖f1 would make his day longer.

38	...	♗xc1!
39	♗xc1	♖xc3
40	f6+	♔g6
41	**White resigns.**	

Answer to the quiz question: 36...♖a2! so that 37 ♖xa2 ♖xe3+ wins. Or 37 ♖ce1 ♖xe2 38 ♖xe2 ♖xc3.

47
Waiting for Magnus

A consequence of playing so much before the world championship match is Fabiano had to determine how much of his opening preparation he was willing to reveal. He risked using up his surprises.

Viktor Korchnoi adopted a traditional policy in the months before his matches with Anatoly Karpov. He concealed the variations he intended to use. But he seemed uncomfortable when he unveiled them. He surprised Karpov but also seemed to have surprised himself.

Caruana's solution was to play his normal game of chess.

Ray Robson – Caruana
US Championship 2018
Petroff Defense,
Nimzovich Variation (C42)

1	e4	e5
2	♘f3	♘f6

In the months before the title match, Caruana played nearly 40 games as Black in which he faced 1 e4.

He defended with the Petroff in 15 of them, even though he would rely on it against Carlsen.

3	♘xe5	d6
4	♘f3	♘xe4
5	♘c3	♘xc3
6	dxc3	♗e7
7	♗e3	

In fact, this is how his game with Carlsen began during the Sinquefield Cup later that summer.

Magnus dodged a theoretical debate, by meeting 7...♘c6 with the rare 8 ♗c4. He nursed a slight advantage well into an endgame before a draw was agreed.

7	...	0-0
8	♕d2	♘d7

This development of the knight, rather than 8...♘c6, was popularized by Boris Gelfand. One idea is to keep c6 free for a pawn that can support ...d5.

9 0-0-0   c6

That plan works well if White goes for the kingside attack we saw in Game 24.

For example, 10 ♗d3 d5 11 h4 ♘c5 can safeguard h7 with ...♘xd3+.

10 ♔b1

White' most promising plan after ...d5 is to undouble his c-pawns with c3-c4.

This works better after 10 ♔b1 than after, say, 10 h4 d5 11 c4 ♘b6 12 cxd5 ♕xd5!.

Then the threat of ...♕xa2 earns Black an equal middlegame.

10 ...   d5

Another of the reasons for revival of the 5 ♘c3 variation is that an exchange on e5, 10...♘e5 11 ♘xe5! dxe5, is more aggressive than it seems.

The e5-pawn becomes a target following 12 ♗d3 ♗e6 13 ♕e2 ♕c7 14 ♖he1 and ♗d2.

11 c4   ♘b6

12 cxd5   ♘xd5

This is much better than 12...♕xd5 13 ♕e1, when White threatens the queen as well as 14 ♗xb6 and ♕xe7.

13 ♗c4

13 ...   ♗f5!

Caruana could have kept this move in his novelty vault just in case he had an opportunity to use it in the November match.

The chief alternative was defending the d5-knight with 13...♗e6. He would be a bit worse after 14 ♖he1 ♖e8 15 ♗g5, for example.

But now 14 ♖he1? ♗b4 costs material.

14 ♗xd5

White has minimally useful alternatives such as 14 ♗b3 and 14 a3. But Black has quiet moves that do more, such as ...♖e8 and ...♗e4.

14 ...   cxd5

15 ♕xd5   ♕c8

For a pawn, Black gets the two bishops and pressure against c2.

The two Bees would embarrass White's rook after 16 ♖d2? ♗b4 17 ♖e2 ♗e6 18 ♕d1 ♗c4 or 18 ♕e4 ♕c4!.

16   ♘d4

Engines claim a substantial White advantage after 14 ♗xd5.

But now they concede some difficulties, such as after 16 ♕b3 ♗e6 17 ♕b5 a6 18 ♕b6 ♗f5 19 ♘d4 ♗g6 followed by ...♖d8 or putting his bishop on c5 or f6.

16   ...   ♗g6

"A computer alone is of no use. It does not generate ideas," Garry Kasparov said in 2000.

Well, maybe. But you can nudge an engine in directions it does not want to go. "If the computer leads the man, then it's bad," Vasily Ivanchuk said. "If man 'leads' the computer, it helps him. This is good."

For example, a computer may claim a +0.50 edge after 17 ♕b3.

But you can lead it and find how principled moves, 17...♗f6 18 ♖d2 ♖d8, tell a different story. White is still better but not by much.

17   ♔a1

Caruana paused to think for the first time. His opponent had spent 40 minutes, half of it on his last two moves.

17   ...   ♖e8

Caruana often reached the end of his prep and remembered only the outlines of why he and his second had agreed the position was good for him.

Here he doesn't need immediate threats as much as a promising plan, such as 18 c3 ♗f6 19 ♕b3 a6 and ...b5.

18   ♖he1   ♗f6

19   c3   ♖e5?

Caruana spent nearly 14 minutes on this move. He could have safely pocketed a pawn with 19...♗e4! and 20...♗xg2.

20   ♕b3   a6!

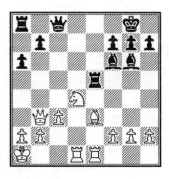

21   ♗f4?

White should insert 21 h3 to stop a future ...♕g4.

Then he can reorganize his minor pieces (♘f3/♗d4).

Black should then admit his 19th was a mistake and retreat 21...♖e8! so that 22 ♘f3 ♗e4 reorganizes his pieces.

21	...	♖xe1
22	♖xe1	♕d7

Baby-step moves keep improving his position. He has more of them (...b5,...♖c8) than White.

For instance, 23 ♕b6 ♖e8!.

Then 24 ♖xe8+?? ♕xe8 loses because of mate threats (...♕e1+ and ...♕e4).

23	♗e5!	♖e8
24	f4	♗d8

Another quickly played move by Caruana. The space-gaining 24...b5 and luft-making 24...h5 offer more.

25	a4

If you are going to play a prophylactic move that is this weakening you better make sure it really does deter ...b5. This doesn't.

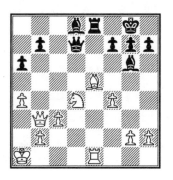

The first thing a grandmaster is likely to notice is that 25...♗b6 is playable (26 ♕xb6?? ♕xa4 mate).

Then he would see how it prepares 26...♗xd4. That would assure him of an almost certain draw in an endgame and likely more after 27 cxd4 ♖c8!.

But he has good reason to expect more than a draw.

25	...	h6

Caruana took nine minutes. That seems like a lot for 25...h6.

But it's not if you realize Black was calculating 25...b5.

Then the opening of the a-file would be fatal, 26 axb5 axb5 27 ♕xb5?? ♕a7+ or 27 ♘xb5? ♗h4! and ...♖a8+.

To play 25...b5 Caruana would have to calculate forcing lines, such as 26 f5! ♗xf5 27 axb5 axb5 28 ♘xf5 ♕xf5 29 ♕xb5!.

Or 28...♕a7+! and 29...♕f2, with equal chances.

In the end, 25...h6 made practical sense. Black will have greater tactical potential (...f6!) once he makes his king safer (...♔h7).

26	♖d1!	♕g4

Now 27 g3 b5! works because after 28 axb5 axb5 White's pieces are very loose (29 ♘xb5 ♗e7 30 ♘a3 ♕e2).

27   ♖d2

Black can maneuver (27...♗e4, 27...♕c8, even 27...♕d7) without cost.

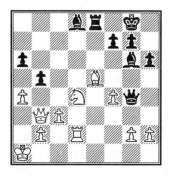

27   ...   b5!

Caruana took only two and a half minutes for this move, indicating he had it in mind when he chose 26...♕g4.

What justifies the pawn sacrifice?

The opening of the a-file is the biggest factor.

But it was near-impossible for a human to evaluate it properly – since even engines got it wrong.

White spent 14 of his remaining 25 minutes on his next two moves to decide whether Caruana was bluffing.

28   axb5

Otherwise Black can force matters on the queenside with 28...♗e7, 29...♕d7 and 30...bxa4.

28   ...   axb5

29   ♕d1?

"The engines just laugh here," *American Chess Magazine* said.

Computers see very little compensation for one pawn, not to mention the two Black has given up, after 29 ♕xb5!.

But Caruana may have noticed how 29...f6 30 ♗b8 would allow 30...♕c8! with a winning threat of 31...♖e1+ 32 ♔a2 ♗e8.

If you catch sight of that you would want to see how different 30 ♗d6 would be.

Then you may realize 30...♕c8! again threatens to win with 31...♖e1+.

Of course, computers saw all this when they were described as chuckling.

They had determined 31 ♕c6 would lead to a trade of queens and a winning endgame.

But 31...♗c7! is a stunning reply.

Engines stop laughing.

The threat is 32...♗xd6 33 ♕xd6 ♖e1+ and wins.

White is also mated after 32 ♕xc7?? ♕xc7 33 ♗xc7 ♖a8+.

Computers eventually indicate the best moves in the diagram are 32 f5! and then 32...♗f7 33 ♘f3 ♔h7!.

Black would not be losing after 34 ♗xc7 ♖e7! or 34 ♗a3 ♕b8 or 34 b3 ♗xd6.

Did Caruana see all of this? Almost certainly not.

But he had faith in Black's tactical chances once the a-file is opened.

29 ...   ♕d7!

In addition to an a-file check, Black readies ...f6. He suddenly has a sizable edge, e.g. 30 b4 f6 and 30 ♘c2 ♕a7+ 31 ♔b1 ♗b6.

30 f5?

White probably counted on this (30...♗xf5 31 ♘xf5 ♕xf5 32 ♖xd8) when he chose 29 ♕d1.

30 ...   ♗g5!

The winning move. White would not have enough compensation for the Exchange after 31 fxg6 ♗xd2 32 ♗g3 ♗e3.

31 ♖d3   ♗xf5

32 ♘xf5   ♕xf5

33 ♗g3

A different pin wins after 33 ♗d4! b4! 34 cxb4 ♖a8+ 35 ♖a3 ♖d8!.

Or 35 ♔b1 ♖d8 (36 ♕c2 ♗f6).

33 ...   ♖a8+

34 ♔b1   ♖d8

35 ♔c2   b4!

340

Those speed games at the Marshall Chess Club paid off. Caruana took four seconds to threaten 36...b3+.

36 cxb4 ♖c8+

37 ♔b3 ♕e6+

Now 38 ♔a3 ♕a6+ 39 ♔b3 ♕c4+ and mates.

38 ♖d5 ♖d8

39 ♔c4 ♕c6+

40 White resigns.

The queen falls after 40 ♖c5 ♕e4+.

Caruana won six Petroffs as Black in 2018, all before the world championship match.

Curiously, Carlsen only played four Petroffs in 2018 – all as White against Caruana. All four were drawn, including two in the championship match.

48
Getting a Game

In the previous Sinquefield Cup, spectators were fascinated as the game Vachier-Lagrave – Karjakin took a complicated course out of a trendy opening. As it reached a head-scratching middlegame, Caruana told the fans it was all pre-game analysis. Probably every player in the tournament had the current position in a well-analyzed file in his laptop, he said.

He was right. The game ended in a draw at move 45. MVL indicated he had prepared almost all of the moves he played. The game "would be pure brilliancy," he said, "if it were not all known already."

But this situation is rare. More often the preparation of the two players ends soon after the start of the middlegame. "We got a game," they say afterward.

Getting a game is harder as the sharpest openings become more deeply explored. There is a better chance for a real struggle when important decisions are deferred. Here Caruana got a game by waiting.

Caruana – Sergey Karjakin
Stavanger 2018
English Opening,
Four Knights Variation (A28)

1	c4	♘f6
2	♘c3	e5
3	♘f3	♘c6
4	e3	♗b4
5	♕c2	♗xc3

This capture puzzles newcomers to the English Opening, especially if they are familiar with the mirror image in the Sicilian Defense.

In the Rossolimo Variation (Game 37), White plays ♗xc6 when it doubles Black pawns or when prompted by ...a6.

Here neither is the case.

The reason for 5...♗xc3 is White was ready to gain a nice edge with 6 ♘d5!.

This would not work well a move ago (5 ♘d5 e4!, when Black is better).

6	♕xc3	♕e7
7	b3	

Of the major alternatives, this is last in popularity, after 7 a3, 7 ♗e2, 7 d3 and 7 d4, for no strong reason.

It has subtle benefits. After ...d5, Black typically continues ...dxc4 and White captures ♗xc4. In contrast with 7 ♗e2, Caruana wanted to save a tempo by playing ♗f1xc4.

| | 7 | ... | 0-0 |

Karjakin also plays a waiting game. He avoids the main line 7...d5 (8 d4 exd4 9 ♘xd4) and defers a choice between pushing his d-pawn one or two squares.

| 8 | ♗b2 | ♖e8 |

Now 9 d3 d5! reveals that Black is better developed after 10 cxd5 ♘xd5 11 ♕d2 ♗g4 12 ♗e2 ♖ad8.

Or after 10 ♗e2 d4!.

| 9 | a3 |

The same goes for 9 d4? ♘e4 10 ♕c2 exd4 11 ♘xd4 ♕b4+ or 11...♘b4.

| 9 | ... | a5 |

Still waiting. At the post-game press conference, Caruana said he expected 9...d5 and a comfortable position after 10 cxd5 ♘xd5 11 ♕c2, since 9 a3 ruled out ...♘db4.

| 10 | h3 |

A new move. On 10...d5 11 cxd5 ♘xd5 12 ♕c2 Black cannot play the desirable 12...♗g4.

| 10 | ... | b6 |

Karjakin, a Nimzo-Indian Defense player, continues to play Nimzo-ish moves.

A good alternative, available for several moves, is ...e4 followed by ...♘e5.

For example, 12...e4 13 ♘d4 ♘e5 followed by ...d6 and ...b6/...♗b7 is fairly solid.

| 11 | ♗e2 |

In the commentator's room, Magnus Carlsen's former trainer Simen Agdestein suggested 11 g4.

When he heard this later, Caruana appeared appalled. "I have a good position," he said, and no reason to create "chaos."

| 11 | ... | ♗b7 |

| 12 | 0-0 |

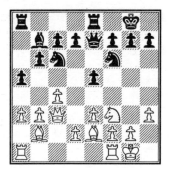

Now a Nimzo-Indian player might adopt another center strategy, 12...♘e4 13 ♕c2 ♘c5.

This discourages b3-b4 while preparing 14 ...e4 15 ♘d4 ♘xd4, with kingside attacking chances after 16...♕h4 or 16...♕g5.

White's queenside pawns would be weak in an endgame after 14 d4 exd4 15 ♘xd4 ♘xd4 16 ♗xd4 ♕e4.

12 ... d5?

This surprised Caruana, for good reason.

13 cxd5 ♘xd5

14 ♕c2

White has a reversed version of an open Sicilian Defense in which Black has little compensation for the loss of the two bishops.

For example, 14...♖ad8 15 d3 followed by ♖ac1.

14 ... e4

Earlier Caruana toyed with the idea of meeting ...e4 with ♘h4 or ♘g5.

Now those moves just hang a knight.

Karjakin must have expected 15 ♘d4.

Then 15...♘xd4 16 ♗xd4 c5! 17 ♗b2 ♕g5 lets his well centralized forces support an attacking plan of ...♖ad8-d6-g6.

White could anticipate that by pushing his f-pawn.

But his position would become static after 18 f4? ♕g3.

Better is 18 f3. Dissolving the e4-pawn should benefit him, at least slightly, because it is a foundation of Black's middlegame.

But 18...♖ad8 19 fxe4? would lose to 19...♘xe3! 20 fxe3 ♗xe4.

15 ♘h2!

This threatens a 16 ♗b5 pin and gains time for White to consider f2-f3! under better conditions.

For instance, 15...♖ad8 16 f3! ♖d6 17 ♖ac1 followed by 18 fxe4 ♕xe4 19 ♗d3 or 19 ♕xe4.

15 ... ♕g5

Caruana pointed out that 15...♘e5 would discourage f2-f3 but allow 16 ♕xe4!.

Then 16...♘c3 looks dangerous.

But after 17 ♕xb7 ♘xe2+ 18 ♔h1 there is no strong follow-up.

White would have sufficient comp for his queen after 17...♖eb8 18 ♕xb8+ ♖xb8 19 ♗xc3.

16 f4 exf3?

This and the equally logical 12...d5 share the blame for the poor middlegame Karjakin gets. No better is 16...♕g3 17 ♗b5!.

But 16...♕h4 and ...♖ad8 would have held White's advantage to a manageable level.

17 ♘xf3 ♕g3

A very similar position would have arisen after 15...♖ad8 and then 16 f3 exf3? 17 ♘xf3. Black's queen would be on e7 and his a8-rook would be on d8.

Karjakin apparently preferred the diagram version because he saw threats of 18...♘f4! and 18...♖xe3! 19 dxe3 ♘xe3.

18 ♖f2!

But this secures White's kingside and also prepares an attack on f7 with ♖af1 and ♗c4/♕f5-g5.

18 ... ♖ad8

What happens next underlines a fundamental difference in how good calculators approach a rapidly improving position.

Some instinctively allow themselves to burn many minutes in search of the absolutely best moves that might get them to the next level, a winning position.

Caruana often did that. But here he took the practical approach.

"I decided to play quickly, not caring whether I was making the most exact moves," Caruana said afterwards.

19 ♗c4

It couldn't be bad to place this bishop on the diagonal leading to f7, he reasoned.

Another version is 19 ♖af1 ♖e6? 20 ♕f5.

Then 20...♘f6 21 ♗c4 ♖ed6 22 ♘g5! and wins.

But if he had taken more time he might have calculated 19 ♗d3! out to a bigger advantage.

There are pretty lines such as 19…h6 20 ♖af1 ♖e7 21 ♗h7+ ♔h8.

Then 22 ♘h4! ♕xh4 23 ♖xf7 wins, e.g. 23…♖xf7 24 ♖xf7 ♘f6 25 ♗xf6 gxf6 26 ♗g8!.

19	...	♘f6

Accepting a ruined kingside pawn structure shows Karjakin's confidence in his "minister of defense" skills.

He could have prepared this move, 19…♖d6 20 ♖af1 ♘f6.

Caruana intended to meet that with 21 ♕f5 and ♕g5. But 21…h6! would put up a defense.

After the game Caruana also mentioned 21 e4!. That turns out to be a powerful shot because of ♖e2 and e4-e5!.

20	♗xf6	gxf6

Now it seemed the position allowed for a calculable, knockout blow.

"I wanted to play 21 ♗xf7+ ♔xf7 22 ♕xh7+," he said at the post-game press conference.

That wins quickly after 22…♔f8 23 ♘h4 and ♖xf6+ or ♘g6+.

It takes longer after 22…♕g7 23 ♘g5+ ♔f8 24 ♖xf6+! ♕xf6 25 ♖f1.

But he had to give up on the sacrifice when he saw a dead end after 22…♔e6!.

21	♖af1	♖d6
22	b4!	

He was trying to expose c7 and make ♗xf7+ work in another way.

For example, 23 b5 ♘e5 24 ♘xe5 ♕xe5 and now 25 ♗xf7+! ♔xf7 26 ♕xh7+ and 27 ♖f5 wins.

22	...	axb4
23	axb4	♖e7

The sacrifice also works with 23…♘xb4 24 ♗xf7+! ♔xf7 25 ♕xc7+ ♖e7 26 ♘g5+! ♕xg5 27 ♕xd6.

24	b5	♘e5
25	♘d4!	

This was another reason for b3-b4-b5. White wants ♘f5.

25	...	♗c8
26	♔h1	♔g7
27	♗e2	♔h8

Now 28 ♖xf6? would allow 28…♗xh3!.

But Karjakin has been reduced to tricks like this and passes with his king.

28	♕c3	♔g7

29 ♝d1!

The passes convinced Caruana he would win if he found a solid plan. An exchange of bishops (♝c2-f5) fits the bill.

29	...	♚g8
30	♝c2	♛h4
31	♜f4	♛g3
32	♝f5!	♝b7
33	♝e4	♝c8
34	♛a3!	

If Black anticipates ♛a8 now with 34...♜e8 he allows 35 ♛a7 ♜d7 36 ♞f5.

34	...	♚g7
35	♛a8	

Karjakin spent more than six minutes here, leaving himself with 31 seconds.

35	...	♝xh3?

After the game, Caruana believed Karjakin panicked twice.

The first was when he allowed 20 ♝xf6.

The second was now when he overlooked how 35...♝d7 36 ♛d8 could be met by 36...♞g6!.

Then 37 ♛xd7 ♜dxd7 38 ♞f5+ ♚f8 39 ♞xg3 ♞xf4 is worth playing out.

Caruana intended to avoid this by answering 35...♝d7 with 36 ♝f5!.

Black cannot avoid a trade of bishops (36...♝e8 37 ♝xh7! and ♞f5).

36	gxh3	♛xh3+
37	♚g1	♜xd4
38	♝g2!	♛g3
39	♜xd4	♞g4

Now 40 ♜xg4 ♛xg4 takes a while to win. Also 41 ♜ff4 ♛e1+ 42 ♝f1 ♛g3+ 43 ♛g2.

40	♜f3	♛e1+
41	♝f1	resigns.

Caruana overcame a first-round loss to Carlsen to clinch first prize with wins over Vishy Anand and Wesley So in the final two rounds. It was his only victory in six attempts in the Norway Chess tournament series.

347

49

Frenemies

When Fabiano returned to play for the United States, the comparison between him and Hikaru Nakamura became a gossip topic among American fans. Caruana is so shy in public that he almost seems to disappear in group photos. He appears smaller than his 5-foot-6, 135 pounds. Nakamura's personality makes him appear larger. He acknowledged, in a 2011 interview, with Riverfront Times, that people found him abrasive. Or more than abrasive. "I know the general idea is that I can be an arrogant asshole," he said. "But that's not all I can be."

"Naka" and "Fabi" had never been buddies, to put it mildly. Nakamura resented being compared with Caruana. "Recently, everyone has made a big deal of Caruana switching federations and is talking about a so-called rivalry between us," he said in 2015. "However, I don't think you can call any matchup a rivalry unless there is a fairly balanced record with many victories on both sides. My rather lopsided score suggests otherwise..."

At the time he was right about their record. Nakamura had the upper hand, four wins and one defeat out of 24 "classical" games. But Caruana more than reversed matters, with five classical wins.

Caruana – Hikaru Nakamura
Sinquefield Cup, St. Louis 2018
Queen's Gambit Declined (D37)

1	d4	♘f6
2	c4	e6
3	♘f3	d5
4	♘c3	♗e7

Caruana needed a new idea in this position. In four other 2018 games with Nakamura, in classical and speed, he played the popular 5 ♗f4. He scored a disastrous ½-3½.

5	g3	dxc4
6	♗g2	0-0

We've transposed into a Catalan Opening with an early development of White's QN.

7	♘e5	

Nakamura had ample experience defending a slightly inferior ending after 7...c5 and 8 dxc5 ♕xd1+ 9 ♘xd1.

348

| 7 | ... | ♘c6 |

This move seemed shocking when it began to appear in GM games in the 1970s. Can't White capture twice on c6?

| 8 | ♗xc6 |

Yes, but if he plays 8 ♘xc6 bxc6 9 ♗xc6, Black gets sufficient play from 8...♖b8 and ...♗b7/...c5.

Then White's b2-pawn will be as vulnerable as Black's c4-pawn.

8	...	bxc6
9	♘xc6	♕e8
10	♘xe7+	♕xe7

White's d4-pawn becomes a tactical problem after 11 0-0 ♖d8! and ...c5.

To avoid getting the worst of that, White should liquidate it with, for example, 12 ♕a4 ♖xd4 13 ♗e3.

| 11 | ♕a4 | c5 |

Anatoly Karpov had given his imprimatur to this way of handling Black, in games that

continued 12 ♕xc4 cxd4 13 ♕xd4 e5 14 ♕h4 ♖b8!.

| 12 | dxc5 | ♕xc5 |
| 13 | ♗e3 | ♕c7 |

But Nakamura was the leading authority on this position. He had shown how the natural 14 0-0 leads nowhere after 14...♘d5!.

A trade of knights (15 ♘xd5) would be a tacit offer of a draw, at the grandmaster level, because of the bishops of opposite color.

Black also has an easy game after (14 0-0 ♘d5) 15 ♗d4 ♗d7 16 ♕a3 a5! and ...♘b4.

| 14 | 0-0-0! |

A stunning innovation.

The conventional wisdom until this game was that White's most important asset was the vulnerability of the c4-pawn.

Caruana overthrew that thinking. His move says: No, it's the d-file that matters most.

| 14 | ... | ♘g4 |

349

Because of the 30-second time delay used in this tournament, neither player had taken any clock time so far.

If 14...♗b7, the move Black would have chosen after 14 ♖d1, White can play on the dark squares, 15 f3 ♘d5 16 ♗d4 ♖fd8 17 e4 ♘xc3 18 ♗xc3.

Is that more than equality? Very slightly, computers say.

15 ♖d2

Analyzing 14 0-0-0 means arguing with your computer. It will keep telling you Black is at least equal.

In fact, some engines recommend 15 ♘b5, so White can draw by repetition, 15... ♕c6 16 ♘c3 ♕c7.

15 ... ♘xe3

16 fxe3

White's pawn structure looks ugly but would improve if he can indirectly swap the e3-pawn for the c4-pawn.

However, computers remain unimpressed after 16...♕c5 17 ♖hd1 ♕xe3 18 ♕xc4 ♗b7 and ...♖fc8.

16 ... ♖b8

17 ♖hd1 a5

18 ♔b1

Members of the on-line audience were still mystified. Surely Black has equalized – if not gotten the upper hand?

But iron control of the only open file is a long-term asset. If queens go off the board, White's rooks would invade, e.g. ♖d6-c6.

18 ... h6

19 ♔a1!

This is both a Caruana "little move" and the kind of prophylactic king shift Magnus Carlsen was known for.

White wants to make better use of his knight and to rule out ...c3 in reply. It also pays to get his king off a light square because of tactics involving Black's bishop.

19 ...   ♖b4

On 19...♗a6 Black allows 20 ♕d7!.

Then 20...♕xd7 21 ♖xd7 is a bad endgame and 20...♕b6 21 ♕d6 ♕b7 is the beginning of a poor middlegame.

20   ♕c2   ♖b8

Nakamura's biggest think of the game was the 20 minutes he invested in this pass.

21   ♕e4!

And this was the first move Caruana spent more than seconds on.

He needed to remember the basic ideas of the position. One is that his queen needs a central post.

After ♕d4 he would be ready for e3-e4-e5!.

In contrast, 21 e4? enables Black's queen to do the centralizing, 21...♗b7 22 ♖d7 ♕c5, with nearly equal chances.

21   ...   ♗b7

22   ♕d4   ♗a8

23   e4

Black could avoid a queen swap, 23 ♕d6 ♕a7.

23   ...   ♖fc8

24   ♕f2   ♗c6

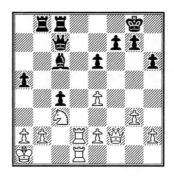

Nakamura stopped White's only tactic, 25 ♖d7.

It was time for long-range thinking:

White could try for e4-e5 after offering a trade of queens, 25 ♕f4.

But even after 25...♕e7 26 e5 ♗d5 it is not clear he is making progress.

For instance, 27 ♘xd5 exd5 28 ♖xd5 c3 or 28...♕b4.

If e4-e5 isn't a good plan, what about a kingside pawn march?

This would show promise after 25 h4 ♗e8 26 g4.

For example, 26...♗c6 27 g5! hxg5 28 hxg5 and ♕h4/♖h1.

But the attack abruptly halts if Black swaps rooks, 26...♖d8! 27 g5 ♖xd2 28 ♖xd2 hxg5 29 hxg5 ♖d8 30 ♖xd8 ♕xd8.

Then White's knight has few good squares. But Black's queen does (31 ♕c5 ♕d2 or 31 ♕f4 ♕d4).

25 ♕c5!

Psychologically, the best move.

It gives Black a choice of playing an inferior endgame -- which is likely to be drawn – or giving up a pawn he might lose anyway.

25 ... ♗e8?

Black would have greater chances with queens on. After 25...♕b7 26 ♕xc4 a4! he is poised for ...a3.

For example, 27 a3 ♗d5 28 ♕-moves ♗b3!.

26 ♕xc7! ♖xc7

27 ♖d6

Computers finally see a White edge, 27...♖c5 28 ♖a6 or 27...♖a8 28 ♖b6!.

27 ... ♔f8

28 ♖a6 ♖c5

29 ♖a7

Now that his rook is ideally placed, White is primed to improve his king with ♔b1-c2 and eventually ♔d2-e3.

29 ... ♖bc8

Black's counterplay lies in attacking his best target, the h2-pawn.

He could start with 29...♖h5 because 30 ♔b1? ♖xh2 31 ♖xa5 ♖g2 approaches equality.

Better is 30 h4 with sharp play after 30...♖c5 31 ♔b1 g5! 32 hxg5 ♖xg5.

Or 32 ♔c2 gxh4 33 gxh4 ♖h5.

30 ♔b1 ♖h5

31 h4 ♖e5

32 ♔c2 g5!

This too, is good, e.g. 33 ♔d2 gxh4 33 gxh4 ♖h5 34 ♖h1 ♖d8+ 35 ♔e3 ♖b8.

Or 35 ♔c2 ♖d7 36 ♖a8 ♖c7.

33 ♖f1 ♔g7

Caruana could defend the kingside with an active rook, 33...gxh4 34 gxh4 ♖h5 35 ♖f4.

34 ♖b7 ♚g6!

Black has a new source of counterplay, a ...♚h5 king raid.

35 ♚d2

White's king is ready for a future without h- and g-pawns.

For example, 35...♚h5 36 ♖f6 gxh4 37 gxh4 ♚xh4 38 ♖xh6+ ♚g5 39 ♖h1.

Then Black lacks a new target and White could seek progress with ♚e3-d4.

35 ... f5?

But Black could neutralize White's best-placed piece with 35...♖ec5 36 ♚e3 ♖8c7!.

Then 37 ♖xc7 ♖xc7 38 ♚d4 ♖b7 39 ♖b1 ♚h5 or 39...gxh4 40 gxh4 ♚h5! is harmless.

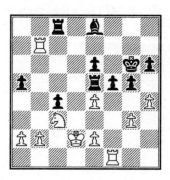

Instead, Nakamura stopped ♖f6 and prepared ...♚h5 as well as ...♗c6 and ...♗xe4.

He would be equal after 36 exf5+ exf5 since White's king loses its shielding e4-pawn.

36 hxg5!

He underestimated this move. Now 36...hxg5 37 ♖h1! and ♖bh7 would threaten ♖1h6 mate.

For example, 37...♗c6 38 ♖bh7 fxe4 39 ♚e3 with the idea of 40 g4!.

The net would tighten after 39...♚f5 40 g4+ ♚xg4 41 ♖7h6 followed by 42 ♖g1+ ♚f5 43 ♖f1+ ♚g4 44 ♘d1! and ♘f2+.

36 ... fxe4?

This cost Black 13 minutes and most of his remaining drawing chances.

Better was 36...♚xg5 with a difficult defense ahead after 37 exf5 exf5 38 ♖f4.

37 ♚e3!

This is the practical alternative to 37 gxh6 e3+.

37 ... ♗c6

He would have won quickly after 37...♚xg5? 38 ♖g7+ ♗g6 39 ♚d4! ♖cc5 40 ♖f8 with zugzwang.

Or 37...hxg5? 38 g4 or 38 ♖f8 and wins.

38 ♖e7 ♖xg5

White would edge closer to a win after 37...h5 38 ♖f6+ ♔xg5 39 ♖exe6 ♖xe6 40 ♖xe6 because his king can penetrate at d4, c5 and b6.

Nakamura pins his hopes on retaining both of his rooks and threatening ...♖xg3+.

39 ♖xe6+ ♔g7

40 ♖e7+ ♔g6

A better try was 40...♔g8 41 ♖f6! ♖xg3+ 42 ♔f4 ♖g7 and then 43 ♖e5 ♖f7 44 ♖xf7 ♔xf7 45 ♖xa5 ♖b8.

41 ♖d1!

Caruana blends in tactics, including a possible mating net.

Now 41...♖xg3+ 42 ♔f4 ♖g5 43 ♖d6+ ♔h5 44 ♖ee6 wins.

41 ... ♔f6

42 ♖a7 ♔e6!

43 ♖h1! h5

Black would be slowly squeezed after 43...♖xg3+ 44 ♔d4 ♖g6 45 ♖h5, followed by ♖c5 or ♖bh7.

44 g4!

Neat. Now 44...hxg4?? 45 ♖h6+ ♔e5 46 ♖xa5+ wins.

44 ... ♗e8

Black would be slowly ground down after 44...♖xg4 45 ♖xh5 ♖g6 46 ♖axa5.

Or 44...♖h8 45 gxh5 ♖hxh5 46 ♖xh5 ♖xh5 47 ♔d4, for example.

45 gxh5 ♗xh5

46 ♘xe4 ♖f5

Now 47 ♖d1 and 47 ♖bh7 win.

47 ♖a6+ ♔e7

48 ♘d6! ♖e5+

49 ♔d4 resigns.

50
Bishops Before Knights

Computers "are really good tactically. And they can't play chess," Magnus Carlsen said in a New Yorker magazine profile in 2011. "It's like playing someone who is extremely stupid but who beats you anyway."

Many of his colleagues trusted engine judgments. "Computers are the ultimate authority. You just automatically accept what they say and move on," Hikaru Nakamura told the New York Times in 2016.

Caruana took a middle ground. Computers are good at refuting your ideas, he said, but not at coming up with new ones. Original ideas are often those that violate general principles and had never been computer-tested. The move 5...♛d7 of Game 46 hadn't passed computer muster before because no one thought it was worth asking an engine if it was playable.

In the following game, Caruana violates different principles. He develops both bishops before his knights and puts one of his knights on the edge of the board. Then he proceeds to beat a former world champion in 26 moves.

Caruana – Viswanathan Anand
Olympiad, Batumi 2018
Catalan Opening,
Open Defense (E03)

1	d4	♘f6
2	c4	e6
3	g3	d5
4	♗g2	dxc4
5	♕a4+	

Regaining the pawn this way has become antique. Instead, the Catalan Opening is usually treated as a possible gambit with 5 ♘f3.

But "if you want to learn the Catalan, study the games of Vasily Smyslov," advised Mikhail Botvinnik. Smyslov played 5 ♕a4+ more than any GM.

| 5 | ... | ♘bd7 |
| 6 | ♕xc4 | a6 |

Black gets the worst of a Catalan most often when he can't smoothly develop his queenside pieces.

This typically occurs because his b7-pawn is pressured by the g2-bishop and he can't free his game with ...c5 and/or ...b5.

7   ♗e3

Another Caruana innovation, at least at the GM level. He tries to slow or stop ...c5.

Instead, White usually settles for modest development (7 b3, 7 ♕d2) or anticipates ...b5 (7 ♕c2, 7 ♕d3).

Anand had achieved equal play previously after 7 ♕c2 c5! 8 ♘f3 b5.

7   ...   ♗d6

8   ♕c2   0-0

Since ...c5 is discouraged, Black prepares the other freeing move, ...e5.

9   ♘h3

When Caruana began testing 7 ♗e3, he must have been disappointed to find 9 ♘f3 can be answered by 9...b5!.

Then White's g2-bishop has discovered attacks on the a8-rook.

But 10 ♘e5, for example, is fine for Black after 10...♘d5 11 ♘c6 ♘xe3 12 fxe3 ♕e8.

He would get ample compensation for the Exchange after 13 ♘e7+? ♕xe7 14 ♗xa8 ♘b6.

9   ...   e5

10   0-0

Black can try to exploit White's odd development with 10...♘g4.

But 11 ♗g5! f6 creates a hole at e6 that White can exploit after 12 dxe5!.

He would be comfortably ahead after 12...♘dxe5 13 ♗d2 c6 14 ♘c3 and 15 ♘f4, for instance.

10   ...   h6!

But now 11 ♘c3? ♘g4!, for example, favors Black after 12 ♕d2 ♘xe3 13 ♕xe3 exd4 14 ♕xd4 ♗e5.

11   dxe5   ♘xe5

356

12	♘c3	♕e7
13	♖ad1	♖e8

Black still has one opening problem: How to develop his c8-bishop. It has no good first-move square except the passive d7.

| 14 | ♘f4 | c6 |

Now that he controls d5, he is ready for 15...g5! 16 ♘d3 ♗f5.

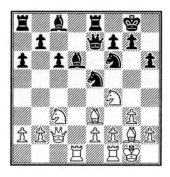

| 15 | ♗d4! |

This eyes ♘a4 – but also frees the e-pawn to advance.

| 15 | ... | g5 |

One more prophylactic move would have nearly equalized – 15...♖b8! (16 ♘a4 g5).

Then 16 ♘e4 ♘xe4 17 ♕xe4 ♘g6 is harmless.

Caruana acknowledged he would have had to try something quiet like 16 a3 or 16 ♖fe1.

| 16 | ♘d3 |

Thanks to his 15th move, White can meet 16...♗f5 with 17 e4! and advance his e- and f-pawns.

For example, 17...♗d7? 18 f4! ♘xd3 19 ♕xd3 and 20 e5!.

Black can disrupt that plan with 17...♗g6.

Then on 18 ♘xe5 ♗xe5 19 ♗xe5 ♕xe5 20 f4 ♕c5+ 21 ♔h1 he has 21...♗xe4!.

But after the careful 18 f4! the tactic fails.

For instance, 18...♘xd3 19 ♕xd3 ♗xe4? 20 ♘xe4 ♘xe4 21 ♖de1.

Instead, 19...♗c5 20 ♗xc5 ♕xc5+ 21 ♕d4 would get White into a nice endgame 21...♕xd4+ 22 ♖xd4 gxf4 23 gxf4.

| 16 | ... | ♘xd3 |

Anand will be lost in six moves. Why?

| 17 | ♖xd3! |

First he counted on 17 ♕xd3 ♗c5!.

Then he could defend after 18 ♗xc5 ♕xc5 19 ♕d4 ♕xd4 20 ♖xd4 ♗e6, for example.

17 ... ♗e5

Now 17...♗c5? 18 ♖e3! costs material, as does 17...♗f5? 18 ♗xf6! (18...♕xf6 19 ♖xd6 or 18...♗xd3 19 ♗xe7).

Anand's move stops the threat of 18 ♗xf6 ♕xf6 19 ♘e4.

18 ♕d2

Another "little" move – yet ranked third-best by some computers.

They prefer 18 e4 and then 18...♗xd4 19 ♖xd4 ♗e6 20 ♕d2 ♖ad8 to hold White to a moderate advantage.

More ambitious is the pinning 18 ♖e3.

But Caruana saw how 18...♘g4! 19 ♖e4? ♗f5 wins the Exchange.

Similarly, 18 ♗xe5 ♕xe5 19 ♖e3 looks good – until you notice 19...♗f5!.

18 ... ♗f5

Black would have had a "really lousy position" if he continued 18...♗xd4 19 ♖xd4 ♗e6 20 ♖d1, Caruana wrote in *New In Chess*.

White could gradually improve his position with e2-e4, b2-b4 and ♘a4-c5, among other plans.

19 e4 ♗g6

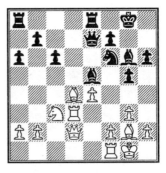

It's been known since the 1940s that White would enjoy a long-term advantage in positions such as 20 ♗xe5 ♕xe5 21 f3.

Then Black's minor pieces are stifled by the e4/f3 pawns. He cannot trade rooks because White controls the only open file (21...♕e7 22 ♖d1).

20 f4!?

Yet this is the move that a modern world champion would choose.

The goal is a strategic wipeout after e4-e5!.

Black can anticipate this with 20...♗xd4+ 21 ♖xd4 ♖ad8 and the pinning 22 e5 ♕c5.

But 23 ♖d1 gets White another nice endgame after 23...♖xd4 24 ♕xd4 ♕xd4+ 25 ♖xd4.

Or 23...♘h5 24 ♕f2.

To play this way, Caruana had to foresee that he would have only one good reply to 23...♗h5 – but it is the unpinning 24 ♔h1!, with a growing edge.

20 ... gxf4?

21 ♗xe5!

Anand made a faulty assumption at move 16 and did it again. He expected 21 gxf4 and then 21...♗xd4+ 22 ♖xd4 ♖ad8.

This would permit him to challenge the d-file in a better way than in the last note, 23 e5 ♕c5 24 ♖d1 ♖xd4 25 ♕xd4 ♕xd4+ 26 ♖xd4 ♘h5! (and 27...f6).

21 ... ♕xe5

22 gxf4 ♕c5+

23 ♔h1

Of course, not 23 ♖d4? ♖ad8.

White is winning because of threats of 24 f5/25 ♕xh6 and 24 ♖d4/25 e5.

For instance, 23...♔h7 24 e5! ♗xd3 25 ♕xd3+ and 24...♘h5 25 ♘e4!.

23 ... ♘xe4

Anand made his remaining moves in seconds. He was playing for traps.

24 ♘xe4 ♖xe4

Black drops a rook after 24...♗xe4 25 ♗xe4 ♖xe4 26 ♕g2+.

25 ♖g3!

Anand was hoping for 25 f5 ♗xf5 26 ♖g3+ ♖g4 27 ♖xg4+? ♗xg4.

Or 26 ♕xh6 ♗g6.

But now 26 ♗xe4 and 26 f5 are decisive threats (25...♕f5 26 ♗h3).

25 ...   ♖d4

Another try for a swindle is 25...♔h7.

To play 26 ♖xg6! White would have to see the one good answer to 26...♖d4.

But once he notices how 27 ♕c3! ♕xc3 28 bxc3 attacks the d4-rook, the game is effectively over.

There is also a win after (25...♔h7) by playing 26 f5 ♗xf5 27 ♖gf3.

For example, 27...♖e5 28 ♖xf5! ♖xf5 29 ♗e4.

Also, 27...♗g6 28 ♖xf7+! ♗xf7 29 ♗xe4+ ♔g7 30 ♕g2+ or 30 ♕f4 ♕e7 31 ♖g1+.

26   ♕e3!   resigns.

The threat remains 27 f5.

The bishop is lost after 26...♔h7 27 f5 ♗xf5 28 ♖xf5 ♕xf5 29 ♕xd4.

Or 27...♗h5 28 ♖h3!.

Anand had not lost a shorter classical game in seven years.

The Olympiad was Caruana's final event before the Magnus match. He scored four wins, six draws and no losses, and his US team garnered the silver medals behind China. Even in the Bobby Fischer years, the Americans had not finished so high in two successive Olympiads

51
Classical Co-Champion

Magnus Carlsen came shockingly close to being dethroned by Sergey Karjakin in his 2016 world championship match. Two years later, Caruana was expected to pose a stronger challenge. He was better prepared, theoretically and emotionally, than Carlsen. "Fabiano's motivation is now clearly higher," GM Sergey Shipov wrote in 64. "For him it will be the match of his life."

When it was over, Carlsen called it his toughest match. All 12 scheduled games ended in draws. This meant Caruana earned the right to call himself Carlsen's equal in classical chess, he said.

"I maybe missed, like, two big chances," Fabiano said afterwards. In one game it was more than a chance.

Magnus Carlsen – Caruana
World Championship match,
sixth game, London 2018
*Petroff Defense,
Irregular Variation (C42)*

1	e4	e5
2	♘f3	♘f6

Magnus had begun 1 d4 and 1 c4 in his first two White games of the match. It was widely expected he would have something new to say in the Petroff during his final four Whites.

3	♘xe5	d6
4	♘d3	

This innocuous move was a letdown for his fans. In *Chess Life*, Ian Rogers said it "will probably now be buried."

Not yet. Ian Nepomniachtchi, Lê Quang Liêm and Pentala Harikrishna have kept it above ground.

4	...	♘xe4

5 ♕e2 ♕e7

6 ♘f4

The threat of 7 ♘d5 might scare Black into 6...c6.

That denies him ...♘c6. It's not much of a concession but would be a minor victory for White.

6 ... ♘c6!

Caruana had studied 4 ♘d3 after Wesley So played it against him three months earlier.

They drew after 6 ♘c3 ♘f6! 7 b3 ♘c6. This showed him the value of a quick ...♘c6-d4.

7 ♘d5

If White prepares ♘d5 with 7 c3, Black would be more than pleased with 7...♘f6! followed by ...♗f5 and ...0-0-0 or ...g5.

7 ... ♘d4

8 ♘xe7 ♘xe2

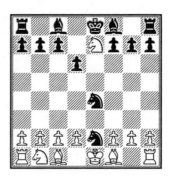

Both knights have become desperados. Since White's captures come before Black's, it is surprising he can't take advantage.

For example, 9 ♘xc8 ♘xc1 10 ♘xa7 ♘xa2?? 11 ♖xa2.

After 10...♖xa7 11 a3 he threatens to emerge a pawn ahead after 11 ♘c3 ♘xc3 12 dxc3 and ♖xc1.

But 11...♘c5! and 12...♘1b3! favors Black.

9 ♘d5! ♘d4!

Actually, this position had been discussed years before when 4 ♘c4, rather than 4 ♘d3, made one of its periodic bids at respectability.

After 4 ♘c4 ♘xe4 5 ♕e2 neither player has better than 5...♕e7 6 ♘e3.

Then 6...♘c6 7 ♘d5 ♘d4 transposes into our game.

10 ♘a3

Attempts to improve White's chances significantly with 10 ♗d3 ♘c5! 11 ♘xc7+ ♔d8 12 ♘xa8 ♘xd3+ 13 cxd3 ♘c2+ have failed.

10 ... ♘e6!

For the trivia-mind, this was the tenth straight knight move.

If, instead, 10...♔d8 11 c3 c6?, Black would be close to losing after 12 d3! and 12...cxd5 13 dxe4!.

11 f3 ♘4c5

12 d4

Internet fans hoping for more excitement saw online computer analysis of 12...c6 13 dxc5 cxd5 14 cxd6 ♗xd6.

They were disappointed to see how balanced 15 ♗e3 ♗xa3 16 bxa3 ♗d7 would be.

12 ... ♘d7

Both players were making their moves quickly. Their home prep must have shown them that 13 ♘b5 ♔d8 14 ♘e3? a6 overextends White's knights.

Better but merely equal is 14 ♘f4 ♘b6 and ...c6.

13 c3 c6

14 ♘f4

Black is not out of the woods yet, as 14...♘xf4? 15 ♗xf4 ♘f6 16 ♘c4 indicates.

14 ... ♘b6!

15 ♗d3 d5

16 ♘c2 ♗d6

17 ♘xe6 ♗xe6

18 ♔f2

With no tactics or obvious principled moves, both players can think of seizing space instead. White prepares g2-g4.

18 ... h5!

Bent Larsen would be proud. The Dane was fond of advancing a rook pawn two squares.

But he might have preferred 18...a5.

Then 19...a4! followed by ...♔d7 and ...♘c4 would grant Black queenside prospects.

How would Carlsen have responded?

Most likely, he would have met 18...a5! with 19 a4!.

19 h4

Computers with a sense of humor consider 19 a4.

Then White prepares to gain space with 20 a5 (20...♘c4? 21 b3).

But Caruana would probably have kept chances even with – guess what? -- 19...a5!.

19 ... ♘c8

20 ♘e3 ♘e7

21 g3

Magnus prepares a favorable exchange of his bad bishop for Black's good one, ♘g2 and ♗f4.

21 ... c5!

Now 22 ♘g2 is ineffective because the d4-pawn becomes a target after 22...cxd4 23 cxd4 ♘c6 (24 ♗e3 ♖c8).

22 ♗c2

The position would have remained dead even after 22 dxc5 ♗xc5 and eventually...d4.

Instead, Carlsen allows an exchange of c-pawns so that his bishop will be well situated on b3.

22 ... 0-0

23 ♖d1 ♖fd8

Now 24 ♗d2 ♘c6 25 ♗e1 ♖ac8 26 ♖ac1 is a safe defensive formation. Hardly what Carlsen wanted five moves ago.

24 ♘g2 cxd4

25 cxd4 ♖ac8

26 ♗b3

Caruana called the position "so sterile I really shouldn't have gotten anything."

A handshake might have been imminent after 26...♗f5 27 ♗f4 ♗c2 28 ♖d2 ♗xb3 29 ♗xd6 ♖xd6 30 axb3.

Or just 27 ♘e3 ♗e6 28 ♘g2 ♗f5, with a repetition of moves.

26 ... ♘c6

27 ♗f4 ♘a5

28 ♖dc1 ♗b4

The doubled pawns are not easily attacked after 28...♘xb3 29 axb3.

Instead, Caruana is beginning to see winning chances from ...♘c4.

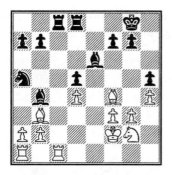

A good way to evaluate the position is to consider how exchanges will change the picture.

A swap of all four rooks, 29 ♖xc8 ♖xc8 30 ♖c1 ♖xc1 31 ♗xc1, favors Black a bit.

Then with 31...♘xb3 32 axb3 g6 he can try to create a passed kingside pawn (...♗e7, ...f6 and ...g5).

29   ♗d1

A better trade for White is 29 ♗c7 ♖e8 30 ♗xa5 ♗xa5 because his remaining minor pieces would be well-placed after 31 ♘f4.

But instead of 29...♖e8? Black should insert 29...♘xb3 30 axb3.

His bishops can come alive after 30...♖e8 31 ♘f4 ♗f5 32 ♘xd5 ♗d2 33 ♖d1 ♗h6.

In this sequence, Carlsen considered going into 31 ♖xa7 ♗d6.

He could get out of the pin with an Exchange sacrifice, 31...♗d6 32 ♖xb7 ♖e7 33 ♗xd6 ♖xb7 34 ♖xc8+ ♗xc8 35 ♘f4.

"I should hold that any day of the week," Carlsen said after the game.

29   ...   ♘c4

30   b3

Not 30 a3? ♗e7 31 ♖ab1 ♗f6, which drops a pawn.

30   ...   ♘a3

31   ♖xc8   ♖xc8

32   ♖c1

White has some counterplay that makes a draw increasingly likely.

After 32...♖xc1 33 ♗xc1, he would threaten ♘f4 and ♘xh5 or ♘xe6.

He should have no trouble after 33...♘b5 34 ♘f4 ♘c3! 35 ♗c2 ♘xa2 36 ♗b2.

In fact, 36...g6?? 37 ♘xe6 fxe6 38 ♗xg6 might cost Black the game.

32   ...   ♘b5

33   ♖xc8+   ♗xc8

34   ♘e3   ♘c3

35 ♗c2

35 ... ♗a3!

Carlsen underestimated this way of stopping a2-a4.

But Black's winning chances are still slim, for example, after 36 ♗d3 ♗e6 37 ♘c2 ♗b2 38 a4 ♘a2 and ...♘c1!.

36 ♗b8 a6

37 f4

True to form, Carlsen prefers active defense. He will push this pawn to f5 so that ♘f4 would win either the d5- or the h5-pawn.

37 ... ♗d7

38 f5 ♗c6

39 ♗d1!

Now 39...g6 40 ♗c2 ♔g7 41 fxg6 and ♘g2-f4 results in White winning a kingside pawn. That offsets the loss of the a2-pawn.

Carlsen famously said he does not believe in fortresses, the impregnable defensive formations that allow seemingly hopeless positions to be drawn.

But potential fortresses are beginning to appear. For example, after 39...♘xd1+ 40 ♘xd1 followed by 41 ♘e3 and ♗a7-c5.

Then Black could not threaten the a2-pawn or easily create a passed kingside pawn.

39 ... ♗b2!

40 ♗xh5 ♘e4+!

Black has greater winning chances with a passed d-pawn than after 40...♘xa2 41 ♗a7.

41 ♔g2

For example, 41 ♔e2 ♗xd4 42 a4 ♘c5 and 43 ♗f3 ♗xe3 44 ♔xe3 ♘xb3 45 g4? d4+.

41 ... ♗xd4

Now on 42 ♘c2 ♗c3! Black prepares a discovered check following ...d4.

White's kingside pawns would also be threatened by 43 ♗a7 ♗e5 44 ♗f2 ♗d7! 45 g4 ♘f6.

42   ♗f4   ♗c5

Caruana thought this would pose "a very difficult decision" for Carlsen.

For example, 43 ♘c2 d4!.

Black would probably win after 44 ♗f3 d3 45 ♘e3 ♗xe3! 46 ♗xe3 d2, with a threat of 47...♘g5!.

43   ♗f3!   ♘d2

Now 44 ♘d1 ♘xf3 45 ♔xf3 d4+ 46 ♔e2 is close to a loss after 46...♗e4 and ...♗b1.

44   ♗xd5?

This move was so astonishing that the Russian magazine *64* found it best to award it the unique notation "?!!?."

It deserves one question mark for a calculation oversight (coming at move 48).

It deserves the second for underestimating the drawing chances after 44 ♘f1! ♘xf3 45 ♔xf3 d4+ 46 ♔f2.

Unlike the scenario with 44 ♘d1 in the previous note, this one should be secure after 46...♗e4 47 g4 ♗b1 48 ♘d2! ♗xa2 49 ♔e2 and ♔d3.

44   ...   ♗xe3

45   ♗xc6   ♗xf4

46   ♗xb7

46   ...   ♗d6!

Black could have slammed the door to the queenside with 46...♗e3.

But even without his king to shepherd them, Carlsen's passed pawns can draw.

For example 47 ♗xa6 f6 48 b4 ♔f8 49 g4 ♔e7 50 a4 ♔d6 51 a5 and ♗d3.

Black can save a tempo in that sequence with 47...♔f8.

But then 48 f6! gxf6 49 b4 is an easier draw because he has to deal with a third passed pawn, on h4.

47   ♗xa6   ♘e4

Black's king and pieces arrive in time to stop the queenside pawn

367

after 48 a4 ♘xg3 49 ♗d3 ♘h5 and ...♘f6/...♔f8-e7.

48   g4

Carlsen thought he would draw after, say, 48...♔f8 49 ♔f3 ♘c3 50 a4 ♗b4 51 g5.

48   ...   ♗a3!

He underestimated ...♗a3 for the second time in the game. Again the a-pawn is blockaded and threatened by ...♘c3.

49   ♗c4   ♔f8

50   g5   ♘c3

51   b4!

As outside pawns go, the a-pawn is "more outside" than the b-pawn and is the one to save.

This is a decision Carlsen could reach by intuition. Caruana could come to the same conclusion by calculating, e.g. 51 ♔f3 ♘xa2 52 ♔e4 ♘b4.

Then White's king is halted – 53 ♔d4 ♗b2+ 54 ♔c5 ♘c2 (55 b4? ♗a3)

And so are his pawns, 53 h5 ♗c1 54 g6 fxg6 55 fxg6 ♔e7.

51   ...   ♗xb4

52   ♔f3   ♘a4

Black must be able to discourage h5-h6 with ...♗d2! and preserve at least one of his pawns, as a potential queen.

White would draw after 52...♔e7? 53 h5 ♘a4 54 h6!.

53   ♗b5   ♘c5

54   a4!

Here 54...♗e1 55 h5 ♗d2 looks like a win – but would allow 56 f6! ♗xg5 57 a5! ♗xf6 58 a6, when Black must give up a piece to stop the a-pawn.

54   ...   f6!

"I was quite worried," Carlsen said.

His king cannot advance the a-pawn or penetrate the queenside, 55 ♔e3 ♗e1! 56 gxf6 gxf6 57 h5 ♗c3!.

Caruana would then pick off one of the kingside pawns with ...♔g7-h6. As long as he preserves his f6-pawn, Black wins.

55   ♔g4   ♘e4

56   ♔h5   ♗e1

57   ♗d3?

57 ...   ♘d6

Ironically, Carlsen is betting on a successful fortess.

For example, he could pass with 58 ♗c2 ♘f7 59 ♗d3 ♘e5! 60 ♗e2 ♔e7 61 ♗b5 ♔d6 62 ♗e8.

His king is stalemated but he would draw after 62...♘f3 64 gxf6 gxf6 65 ♔g4 ♘xh4 66 a5! ♘f3 66 ♔f3.

But Black has 62...♔d5 instead of 62...♘f3?.

Broken fortress

He would pick off the f5-pawn with ...♔e4.

It is too late for 63 a5 ♗xa5 64 gxf6 gxf6 65 ♔h6 ♔e4.

58   a5!

White might have avoided that loss if he had chosen 57 ♗c4 ♘d6 58 ♗e6!.

Now he has to try for a Carlsen miracle.

58 ...   ♗xa5

59   gxf6   gxf6

60   ♔g6   ♗d8!

Black needs the bishop on d8 so it protects the f6-pawn after ...♘f7-e5+.

His king can mind the h-pawn, 61 h5 ♔g8 62 h6 ♔h8 and eventually ...♘e5+ followed by ...♔h7.

61   ♔h7!!

Carlsen foresees a new fortress based on stopping ...♔g8!.

369

61	...	♘f7
62	♗c4	♘e5
63	♗d5	♗a5

Now ...♗e1 will force h4-h5.

If White defends it, 64 ♔h6 ♗e1 65 ♔h5, his king will be frozen.

Black would win with a king march on dark squares ...♔e7-d6-c5-d4-e3-f4!.

64	h5	♗d2
65	♗a2	♘f3
66	♗d5	♘d4

67 ♔g6?

A remarkable defense was later found in 67 ♗c4!! ♘xf5 68 ♔g6 ♘d6 69 ♗e6.

Despite freeing his f-pawn, Black cannot win.

For example 69...♔e7 70 ♗d5 f5 71 h6 ♗c3 72 h7 ♗d4 73 ♔g5 ♔f8 74 ♗e6 and ♗xf5.

67	...	♗g5

White is lost. Computers were showing on-line spectators a forced mate.

The shortest version is 68 h6? ♘e2 69 h7? ♘f4 mate.

Or 69 ♔h7 ♘f4 and the knight maneuvers to g4 and picks off the h-pawn.

68 ♗c4

The stage is set for one of the most remarkable events in a world championship match.

The critical variation is 68...♗h4. After passes such as 69 ♗d5 ♘e2 70 ♗f3 Black plays 70...♘g1!! and allows 71 ♗g4.

"No human" stalemates his own knight.

370

Black stalemates his knight in order to set up zugzwang.

It looks like a fantasy variation, something that can be enjoyed only by fans of composed studies.

In other words, endgame porn.

But computers found that it is the only way for Black to win, after 71...♔g8 72 ♔h6.

He needs to lose a tempo and does it with 72...♗g3 73 ♔g6 ♗e5 74 ♔h6 ♗f4+ 75 ♔g6 ♗g5.

Then 76 ♗d1 ♘h3 and ...♘f4+ would win.

The main line is 76 h6 ♔h8! 77 h7 ♗h4 and the h-pawn eventually falls.

This is a fraction of the complications. There are even logical sequences in which White's king gets mated on h8.

But Caruana played **68...♘f3?** and the win was gone. As Kasparov said, "No human would willingly trap his knight like that."

Caruana played another 12 moves and conceded the draw, which, even then, was too early, according to Jan Timman:

**69 ♔h7 ♘e5 70 ♗b3 ♘g4
71 ♗c4 ♘e3 72 ♗d3 ♘g4
73 ♗c4 ♘h6 74 ♔g6 ♔e7
75 ♗b3 ♔d6 76 ♗c2 ♔e5
77 ♗d3 ♔f4 78 ♗c2 ♘g4 79 ♗b3
♘e3 80 h6! ♗xh6 draw**

After the game Carlsen joked about his earlier comments on fortresses. "It's a good thing they exist, right?"

He was energized by the draw and felt motivated by the end of the match. "I was the opposite," Caruana said. He was exhausted, physically and emotionally. Although he managed to end the 12 regulation games in a tie, he was outplayed badly in the speed playoff. Carlsen retained his title. Caruana had to start over again in the next world championship cycle.

But not immediately. "I didn't look at chess for, like, two months after the match," he said.

52

The Armageddon Philosophy

The Armageddon method of breaking ties has no close analog in other games and sports. It is a speed game with two special rules (a) White begins with more time but (b) Black has "draw odds." That is, Black is declared the tie-break winner if the game ends in a draw.

The Norway Chess tournaments of 2019 and 2021 built Armageddon into a new scoring system. If a player won a regularly scheduled game, he earned two points. In case of a draw, each player received half a point. A second game, played with Armageddon rules, was held to determine who got an additional one point.

In the seventh round of the 2019 tournament, Caruana amassed what computers called a +13 advantage against Vishy Anand. He only drew, a dramatic case of wounding, not killing. But he partially made up for it in the Armageddon.

Caruana – Viswanathan Anand
Stavanger 2019
Giuoco Piano (C53)

1	e4	e5
2	♘f3	♘c6
3	♗c4	♗c5
4	c3	♘f6
5	d3	d6

Like all elite players of the 2020s, Caruana had considerable experience with Giuoco Piano lines featuring the auto-pilot moves 0-0, ♘bd2 and ♗b3, in one order or another.

6	♗g5	a6

7	a4	♗a7
8	♘bd2	

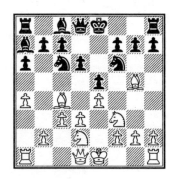

One benefit of ♗g5 occurs if Black tries to maneuver his c6-knight to g6.

This is common in similar positions. But after 8...0-0 9 b4

♘e7, for example, it allows kingside damage, 10 ♗xf6! gxf6 11 ♘h4 and ♕f3.

8	...	h6
9	♗h4	♕e7

Black can disguise his intentions for another move with 9...♗d7, and then 10 0-0 g5 11 ♗g3 ♕e7.

But queenside castling rarely works well when White can open the queenside (12 b4 0-0-0? 13 b5).

10 b4

Caruana had been moving almost instantly. But he took 15 seconds to choose this move and found himself in serious trouble.

10	...	g5!
11	♗g3	♘h5!

Now 12 0-0 ♘xg3 13 hxg3 g4 14 ♘h4 ♕g5 15 b5 looks like a Morphy-era example of how

Black can over-estimate his kingside chances.

However, if we replace 13...g4 with 13...h5! Black is much better. He can play 14...h4 15 gxh4 g4!, when the key defensive move ♘h4 is impossible.

12 b5

This is beginning to look like another whoever-opens-files-first-will-win game.

But there is a big difference in files.

Opening the h-file would be a major, if not decisive, plus for Black as in the last note.

Opening the a-file, 12...axb5? 13 axb5, is very bad for him because of the pin (13...♘d8 14 ♖a4 with the idea of ♕a1).

But opening the b-file is merely good for White.

12	...	♘d8

Anand foresees ...♘e6-f4. Yet the knight never moves again in this game.

Better is 12...♘a5!. Black would have excellent play after 13 bxa6 bxa6 14 ♗a2 ♕f6 or 14 0-0 ♘xc4 15 ♘xc4 f5!.

13 bxa6 bxa6

14 ♖b1

The intended 14...♘e6 allows 15 ♗d5!.

Then 15...♖b8? 16 ♖xb8 ♗xb8 17 ♘xe5! and ♕xh5.

Or 17...♘xg3 18 ♘c6.

Black can insert 14...♘xg3 15 hxg3 before 15...♘d8.

But the positional difference between playing ...♘f4! and ...♘xg3 is substantial. Black would be worse after 16 ♗d5 ♖b8 17 ♖xb8 ♗xb8 18 ♘c4 followed by ♘a5 or ♘e3-f5!.

14 ... ♕f6

15 d4!

This pawn sacrifice is the only good answer to the threat of ...♘xg3/...g4.

It was well worth an Armageddon minute, Caruana's biggest think of the game.

Black would have been better after 15 0-0? ♘xg3 16 hxg3 h5 and ...h4.

15 ... ♘xg3

Not 15...exd4? 16 e5! (and 16...dxe5?? 17 ♗xe5).

16 hxg3 g4!

White would get some – but not a lot of – compensation after 16...exd4 17 cxd4 ♗xd4 18 ♘xd4, 18 ♗d5 or 18 ♕c2.

17 ♘h4 exd4

18 cxd4 ♗xd4

Also good is 18...♕xd4. The queen cannot be easily harassed on d4 and can support ...d5.

Black would then have nothing to fear from 19 0-0 0-0 20 ♘g6 ♖e8 and can meet 20 ♕c2 with 20...♖e8 (21 e5? d5!).

19   0-0   0-0

By traditional standards, chances are in rough balance. White can take aim at three weak pawns, at a6, c7 and g4.

But Armageddon adds a new factor to the evaluation metric: White cannot permit a simplification that leads anywhere near a drawish position.

20   ♔h1

Caruana takes a much more ambitious path, towards 21 f4 and the tactics of e4-e5.

He would be worse off now after 21...♕g7 22 f4 gxf3 23 ♘dxf3 ♗f6 24 ♘f5 ♗xf5 than if he had regained his lost pawn with, say, 20 ♘b3 ♗a7 21 ♗e2.

But 20 ♔h1 gives him greater winning chances. It doesn't matter that it also increases his chances of losing, according to the Armageddon philosophy. Since he is White, a loss is no worse than a draw.

20   ...   c6?

Also bad was 20...♗d7 21 f4 h5?? 22 e5!.

Then 22... dxe5 23 ♘e4 ♕g7 25 fxe5 exploits the unprotected d7-bishop.

And   23...♕c6   24   ♗d5 (24...♕xd5? 25 ♘f6+) exploits the a8-rook.

21   f4!

Suddenly Black is in trouble. After 21...gxf3 22 ♘dxf3 his attacked bishop has no good retreat.

White can muster his unopposed army after 22...♗c5 23 e5! dxe5 24 ♕d3 and ♖ae1, followed by a winning capture on e5.

21   ...   d5

This looked promising: 22 exd5 ♗f5 23 ♘xf5 ♕xf5 and White has

375

only one good way to avoid ...♛h5 mate.

But 24 ♞f3! is good enough. White's superiority would be clear after 24...♛h5+ 25 ♞h2 or 24...gxf3 25 ♛xd4.

But this is unnecessary. Instead of 23 ♞xf5, the simple 23 ♖b3 keeps a big edge.

22 ♗d3

Best of all was 22 e5!.

Then 22...♛g7 23 ♗d3 resembles what happens in the game.

But 23 ♞e4! would be winning after 23...dxe4 24 ♛xd4 and ♛xe4.

Or after 23...♗xe5 24 fxe5 dxe4 25 ♖f6!.

22 ... ♛g7

A pawn structure with 23 e5! would likely be fatal. But so would 22...dxe4 23 ♞xe4 ♛-moves 24 f5!.

23 e5! f5

Anand moved instantly. He understood how routine White's winning task would be if he can occupy f5 with pieces or a pawn.

Computers look at defenses such as 23...♗c5 24 ♞b3 ♗e7 25 ♞d4 ♗xh4 26 gxh4.

But 26...♗d7 27 f5 or 26...c5 27 ♞e2! followed by ♞g3 and f4-f5 should finish Black off.

24 ♛c2

This quick move is the first step in a plan to exploit the dark squares with ♞b3 and ♞d4 or ♞c5.

Faster is 24 ♞c4 and 25 ♞d6 (24...dxc4? 25 ♗xc4+ and ♛xd4).

24 ... ♛f7

25 ♞b3

If Black gives up his dark-squared bishop, 25...♗a7 26 ♛c3 and 27 ♞d4 ♗xd4, he is strategically lost. Caruana can also provoke that exchange with ♞c5.

25 ... ♗e3

26	♖fe1	♗a7
27	a5	♗e6
28	♘c5!	

If Black offers the a6-pawn, 28...♖c8 29 ♗xa6 ♖c7, White's best policy is to double rooks on the b-file with 30 ♖b6! and ♖eb1.

For example, 30...♗xb6? 31 axb6 ♖e7 32 ♖b1 and eventually b6-b7.

28	...	♗xc5
29	♕xc5	

This is a classic dark-square bind. White can slowly bring his heavy pieces to bear on the weakest points, a6 and c6.

For example, 29...♘b7 30 ♕b6 ♘d8 31 ♕b4 ♕c7 32 ♖ec1 followed by ♕a3 and ♖b6.

29	...	♖e8
30	♖b6!	♕f8

White has many ways of winning now but taking the

f5-pawn and pushing his own f-pawn is fastest.

Even 31 ♕c3 c5 32 ♗xf5! was possible (32...♗xf5 33 ♖f6).

31	♕c2	♖a7
32	♗xf5	♗xf5
33	♘xf5	h5

By moving fairly quickly, Caruana had overlooked faster wins (22 e5 and 24 ♘c4 among them).

But he preserved his Armageddon time edge. The game began with ten minutes for White to seven for Black. Now it was more than five minutes for White to Anand's three-minutes-plus. There was little chance Caruana would make a *zeitnot* blunder.

34	♘h4	♖g7
35	f5	♕a3
36	♔h2	♕xa5
37	♖bb1	

He spent another six seconds on this, rather than calculate 37 ♖eb1 ♖xe5 38 f6.

That wins, 38...♖f7 39 ♕g6+ ♔f8 40 ♖b8.

37	...	♕c7
38	e6	♕e7
39	♕c3	

The easiest way to win now is to maintain a threat of f5-f6 while penetrating with his heavy pieces. This will eventually run Black out of useful moves.

39	...	♖f8
40	♖b8	c5
41	♕e5	

Anand doesn't even get to play a piece-down endgame after 41 f6 ♕xf6 42 ♕xf6 ♖xf6 43 ♖xd8+.

41	...	d4
42	♕d5	

Swindlers might appreciate 42...♖g5 because 43 ♖a1 allows 43...♕xe6! 44 ♕xe6+? ♘xe6 and Black is better.

But White can short-circuit this with 44 ♕xd8!, among others.

42	...	♔h7
43	♖e5	♕f6
44	♘g6!	resigns.

Enough (44...♖e8 45 e7!) is enough.

Conventional wisdom and a wealth of statistical experience says it is better to be Black in Armageddon. In this tournament, White won 15 Armageddon games and suffered six losses. But 13 games were drawn so the player with Black came out ahead, 19-15.

53
Winning The Fifth Hour

When a master's prepared moves are so surprising and strong that he quickly gains a significant advantage, he "wins the first hour." That may be enough if he can nurse his edge into a decisive endgame.

But more games are won in the fifth hour. This is when critical decisions are made and mistakes multiply, because of the position, the clock or both.

In the following game, Caruana's early advantage dissipates. After winning the first hour, he loses the second, matches wits with his opponent in the third and fourth and outplays him again in the fifth.

Levon Aronian – Caruana
Stavanger 2019
English Opening,
Smyslov Variation (A22)

1	c4	e5
2	g3	♘f6
3	♘c3	♝b4

This reversed version of the Rossolimo Sicilian was a natural fit for Caruna. Yet he had rarely played it before this game.

4   e4

As in the Rossolimo, 1 e4 c5 2 ♘f3 ♘c6 3 ♝b5 g6 4 ♝xc6, the next capture forces the opponent to commit to a pawn structure.

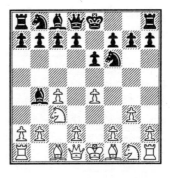

4	...	♝xc3

If Black waits to play ...♝xc3, after 4...0-0, White can play 5 ♘ge2 so he can retake on c3 with a knight.

Caruana knew that move order well: Magnus Carlsen used it to win one of the painful playoff games in their 2018 match.

5   dxc3

In the comparable Rossolimo position, the recapture ...bxc6 (after 4 ♗xc6) invites White to prepare a two-square push of the d-pawn.

Here this means after 5 bxc3 Black would shoot for ...c6/...d5.

That is what Caruana likely intended. Three months after this game, his trainer Rustam Kasimdzhanov quickly equalized as Black, 5...0-0 6 ♗g2 c6 7 ♘e2 d5 8 cxd5 cxd5 against Evgeny Bareev in the 2019 World Cup.

5   ...   d6

6   ♕c2

Aronian wants his knight on f3 so he protects the e4-pawn first. Carlsen has preferred the equally good 6 f3 and ♘h3-f2/♗e2.

6   ...   0-0

7   ♘f3   ♗e6

In addition to ...c6/...d5, Black can work against the doubled c-pawn following 8 b3 a5!.

Then 9 ♗g2 a4 favors him. Also 9 a4 ♘a6 10 ♗g2 ♘c5.

8   ♘g5   ♗d7

9   f3

White's options include 0-0-0 and a kingside pawn advance.

For example, 9...a5 10 ♗e3 ♘a6 11 0-0-0 ♕e7 12 h4 ♘c5 13 g4 a4 is fairly balanced. Neither side can quickly force an attack-friendly file open.

9   ...   a5

10   ♘h3   a4!

11   ♘f2   ♘c6

Black can attack the c4-pawn *a la* Nimzovich with ...♘a5 and ...♗e6.

A reasonable alternative is ...♘a6-c5 and ...a6/...b5.

That means White has pawn problems, and 12 ♗e2 ♗e6 13 0-0 ♘a5 14 ♕xa4 ♘xc4 15 ♕c2 and 16 b3 would solve some of them.

But care is needed. The logical 13 ♗e3 ♘a5 14 b3? allows 14...axb3 15 axb3 ♘xc4! 16 ♖xa8 ♘xe3! (17 ♖xd8 ♘xc2+).

White can avert this with 14 c5. The pawn is gone from c4, but as Nimzovich would say, the square is still weak.

Black would have a growing positional edge after 14...♘c4! 15 ♗xc4 ♗xc4 16 cxd6 ♕xd6.

12 ♗e2 ♘a5?

Caruana may have rejected 12...♗e6 because White would have time to protect his c4-pawn with 13 ♘d1 and 14 ♘e3.

Nevertheless, 13...♘d7 14 ♘e3 ♗h3 and ...♘e7/...f5 is nice for Black.

13 b4!

He misjudged this. The c-pawn would be optically weak after 13...♘c6?. But Black has no way of attacking it.

13 ... axb3

14 axb3 ♘c6

15 ♖b1

Also equal is 15 ♖xa8 ♕xa8 16 0-0 and ♘d1-e3.

Caruana's advantage has evaporated

15 ... ♗e6

16 ♘d1

White prepares to improve his prospects with ♘e3, 0-0 and either ♖d1 or some preparation for f3-f4.

16 ... ♘e7

There is less Black can do until the center pawn structure is changed. For example, 16...♕b8 17 0-0 ♕a7+ 18 ♗e3 ♕a2 is halted by 19 ♖b2.

White would benefit from a change in the queenside structure, such as 16...♘d7 17 ♘e3 ♘c5 18 b4! and 18...♘d7 19 0-0 b6 20 f4!.

17 0-0

Black's choice of pawn changes boils down to ...f5 or ...d5.

There was nothing very wrong with 17...♘d7 18 ♘e3 f5.

Chances would remain in rough balance after 19 exf5 ♘xf5 20 ♗d3 ♕f6 and ...♘c5.

17 ...   c6

Going for ...d5 makes more sense because White is one move short (18 ♘e3 and 19 ♖d1) of stopping it.

That break would undouble White's pawns. But gaining squares for Black's knights is more important.

For example, 18 ♗e3 d5 19 cxd5 cxd5 20 exd5? ♘fxd5! and Black follows with a favorable 21...♗f5 or 21...♘xe3.

Or 18 ♘e3 ♛b6 and then 19 ♔h1 d5 20 cxd5 cxd5 21 exd5 ♘exd5 22 ♘xd5 ♘xd5, also with advantage.

But on 18 ♗e3 d5 Black should avoid two instructive mistakes.

One is 19 ♘f2 dxc4? 20 bxc4.

White's pawns remain damaged. But they keep a Black knight off d5 and allow White pressure on the b-file.

Another error is 19...d4? 20 cxd4 exd4, to create a passed pawn.

But it is easily blockaded, Black's minor pieces remain restricted and he has granted White a strong pawn plan of f3-f4 and e4-e5!.

18	♗g5	♘d7
19	♛d2	h6
20	♗e3	♘f6
21	♘f2	d5

Black's ...d5 plan was slowed by 18 ♗g5 and the positional threat of ♗xf6.

But his knights would still benefit from 22 cxd5 cxd5 23 exd5 ♘exd5 and the tactic 24 ♗c5? ♘f4! and ...♘xe2+.

22 ♖fd1   ♛c7

There's little to be gained from ...dxe4 until Black can exploit fxe4 by planting a piece on g4.

The only real advantage Caruana has now was on the

clock. He had nearly twice as much time as Aronian's remaining 34 minutes.

23 ♗c5

Now 23...♖fd8 24 ♕e3 would threaten ♗b6.

One of many ways the position could be simplified is 24...dxe4 25 ♘xe4 ♘xe4 26 ♖xd8+ ♕xd8.

Then 27 ♖d1! ♕a5 28 b4 ♕a2 29 ♕xe4 ♘g6 – with enough pieces left to make for an interesting fifth hour.

23 ... b6

24 ♗xe7 ♕xe7

25 cxd5 cxd5

26 exd5

26 ... ♗xd5!

The endgame would be even after 26...♘xd5 27 c4 ♘-moves 28 ♕d6 ♕xd6.

Retaking 26...♗xd5 is Caruana's recognition that his best winning

chances lay on the kingside and in the prospect of ...e4.

27 c4 ♗c6

For example, 28 ♖b2? e4! 29 fxe4 ♘xe4 30 ♕e3 ♕f6 31 ♖c2 ♖fe8.

Or 28 ♕d6? ♕b7 29 ♕xe5 ♖fe8 30 ♕b2 ♗xf3, also with a Black advantage.

28 ♕e3 ♖a2

29 ♖a1! ♖xa1

30 ♖xa1 ♘d7

Chances would be roughly equal after 31 ♘e4 or 31 ♖a7. But this is the fifth hour and it has its own rules. Aronian had 20 minutes to make the final ten moves of the time control.

31 ♗d3? f5!

Black would be better in the endgame after 31...♕c5 32 ♕xc5 ♘xc5.

But after 33 b4! ♘xd3 34 ♘xd3 White threatens ♘xe5.

This would enable him to play a few intuitive moves (34...f6 35 ♔f2) and reach move 40 with a sound position.

Worse is 32...bxc5? 33 ♗f5 and the c5-pawn is as weak as the b3- and f3-pawns.

For example, 33...♖b8? 34 ♘d3 and ♗xd7/♘xc5.

32 ♗c2

Caruana prepared ...f4 but also ...e4.

After 32 ♖e1 ♛f6 White can defend with 33 f4 exf4 34 ♛e6+! ♛xe6 35 ♖xe6.

His pieces are sufficiently active, 35...fxg3 36 hxg3 ♗b7 37 ♖d6.

But 33...e4 followed by ...♖a8 and a knight maneuver to d4 would be difficult.

32 ... e4

Objectively, 32...f4 is just as good.

But after 32...f4 33 gxf4 ♖xf4 White can play safe moves, 34 ♗e4 ♗xe4 35 ♘xe4.

A draw would be likely after 35...♘c5 36 ♘xc5 dxc5 37 ♔h1.

33 fxe4 ♘e5

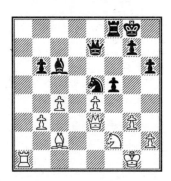

Now on 34 ♖e1 Black can play a series of forcing moves, 34...fxe4 35 ♗xe4 ♗xe4 36 ♛xe4 ♘f3+.

After 37 ♔h1 he could pause and use his advantage in time.

He could calculate the possible queen moves, to f7, f6 or c5, to see if they yielded winning chances.

If they don't, he could continue 37...♛xe4 38 ♖xe4.

Then 38...♘d2! would force a drawish endgame, 39 ♖e2 ♘xb3.

(He would, in fact, have some slim chances after 37...♛f7 38 ♖e2 ♘d4!, e.g. 39 ♛xd4? ♛f3+ or 39 ♖b2 ♘xb3 40 ♛d5 ♘a5!.)

34 ♗d1

White protects the vital f3-square but it's a minor error – and a prelude to a major one.

It was difficult to see how safe 34 ♖f1! was.

Then there is nothing in 34...fxe4? 35 ♘xe4.

Black could go for a draw by repetition, 34...♛d8 35 ♖d1 ♛f6 36 ♖f1 ♛d8.

34 ... fxe4

White had visualized this position when he chose 34 ♗d1.

He had seen 35 ♘xe4? walks into 35...♘f7 36 ♗c2 ♘g5. He moved instantly.

35   ♗e2?

The only move to keep matters in doubt was 35 ♘g4!.

Then 35...♘f3+ 36 ♗xf3 ♖xf3 37 ♕xb6 resembles what happens in the game – except with the extra, saving move ♘g4.

Instead, Black can play a favorable endgame after 35...♕f7! 36 ♕f4 ♕xf4 37 gxf4 ♖xf4.

35   ...   ♘f3+!

36   ♗xf3

Putting his king on the bishop's diagonal, with 36 ♔g2 or 36 ♔h1, makes 36...♘d4! decisive.

For instance, 36 ♔h1 ♘d4 37 ♕xd4 ♖xf2.

36   ...   ♖xf3

37   ♕xb6   ♕f6

Also winning was protecting the c6-bishop, with 37...♕e8 or 37...♕e6. Each makes 38...e3 deadly. But 37...♕f6 also threatens the a1-rook.

38   ♖d1

Or 38 ♖e1 e3 39 ♘g4 ♕g6 and 39...♕c3.

38   ...   e3

The poignant point is 39 ♕d8+ ♕xd8 40 ♖xd8+ ♔h7 and now 41 ♘d3 e2! queens or mates.

39   ♘g4   ♕e6

The only move. Now 40 ♕d8+ ♔h7 41 ♕d3+ ♗e4.

40   ♕b8+   ♔h7

41   ♘e5   ♕h3

42   White resigns.

Yes, 41...e2 would have mated one move faster.

54
A Magnus Tutorial

"You certainly learn a lot of things from Magnus," Caruana said after their world championship match. By the time he had recovered fully from the ordeal, he called it a great learning experience. "In general I definitely improved my chess from that match," he said.

Few world championship challengers could make that claim. Others who had lost a title match in the recent past – such as Veselin Topalov, Boris Gelfand and Nigel Short – were never quite the same.

What did Caruana learn? This game provides clues.

Caruana – Magnus Carlsen
St. Louis Rapid and Blitz (rapid)
2019
Sicilian Defense,
Rossolimo Variation (B30)

1	e4	c5
2	♘f3	♘c6
3	♗b5	e6
4	♗xc6	bxc6!

Unlike the situation after 3...g6 4 ♗xc6, Black usually retakes with the b-pawn here.

It gives him more flexibility if, as expected, White advances e4-e5.

In contrast, 4...dxc6 5 d3 ♕c7 6 e5! would sentence him to a sterile position with an inferior pawn structure that he can't try to change with ...♗g4.

For example, 6...♘e7 7 0-0 ♘g6 8 ♖e1 ♗e7 9 ♘bd2 and 10 b3.

5   d3

Opening the center with d2-d4 is dubious as Caruana learned as a ten-year-old.

In the 2003 World Open he played 5 0-0 ♘e7 6 d4 cxd4 7 ♕xd4.

He found his advantage in space was negated by Black's preponderance of center pawns.

He was worse after 7...♘g6 8 e5? ♗e7 9 ♖d1 0-0 because Black could alter the structure, with ...f6/...c5.

5   ...   ♘e7

Carlsen prepares ...♘g6 and ...e5.

He would get out of the opening in splendid shape after 6 0-0 ♘g6 7 b3 e5! 8 ♗b2 d6.

In the middlegame he can aim to change the pawn structure favorably with ...f5.

6   b3   ♘g6

Control of e5 is crucial in this variation. If White can maintain a pawn on that square he is better.

If Black can liquidate it, he should have no problems. Experience has shown that 7 ♗b2 f6 8 e5 ♗e7 is harmless.

For example, 9 ♘bd2 0-0 10 0-0 fxe5 10 ♘xe5 ♘xe5 11 ♗xe5 d6 and ...e5!.

7   h4

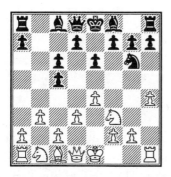

This move was new to grandmaster practice, although it had long been seen in other move orders (6 h4 and 6 ♕e2 ♘g6 7 h4, for examples).

White's intent, of course, was to humiliate the knight with 8 h5 and thereby cement his hold on e5.

7   ...   h5

To play 7 h4 Caruana had to have a good answer to 7...♕f6.

Clearly, 8 e5? ♘xe5 9 ♗b2? ♘xf3+ doesn't work.

Black would stand well after 8 c3 e5 9 h5 ♘f4.

The answer is 8 d4!, with its threat of 9 ♗g5.

For example, 8...h6 9 h5 ♘e7 10 ♗b2 or even 10 g4 with a new threat, 11 e5!.

8   e5

How can this be good now if it was innocuous earlier (7 e5 ♗e7 and ...f6)?

The reason, Caruana hoped, is ...h5 has opened tactical gates for him.

8   ...   f6

But his h2-h4 was also weakening. One way that this matters is 8...c4, threatening 9...♘xe5 10 ♘xe5 ♕a5+.

Had this happened a move earlier, 7 e5 c4, White could just castle and retain a small edge (8 0-0 cxd3 9 ♕xd3).

But here 8...c4 9 0-0 allows 9...♘xh4!.

Instead, White should settle for a lead in development with 9 dxc4 ♘xe5 10 ♗b2 ♘xf3+ 11 ♕xf3.

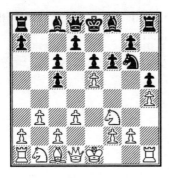

9   ♘bd2!

Another Caruana gambit.

Instead of 9 ♗b2, he can post the bishop or a knight on g5 and obtain some compensation after 9...♘xe5 10 ♘xe5 fxe5 11 ♘e4 followed by ♕e2 or ♕f3.

Or 9...fxe5 10 ♘c4 d6 11 ♕e2 and 11...♗e7? 12 ♕e4!.

9   ...   d6?!?

Carlsen is willing to permanently isolate his doubled c-pawns in order to buy more center space.

The new pawn structure would likely be fatal in an endgame because ♗a3/♘e4 would doom the c5-pawn.

But endgames are a long way off.

On-line spectators were surprised Carlsen took only 20 seconds to play 9...d6. But he had a similar experience.

Two months earlier, in a rapid tournament in Zagreb, Anish Giri

had played 6 h4 h5 7 e5 against him.

Carlsen replied 7...d6 8 exd6 ♘g6 and ...♗xd6. White was comfortably better – until he was outplayed.

10   exd6

Caruana had no choice since he would be worse after 10 exf6? ♕xf6 and much worse after 10...gxf6! and ...e5/...d5.

10   ...   e5

White's next task is to decide where his queen and knights serve best.

His queen would stand well on e2. But f3 may be better.

For example, 11 ♘c4 ♗xd6 12 ♘fd2 ♗e7 13 ♕f3 (13...♕d5 14 ♕g3 ♘f4 15 ♘e4).

11   ♗b2   ♗g4

12   ♕e2

Given time, Black will catch up in development. Then tactics may begin to flow in his direction.

But now they benefit White: 12...♘f4 13 ♕e4 ♕d7? is short-circuited by a winning knight or bishop sacrifice on e5.

12   ...   ♕xd6

13   g3   ♗e7

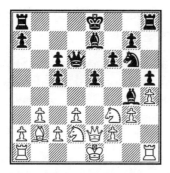

Black's queen would work well on d5 and his knight could reposition, ...♘f8-e6-d4.

For example, after 14 ♕e4 ♘f8 15 ♘c4? ♕d5 he threatens to win a piece with ...♕xe4+.

He would be at least equal (16 ♘fd2 ♗f5!).

White's error was disconnecting the knights. After 15 0-0-0 ♕d5 16 ♖de1, for example, his positional edge remains solid.

14   0-0-0

A potential wild card is a radical change in the pawn structure from ...c4.

For example, 14...♕d5! 15 ♕e4? invites 15...♕xe4 16 dxe4 c4!.

Then 17 bxc4 ♔f7 followed by ...♗c5 and ...♖ab8 is more than worth a pawn.

The sacrifice is also available after 15 ♖de1 c4 16 dxc4 ♕a5 17 ♔b1 ♖d8 and ...♗b4.

14   ...   ♘f8?

White can stop ...♘e6-d4! with c2-c3.

But this is a grave error that weakens the d3-pawn.

For example, 15 ♕e3 ♘e6 16 c3? ♖d8 17 ♘c4? ♕d5 wins material.

Or 17 ♘e4 ♕c7 and ...♕a5, with advantage.

15   ♖de1!

When White committed his h-pawn at move seven he made ...♗g4 a stronger pin. It can't be broken by h2-h3.

But now he can get out of it with ♕e4 or ♕e3 and ♘h2.

15   ...   ♘e6

16   ♕e4!

Now 16...♘d4 17 ♘xd4 cxd4 allows him to exploit the uncastled Black king with 18 f4.

For example, 18...exf4? 19 ♘c4 ♕d7 20 ♗a3 and wins.

16   ...   ♕d5

It was too late for 16...♔f7 because of the combination

389

17 ♘c4 ♛d5 18 ♘fxe5+! fxe5 19 ♘xe5+ and ♘xg4.

Despite the critical situation on the board, both players had been moving fairly quickly and had more than 21 of their 25 minutes left.

Caruana took two minutes to make a difficult choice among three attractive moves.

The natural 17 ♛g6+ would win after 17...♚d7 18 c4!.

For example, 18...♛d6 19 ♗xe5! fxe5 20 ♘xe5+ and ♘xg4.

But 17...♚d8! is not so clear.

White can even lose after 18 ♗xe5? ♖h6!.

17   ♘xe5!

Attractive but second-best is 17 ♘h2.

If Black avoids 18 ♘xg4 with 17...♗h3 he is worse following 18 ♘hf1 ♛xe4. But not lost after 19...♗g2.

17   ...   ♛xe4

Caruana's combination is essentially just a forcing trade of wood that exposes Black's pawn weaknesses (17...fxe5 18 f3! ♛xe4 19 dxe4 with a winning endgame).

18   dxe4   fxe5

Trying to confuse White with 18...♘d4 would drop another pawn after 19 ♘xg4 hxg4 20 ♘c4 and ♘e3xg4.

19	f3	♘d4
20	fxg4	hxg4
21	♘c4	0-0

At least now Carlsen has an f-file to play with, a target at g3 and some ways for White to err.

He would have a glimmer of hope after 22 c3 ♘e6 23 ♖hf1 ♖ae8 or 22 ♘xe5 ♗d6 (23 ♘xg4 ♗xg3 24 ♖ef1 ♖ae8).

22   ♚b1!?

This was Caruana's second two-minute think and it required quite a different kind of calculation than 17 ♘xe5.

390

It safeguards against checks from ...♞e2 or ...♜f2xc2.

He would have had a much harder task after 22 ♜hf1? ♞e2+! and ...♞xg3.

22 ... ♜f2

23 ♞xe5 ♞xc2

Against a less vigilant player, 23...♞f3 might have worked, e.g. 24 ♞xf3? ♜xf3 25 ♝e5 c4! 26 bxc4? ♝a3 with a likely draw.

But Caruana would have won after 24 ♞xg4 ♜g2 25 ♜d1 ♜xg3 26 ♞e5.

24 ♞xg4

Caruana had another way to win, 24 ♜c1! ♞d4 25 h5!.

He would threaten a mating attack with 26 h6 gxh6 27 ♜xh6 and ♜g6+.

24 ... ♜g2

Carlsen had played quickly since spending five minutes on 22...♜f2.

He could have complicated Caruana's life with 24...♞xe1 25 ♞xf2 ♜f8.

For example, 26 ♜xe1 ♜xf2 27 ♝e5 ♚f7.

25 ♜eg1 ♜e2

26 h5!

Now the mating attack is more visible (27 h6).

26 ... c4?

Carlsen evaluated 26...♜xe4 27 ♚xc2 ♜g4 28 h6! ♝f6 29 hxg7 as lost.

But there would be technical difficulties after, for example, 29...♝xg7 30 ♜h4 ♜g5 31 ♜a4 ♝xb2 32 ♚xb2 a5.

27 h6!

Caruana played 56 games against Carlsen before their 2018 match. That seems like a lot. But he played 54 games with Carlsen in the next three years.

What had he learned from that experience?

"He puts pressure on you in every game and he forces you to defend," he said. "You have to stay vigilant because there's always chances to lose a position."

Here 27 bxc4?? ♜b8 was one of those chances.

27 ... c3

This was Carlsen's longest think of the game.

Why? Because 27...♘a3+ would turn the tables after 28 ♔c1?? ♖c2+.

And it might save him after 28 ♔a1 c3!

Then 29 ♗xc3 ♘c2+ 30 ♔b1 ♘a3+ is a perpetual check.

Better is 28 ♗xa3 ♗xa3 29 h7+ ♔h8 30 ♘e5 with a threat of ♘g6 mate or ♘f7 mate.

But the story goes on: After 30...g5! White should avoid 31 ♘g6+ ♔g7 32 h8(♕)+ ♖xh8 and 32...c3!.

There is a simple win, however, in 31 ♘xc4!.

28   h7+

28   ...   ♔f7

A final try. After 29 h8(♕)? ♖xh8 30 ♖xh8 cxb2 White has to be wary of 31 ♘e5+ ♔e6 32 ♘c4 ♘d4!.

That threatens ...♘b5-c3 mate and might save him after 33 a4 ♘xb3.

29   ♖f1+   ♗f6

A cute finish is 29...♔g6 30 ♘e5+ ♔g5 31 ♖f5 mate.

30   ♗c1!

Simplest. White wins a piece (30...♘d4 31 e5) and has h8(♕) in reserve.

30   ...   ♘b4

31   e5   ♖xa2

32   ♘e3!

No more tricks (if 32...c2+ 33 ♘xc2 ♖xc2 34 exf6 and queens).

Carlsen did not resign until after: **32...♖h8 33 exf6 g5 34 ♖d1 a5 35 ♖d4 c2+ 36 ♘xc2 ♖xc2 37 ♖xb4 ♖xc1+ 38 ♔xc1 axb4 39 ♖h6.**

He was helpless in the rook endgame, 39...c5 40 ♔d2 ♔e6 41 ♔d3 and so on.

55
Too Strong

By the end of 2019 Fabiano seemed to have taken up permanent residency on the Elo list as the second highest-rated player. When he and Carlsen entered the FIDE Grand Swiss on the Isle of Man in October 2019 they were criticized for being too strong for the competition.

At stake was $432,500 in prize money – but also a seed in the 2020 Candidates tournament. Since neither Carlsen nor Caruana needed to qualify for the Candidates, their presence seemed vaguely unfair. So, for the first time in history, the world's two best players were maligned for playing too much chess. Nevertheless, Caruana ended up sharing first prize and winning one of the most remarkable endgames in years.

Caruana – Samuel Sevian
Isle of Man 2019
English Opening,
Reversed Dragon Variation (A20)

1	c4	e5
2	g3	♘f6
3	♗g2	

The chief benefit of delaying ♘c3 is to deny Black lines with ...♗b4xc3. But there are other ways of developing the b1-knight, as we'll see.

3	...	d5
4	cxd5	♘xd5
5	♘f3	♘c6
6	0-0	

White can transpose into a reversed form of the Dragon Sicilian with ♘c3.

By delaying that, he might tempt 6...e4?.

Then 7 ♘e1 f5 8 d3 exd3 9 ♘xd3 shows why the Hypermoderns had a point. White could exploit open lines after 9...♗e7 10 ♕b3 ♘b6 11 ♗e3, for example.

6 ... ♘b6

This looks like a loss of time but it is often necessary in the Dragon to deter a two-square advance of the d-pawn.

For instance, 6...♗e7 7 d4 exd4 8 ♘xd4 or 7...e4 8 ♘e5!, with a small White plus.

7 b3 ♗e7

8 ♗b2

Now 8...e4? is no longer possible because the e- and g-pawns are under attack after 9 ♘e1.

8 ... f6

Black might not want to play ...♗f6 until after ...f5.

But here 8...♗f6 9 ♘c3 0-0 10 ♘e4! and 11 ♘xf6+ is poor for him.

So is 9...e4 10 ♘e1 ♗f5 11 d3 exd3 because of 12 e4! and ♘xd3.

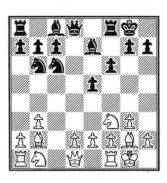

9 ♘a3

If White can liquidate Black's center pawn, 9 d4 exd4 10 ♘xd4 ♘xd4 11 ♗xd4, he would get nice pressure on the queenside, reminiscent of a favorable Catalan (11...0-0 12 ♘c3 c6 13 e4).

But 9...e4! and 10...f5 would be splendid for Black despite the loss of time.

For example, 10 ♘fd2 f5 11 f3? ♗f6! 12 e3 ♘xd4! (13 exd4 ♗xd4+).

9 ... ♗e6

10 ♘c2

Once he went for 7 b3/8 ♗b2, White's only chance for a significant advantage lay in changing the center with d2-d4.

He could have prepared it with 10 ♕b1 and ♖d1. But not 10 ♕c2? ♘b4! and 11...c5.

10 ... 0-0

11 e4!

Caruana, moving instantly, had come to the board with an original idea.

Black was still poised to meet 11 d4? with 11...e4! 12 ♘d2 f5.

394

11 ... ♛d3

There was no other way to stop 12 d4! from earning White a superior middlegame.

For example, 11...♛d7? 12 d4! exd4 13 ♘cxd4 ♘xd4 14 ♘xd4 ♝f7 15 ♘f5!.

Or a superior endgame after 11...♝g4 12 d4! exd4 13 ♘cxd4 ♘xd4 14 ♛xd4 ♛xd4 15 ♘xd4.

12 ♖e1

The reason 11 e4 is so striking is that it made the d2-pawn backward on an open file.

It works because Black cannot stop 13 ♝f1 and 14 d4.

He would be very slightly worse after 12...♝c5 13 ♝f1 ♛d7 14 d4 exd4 15 ♘cxd4 ♘xd4 16 ♘xd4 ♝g4!.

12 ... ♖ad8?

Annotators used to shout "Wrong rook!" when a player had a better use of his heavy pieces. We'll just whisper it, because

12...♖fd8! is only superior because of a subtle tactical reason.

13 ♝f1 ♛d7

14 d4 exd4

15 ♘cxd4

The difference between 12...♖ad8 and 12...♖fd8 is revealed by 15...♝b4.

Then 16 ♖e3 is the only good White move.

It leads to 16...♘xd4 17 ♘xd4 c5 (17...♝c5 18 ♖d3) 18 ♘xe6 ♛xd1 19 ♖xd1 ♖xd1 20 ♘xf8.

Then White has the two bishops and the same long-term edge he enjoys in the game.

But if 12...♖fd8! had been played, the same sequence would fail because there is no rook to capture on f8 at move 20.

White could settle, instead, for the equal chances of 15 ♘fxd4 ♘xd4 16 ♝xd4 c5 or 16...a5.

15 ... ♝g4

16	♕c2	♘xd4

17	♘xd4

That key ♖e3 move also figures in 17...♗b4.

Then 18 ♖e3 ♖fe8 19 ♖d3 or 18...c5 19 ♘f3 and 20 a3 is excellent for White.

17	...	♖fe8

18	♖ac1	c6

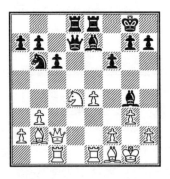

19 b4!

This pawn structure favors White. The b-pawn stops ...c5 and gives White the opportunity for a minority attack (b4-b5).

Also, the open diagonal created by Black's f6-pawn allows tactics (19...♗xb4? 20 ♕b3+).

19	...	♔h8

20	b5

There is nothing wrong with 20 f3 ♗h5 21 a3 and then ♘f5.

20	...	c5

21	♘f5

But this procedure gives White more active plans, e.g. 21...♗xf5 22 exf5 followed by ♖ed1 and a2-a4-a5.

21	...	♗f8

22	h3

On 22...♗f3 Black has the annoying resource 23 ♖e3 ♗d1!.

Instead, White can play on the queenside with 23 a4.

Or in the center with 23 ♘h4 ♗h5 24 e5 fxe5 25 ♗xe5 followed by g3-g4 and ♘f5. Both offer a small plus.

22	...	♗xf5?!

23	exf5	♖xe1

24	♖xe1

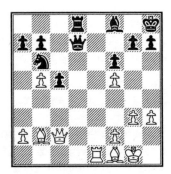

Now 24...♕d2 leads to an unpleasant endgame, 25 ♕xd2 ♖xd2 26 ♖e2.

And 26 ♗c1 ♖xa2? 27 ♖e8 ♔g8 28 ♗f4 would be much worse.

24 ... c4!

When he calculated 22...♗xf5, Black correctly bet that the worst that can happen is a swap of his c-pawn for White's a-pawn. White cannot safely allow 25...♕xb5.

25 a4! ♗b4

Now 26 ♖c1 ♖c8 or 26 ♗c3 ♗xc3 27 ♕xc3 ♖c8 offers counterplay.

26 ♖e4! ♕d2

27 ♕xd2 ♗xd2

28 ♗xc4

A good alternative is 28 ♗a3 because the c-pawn can be halted after 28...c3 29 a5 ♘c8 30 ♗b4 or 30 ♖c4.

28 ... ♘xa4

29 ♗a3 ♘b6

30 ♗b3 ♘c8

Otherwise 31 ♖e7 begins a seventh-rank pillage.

Computers can smell zugzwang. They begin to sniff one here, with 31 ♖a4 followed by 32 ♗e6.

There are elegant ways to win, such as 31...g6 32 b6!!.

The points include 32...♘xb6 33 ♗e7! (threat of ♗xf6 mate).

Also 32...axb6 33 ♖a8 ♔g7 34 ♗e6.

The prettiest is 32...a6 33 ♖xa6! bxa6 34 b7 ♘a7 35 ♗e7! and wins.

31 ♗d5

This is second best but has its charms.

It threatens ♗xb7 and is tactically justified by 31...♖xd5?? 32 ♖e8 mate.

If it induces 31...b6?, the knight loses its only safe square and would be condemned by 32 ♖c4 and 33 ♗e6.

For example, 32...h5 33 ♗e6 ♘d6 34 ♖d4 ♘b7 35 ♖xd8+ ♘xd8 36 ♗d5 and ♗e7.

31 ... a6!

32 b6!?

If White has to trade bishops, 32 ♗xb7 axb5 33 ♗a6 b4 34 ♗xb4 ♗xb4 35 ♖xb4, his chances of creating a winning passed pawn plunge.

They would drop further after a trade of rooks, 35...♘d6 36 ♖d4 ♘f7 37 ♖xd8+ ♘xd8 and ...g6.

32 ... ♘xb6

33	♗xb7	a5

| 34 | ♗c5! | |

Caruana's best chance is to exploit the knight tactically. For example, 34...♘d7? 35 ♖d4 pins and wins.

34	...	♘a8

Of course, Black knew a8 is usually an awful square for a knight.

But it might seem more secure there than after 34...♘c8 35 ♖c4 in view of tactics (36...♘d6? 37 ♗xd6).

A difficult ending, most likely drawable, would come about after 35...♔g8 and ...♘d6 and/or ...♗b4.

35	♖c4	♗b4

| 36 | ♗e3 | |

Even with the poorly placed knight, there were few chances for White after 36 ♗xb4 axb4 37 ♖xb4 ♘c7.

36	...	h6

Now he has another way to make progress, with g3-g4-g5!.

Black could anticipate that with ...g5. But that is a difficult decision to make because it creates an irreparable weakness at f6.

For example, 36...g5 37 ♗d4 ♔g7 38 ♔g2 ♖e8? 39 ♖c6 wins a pawn (39...♗e7 40 ♖a6).

Winning the a-pawn – without a trade of bishops – is not necessarily a forced win. But it would be getting closer.

37	h4!	♔h7

38	g4	♖b8

Now 38...g5? leaves Black's king in a tightening noose after 39 fxg6+ ♔xg6 40 ♗e4+ and ♔g2, h4-h5 and ♗g6.

39	♗e4	♘b6

| 40 | ♖c7 | |

The threat is 41 g5 because …fxg5 will allow a discovered check with the f-pawn.

A crucial question is what happens after 40…♘c8 41 g5 hxg5 42 hxg5.

Then 42…♗d6? 43 g6+ ♚h8 44 ♖d7 ♗e7 45 ♗c5! is a win.

Also, 42…♘d6 43 g6+ ♚h8 44 ♗c2 sets up a threat of 45 ♖d7 and 46 ♗f4.

The last-rank mate would doom Black after 44…♖c8 45 ♖d7.

He would also lose after 44…♖d8 41 ♗h6! ♘e8 42 ♖f7! because of ♗a4xe8!.

40 … ♘a4

The a-pawn is not enough to distract White – 40…a4 41 g5 hxg5 42 hxg5 ♗d6 43 g6+ ♚g8 44 ♖a7.

Then 44…a3 45 ♗xb6 ♖xb6 46 ♗d5+! ♚h8 47 ♖d7! and mates.

41 g5

Now 41…hxg5 42 hxg5 creates a new way to lose – getting mated on the h-file after 43 g6+ ♚h8 and ♚g2/♖c1-h1.

41 … ♘c3!

So that 42 ♗c2 ♘d5! and Black is drawing (43 g6+ ♚h8 44 ♖d7 ♘xe3).

42 ♗f3!

There is no longer a discovered check after 42…hxg5 43 hxg5 fxg5.

But 44 f6 still wins, e.g. 44…♚h6 45 fxg7 and ♗d4.

For instance, 45…♖g8 46 ♗d4 ♘b5 47 ♖c6+.

Then 47…♚h7? 38 ♗e4 is mate and 37…♘d6 48 ♗e5.

Love those bishops.

42 … ♘b5

43 ♖d7 hxg5

44 hxg5 ♚h8

45 g6!

This looks conclusive because ♗h6! is in the air.

For instance, 45...♗c3? 46 ♗h6! ♖g8 47 ♗d5 and mates.

But there is one more twist.

45 ... ♘c3

46 ♗d2 a4

47 ♖d3!

White has another h-file mate: 47...♖c8 48 ♗xc3 ♗xc3 49 ♗d5 and ♖h3.

A more elaborate version is 47 ♖d4! ♔g8 48 ♗f4 ♖b6 49 ♖d8+ ♗f8 50 ♗c7!

The rook is trapped (50...♖a6 51 ♗b7! ♖a7 52 ♗d6 and mates).

White can allow Black to queen, 50...a3 51 ♗xb6! a2 52 ♗c5 a1(♛)+ 53 ♔g2 because he mates.

47 ... a3

48 ♗xc3 ♗xc3

49 ♗d5 ♗d2

The only way to delay mate.

50 ♖xd2 ♖b1+

51 ♔g2 a2

Suddenly it looks like Black can escape with a stalemate, 52 ♗xa2 ♖g1+!.

Then White can win by finding an elusive king dance.

It begins with 53 ♔f3 ♖g3+ 54 ♔e4! and takes several moves after 54...♖e3+ 55 ♔d5 or 54...♖d3 55 ♖b2.

But simpler is:

52 ♗b3! ♖g1+

53 ♔f3! resigns.

56
Poise Under Pressure

Despite his enormous pre-game labors, Caruana is still surprised from time to time by an opponent's innovation. The world's newest elite player, 16-year-old Alireza Firouzja, blitzed his opening moves against him at Wijk aan Zee 2020 as Black: 1 d4 ♘f6 2 c4 g6 3 ♘c3 ♗g7 4 e4 d6 5 h3 O-O 6 ♗e3 ♘c6 7 d5 ♘e5 8 f4 ♘ed7 9 g4 c6 10 ♘f3 cxd5 11 cxd5 and now 11...b6.

His new move has an evident drawback, the hole at c6. After three minutes, Caruana replied, 12 ♘d4 ♘c5 13 ♕f3.

Knowing his opponent had prepared the opening, he nevertheless provoked a sacrifice as well, with 13...♗b7 14 g5! ♘fxe4 15 ♘xe4 ♗xd5 16 ♘f6+ exf6 17 ♕xd5.

Black had ample compensation for a piece. Chances were quite balanced until move 30, when Caruana began to pull away.

His poise under pressure prevailed. One round later:

Vladislav Kovalev – Caruana
Wijk aan Zee 2020
Ruy Lopez,
Neo-Arkhangel Defense (C78)

1	e4	e5
2	♘f3	♘c6
3	♗b5	a6
4	♗a4	♘f6
5	0-0	b5
6	♗b3	♗c5

There has been a sophisticated debate about whether 5...♗c5, the related Møller Defense, is a more accurate move order.

The two often transpose after 5...♗c5 6 c3 b5 6 ♗b3.

There are minor differences: In the second move order White can retreat the bishop to c2. Also, White can complicate with 6 ♘xe5 ♘xe5 7 d4.

7	c3	d6
8	a4	

How to meet the threat of axb5 is a recurring question for Black in the Lopez and a significant one in this variation.

Usually ...b4 is considered too weakening, and Black chooses between ...♗b7 and ...♖b8.

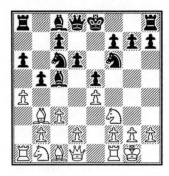

The bishop move appears more active. Black always played ...♗b7, even without a2-a4, in the old Arkhangel move order.

But after 8...♗b7 here, White can choose a different center strategy, 9 d3!?.

Then the bishop is moderately misplaced. However, it can be repositioned to g4.

Caruana's game with Vachier-Lagrave from Zagreb 2019 went 9...h6 10 axb5 axb5 11 ♖xa8 ♕xa8!. He went on to a neatly finessed victory.

Retaking with the bishop, 11...♗xa8, only delays its usefulness and White stands well after 12 ♘h4 ♘e7 13 ♕f3.

Play went (11...♕xa8!) 12 ♘h4 ♗c8 13 ♘a3? ♗g4! and Caruana eventually won.

8   ...   ♖b8

9   d4

Caruana has played this position as Black at least 15 times in big-league chess and achieved a nice plus score.

9   ...   ♗b6

A fundamental Lopez error is to exchange on d4 without a very good reason.

After 9...exd4? 10 cxd4 ♗b6 Black is ready to play 11...♗g4! and 12...♘xd4.

But 11 h3 stops him. White can develop his QN on c3 and watch for a good opportunity for ♘d5 or e4-e5.

10   axb5

For a while, circa 2012-7, the strange 10 a5 was played by elite GMs.

Black should probably avoid 10...♘xa5 11 ♖xa5! ♗xa5 12 dxe5 and the complications of 12...♘g4 13 ♗g5.

Two of Caruana's 2012 games went 10...♗a7 11 h3 0-0 12 ♖e1 h6 13 ♗e3 and then 13...♖b8 allowed him to meet the threat of 14 d5.

10   ...   axb5

11   ♘a3!

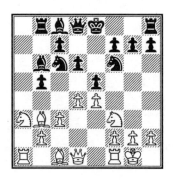

This threat to the b5-pawn is considered the only way to seek a White advantage.

There is no danger of ...♘xe4, now or earlier, because of ♗d5.

11 ... 0-0

12 ♘xb5 ♗g4

This is the starting point for many a grandmaster game. GM Alexey Shirov has offered Black's gambit at least 22 times.

As compensation, he has pressure on both White center pawns, e.g. 13...exd4 14 cxd4 ♘xd4 15 ♘bxd4 ♗xd4 16 ♕xd4? ♖xb3.

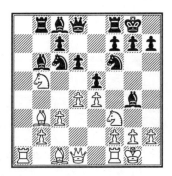

13 ♖e1

White has a book's worth of alternatives, including 13 ♗c2, 13 d5, 13 ♖a4, 13 ♖a3, 13 ♕d3, 13 ♗a4 and 13 ♔h1.

The logical defense of the d4-pawn, 13 ♗e3, allows the equalizing 13...exd4 14 cxd4 ♘xe4!, since 15 ♗d5 ♕e8.

13 ... ♗xf3

This is the only valid bid for compensation. Now 14 ♕xd3 exd4 gets back the pawn.

14 gxf3 ♘h5

Caruana goes for kingside attack (...♕h4 or ...♕f6 and ...♘f4) while keeping pressure on the d4-pawn.

Black's gambit gained respectability after an Ivanchuk – Shirov game in 1997 that went 15 ♗e3 ♕f6 16 ♔h1 exd4 17 cxd4 ♗a5 and ended in a draw.

Experience circa 2012-2015 indicated 15 ♔h1 was insufficient after 15...♕f6 16 ♖g1 ♘f4. White needed a new idea.

15 f4

Actually, this is a borrowed idea.

Giving back the gambit pawn had been tested in the slightly different variation with ♗c2 in place of ♖e1. (That is, 13 ♗c2 ♗xf3 14 gxf3 ♘h5 15 f4.)

15	...	♘xf4
16	♗xf4	exf4

White's center is secure and his pawn structure is superior.

But after GM Eric Hansen introduced this version at Wijk aan Zee 2017 he continued 17 ♗a4?.

He should have gotten into serious trouble after 17...♕h4! followed by ...♘e7-g6.

17 ♔h1!

White will play ♖g1. By not playing ♗c2 he seems to have improved on the earlier f3-f4 idea.

When confronted with a new opening position, like this one, there is a natural tendency to try to calculate your way to a safe harbor.

For example, Black can begin a process of elimination by seeing how 17...♕h4 18 ♖g1 ♕xf2? gets into trouble after 19 ♕g4 g6 20 ♗c4!.

It is not only the attack on the f-file to be feared but the threat to trap Black's queen, 21 ♖af1 ♕xb2 22 ♖g2.

17 ... ♘e7!

But Black can also find the best move by thinking in general terms.

Question: Which is his worst piece?

Answer: His bishop, hampered by the d4-pawn. He needs to get it into the game after ...♘e7 and ...c5!.

Another question: What is the best defense to a White attack on the g-file?

Answer: Plugging the file with ...♘e7-g6.

18 ♗c2

White's most vulnerable targets are on the b-file and this move prepares b2-b4.

If he anticipates a threat to his b5-knight with 18 ♕d3 Black can point out his problem on the other wing, with 18...c6 19 ♘a3 ♗c7!.

For example, 20 ♕c2 defends White's bishop and b2-pawn.

But there is little to protect his king after 20...d5!, e.g. 21 exd5 f3 threatens to win with ...♕d6xh2 mate.

Or 21 e5 f6, with advantage.

18	...	♘g6
19	b4	c6

Adequate are 19...c5 or 19...♕d7. But it is Caruana's next move that discredited White's innovation.

| 20 | ♘a3 | c5! |

Suppose White's bishop were on d5. Whose bishop would be better?

In terms of scope, the answer is White's.

But what matters more are targets.

White's bishop has no real targets, on d5 or c2. But Black's bishop hits at the d4-pawn and potentially at f2.

21	bxc5?

This is bad and 21 d5? cxb4 is worse.

Only somewhat better is 21 ♘c4 cxb4 22 cxb4 ♗c7 23 ♕d2 d5.

If he tries to block the b-file with 21 ♘b5 ♕d7 22 ♗d3, Black

remains on top with 22...♗d8 (23 ♖a7 ♕c6).

21	...	dxc5
22	♘c4	cxd4
23	♘xb6	

23	...	♖xb6!

Caruana took 22 minutes to reject 23...♕xb6, when White might survive (24 cxd4 ♖fd8 25 ♖b1 or 24...♕c6 25 ♖b1).

There was a third possibility, the zwischenzug 23...d3.

Black would have a solid plus after 24 ♕xd3 ♕xb6 because the c-pawn is weak and ...♘e5 is coming.

But 24 ♘d5 dxc2 25 ♕xc2 isn't as certain.

24	cxd4

White would be nearing a loss after 24 ♕xd4 ♖b2.

For example, 25 ♕xd8 ♖xd8 26 ♖ed1 ♖c8. Or 25 ♖ac1 ♕h4.

| 24 | ... | ♖d6 |

25 ♖a4

Or 25 d5 ♘e5 with the ideas of ...♖h6/...♕h4 or ...f3/...♖g6-g2.

| 25 | ... | ♘e5 |

Black threatens to win immediately with a mate threat, 26...♕h4! and 27...♖h6.

26 f3

Again, Black could try to find the best path by calculation or following basic principles.

For example, 26...♕d7 would prepare both 27...♖d8 and 27...♕h3.

Black is definitely superior after 27 ♖f1 ♖c8 or 27...♖d8 28 ♕c1 ♖xd4 29 ♖xd4 ♕xd4 30 ♕xf4 ♕c3, for instance.

Some computers even say 26...h6 is best because it eliminates last-rank mating tactics for White.

| 26 | ... | ♘c6! |

But securing e5 for his knight and making the bad bishop worse (27 d5 ♘e5) was the surest method.

There is no forced win after, say, 28 ♖g1 g6 29 ♕e2 ♖b6.

But ...♕h4 and ...♖fb8 would slowly build pressure to the breaking ploint.

27 e5?

Facing a grim defensive task against a stronger opponent, White tries for a kingside fortress.

| 27 | ... | ♖xd4 |

| 28 | ♖xd4 | ♘xd4 |

Not 28...♕xd4? 29 ♗xh7+! ♔xh7 30 ♕c2+ and ♕xc6.

29 ♗e4

Black would likely have won a queen endgame after 29 ♕d3 ♕h4 30 ♖d1 ♘e6 and ...♖d8.

Or the rook and minor piece endgame of 29 ♖e4 ♘e6 30 ♕xd8 ♖xd8.

But they would be more difficult than what happens now.

| 29 | ... | ♕h4 |

| 30 | ♖g1 | ♖d8 |

The threat is 31...♘f5 and 32...♖xd1 or 32...♘g3+.

31 ♕f1

The potential queen endgames are lost, e.g. 31 ♕a4 ♘e2 32 ♖d1 ♖xd1+ 33 ♕xd1 ♘g3+ and 34...♘xe4.

31 ... g6

32 ♖g4?

White tries to swap off his doomed e5-pawn for the f4-pawn.

He would have been lost in endgames such as 32 ♕g2 ♕e7 33 ♕g5 ♕xg5 34 ♖xg5 ♘e2 35 ♔g2 ♘c3 36 ♗c6 ♘d1.

32 ... ♕e7

33 ♖xf4 ♕xe5

The White rook is embarrassed (34 ♕c1 ♘e2; 34 ♖g4 f5).

34 ♖h4 ♘e6!

It would be trapped after 35...h5 and ...♕g5 – although 35...♖d2 and ...♕d6/...♖d1 would win faster.

35 ♖h3 ♘f4

36 ♖g3 ♖d2

37 White resigns.

The threats included 37...♕b2/ ...♖xh2+, 37...♕d4/38...♖d1 and 37...♖a2/38...♖a1.

Caruana won the tournament, two points ahead of Carlsen, and with a performance rating of 2945.

His recovery from their 2018 match was complete. He was ready for a big year, with invitations to several major tournaments.

But two months later, chess shut down.

57
Locked In

"I don't like to go for a month without playing in anything,"
Caruana said in 2008. But when the Covid lockdown began, it
appeared he would go much longer. He only played in one
over-the-board tournament in the nine months following the
abrupt suspension of international chess during the 2020
Candidates tournament.

However, OTB chess was quickly replaced by on-line speed
tournaments. Sponsors invited the highest-rated, best known
grandmasters. The practical effect was a lock-out for players who
were not considered elite. Hundreds of grandmasters could not
earn a living doing what they had done before Covid.

For the fortunate few, such as Caruana, the new normal meant
playing the same opponents over and over, often in the same day
during tightly scheduled rapid and blitz tournaments. They were
locked in: Fabiano played Magnus Carlsen 23 times in on-line
games in 2020.

This posed new problems for Caruana. Speed chess is not his
long suit. And his opening preparation could be quickly
exhausted when he had to find new ideas in the same variation,
against the same opponent, over a period of a few days.

One of the most-watched of the on-line Covid tournaments was
the $265,000 Clutch Chess International in June 2020. To reach
the 10-minute-game finals, Fabiano defeated Leinier Dominguez
and Wesley So in best-of-12 matches. That set the stage for one of
the great speed marathons.

Caruana – Magnus Carlsen
Clutch (internet) 2020
Sicilian Defense,
Rossolimo Variation (B30)

1	e4	c5
2	♘f3	♘c6
3	♗b5	e5
4	0-0	♗d6!?

Before this match, Black's third
move was rare and his fourth
move even rarer.

Together they make some sense.

If White captures ♗xc6, Black will develop smoothly after …dxc6!. He has already achieved the …e5 advance that Black often seeks.

Of course, if White doesn't play ♗xc6, Black has blocked the d7-pawn and made it harder to develop his c8-bishop.

5   c3

Carlsen stuck to this variation during the finals match until Caruana found a good answer.

He hadn't when he tried 5 d3 ♘f6 6 ♗g5 in another game of the match.

He had little to show after 6…h6 7 ♗h4 a6 8 ♗c4 ♗e7, despite the loss of time of Black's bishop.

That bishop would be well placed after 5 ♘a3 ♘ge7 6 ♘c4 ♗c7.

5   …   a6

Carlsen was less concerned about the loss of a tempo from 6 ♗xc6 dxc6 than by the opened center that would occur after 5…♘ge7 6 d4!.

6	**♗a4**	**b5**
7	**♗c2**	**♘ge7**

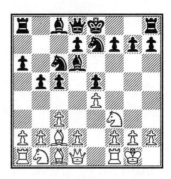

Black's position looks odd, if not bizarre.

But compare it with a standard Rossolimo line that runs 3…e6 4 0-0 ♘ge7 and then 5 c3 a6 6 ♗a4 b5 7 ♗c2 ♗b7.

Theory rates this as quite sound for Black. The differences between it and the diagram version are …♗d6, instead of …♗b7, and …e5, rather than …e6.

This can help Black tactically. For instance, 8 d4 cxd4 9 cxd4 exd4 10 ♘xd4 and now 10…♘xd4 11 ♕xd4 ♕c7, with a double attack on c2 and h2.

The example of 8 d4 that has gotten the most attention saw 10 ♘bd2 played.

Black equalized after 10…♗b7 11 ♘b3 ♕c7.

The game? Grandelius-Caruana, Wijk aan Zee 2021.

8   d3!

Caruana plays the position like an Anti-Marshall Ruy Lopez. He gets the same kind of pawn structure, with the d6-bishop sticking out like a sore thumb.

8   ...   0-0

In another game of the finals, Carlsen improved with 8...♘g6 9 ♗e3 0-0.

He had a more playable game after 10 ♘bd2 ♗e7 11 ♗b3 d6 12 ♗d5 ♕e8.

9   ♗e3

This stops ...♗c7/...d6 because of ♗xc5.

9   ...   ♗b7

Black would equalize with 9...f5 and ...f4!.

But 10 ♗b3+ ♔h8 11 exf5 is a problem because White can dominate light squares.

For example, 11...♘xf5 (else 12 ♘g5!) 12 ♘bd2 ♘xe3 13 fxe3 ♗b7 14 ♘e4 and 15 ♗d5 favors him.

10   ♘h4!

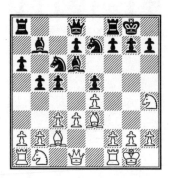

Caruana has found one of the few ways to exploit the d6-bishop and pawn structure – 10...♘g6 11 ♘f5.

10   ...   ♖e8

Black can try to regroup with 10...g6 11 ♘d2 ♘c8 and ...♗e7/ ...d6

But White would be better after 12 ♘hf3 and much better after 12 ♕g4!.

11   ♘d2   ♘g6

12   ♘f5   ♗f8

13   ♕g4!

Caruana is primed for h2-h4-h5. Black cannot move the g6-knight because of ♘h6+.

The White queen would also look nice on h5, where it could be followed by 14 ♘f3 and 15 ♘g5 h6 16 ♘xf7! ♔xf7 17 f4 or 17 ♗b3+.

But 13 ♕h5? ♘f4! would have set him back.

410

13 ... d6

More Magnus-like is 13….d5 so that 14 h4 ♗c8 15 h5 d4.

In a speed game, Caruana might play 14 exd5 quickly and weigh his options after 14…♕xd5.

Then 15 ♘e4 threatens to win with 16 ♘h6+! gxh6 17 ♘f6+ or 16…♔h8 17 ♗b3.

But in a classical game he would probably take time to see if 15 ♗b3 ♕xd3 16 ♘e4 is better.

14 h4 ♔h8

The threat of 15 h5 forced Carlsen to consider semi-desperate measures.

Least expensive is a pawn sacrifice.

He would have compensation after 14…♗c8 15 h5 ♗xf5 16 exf5 ♘f4 17 ♗xf4.

But 17 h6!, instead, gets bad for him after 17…g6 18 g3 ♘d5 19 fxg6 and 20 ♗b3.

15 ♗b3! ♕c7

After playing Carlsen more than 100 times, Caruana knew how much the initiative meant to the world champion.

He took his longest think of the game, well over a minute, to consider 16 h5.

It wins a pawn (16…♘ge7 17 ♗xf7).

Again Carlsen would get some compensation after 16…♘f4 17 ♗xf4 exf4 18 ♕xf4.

For instance, 18…♘e5 19 ♕g3 c4!.

16 ♘f3

This guarantees a positional, rather than material, advantage.

It also carries the playability benefit: It is easier to blunder and harder to find good moves.

For example, Black could resign after 16…♘ce7? 17 ♘g5!.

411

16   ...   ♘a5

If Black covers f7 with 16...♘d8, White replies 17 ♘g5 with a threat of 18 ♕h5 h6 19 ♘xf7+ ♘xf7 20 ♕xg6.

Then 17...c4 18 dxc4 bxc4 19 ♗a4 gets White a no-risk positional advantage.

For instance, 19...♗c6 20 ♗xc6 ♘xc6 21 ♖ad1 or 21 g3 and 22 h5.

17   ♗d5   ♗xd5

18   exd5

Now 18...♘e7 19 ♘xe7 ♗xe7 allows White a powerful queenside initiative, 20 b4 ♘b7 21 a4!.

Similar to the game is 19...♕xe7 20 ♘g5 and ♘e4 but...

18   ...   f6

19   h5   ♘e7

The pawn offer 19...♘f4 20 ♗xf4 exf4 no longer works

because White can go for mate with 21 ♘3h4! and ♘g6+!.

For example, 21...♔g8 22 ♘h6+ ♔h8 23 ♘g6+! hxg6 24 ♘f7+ ♔g8 29 hxg6 and ♕h5.

20   ♘xe7

20   ...   ♕xe7

White's most promising positional plan includes putting pawns on b3 and c4.

For instance 20...♖xe7 21 ♘h4 ♕d7 22 ♕e4 ♔g8 23 b3 ♖ee8 24 c4!.

Then White can turn to the kingside, e.g. 24...♖eb8 25 h6 g5 (25...g6 26 ♘xg6) 26 ♘f5 and eventually f2-f4.

21   ♘h4!   ♕f7

Now 22 ♕f3 would keep control, e.g. 22...♘b7 23 c4! or 22...c4 23 d4.

22   c4?   bxc4

23   dxc4

412

23	...	e4?

Carlsen was more than three minutes behind on the clock and both players were making quick moves.

He missed his chance for 23...f5! and then 24 ♘xf5 ♘xc4, when his deficit is drastically cut.

Caruana would still be better after 25 b3 ♘b6 – not 25...♘xe3? 26 fxe3! ♕xd5? 27 ♖ad1 ♕e6 28 ♖xd6!.

24	b3	♔g8
25	♗d2!	♘b7
26	♗c3	

The position is strategically won for White.

He can win the e4-pawn whenever he wants with ♖ae1 and ♖xe4.

Black cannot defend with ...♖e7 because of ♘f5.

White is in such command that he can delay capturing on e4 until after he has doubled rooks and played ♘f5.

For example, 26...♔h8 27 ♖ae1 ♘d8 28 ♖e3 ♘b7 (nothing better than a pass) 29 ♖fe1 and now 29...♖ad8 30 ♘f5 ♕d7 31 h6! wins.

Or 30...♖b8 31 ♖xe4 ♖xe4 32 ♖xe4 ♖e8 33 ♘h6! gxh6 34 ♖xe8 (34...♕xe8 35 ♗xf6+).

26	...	♖e5
27	♗xe5	dxe5
28	♖ae1	

Smoother than 28 ♕xe4 ♕xh5 and ...♘d6.

28	...	♘d6
29	♘f5	g6
30	♘xd6	♗xd6
31	♕xe4	

Now 31...gxh5 32 ♕f5 would eliminate virtually all remaining

counterplay. White could finish off with ♖e4-h4 or ♖e3-f3.

31	...	f5
32	♕h4	♖e8
33	f3!	gxh5
34	♖e3	♔h8
35	♖fe1	♕g6
36	♕h3	

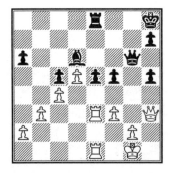

White has made sure there are no tricks involving a mate threat on g2 or on a dark square.

36	...	a5

The e-pawn dies after 36...e4 37 fxe4 fxe4 38 ♕h4.

White also has ways to win by giving back the Exchange, e.g. 36...♖g8 37 ♖xe5! ♗xe5 38 ♖xe5.

37	♔h1	♕f7
38	a3	♖e7
39	♕h4	♕g6

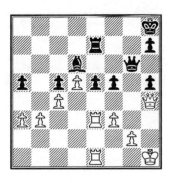

40	b4!	

If Black had prevented this liquidation there was bound to be another. No fortress for Magnus today (40...cxb4 41 axb4 ♗xb4 42 ♖xe5).

40	...	♖g7
41	♖1e2	cxb4
42	axb4	axb4
43	c5!	f4

The simplest win after 43...♗xc5 44 ♖xe5 b3 is 45 ♖e8+ ♖g8 46 ♕d8.

44	♖e4	♗xc5
45	♖xe5	♗e3
46	♖e6!	

It's far from necessary but White can now beat 46...♕f7 with 47 ♖2xe3! fxe3 48 ♕e4 and ♖e8+.

46	...	♕b1+
47	♖e1	♕b2
48	♖e8+	♖g8

49	Rxg8+	Kxg8

| 50 | Qd8+ |

There was a fancy finish for computers and grandmasters with more time on their clock (50 d6 Qd2 51 Ra1 Qxd6 52 Ra8+ etc.).

Instead, Caruana forces his queen's way to e7, where it controls the queening square.

50	...	Kf7
51	Qd7+	Kg6
52	Qe8+	Kg7
53	Qe7+!	Kg6
54	d6	Qd2
55	Rb1	b3

56	d7	b2
57	d8(Q)	resigns.

This match was an extraordinary back-and-forth battle. Carlsen and Caruana alternated wins with White. Carlsen broke serve by winning a game as Black. Then Caruana's win in the 11th game tied the match. But Carlsen clinched victory with a win in the 12th.

The other Magnus-Fabiano competition remained on hold. This was for rating supremacy.

After Caruana qualified for the 2018 world championship match he trailed Carlsen by more than 20 rating points. But he had narrowed that to a mere three points when the match was over.

However, in 2019 Carlsen's lead grew to more than 40 points as he regained his form. It was frozen at 55 points when Covid virtually halted rated "classical" play. Fans of both players awaited the return of over-the-board chess in 2021 to see if Caruana could resume his pursuit of the number one rating position.

58
Belated Rivals

When Ian Nepomniachtchi qualified for the 2021 world championship match, he had an envious record. He had beaten Magnus Carlsen four times and lost once in their previous classical time limit games.

"Fabi" and "Nepo" had been somewhat distant rivals since their first game in 2006. They had played only one decisive "classical" game, a Nepo win. For years they didn't seem to be in the same elite class. The Russian was only ranked 27th in the world in December 2017.

Their rivalry became intense when they were locked-in. They played 24 on-line games during 2020-21. This is arguably the best.

Caruana – Ian Nepomniachtchi
Chessable (internet) 2020
English Opening, Reversed Dragon Variation (A22)

1	c4	♘f6
2	♘c3	e5
3	g3	d5
4	cxd5	♘xd5
5	♗g2	♘b6
6	d3	

This was once played as a waiting move. White delays ♘f3 so he can consider doubling Black's pawns after ...♘c6 with ♗xc6+.

6	...	♗e7

7	♗e3	

But as often happens with move order finesses, new purposes were found for 6 d3. One of them, pioneered by Vasily Ivanchuk, was to quickly occupy the c5-square after ♖c1 and ♘e4.

7	...	0-0
8	♖c1	

White hopes a quick ♘c5 will prevent Black from harmonizing his forces with ...f6, ...♗e6 and ...♕d7.

In general, if Black keeps his pieces centralized and avoids pawn weaknesses, he should equalize in this variation.

8	...	♖e8

Black may also have doubts about 8...♘c6 and now 9 ♗xc6 bxc6.

But he wants to play ...♘c6 eventually. So he avoids 8...c6? 9 ♘f3.

9　♘f3　♘c6

With his e5-pawn protected, he can continue ...♘d4, since ♘xd4/...exd4 is a nice pawn structure for him.

10　0-0　♗f8

The generic English Opening moves are 11 ♘e4 and 11 a3. Both are adequately met by 11...♘d4.

Nepo knew these positions because he had played the White side. He had tried 11 a3 ♘d4 12 ♘e4 c6 13 ♗g5 against Sergey Karjakin in the World Blitz Championship in 2016.

He induced a slight weakening, 13...f6. But Karjakin had nicely centralized power after 14 ♘xd4 exd4 15 ♗d2 ♗e6 and 16...♗d5.

11　♗g5　♕d7

Nepo's move is new: He wants to kick the bishop with ...h6 rather than ...f6.

12　a3　h6

13　♗d2　♕d8

He might have said, "This is basically the same position we had three moves ago. Show me what you've gotten out of this."

14　♘e4　a5

Black often plays ...a5 earlier, to stop b2-b4.

Then if White replies ♘a4!, a trade of knights would weaken Black's queenside (♘xb6/cxb6) or mildly expose b7 (...♘xa4/♕xa4).

15　♘c5　a4

Chances are roughly equal and that would also be the case after 15...♘d7 or even 15...♖a7.

A minor drawback to 15...a4 is that this pawn would hang after ...♘d5 or ...♘d7.

16　♕c2　♖a7

417

Nepo protects b7 so he can play ...♞d4 without fear of ♘xd4 and ♘xb7.

He can't move his c8-bishop because of ♘xb7! and ♕xc6.

But he can nudge the needle in his favor by swapping his b6-knight for the one on c5.

For example, 17...♞d7 18 ♘xd7 ♝xd7 followed by ...♝g4 or ...♝e6 and ...♕d7.

17   ♖fe1!

Prophylaxis. Now on 17...♞d7 White can play 18 ♘xa4.

Then on 18...♞d4 19 ♘xd4 exd4, Black would threaten to trap the knight with ...b5!.

This can get complicated but White could meet 18...♞d4 with the simple 19 ♕d1. Thanks to 17 ♖fe1! his e2-pawn is safe.

17   ...   ♞d4

Continuing the waiting game with 17...♕e7 was wiser because White has no particularly good, non-committal reply.

For instance, 18 ♘c4 allows 18...♝e6! with the idea of ...♝b3. And 18 ♝e3 invites 18...♞d5.

White could rule out ...♞d4 with 18 e3.

But then 18...♕d8! threatens 19...♝xc5 20 ♕xc5 ♕xd3.

18   ♘xd4

Not 18...♕xd4? 19 ♝e3 ♕d8 because of 20 ♘xa4! ♖xa4 21 ♝xb6.

18   ...   exd4

This would be a nice pawn structure for Black if it is allowed to stand.

He prepares, for example, 19...♖e5 20 ♘e4 ♖b5! and ...f5.

Or 20 ♝b4 ♞d5! with a slight edge.

19   e4

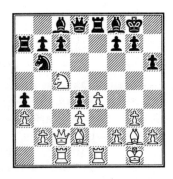

And this looks like a favorable structure for White because the e4-pawn stops Black from reorganizing with ...♞d5!/...c6.

19   ...   dxe3

But 19...c6 and 20...♘d7 was preferable. White cannot reply ♘xa4 when the reply ...b5 would trap the knight.

20   ♗xe3

But now 21 ♘xa4 is a real threat (21...♖xa4 22 ♗xb6).

20   ...   c6

21   ♘e4

Black finally solved the problem of defending the c7-pawn. This leaves White trying to exploit d6 and other dark squares with ♗c5 and a trade of bishops.

21   ...   ♗e6

22   ♗c5

Nepo spent ten of his remaining 14 minutes here.

22   ...   ♖a8

There were two forcing variations worth his time calculating.

One is 22...f5 23 ♘d2 (23 ♗xf8 fxe4) ♗xc5 24 ♕xc5.

White would rather have his knight on c5. But the trade of bishops made ♘f3-d4 very good for White.

Since ...f5 looks antipositional, Black must have calculated 22...♗xc5 23 ♘xc5 ♗f5.

Then the sacrifice 25 ♘xb7 fails to 25...♖xe1+.

But White can improve incrementally, such as with 23 ♕c3.

23   ♗xf8   ♖xf8

24   ♘c5   ♗c8

Caruana can claim a plus-over-minus advantage but he needs a new plan. Or two.

25   ♖e4!

This eyes ♖b4 and/or ♘xa4.

25   ...   ♖e8

Not 25...♗f5 because of 26 ♘xb7 ♕c7 27 ♖f4, for example.

Or 25...f5 when 26 ♖b4 is good and 26 ♖e5 (26...♕d6 27 f4) is better.

26   ♖ce1   ♖xe4

27   ♖xe4

Computers debate with themselves for a while over whether 27 dxe4 is better. Recapturing with the rook prepares a specific follow-up, 28 ♕e2 and ♖e8+. And ♘xa4 remains a future possibility.

27 ...   ♖a5

So that 28 ♘xa4? ♗f5! or 28 ♖b4 ♕e7!.

Now after 28 ♕e2 ♔f8 White has to defend his c5-knight, and 29 d4 ♘d7! doesn't help.

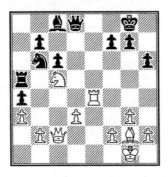

28   h3

Almost anything Black does would worsen his position, so Caruana can afford a little move like 28 h3.

But 28 ♖e1! was a better waiting move – waiting, for example, for 28...♔f8, when 29 d4! would threaten ♕h7 and ♕h8 mate.

If Black also passes, 28...♖a7, White can reverse the queen+rook battery with 29 ♕e2.

He would be making progress after 29...♖a5 30 d4 and ♗e4-c2/♕d3.

That also sets a trap, 30...♕xd4 31 b4! axb3 32 ♘xb3, forking.

28   ...   ♔f8

29   d4!   ♖a8

With his rook on a5, the knight fork (29...♗f5? 30 ♘xb7) is always present.

30   ♖e1

White threatens ♕h7!.

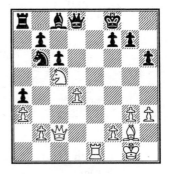

30   ...   g6

Nepo is struggling to find a defensible kingside formation.

If he temporizes, 30...♔g8 31 ♕e4 ♕f8, White's queen penetrates, 32 ♕e5.

Black can delay for a while, 32...♘c4 33 ♕c7 ♘d6 (not 33...♘xb2? 34 ♗f1! traps the knight).

But such a defense only succeeds in a fantasy world of perfect computer play. The same for 32...♘d7 33 ♕c7 ♘xc5 34 dxc5.

31   ♕d2   ♔g7

32 ♕f4

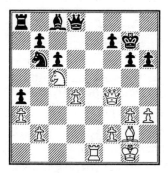

Now Black had to consider 32...♘d5 so that 33 ♕e5+ ♘f6.

But he must have feared 33 ♗xd5! exd5 34 ♕e5+ and then 34...♔h7 35 ♕e8 or 34...♕f6 35 ♕xf6+ ♔xf6 36 ♖e8.

There is a swindle try in 33...♕xd5 34 ♖e8 ♗xh3 because of the ...♕g2 mate threat.

But this blows up if White finds his only good move, 35 ♘e6+! (35...fxe6?? 36 ♕f8+; 35...♗xe6 36 ♖xa8 and wins).

32 ... ♘d7

With 32...♘c4 Black prepares 33...♕d6!.

White keeps his large positional plus with 33 d5! cxd5 34 ♕d4+.

But after 34...f6! it is far from decisive.

33 ♘e4!

Black can't stop ♘d6 or ♕e5+ for long (33...♕e7 34 ♖e3).

33 ... ♖a5?

34 ♘d6 ♘f6

If this were a quiz position, many players would stop once they spotted 35 ♕xh6+ ♔xh6 36 ♘xf7+.

35 ♖e8!

Now 35...♘xe8 36 ♕xf7+ ♔h8 37 ♘xe8 ♕xd4 38 ♘f6! is over.

Or 35...♕xe8 36 ♘xe8 ♘xe8 37 ♕b8.

35 ... ♕d7!

36 ♖xc8 g5

And if this were a quiz position, some players would try to be brilliant with 37 ♕e5 ♖xe5 38 dxe5.

They would foresee a win after 38...♘-moves 39 ♖b8 and ♖xb7.

But 38...♕e6 39 exf6+ ♔xf6 is not nearly as easy as the boring way Caruana chooses.

37 ♕d2! ♖a6

38 ♕b4 c5

Once he saw 34 ♘d6, he played these moves quickly.

But he paused here to evaluate the various ways of banking his extra material.

They include (a) 39 ♕xb7 ♖xd6 40 ♖c7, (b) 39 ♕xc5 ♖xd6 40 ♖c7 and (c) 39 ♘f5+ ♕xf5 40 ♕xc5. Each would have won.

39 dxc5! ♖xd6

40 cxd6 ♕xc8

41 ♗xb7!

Going for passed a- and b-pawns is a bit faster than 41 ♕xb7 ♕c1+ 42 ♔h2 ♕d2.

41 ... ♕xh3

42 ♕xa4 h5

There are no real Black mating chances (42...♘g4 43 ♗g2) so Nepo tries for perpetual check.

43 ♕d4 ♕d7

44 ♗f3 h4

45 gxh4 gxh4

46 ♕xh4 ♕f5

Of course, 46...♕xd6 47 ♕g3+ is hopeless.

The rest deserves little comment:

47 ♔g2 ♔f8 48 a4 ♕g6+ 49 ♕g3 ♕f5 50 b4 ♘d5 51 ♕g4 ♕e5 52 ♕c8+ ♔g7 53 ♕g4+ ♔f8 54 d7 ♔e7 55 ♕e4 ♕xe4 56 ♗xe4 ♘xb4 57 ♗f5 ♘c6 58 ♔f3 ♔d6 59 ♔f4 f6 60 ♗e4 ♘d8 61 ♔f5 ♔xd7 62 ♔xf6 ♔d6 63 a5 ♘e6 64 a6 resigns.

59
The 389-Day Wait

The 2020 Candidates tournament was abruptly halted midway when Russian hosts feared that the players would be trapped by the Covid crisis in their Siberian playing site. "Not entirely certain we'll be allowed out of the country," Caruana tweeted to his fans when he tried to head home. "Complete farce."

After many attempts, the most prestigious tournament in chess resumed in the same Ekaterinburg location in April 2021, after a break of 389 days. Guest of honor Anatoly Karpov played the symbolic first move in the marquee game of the round, Caruana – Vachier-Lagrave. A worldwide audience knew this was the American's best chance to get back into contention. Perhaps no game outside of a world championship match elicited so much expectation for so long.

Caruana   Maxime Vachier-Lagrave
Candidates tournament,
Ekaterinburg 2021
*Sicilian Defense,
Najdorf Variation (B97)*

1	e4	c5
2	♘f3	d6
3	d4	cxd4
4	♘xd4	♘f6
5	♘c3	a6
6	♗g5	e6
7	f4	♛b6

Caruana has a remarkable record with the Poisoned Pawn Variation in international chess: Four games, four victories. One was against Hikaru Nakamura and all three others against MVL.

8	♕d2	♛xb2
9	♖b1	♛a3

423

10   e5

Vachier-Lagrave seemed caught off guard at Wijk aan Zee 2021 when Caruana chose the below-the-radar 10 ♗e2.

After 20 minutes he replied 10...♘c6 and then took another 20-plus minutes after 11 ♘xc6 bxc6 12 e5.

This was still book and his new move, 12...♘d5, was not a bad idea. But his next two were dreadful, 13 ♘xd5 exd5? 14 e6! f6?.

The game was virtually over after 15 ♗h5+ ♔d8 16 ♗h4.

10   ...   h6

The insertion of ...h6 was considered critical to the Poisoned Pawn Variation when it was a new, experimental opening. Then it was forgotten for half a century.

Vachier-Lagrave played a pivotal role in its revival and Caruana said it should be known as "the MVL Variation."

11   ♗h4   dxe5

12   fxe5   ♘fd7

The difference ...h6/♗h4 makes is purely tactical – and the tactics initially benefit White. A sacrifice on e6 may set up a winning check on the h5-e8 diagonal after ...fxe6.

13   ♘e4

The position is becoming so double-edged it defies normal moves.

Black can forget about trying to castle. He would get slaughtered soon after 13...♗e7 14 ♗xe7 ♕xe7 15 ♘d6+.

Or after 14...♔xe7 15 ♖b3 ♕a4 (15...♕xa2 16 ♕b4+) 16 ♗e2 ♖d8 17 ♘xe6!.

13   ...   ♕xa2

Nor would he last long after 13...♘c6 14 ♘xc6 bxc6 because 15 ♗e2 mounts threats to f7 with 0-0/♗h5.

14   ♖d1!

This move brought the ♘e4 attack back from the cemetery of dead opening ideas.

It had been buried more than 60 years before when White played 14 ♖b3 and the Soviet star Alexander Tolush replied 14...♕a1+ 15 ♔f2 ♕a4.

In one game (without …h6/♗h4) Mikhail Tal beat him with a stunning bishop sacrifice that made Tal internationally famous.

But Tolush soon repeated the opening, with the insertion of …h6/♗h4, against Viktor Korchnoi. When Korchnoi used the Tal idea, 16 ♗b5 axb5 17 ♘xb5, Tolush surprised him with 17…♗c5+!.

White's h4-bishop was unprotected and he lost after 18 ♘xc5 ♕xh4+.

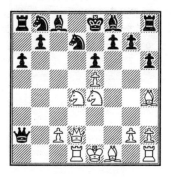

14   …   ♕d5

Before 2000, the idea of deeply analyzing an opening move for use in a speed tournament was laughable to grandmasters. "Prep" was for classical chess.

What gained respectability for 14 ♖d1! was a rapid game, Radjabov – Karjakin, Cap d'Agde 2006.

Karjakin played 14…♕b2 with the idea of 15…♗b4.

But Radjabov had discovered that White's queen stands well on e3 in this variation.

After 15 ♕e3! ♗c5 16 ♗e2 ♘c6 he missed a neat knockout with 17 ♘xe6! ♗xe3?? 18 ♘d6 mate.

But he won anyway. Later that year Radjabov beat Vishy Anand in the World Blitz Championship: 13…♕a4 14 ♗e2 ♘c6? 15 ♘xe6! g5 16 ♘f6+ resigns.

15   ♕e3!

Now 15…♗c5 16 ♘xe6! works (17 ♘c7+).

This has been tested in games that went 16…♗b4+ 17 c3, with unclear chances.

15   …   ♕xe5

Now 16 ♗g3 ♗c5 had been tried, without notable success.

16   c3

Both players had prepared the first 15 moves with their computers, which recommended 16 c3. But MVL took 17 minutes to reply because he couldn't remember his analysis, he admitted after the game.

16 ... ♗c5

17 ♗g3 ♕d5

Black's queen has to guard d6, otherwise 18 ♗d6! is too strong.

After 17...♕h5 18 ♗d6 Black's king is caught in the center, e.g. 18...♗xd6 19 ♘xd6+ ♔e7 20 ♘4f5+ ♔f8 21 ♗e2 ♕g5 22 0-0 and wins.

Or 18...♗a7 19 ♗a3 and ♘d6+.

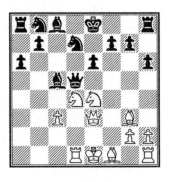

Computers were now telling on-line spectators that 18 ♗d6 ♗xd6 19 ♘b5 was by far the best White can get for his three sacrificed pawns.

Engine analysis well past move 30 assured fans 19...♕xd1+ 20 ♔xd1 ♗e5 would favor Black.

18 ♗c4!

Another case of "if man leads the computer," as Ivanchuk had put it.

Caruana credited his second, Rustam Kasimzhdanov, for suggesting the move and forcing engines to try to refute it.

Caruana said they had tested the bishop sacrifice "for quite some time" before the tournament. But the consequences were too complex even for engines to be certain it worked.

18 ... ♕xc4

19 ♗d6

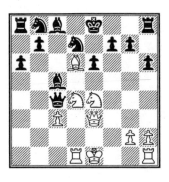

Cyber skeptics claimed 19...♗xd4 20 ♖xd4 ♕b3 (or 20...♕a2) would have won for Black.

But when given time to consider 21 ♕g3, they saw that 21...♕b1+ 22 ♔d2 ♕xh1? 23 ♕xg7 was lost.

And 22...♕b2+ 23 ♔e3 g5 would allow a perpetual check, such as 24 ♗b4 and ♘d6+.

19 ... ♘f6!

"I was kind of sad that he played this," Caruana said after the game.

426

This was a very difficult move to find and he rated it best.

20   ♘xc5

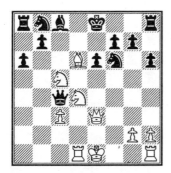

White threatens to capture on g7 and win, after 20 ♕g3 or 20 ♘f5.

For example, 20...b6 21 ♘f5! bxc5 22 ♗xc5, when Black must play 22...♕g4 and try to hold on after 23 0-0.

Best, according to engines, is 21...♘d5! 22 ♖xd5! ♕xd5 23 ♘xg7+ ♔d8.

Then it leads to an almost equal endgame, 23 ♘cxe6+! ♔d7 24 ♘c7 ♕xd6 25 ♘xa8 ♕c5.

20   ...   ♘d5

21 ♕e5

Still moving instantly, Caruana was an hour ahead on the clock.

But he had been in a very similar situation more than a year before, when Ding Liren fell into another Caruana analysis.

Fabiano had sacrificed two pawns for reasonable compensation and was still in his prep at move 17. But the Chinese GM outplayed him and was winning within ten moves.

21   ...   ♖g8

Some engines still prefer Black's winning chances, rather than a draw by repetition after 21...♕xc3+ 22 ♔f2 ♕b2+ 23 ♔f3 ♕c3+ 24 ♔f2.

Other computers point out 24 ♖d3!.

Then 24...♘c6 25 ♘xc6 ♕xe5 26 ♘xe5 gets Black to an endgame with four pawns for a piece. But White is for choice.

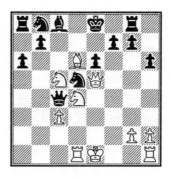

22 ♘dxe6!

Even this was analyzed by the triumvirate of Caruana+ Kasimzhdanov+computer.

Now 22...♗xe6 23 ♘xe6 ♕xc3+ 24 ♕xc3 ♘xc3 25 ♘c7+ is very similar to what happens in the game. The difference is

Black's bishop would be gone and his f7-pawn would remain.

White would be better in that case, with a piece for three pawns, but a win would be far from certain.

22 ... fxe6

23 ♘xe6

He might have to settle for a perpetual check after 23...♔f7 24 ♖f1+ ♘f6 25 ♕h5+ ♔xe6 26 ♕e5+ ♔f7 27 ♕h5+.

23 ... ♕xc3+

One of the many questions that lingered after the game was whether Black can play for more with 23...♘f6.

Incredibly, White has no discovered check better than 24 ♘xg7+.

Then 24...♔f7 25 ♖f1 ♕xf1+! 26 ♔xf1 ♘c6! appears, if anything, good for Black.

24 ♕xc3 ♘xc3

25 ♘c7+ ♔f7

Carlsen later praised MVL's "super-human defense" in threading his way to a drawable endgame.

Caruana finally paused to think about a move. Thanks to increments, he had more time than when the

game began, 1 hour, 43 minutes, 14 seconds.

MVL was down to 32 minutes, 48 seconds.

26 ♖d3

White is still down a piece and two pawns. But after 26...♖a7 27 ♖xc3 ♘c6? he would regain it and more, with 28 0-0+ ♔g6 29 ♗c5!.

Caruana had prepared 26...♖a7 and pronounced it "just a draw" after the game, perhaps because of 27 ♖xc3 ♔g6!.

This reflected what Vladimir Kramnik had said. "Even if you work like crazy, even if you're incredibly imaginative in the opening...Hardly any games are won in the opening now."

26 ... ♘e4?

What deep prep can provide are opportunities for the opponent to go wrong in a middlegame (or, here, an endgame).

428

MVL will have two pawns for the Exchange. But the White rooks have excellent chances of picking off both queenside pawns.

27	0-0+	♔g6
28	♘xa8	♘c6

The usual rule when down the Exchange is to preserve your remaining rook. But here 28...♖d8! 29 ♖fd1 ♘c6 30 ♗a3 ♖xd3 offered a better defense.

29	♘b6	♖d8
30	♘xc8	♖xc8
31	♗a3	

The rooks would exert greater pressure on the queenside pawns after 31 ♖e1! ♘xd6 32 ♖xd6+ and 33 ♖d7.

Or 31...♘f6 32 ♖b1.

31	...	♖c7
32	♖f4	♘f6
33	♗b2!	

This prepares ♖d6 and ♗xf6.

33	...	♘e7
34	♗xf6	gxf6
35	h4?	

This move came back to haunt Caruana. Much better is 35 ♖d6 ♘f5 36 ♖b6.

35	...	h5!
36	♖g3+	♔f7
37	♖g5	

This seems to punish 36...h5. White would be winning after 37...b5 38 ♖xh5 ♔g6 39 ♖h8 a5 40 ♖a8.

But Caruana misjudged the trade of h-pawns that Black now forces.

37	...	♖c1+
38	♔h2	♘g6!
39	♖f2	♘xh4
40	♖xh5	♘g6
41	♖h7+	♔e6
42	♖xb7	♘e5

If White preserves rooks, 43 ♖a2 ♔f5 44 ♖xa6 ♔g5, for example, he will have to seek a trade later to make progress.

43	♖b6+	♖c6
44	♖xc6+	♘xc6

This position fascinated on-line spectators because their computers told them Black was inches away from a "table-base draw."

That is, a position in which computers have exhausted every winning attempt.

The game landed in tablebase range after **45 ♔g3 ♔f7 46 ♖c2 ♘b4 47 ♖d2 ♘c6 48 ♔f4 ♔g6 49 ♖d6 ♘e5 50 ♖xa6 ♘f7 51 ♔e4**.

Black has three moves that would maintain the draw, 51...♔g5, 51...♘h6 or 51...♘g5+. The other eight legal moves lose, according to the tablebase.

This is the kind of position that is maddening to amateurs *and* masters. A move that draws in one scenario would lose in a very similar one.

That was the case here after **51...♘h6 52 ♖a5 ♘f7 53 ♖a3 ♘d6+ 54 ♔f4 ♘f5 55 ♖d3**

55 ... ♘h6?

The same ...♘h6 that was safe in the previous diagram was potentially fatal here.

White's only winning chance is to penetrate with his king to a vulnerable square, such as f8.

Black could have shut off access with 55...♘g7! or 55...♘e7!.

This was certainly not visible here. There followed **56 ♖g3+ ♔f7 57 ♔e4 ♘g8 58 ♔f5 ♘e7+ 59 ♔f4 ♘d5+ 60 ♔g4?**

The only forced win comes about after 60 ♔f5!. That would transpose into what happens in the game after 64 ♔f5!.

430

60...♚g6 61 ♔f3+ ♚f7 62 ♔e4

62   ...   ♘e7?

This was the final error. The intuitive defense is to keep the knight close to the king. But 62...♘c7! was the only drawing move, as the knight can reach the key g7 square.

The finale was: **63 ♔f4 ♘d5+ 64 ♔f5! ♘e7+ 65 ♔e4 ♘g8 66 ♖h3 ♚g6 67 ♖a3 ♚f7 68 ♔f4 ♘h6 69 ♖g3 ♘g8 70 ♔g4 ♘e7 71 ♔h5! ♘d5 72 ♖f3!**

Now 73 g4 and 74 g5 is a decisive threat.

72	...	♚e6
73	g4	♚e5
74	♔g6	resigns.

Fabiano "absolutely had to win" this game to save his chances, his second said. It was a repeat of what happened when the second half of the 2016 Candidates began and he won Game 34.

But after beating MVL, "he strangely had no more energy," Kasimzhdanov said. Caruana played listlessly in the next three games. Then a loss to Giri put an effective end to his latest bid for the world championship. He was deeply disappointed but, as his second put it, "he is not the type to let things out." However, the tournament put a strain on their relationship. By the end of 2021, Caruana and Kasimzhdanov agreed their six-year partnership had come to an end.

60
Two Wings

One of Caruana's salient qualities is the ability to play on both wings of the board simultaneously. Every aspiring player is taught to watch for sudden tactical opportunities on the opposite wing. Better students learn how to conduct continuous pressure on both sides of the board. Previous generations learned this from Alekhine games and Kasparov games. Now they learn from Carlsen and Caruana games.

The following is distinctive because of what Caruana does not do. Virtually all computers – and perhaps a majority of grandmasters – would seize the opportunity to launch a queenside initiative at move 20. It opens the door to a very favorable endgame. But it would close the door to a kingside initiative. Caruana chose a more practical path.

Caruana – Peter Svidler
St. Louis (blitz) 2021
Ruy Lopez, 6 d3 Variation (C84)

1	e4	e5
2	♘f3	♘c6
3	♗b5	a6
4	♗a4	♘f6
5	0-0	♗e7
6	d3	d6

Black inserts ...b5 so often and so early in the Ruy that 6...d6 is somewhat rare.

This version is similar to 6 ♖e1 d6, which is considered dubious because 7 ♗xc6+ bxc6 8 d4 would put Black's center under pressure.

But the quiet 6 d3 justifies the quiet 6...d6. White would be a tempo behind the 6 ♖e1 d6 line after 7 ♗xc6+ bxc6 8 d4? ♘xe4 or 8...♗g4.

7	c3	0-0
8	♖e1	♖e8

A benefit of Black's delay of ...b5 is that it denies White the generic Lopez strategy of targeting the b-pawn after a2-a4.

432

9	♘bd2	♗f8

Now on 10 d4 Black exerts his own pressure on the center with 10...b5 11 ♗c2 exd4 12 cxd4 ♗g4! and later ... ♗xf3, as Magnus Carlsen showed in a 2020 game with Nepomniachtchi.

10	h3	h6
11	d4	b5
12	♗c2	♗b7

By a relatively rare sequence of moves, Black has set up a version of the Zaitsev/Breyer variation.

He can continue 13...♘b8 and ...♘bd7 if White plays an innocuous move like 13 a3.

13	d5!

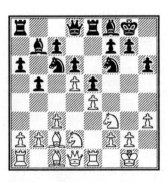

The diagram wouldn't confuse a human familiar with Lopez patterns. This is how White often gains space and begins a queenside initiative.

But some computers suggest 13 ♔h2 as one of White's best options – followed, of course, by 14 ♔g1. Silly computers.

13	...	♘b8!

As noted earlier, this knight has a much better future on the queenside than on e7.

14	b3	c6

It is easy to confuse Ruy Lopez pawn structures. But a basic guideline here is Black needs his own fluid queenside play with ...c6.

Instead, 14...c5? is a positional blunder. Black's pieces would lack good queenside squares after 15 a4!, e.g. 15...♘bd7 16 ♗d3 and ♗b2.

15	c4

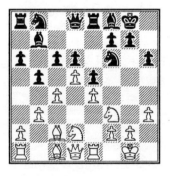

Look familiar? Yes, in Game 7 we saw virtually the same position after 17 b3.

There is one difference. David Navara had played ...g6 instead of ...h6.

This enabled him to swap dark-squared bishops with ...♗h6.

15	...	♕c7

| 16 | ♘f1 | ♘bd7 |

Black's best policy is to slowly organize a queenside defense. When he is ready, he can try to blockade the files as Navara did or open the b- and c-files for his heavy pieces.

The dangers of trying to liquidate pawns quickly was shown by a 2016 Caruana – Ding Liren game that went 17 ♗e3 a5 18 ♖c1 ♗a6 and now 19 cxb5 ♗xb5 20 ♗d3!, with advantage to White.

| 17 | ♘g3 | |

A relatively new move. This variation has been so well trod that a stem game was played by then-world champion Anatoly Karpov in 1979.

| 17 | ... | bxc4 |
| 18 | bxc4 | a5 |

Black is poised to equalize with ...♖ec8, ...♖ab8, ...♘c5, ...♗a6 and eventually ...cxd5.

Timing is subtle because 18...cxd5 would allow White a slight positional pull after 19 cxd5

♖ec8 20 ♗d3 ♘c5 21 ♗e3 ♘xd3 22 ♕xd3 and ♖ab1/♖ec1.

| 19 | ♗e3 | ♘c5? |

But 19...cxd5 20 cxd5 ♘c5 would be fine because of 21 ♗d3? ♘xd3 22 ♕xd3 ♗a6.

| 20 | ♘d2!? | |

Caruana later sacrifices a knight and then one rook after another. But to a master, this can be the most surprising move in the game.

The reason is Caruana rejected 20 ♗xc5 dxc5 21 ♗a4!.

After the eventual dxc6 and swap of bishops, he could occupy b5 and/or d5 with a knight.

This is textbook positional chess. White's advantage would be undisputed. But it virtually gives up any hope of making a dent on the kingside.

| 20 | ... | cxd5 |

Svidler would be worse after 21 cxd5 ♖ec8 but well within the radius of a defensible position.

21 exd5!

This explains more of Caruana's thinking: He is looking at the kingside.

He opens the way for 22 ♕f3, with a threat of ♗xh6, and then 22...♘fd7 23 ♘h5.

If Black retreats ...♘cd7 instead, White can play on both wings simultaneously by looking for c4-c5!.

For example, 21...♖eb8 22 ♕f3 ♘cd7 23 ♖ac1 ♗a6 24 ♘de4.

Then 24...♘xe4 25 ♘xe4 ♖b2? 26 c5 dxc5 27 d6!.

21 ... g6?

So that 22 ♕f3 ♗g7! would approach equality.

22 ♗xc5!

Caruana quickly spotted a tactical flaw. The f6-square is weakened.

He would win the Exchange after 22...♕xc5? 23 ♘de4.

22 ... dxc5

23 ♖b1 ♖eb8

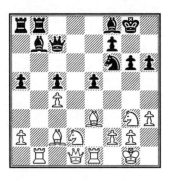

This is similar to the pawn structure Caruana could have had with 20 ♗xc5. He could still pursue the favorable strategy of 24 ♗a4.

There is another option. The e5-pawn is more vulnerable. White could gain an edge from 24 ♘f3 ♖e8 25 ♗a4 or 24...♗d6 25 ♕d2 ♔g7 26 ♕c3.

24 ♕f3

Now on 24...♗g7 White would have a choice of wings to focus on.

He would have excellent winning chances after 25 ♗a4 ♗a6 26 ♗c6 even if all the rooks are traded (26...♖xb1 27 ♖xb1 ♖b8 28 ♖xb8+ ♕xb8 29 ♕d3).

But he could play on both wings with 25 h4 and then 25...h5 26 ♘de4 ♘xe4 27 ♘xe4 and 28 ♖b5.

This also prepares to push the d-pawn (27...♗a6 28 d6).

A key continuation would be 27...f5 28 ♘g5 e4.

Then the sacrifice 29 ♗xe4 fxe4 30 ♕xe4 would bring decisive pressure on both wings (30...♕d6 31 ♖b3 or 31 ♘e6).

24   ...   ♘e8?

Black follows a different textbook, with ...♘d6 in mind.

25   h4!

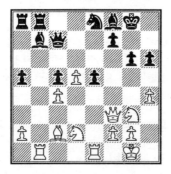

25   ...   h5

The light squares would have been terminally weak after 26 h5.

For example, 25...♗c8 26 h5 g5 27 ♗f5 and then 27...♖xb1 28 ♖xb1 ♖b8 29 ♖xb8 ♕xb8 30 ♗xc8 and ♘de4.

Or 27...♘d6 28 ♘de4 ♘xf5 29 ♘f6+ ♔h8 30 ♘xf5 and ♕e4.

26   ♘xh5!   gxh5

27   ♕xh5

He has three weapons to assist the queen – a rook lifted to the third rank, his knight and h-pawn.

For example, 27...♘f6 28 ♕g5+ ♗g7 and now either 29 ♖b3 or 29 ♖e3 is strong. But 29 h5 is faster because of the 30 h6 threat.

One of the cute lines runs 29 h5 ♘h7 30 ♗xh7+ ♔xh7 31 ♘e4 ♗c8 and now 32 ♖xb8 ♖xb8 33 h6! f6 34 d6! and wins.

27   ...   ♗g7

28   ♖b3

28   ...   ♖a6

This shortens matters. After 28...♔f8 29 ♖g3 White would threaten 30 ♖xg7!.

For example, 30...♘xg7 31 ♕h8+ or 30...♔xg7 31 ♕h7+ ♔f8

436

32 ♕h8+ ♔e7 33 ♖xe5+ ♔d7?
34 ♗f5+ and mates.

Black can keep the game going with 29...♘f6 30 ♕g5 ♘e8.

29	♖g3	♔f8
30	♖xg7!	♔xg7
31	♕h7+	♔f8
32	♕h8+	♔e7
33	♖xe5+	♖e6

Caruana took a minute to decide on 30 ♖xg7.

Virtually all of the moves since then have been forced on both sides (33...♔d7 34 ♗f5+).

But to choose 30 ♖xg7 he needed to see four moves further.

| 34 | dxe6 | ♘f6 |

| 35 | ♖xc5! | |

Now 35...♕xc5 36 ♕xb8.

| 35 | ... | ♕d6 |

| 36 | ♕g7 | ♖f8 |

The true end of the 30 ♖xg7! combination lies after 36...♕xc5 37 ♕xf7+ ♔d6 38 ♕xf6.

White's threats include 39 ♗a4 and 40 e7+.

37	♘b3	a4
38	♖f5!	♕xe6
39	♘c5	♕e1+
40	♔h2	resigns.

After this game, Caruana finished a creditable second in the Sinquefield Cup and looked forward to making on-line commentary when Magnus Carlsen defended his world championship title against Ian Nepomniachtchi.

Fans wondered if he would ever return to a championship match of his own. He still had a great future ahead and may not have reached his peak. After all, Vishy Anand was nearly 40 when he won the uncontested world championship. And Fabiano indicated he still had his determination. After his title match with Carlsen, he told *Forbes* magazine, "I can't say it's a pleasant experience... The pressure is enormous."

"But I want nothing more than to play again."

Index of Opponents

(Numbers refer to games)

Index of Openings

(Numbers refer to games)

ECO Opening Index

(Numbers refer to games)

Index of Middlegame Themes

(Numbers refer to games)

Center breakthrough – 2, 3, 5, 10, 25, 29, 53, 55

Combination – 3-5, 10-11, 24, 28-29 32, 36-39, 42, 44, 53-4, 60

Counter-attack – 6, 8, 11, 18-19, 37-38, 43

Deep-dive calculation – 6, 18-19, 26, 34, 44, 47

Defense, critical – 8, 10, 13-14, 18, 26, 28, 32, 34-5, 59

Hypermodernism – 1, 13, 25, 36, 45, 55

Kingside attack – 1, 4, 9, 10, 13, 18, 22, 24-27, 34-5, 37, 42-43, 48, 53, 56, 60

"Little" moves – 16, 23, 47, 49-50, 58

Mating attack – 1, 6, 11, 13, 22, 24-25, 37-39, 42, 44, 60

Opening preparation , deep – 6, 12, 19, 27, 39, 43, 45, 47, 49, 55-56, 59

Passed pawn(s) – 7, 10, 15, 19, 26, 29, 33, 46

Patience – 2, 12, 17, 27

Playability decisions – 8-9, 14, 20, 27, 58

Prophylaxis – 5, 15, 19, 26, 35, 37, 47, 49-50, 54, 57-58

Queenless middlegame – 12, 49, 51

Queenside attack versus kingside attack – 1, 9, 10, 11, 34-35, 47

Sacrifice of Exchange – 12-13, 17, 20, 23, 42-5, 57

Sacrifice of minor piece – 3, 4, 6, 9, 14-15, 17, 24, 26, 42, 59, 60

Sacrifice of a pawn – 7, 9, 10, 14, 19, 21, 39, 43, 44-5, 47, 52-53, 56, 59

Sacrifice of a queen – 5, 37-39

Small chess decision – 17, 20

Space advantage – 5, 16, 24-25, 37, 39, 41-42, 45, 52

Strategically won position – 1, 17, 37, 48, 52, 57

Superior pawn structure – 1-2, 6, 17, 25, 33, 35-6, 39, 42, 46, 48-49, 52-55, 57-58

Surprise in the opening – 6, 12-13, 46-7, 50, 56, 59

Swindle attempt – 8-9, 19, 36-39, 44, 46, 54

Time pressure – 7- 9, 11, 17, 19-20, 22, 35-37, 42-43, 47-48, 53

Two-bishop advantage – 11, 17, 19, 21, 26, 28, 32, 46-47, 55

Two-wing play – 1, 10, 17, 20, 24, 27, 29, 39, 46, 48-49, 56, 58, 60

Waiting move – 3, 5, 12, 20, 22, 24, 27, 28, 35, 38, 40, 48-49, 58

Index of Endgames

(Numbers refer to games)